Routledge Revivals

Maternal and Child Health in Rural Kenya

Maternal and Child Health in Rural Kenya (1984) is based on a longitudinal, multi-disciplinary, population-based research study in the Machakos district, a rural area of Kenya. The purposes of the project were to obtain accurate data on morbidity and mortality from a number of acute infectious childhood diseases and on the outcome of pregnancy; to investigate nutritional factors and those of the social, biological and physical environment which may have a bearing on the observed disease pattern; and to develop a system of registration for births, deaths and morbidity suitable for use in an area of limited resources. Data for this study was collected over a seven-year period and the book has major implications for those concerned with health care in less-developed countries.

Maternal and Child Health in Rural Kenya

An Epidemiological Study

Edited by
J.K. van Ginneken and A.S. Muller

Routledge
Taylor & Francis Group
Routledge Revivals

First published in 1984
by Croom Helm Ltd

This edition first published in 2026 by Routledge
4 Park Square, Milton Park, Abingdon, Oxon, OX14 4RN

and by Routledge
605 Third Avenue, New York, NY 10017

Routledge is an imprint of the Taylor & Francis Group, an informa business

A Library of Congress record exists under LCCN: 85129781

ISBN: 978-1-041-30436-4 (hbk)
ISBN: 978-1-003-77455-6 (ebk)
ISBN: 978-1-041-30438-8 (pbk)

Book DOI 10.4324/9781003774556

MATERNAL AND CHILD HEALTH IN RURAL KENYA

AN EPIDEMIOLOGICAL STUDY

Edited by
J.K. VAN GINNEKEN
A.S. MULLER

CROOM HELM
London & Sydney

Croom Helm Ltd, Provident House, Burrell Row,
Beckenham, Kent BR3 1AT

Croom Helm Australia Pty Ltd, First Floor, 139 King Street,
Sydney, NSW 2001, Australia

British Library Cataloguing in Publication Data

Maternal and child health in rural Kenya.
1. Children – Care and hygiene
2. Mothers – Health and hygiene
I. Ginneken, J.K. van II. Muller, A.S.
613'.0432'V96762 RJ101

ISBN 0-7099-2608-1

Printed and bound in Great Britain by
Biddles Ltd, Guildford and King's Lynn

Contents

Foreword

The studies reported in this monograph have in common the fact that they were based on a disease and demographic surveillance system that was maintained for nearly eight years in a rural area of Machakos District, Kenya, by the Medical Research Centre, Nairobi, which until the middle of 1982 was a department of the Royal Tropical Institute, Amsterdam.

This surveillance system made it possible for population-based longitudinal studies on a variety of aspects of mother and child health to be conducted. There is no need to emphasize the urgent need for such epidemiological studies, not only in Kenya but in Africa at large, where little work of this nature has so far been undertaken. Yet, since over 80 percent of our population is non-urban, the understanding of the patterns of disease in the rural setting and its alleviation is a matter of fundamental importance.

The infrastructure of the Machakos Project was also used for other purposes. Scientists and students from Kenya and from several other countries took advantage of its existence to carry out other studies in epidemiology, nutrition, demography, medical sociology, anthropology and agricultural economics. The project thus provided teaching and research facilities not only for the staff of the Medical Research Centre but for other institutions as well.

The organizers of the Machakos Project have displayed commendable initiative in assembling in one volume the results of most of the studies done. The various chapters in this book show that the results have made a contribution to our knowledge of disease and related problems affecting mothers and children in Kenya. The studies are also important because conclusions that have important implications for the formulation of public health policies in the country were reached.

This latter achievement is particularly important because in Africa the greater share of the funds for medical research should be used for investigations directed towards the solving of Africa's most immediate health problems.

The Machakos Project of the Medical Research Centre has set an example of the type of research that I hope will be undertaken in the future within the framework of the Kenya Medical Research Institute, of which the Medical Research Centre, Nairobi, is now part. The authors are to be highly commended on the quality of research and training undertaken in this project.

Prof. M. Mugambi
Director
Kenya Medical Research Institute
Nairobi

Preface and acknowledgements

The results that are reported in this book are the product of a vast amount of work that has been undertaken over the last 12 years. The earliest discussion on the design of the project took place in the latter half of 1971 and 1½ years were needed to finalize the design and to make other preparations. Data collection in the study area in Machakos district (including the demographic baseline survey) continued for 8½ years up to April 1981; analysis of the data and writing up the studies took another 2 years.

The editors of this volume were the project leaders—ASM until the middle of 1977, JKvanG thereafter; on behalf of themselves and of the authors they would like to thank the large number of organizations and persons who have contributed in so many ways to the Machakos Project through all its stages.

We are indebted in the first place to the Director and staff of the Medical Research Centre, Nairobi; the Machakos study was the largest of its projects. We wish to thank Dr Th. Hanegraaf, Director of the Centre until mid-1982, for his continuous support. We also received a great deal of assistance from the scientific staff of the Centre, many of whom, from different departments, contributed to the various investigations, as the authorship of the chapters shows. Several of them were also members of the project team, participating in its management, supervision and co-ordination. We are very much indebted to the statistical and administrative staff, and the secretaries and technical support staff of the Centre; and we appreciate the help of Dr S. Kinoti, the present Director of the Medical Research Centre, now a department of the Kenya Medical Research Institute.

We also owe a great deal to the field-workers from the study area, who were employed by the Medical Research Centre. Without their conscientious and highly motivated work, making their daily rounds for many years, the project would have been impossible to conduct.

We are much indebted to the staff of the Department of Tropical Hygiene of the Royal Tropical Institute of Amsterdam, with whom, in fact, the Machakos Project was in many ways a joint undertaking. In particular, members of the sub-departments of tropical health and nutrition made scientific contributions to the project, as can again be seen from the list of authors; some few of them also provided logistic and administrative support for the project throughout the 12 years of its existence.

We must also express our gratitude for the financial support, continued over many years through the Medical Research Centre and the Royal Tropical Institute, of the Directorate-General for International Co-operation of the Ministry of Foreign Affairs in the Netherlands.

It is impossible to mention all those in Kenya who gave support and advice, but we would like to mention specifically Dr W. Koinange Karuga, Director of Medical Services of the Ministry of Health, formerly Director of the Division of Communicable Diseases Control in the Ministry of Health; Dr T.K. Arap Siongok, Director of the Division of Communicable Diseases Control in the Ministry of Health; Prof. F.D. Schofield, formerly Chairman, Department of Community Health of the

University of Nairobi; Dr D.H. Smith, formerly of the British Medical Research Council in Kisumu; Prof. P.M. Mbithi and Mr H. van Doorne of the Department of Sociology of the University of Nairobi; Dr J.J. Kornman, former Provincial Obstetrician and Gynaecologist in Machakos Town; Prof. K. Lorenzl of the Faculty of Agriculture of the University of Nairobi; and Dr M. Collinson of C.I.M.M.Y.T. in Nairobi.

Similarly we would like to thank the following in the Netherlands and elsewhere for contributions mostly to the early stages of the project: Prof. H.A. Valkenburg, Department of Epidemiology, Erasmus University, Rotterdam; Prof. P.R. Odell and Mr C. Moore of the Economic-Geographical Institute of the same university; Dr J.D. Heynen of the Geographical Institute of the University of Utrecht; Mr J.T.P. Bonte, Department of Health Statistics of the Netherlands Central Bureau of Statistics in Voorburg; and Prof. A.M. Davies of the Hebrew University Hadassah Medical School in Jerusalem.

For assistance provided in the final stages of the project we are grateful to Prof. D. Morley, Institute of Child Health, University of London, who strongly encouraged the publication of this book; to Dr H. de Glanville and Mrs N. de Glanville of Meditext, Weybridge, Surrey, England, who provided much-needed editorial and technical assistance during its preparation; and to Mrs L. van Ginneken, who greatly assisted the first editor with the completion of the manuscript.

Several chapters in this volume were published earlier in *Tropical and Geographical Medicine*. We are grateful to the former and present editors of this journal, Prof. H.A.P.C. Oomen and Dr L.C. Vogel, for editorial assistance in the preparation of these articles and for permission to use them.

Last, but not least, we would wish to thank the people themselves in the study area of Matungulu and Mbiuni locations in Machakos district. The chiefs of those locations, Chiefs Savano Maveke and Joseph Kunuva, and the subchiefs of the various sublocations were extremely helpful in introducing the project to the people and in organizing regular *barazas* that enabled the project staff to inform the public from time to time about its progress and about future plans.

We are especially grateful to the people in the study area for their unfailing willingness to co-operate throughout these years; they almost never refused to participate during 8½ years of data collection. This applies particularly to the mothers and other household members who co-operated in the several intensive studies—on food intake, lactation, agricultural production, utilization of health services—that took a considerable amount of their time.

We express the hope that this collaboration given by the people in the area will lead, directly and indirectly, to the formulation and implementation of health policies that will be of benefit, not only to themselves, but also to those in other parts of Kenya and in other African countries.

J.K. van Ginneken
A.S. Muller
Dept. of Tropical Hygiene
Royal Tropical Institute
Amsterdam

Contributors

At the time of the study the following contributors were with the Medical Research Centre in Nairobi, Kenya:

D.M. Blankhart (the late); P.G. Blok, W. Gemert, A.A.J. Jansen, P.W. Kok, S.A. Lakhani, J Leeuwenburg, B. Maina-Ahlberg, F.M. Mburu, A.S. Muller, Omondi-Odhiambo, S.R. Onchere, C. Patel, T.W.J. Schulpèn, W. 't Mannetje, B. Thiuri, J.K. van Ginneken, M. van Rens, A.M. Voorhoeve and H. W'oigo.

K. de With, J.W.L. Kleevens, J.A. Kusin, H. Nordbeck, H.A.P.C. Oomen, U. Renqvist, R. Slooff, J.N. van Luyk and W.M. van Steenbergen were with the Department of Tropical Hygiene of the Royal Tropical Institute in Amsterdam, the Netherlands. C. Kars was with the Department of Anthropology, Leyden State University, Leyden, the Netherlands.

K.S. Warren, and A.A.F. Mahmoud were at the Division of Geographic Medicine, Department of Medicine, Case Western Reserve University Cleveland, Ohio, USA and T.K. Arap Siongok and J.H. Ouma with the Division of Communicable Diseases Control, Ministry of Health, Nairobi, Kenya.

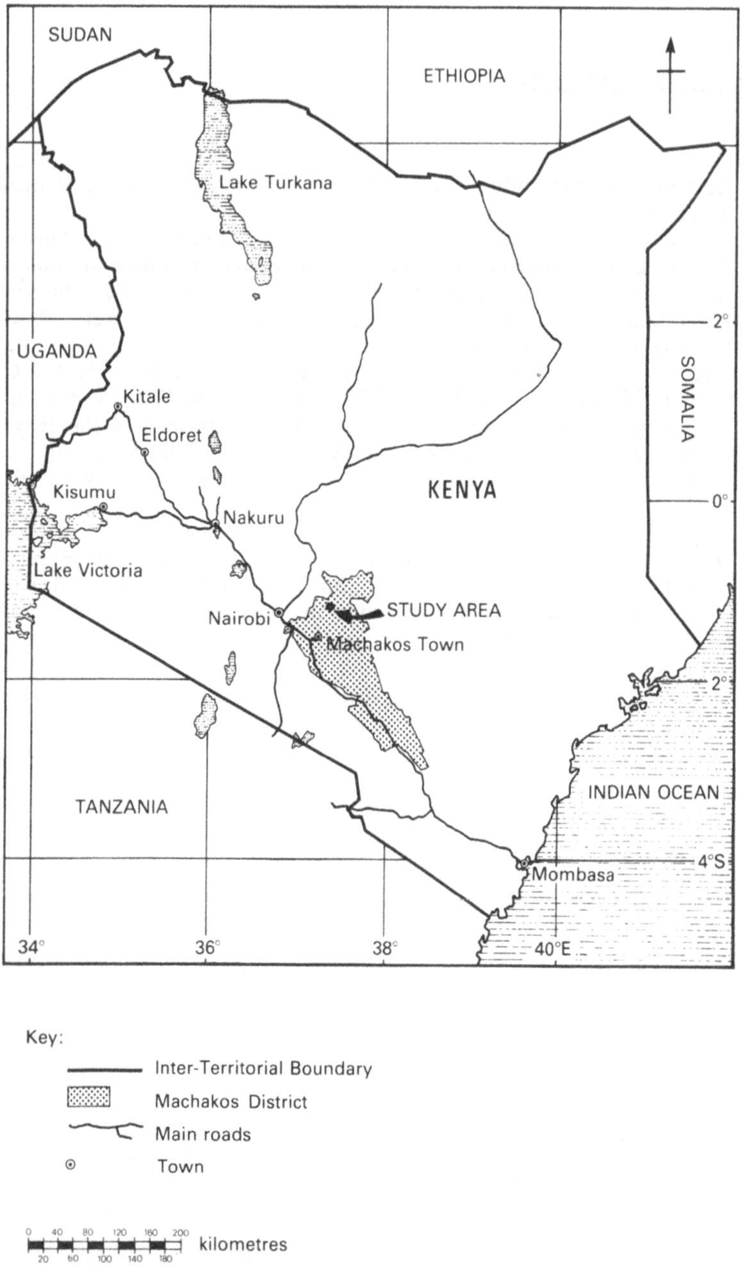

Figure 1. Position of study area in relation to Machakos district of Kenya.

Part I
Introduction

1

Study design and methodology

A.S. Muller
J.H. Ouma
F.M. Mburu
P.G. Blok
J.W.L. Kleevens

It is generally accepted that allocation of limited resources to health services should be based on the relative importance of different health problems. Such estimations in developing countries depend on available information on patterns of disease and the factors determining them, compiled as a rule from official returns of health institutions.

On the other hand returns from hospitals, health centres and dispensaries in developing countries are often incomplete and inaccurate. Furthermore, only a small proportion of the population makes use of these health services and the morbidity and mortality experience of the population at large remains largely unknown. Longitudinal population-based studies from which disease incidence and mortality can be measured have been few, the most notable being those in Bangladesh on a number of infections (International Centre for Diarrhoeal Disease Research, Bangladesh, 1978, 1979, 1980), in Guatemala and India on the interaction of nutrition and infection (Scrimshaw et al., 1968) and the Danfa project on rural health and family planning in Ghana (Neumann et al., 1974).

In 1971 a longitudinal population-based project was initiated in a part of the Machakos district of Kenya with a view to developing means of improving mother and child health in a rural area. The objectives were as follows:

1. to obtain accurate data on morbidity and mortality from measles, whooping cough, other acute respiratory infections and acute diarrhoeal disease in children 0–4 years of age;

2. to obtain data on nutritional status, social behaviour and attitudes, socio-economic status, and biological and physical environment, and to study the influence these may have on observed disease patterns;

3. to obtain accurate data on maternal and perinatal morbidity and mortality in relation to antenatal and delivery care received;

4. to develop a system for registration of births, deaths and causes of death for all age groups and for the diseases mentioned in (1) among children 0–4 years of age, capable of producing data useful for the planning, operation and evaluation of health services and suitable for use in a typical district in Kenya with limited resources;

5. to study and measure the influence, if any, of the presence of a medical research team on mortality.

In the course of the project two more objectives were added:

6. to test the impact of several health interventions under field conditions and to determine in particular the clinical efficacy of two rather than three pertussis vaccine immunizations during infancy;

7. to study the relationship between nutritional status during pregnancy and birth weight, lactation performance and growth during infancy.

During the implementation of the project it was decided in view of methodological problems and staff constraints not to pursue objectives 4 and 5.

Study design

The core of the project was the demographic and disease surveillance system whereby each of the approximately 4000 households in the study area were visited fortnightly (until September 1978) and then monthly (until April 1981) by field-workers who recorded pregnancies, births, deaths and migrations, and morbidity from measles, whooping cough, other respiratory infections and acute diarrhoea among children 0–4 years of age (see objective 1;

in practice all cases of measles and whooping cough were recorded, regardless of age). The study design was of a semi-longitudinal type (Thomson et al., 1968), i.e. at the start it included all children under 5 years of age. Newborn babies and immigrant children under 5 were continuously entered into the study, while follow-up was discontinued as soon as the child reached its fifth birthday or had permanently left the area.

Based on the surveillance system, longitudinal and cross-sectional studies were carried out. The longitudinal studies covered child growth, outcome of pregnancy and nutritional status during pregnancy and infancy, and two vaccine trials. The cross-sectional surveys dealt with a number of explanatory variables in the environment.

Study area

Originally two areas approximately 80 km east of Nairobi were selected for the study. All research activities took place in one area (B), while in a nearby control area (A) only an annual census to obtain information on vital events was carried out. For several reasons the results of the demographic studies in the control area A have never been fully analysed (see Chapter 26) and the results reported in this book refer nearly everywhere to studies undertaken in experimental area B.

The area selected is part of the northern division of Machakos district (see Figs. 1 and 2). Table 1 shows the sublocations involved, the de facto number of inhabitants and the population density according to the baseline survey in November 1973.

The area is divided into two parts by the Kanzalu range of hills.

Table 1.
Study area, total population and population density according to 1973 survey.

	Study area (surveillance area, area B)		
Location and Sublocation	*Total inhabitants*	*Surface area (sq km)*	*Population density per sq km*
Matungulu			
Kambusu (West)	4258	8	532
Kingoti (West)	6497	17	382
Katheka (East)	1847	15	123
Mbiuni			
Ulaani (East)	3413	29	118
Katitu (East)	2568	18	143
Total	18 583	87	214

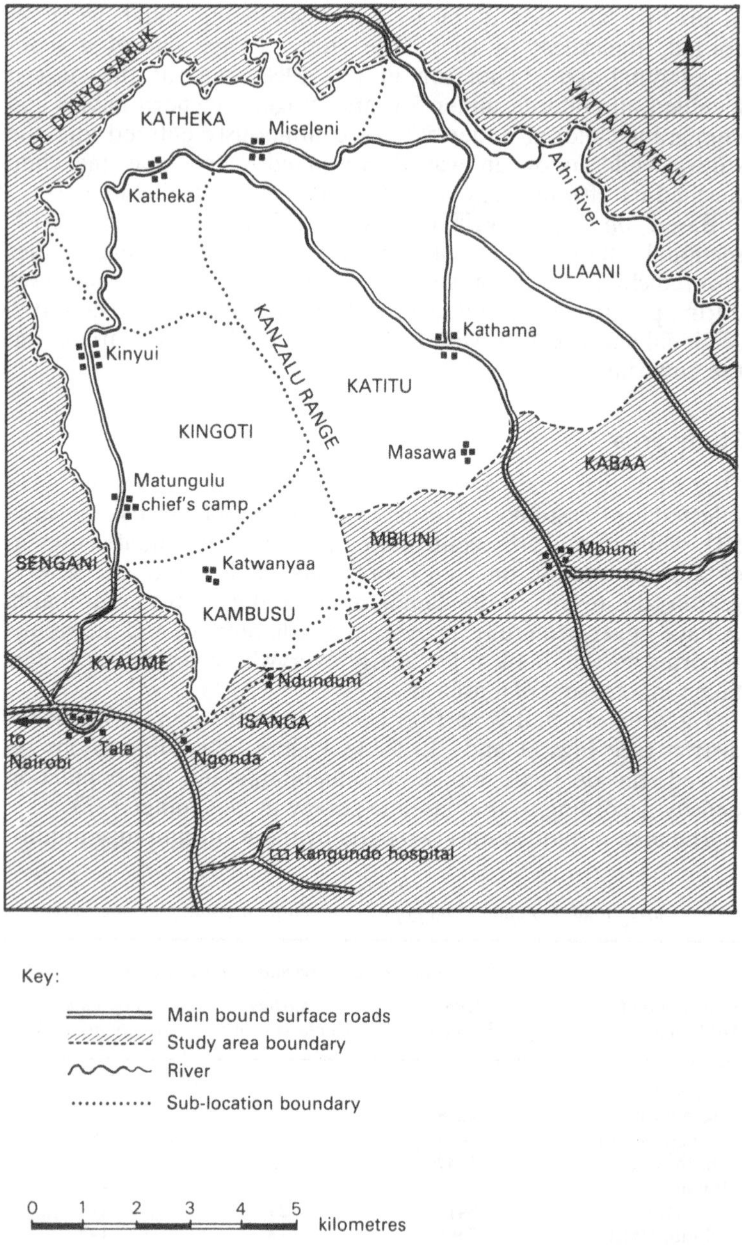

Figure 2. Machakos study area.

The sublocations of Kambusu and Kingoti belong to the western part, which is relatively fertile. Katheka, Ulaani and Katitu are on the flat, semi-arid eastern side of the Kanzalu range. Coffee is an important cash crop in the western part while subsistence farming (cow-peas, maize, cattle) predominates in the eastern part. The altitude ranges from approximately 1300 to 1700 meters. Mean annual rainfall is 900 mm.

The population belongs to a Bantu tribe, the Kamba. Most people live in compounds consisting of 2–4 huts and a food store; the compounds are scattered throughout the area. There are no villages in the sense of concentrations of a large number of homesteads, except to a certain degree around trading centres. The sublocations are subdivided into 6–8 *utui* (villages); these often do not form geographically well-defined units, but for the purposes of the project they have been used to number the households. There are also a number of market places in the area. The largest—Kinyui—consists of 30–50 shops on both sides of the main road but very few shop owners actually live in the market area.

In four of these market places in the study area (area B) a small room was rented to serve as a field office. In Tala, a larger trading centre just outside the study area, a field headquarters was established in a duplex house on a small housing estate, providing lodging facilities for 6–8 staff members from Nairobi at any one time and a small field laboratory.

From Tala an all-weather murram road runs through the area and a 4-wheel-drive vehicle is only required for a few weeks each

Thorn trees and shrubs in the eastern part (Ulaani).

Terraces in the western part (Kambusu).

year after excessively heavy rains. A bus service is available once a day in both directions and frequent taxis ply between Kinyui and Tala. Within the study area there is a government dispensary near Kinyui, staffed by an enrolled nurse. There used to be privately operated clinics in Kinyui, Katwanyaa and Kathama, usually manned by unqualified staff, but these ceased operating in 1977.

Outside the area, there is a 50-bed government hospital in Kangundo, a sub-health centre in Mbiuni, a 20-bed mission maternity hospital in Misyani and a small private clinic in Tala.

The average de jure number of household members is six. As in many parts of Kenya, there is considerable migration. About a quarter of all heads of households have a job in one of the larger towns in Kenya—most of them in Nairobi—and come home for the weekend or once a month. Because of shortage of land a considerable number of families move out of the study area or maintain one farm within and one outside the area, moving back and forth several times a year.

Disease and demographic surveillance

The disease and demographic surveillance system was established in four stages:

1. *The establishment of close links with the chiefs, subchiefs and other local leaders of the area.*

The chiefs organized open-air meetings (*barazas*) with the people in various parts of the study area during which the project staff introduced themselves and explained the aims of the project.

During these *barazas* it was stressed that a considerable amount of co-operation was being requested, in particular a willingness to accept, for several years to come, frequent home visits by the field staff to question members of the household about a variety of items. Medical treatment was offered through the local field staff for small children whenever required and the people were told that transport to the nearest hospital, about 15 km outside the study area, would be made available for emergency cases. The *barazas* continued to take place on a yearly basis to keep the population informed on what had been accomplished and what type of activities were planned for the coming year.

2. *A demographic baseline survey of the entire population, including the preparation of detailed maps of every village and the numbering of every household.*

Initially these maps consisted of crude sketches made by the field-worker on the spot. At a later stage the quality of the maps was improved by use of fairly recent aerial photographs of the area obtained from the Office of Lands and Surveys. The demographic baseline and follow-up demographic surveillance provided a register that could also be used to study other groups besides 0–4-year-old children and fertile women.

A slightly modified version of a form designed by JGC Blacker for the Uganda census, identical with the one used for the British Medical Research Council's Kano Plain Project near Kisumu, Kenya, was used. This form provided for the following information on every member of a household: name, relationship to the head of the household, sex, age, whether present or absent, whether father and mother were alive, and fertility information on females aged 12 years and over.

A household was defined as a group of people habitually eating and sleeping together on the same compound and one demographic survey form was used for each household. It became clear that not all field-workers applied the same criteria when entering a person on the form as a member of the household; therefore it was decided to register only the de facto population, i.e. only those who had slept in the household during the night immediately preceding the interview. Every person considered to be a member of the household by its head, whether present or not (de jure population) was later added to these rolls in order to provide the denominator for vital events and incidence rates.

After two months of initial training and testing of questionnaires the actual demographic survey was started. This included mapping of all the *utui* in one of the five sublocations comprising the study area. All households were given a card marked with a number, which was also painted on the door after permission had been obtained from the chief and the people at a *baraza*. The households were listed according to number, and the name of the head of the household was entered after each number. With these lists and the maps drawn by the field staff, field-workers were assigned 12–15 households per day for which they had to complete demographic survey forms. After finishing with all the *utui* in one sublocation the entire staff moved on to the next.

It was found that many people did not know their age in calendar years and use was made of a 'calendar of events' that listed all important events that had taken place in the area since approximately 1880 that were known or remembered from hearsay. For children 0–4 years of age it was usually possible to obtain a birth date accurate to a month from a birth certificate or a record of baptism kept by the parents.

As a rule the informant was the head of the household or his wife. If necessary, field-workers were allowed to obtain information from any other member of the household over 15 years of age who happened to be available for interview.

An attempt was made to assess interviewer variation. Every 3–4 weeks a number of households were revisited by the same or a different field-worker. Discrepancies between the two interviews were discussed at regular meetings between field staff and supervisory staff. It was often not possible to determine with certainty whether discrepancies were the result of interviewer errors or real differences in the information given by different respondents. The most common discrepancies concerned the year of birth and the number of a woman's live-born children, especially of children no longer alive.

The demographic baseline survey, including recruitment and training of field staff, took 10 months; at the end of this all demographic information was completely updated (Sept./Oct. 1973).

3. *The introduction of fortnightly demographic data collection (demographic surveillance) in Nov. 1973.*

At first all households in a sublocation were visited every 2 weeks by three field-workers to obtain information on births, deaths and migration. After 3 months demographic surveillance was introduced in the entire study area, which had been divided into 12 clusters of approximately 300 households. Each field-worker was assigned to one cluster, whenever possible to that in which he himself lived.

4. *Consolidation of the surveillance system and the training of field*

staff in the recognition of specific signs and symptoms of disease in infancy and childhood.

This stage lasted 5 months (Nov. 1973–April 1974). A disease surveillance form was designed that included two screening questions: 'Has the child been ill since the previous visit?' and 'Does the child look ill?'. If the answer to both questions was no, the field-worker was required only to observe and record whether a child had a running nose and cough. If the answer to either question was yes, the mother was asked about vomiting and diarrhoea during the past two weeks, the temperature was taken and defined observations relating to measles, respiratory distress and dehydration were recorded. Every suspected case of measles or whooping cough was reported by the field-worker to the doctor during his regular clinic visit. The doctor verified the diagnosis according to a standardized list of clinical signs. If the mother allowed, nose swabs for culture and finger-prick blood for the determination of serum antibody levels were taken as well. During these clinics any other children accompanying the mother were also examined and treated.

Because an increasing number of measles and pertussis cases were being seen at nearby health facilities, disease surveillance was started one month ahead of schedule. As a result the documentation of epidemics of these diseases was begun in their early stages. No doubt this was at the expense of training, but this was compensated for by the considerable amount of on-the-job training provided by the medical project staff. Therefore case-identification is assumed to have been fairly accurate even during the early days of the measles and whooping cough outbreaks. Owing to the work involved in covering epidemics of measles and whooping cough at the same time, surveillance of acute diarrhoea and acute respiratory illness was not considered sufficiently standardized to be included in the system until 1976.

Demographic surveillance was continued for a period of about 7½ years from November 1973 to April 1981, while disease surveillance was in operation for 7 years from April 1974 to April 1981. Up to August 1978 surveillance took place on a fortnightly basis; from September 1978 to April 1981 field-workers visited all households every 4 weeks. Disease surveillance was also simplified in August 1979, thereafter being restricted to measles and whooping cough.

Other studies

In addition to the disease and demographic surveillance a number of other studies have taken place. Many of these have been longitudinal studies such as the DPT vaccine trial, the study on the outcome of pregnancy and the nutrition studies of pregnant and lactating women and children under 5. Cross-sectional surveys included the collection of information on socio-economic status and environmental sanitation in 1974/1975 and again in 1978 and sociological studies on attitudes and behaviour in relation to pregnancy, measles and diarrhoea. Demographic studies were carried out on migration patterns and on the impact on fertility of length of emigrants' residence in urban areas. Agricultural investigations focused on food production patterns and on food availability and its impact on food intake in the eastern part of the study area. Five weather stations were in operation for several years to monitor rainfall, temperature and humidity.

Staff

Initially the responsibility for the project at the academic level rested with an epidemiologist project leader, a biologist, a sociologist and a demographer. Only the epidemiologist had practical experience with field work, the other three members of the team having just graduated from university. In Nairobi a statistician was available, reinforced at a later stage by a part-time computer programmer and three assistants for checking, coding and filing records. A few months before the start of disease surveillance a paediatrician and a public health specialist joined the project team. Further expansion of the project team took place with intensification of research in nutrition, sociology and agriculture (see below), while the original project members were replaced by others. Throughout the project nearly all the Kenyan project members pursued higher studies at the University of Nairobi or at other universities, sponsored by the Medical Research Centre. They carried out their field work in the study area on topics in nutrition, demography, medical sociology and agriculture. In addition a number of scientists from the Department of Tropical Hygiene of the Royal Tropical Institute in Amsterdam, the parent institute of the Medical Research Centre, participated in specific studies.

The local field staff started with 5 interviewers and one field supervisor, all with 1–4 years of secondary schooling. Later on the field staff was increased to 12 interviewers and 3 field supervisors. With the expansion of research in nutrition the field staff was further increased to 19 interviewers and 4 field supervisors. All the field-workers could speak both English and Swahili as well as their own language. Both male and female field-workers were recruited. All of them were permanent residents of the study area.

Discussion

Ideally a study of this nature would include several ecological zones in the country, or in tropical Africa for that matter. Because of limitations of manpower and finance it was decided to use only one part of Kenya, within easy reach of Nairobi, where the Medical Research Centre is located, for the study. We believe that the area was reasonably representative of many parts of Central Kenya in terms of agricultural potential and standard of living. The scattered distribution of the population over the area made collection of data a laborious and time-consuming exercise.

Initially, because of the lack of experience of some of the academic staff in organizing and supervising an extensive longitudinal field study using unskilled field-workers, there was some doubt about the feasibility of the undertaking. Once the field-workers fully realized what was expected of them, however, which took 1–5 months, they usually carried out the tasks diligently and conscientiously provided continuous supervision was maintained. In general they quickly mastered the observational skills needed for the diagnosis of disease but experienced considerable difficulty in recording their observations correctly and in maintaining a system of administration understandable to others.

Each member of the academic staff had to spend on average 1–2 days a week with the field staff. Detailed field maps were thus needed in all four offices in the study area; daily messages had to be left behind by field-workers, specifying which households they were visiting and in which order, and field-workers' records had to be checked for accuracy and completeness. For the major activities—demographic baseline survey, demographic surveillance and disease surveillance—extensive instruction manuals were written and periodically revised (Omondi-Odiambo, 1979). Approximately once a month meetings were held with the field staff at which the written instructions were discussed and any new procedures explained. During these meetings it became apparent that many of the field-workers had not studied the instruction manuals properly. They preferred verbal instructions and usually followed these better.

One of the problems was a shortage of middle-level staff competent to handle the numerous administrative details. Others have had similar experience elsewhere in Africa (Neumann et al., 1973). This may or may not be a universal problem for longitudinal field projects in developing countries but an epidemiologist planning such research should be prepared to have to be involved in the most simple and seemingly straightforward details if he expects to obtain data of acceptable quality.

On the whole collection of data in the field for the various studies was carried out on schedule and satisfactorily by a well-motivated staff. A problem encountered in later stages of the project was how to maintain field-workers' motivation. Their work was mainly routine and not all of them were able to keep up a high standard; as a result several had to be replaced. One method of maintaining their motivation was to provide them with the results of the studies in which they were involved in and ask for their views and comments on the findings.

Co-operation by the study population was excellent. Virtually all households provided the necessary demographic baseline information and continued to co-operate in the course of the surveillance and various other surveys. No cultural inhibitions against discussing matters related to births and deaths came to light. Only the taking of capillary blood samples proved very unpopular and a variable proporation of mothers refused to have their children bled. In the course of 7½ years' surveillance only 9 of 4000 households refused to participate, an indication of the study population's excellent collaboration.

Data processing constituted a major bottleneck. This is not unusual with longitudinal epidemiological studies involving the frequent collection of demographic and morbidity information (Behar et al., 1968; Neumann et al., 1973), and it was partly due to inadequate planning in terms of staff and computer facilities at the start. More important, however, was that if the adequacy of the data for processing had been verified at the pilot study stage a number of pitfalls that only emerged later could have been avoided.

References

International Centre for Diarrhoeal Disease Research, Bangladesh, Annual Reports 1978, 1979, 1980, ICDDR, B, Dacca.

Omondi-Odhiambo, Ed, Manual of Instructions to Fieldworkers, Medical Research Centre, Nairobi, 1979.

Behar M, Scrimshaw NS, Guzman MA and Gordon JE, Nutrition and infection field study in Guatemalan villages, 1959–1964. VIII. An epidemiological appraisal of its wisdom and errors, Arch Environm Hlth, 17 (1968) 814.

Scrimshaw NS, Taylor CE and Gordon JE, Interactions of Nutrition and Infection, World Health Organization, Geneva, 1968.

Neumann AK, Sai FT, Lourie IM and Wurapa FK, Focus: Technical Cooperation, 2 (1973) 11.

Neumann AK, Sai FT and Dodu SRA, Environm Child Hlth, Monograph 32 (1974) 40.

Thomson AM, Billewicz WZ, Thomson B, Illsley R, Rahman AK and McGregor IA, A study of growth and health of young children in tropical Africa, Trans R Soc Trop Med Hyg, 62 (1968) 330.

Part II
Characteristics of the study area

2

Agricultural and economic characteristics

S.R. Onchere

Introduction

This chapter consists of two sections: in the first the physical, agricultural and economic conditions of the Machakos study area in general are described, while the second part deals with the results of a longitudinal study of patterns of food production, storage and consumption in household groups of varying nutritional vulnerability.

1. Agricultural and economic data from previous investigations

Seasons, rainfall and ambient temperatures

If we loosely define a season as a period of the year characterized by special climatic conditions, rainfall is perhaps the most important seasonal indicator in the Machakos study area, and indeed in most of the seasonally arid tropics. The Kenya National Agricultural Laboratories have demonstrated that there are considerable variations in onset, amount, reliability and duration of rainfall throughout the Machakos and Kitui districts (Braun, 1977). Thus in the study area the rains can be insufficient, or fail completely, leading to occasional droughts, as is well documented in the Kenyan literature. It follows that, when rainfall is ample, harvests tend generally to be bountiful, but when Nature is less generous, they can fail. In most years, however, it is the actual variation in the two cropping seasons that counts. These are referred to as the short rains (SR) starting in September or October, and the long rains (LR) starting in March or April. The actual total number of rainy days in the whole year is less than 70 (Gemert, 1980).

In general the short rains are more reliable than the long rains. The probability of crop failure in the Machakos area, using Woodhead's potential evaporation equation, is 35 percent in the long-rains period and 25 percent in the short-rains period (Onchere, 1982). Based on rainfall and a seasonal crop (Katumani maize) that takes 90 days to mature, Braun (1977) calculated the probabilities of having two crops, one, no good crop or none at all in this agro-ecological zone at 22 percent, 51 percent, 18 percent and 9 percent respectively for any one year.

The study area characteristically experiences intense sunshine. Mean ambient temperatures are generally high, calculated to be 20°C, with a low of 15° in July and August and a high of 25° in January and February (Gemert, 1980). The maximum mean humidity fluctuates between 93 and 95 percent, and the minimum between 42 and 52 percent.

Table 1 summarizes the climatic contrasts between the eastern and western parts of the study area.

Table 1.
Climatic differences between western and eastern part between 1975 and 1979.

Weather component	*Western part*	*Eastern part*	*Absolute mean difference*
Rainfall (mm)	1086	932	154
Rainy days (no.)	69	61	8
Min. mean temp. (°C)	14.4	15.9	1.5
Diurnal mean temp. (°C)	19.7	21.1	1.4
Max. mean temp. (°C)	24.8	26.2	1.6
Min. mean humidity (%)*	47.8	45.8	2.0

*Max. mean humidity does not fluctuate markedly. It stays within the limits of 90–99% for the whole area, throughout the year.

Source: Adapted and modified from Gemert (1980) pp.5–10.

The climate thus tends to be more severe on the eastern part of the Kanzalu ridge, with relatively less rainfall, fewer rainy days, and higher ambient temperatures.

Soils, geology and topography

A number of Kenyan geological and soil survey studies also cover the study area (Fairburn, 1963; Mbuvi et al., 1974). These have established that the soils found on the eastern part of Kanzalu ridge have developed from rocks that come under the Basement System, mainly differentiated by banded gneisses, while the western part is covered by volcanic rocks known as tuffs. Soils on the tuffs are deeper, and are mainly red clays referred to locally as *kitune*.

The Kanzalu ridge is composed of hard granitoid gneisses, which are actually metamorphic rocks very rich in quartz—hence their greater resistance to erosion. These have given rise to sandy weathering materials. The soils east of Kanzalu are less resistant to erosion and form red to brown soils of varying textures. In some places imperfectly drained soils (so-called 'black cotton' soils) occur. Kaolinite is dominant in the top 15 cm of soils, which is considered important for agricultural purposes. It shows intensities of 7.25 to 7.49Å spacings and is classified as metahallolysiteillites, decreasing with depth. Soils on both sides of Kanzalu are considered to be fertile enough if sufficient moisture is retained.

The vegetation

Much of the study area has little or no original natural vegetation left. Much of it has been destroyed by cultivation and cutting of wood for charcoal, firewood and fencing, and little or no effort has been made to replace it, except for the planting of 'sausage' trees, (*Kigelia anthiopium*), the fruits of which are used to brew traditional beer. The many goats seen in the area have also helped in the 'defoliation' process. For this and other reasons the dominant visible vegetation found west of Kanzalu ridge is composed of coffee bushes and bush grass, while to the east pigeon peas and thorny bushes dominate the scene.

The infrastructure

Just outside the study area a bituminized all-weather road links Kangundo and Tala market centres with Nairobi, and two well-paved roads link these two centres with Machakos and Thika towns. The road from Kangundo to Mwala is also fairly good, while that joining Tala to Kinyu, Kathama and Mbiuni has recently been paved and can be regarded as an all-weather road. There are, however, numerous feeder roads radiating from the all-weather roads, leading mainly to schools or churches. Nearly all

The road to Kathama during the rainy season, before resurfacing.

these are rough and impassable in wet weather: rain cuts deep gullies across them, making them virtually unusable, especially in the area east of Kanzalu; also feeder roads through the so-called black cotton soils are sticky and impassable for days after rain.

Regular *matatu* services operate between Tala and Kinyui markets. These are usually old, ill-maintained small vehicles that seem to have no limit to the number of people they will hold. The new paved road to Kathama has improved these services but, on the whole, most people have to walk long distances to catch a *matatu*.

Further into the study area the oxcart and the bicycle are the commonest means of transport, used to carry people, water, building materials, seed and farm produce such as cotton and coffee. Women are also culturally and physically accustomed to carrying almost every kind of load on their backs with a head-band.

There are no telephones, post offices or electricity in the study area. There is also no pipe-borne water supply, except for the area in and around Kinyui market, where there is an intermittent supply of untreated tap-water.

There are agricultural co-operatives on both sides of Kanzalu ridge. The large Matungulu Farmers' Co-operative Society handles coffee production, pulping and forwarding the coffee to other national agencies, while the New Mbiuni Farmers' Co-operative Society deals mainly with cotton and sunflower seed.

The agricultural extension service has a few junior agricultural assistants and animal health assistants, mainly stationed at Kingoti in Matungulu, and in Miseleni and Mbiuni to the east of the Kanzalu ridge.

The main market centres of Kinyui, Katwanyaa, Katheka, Miseleni and Kathama have 10–30 simply constructed *dukas* (shops) selling a variety of commodities, including salt, kerosene, maize, beans and simple clothing. Small amounts of fruit and vegetables are also sold in the open areas of these market centres. The more important centre with fixed market days are outside the study area; the most important of these are Tala, Kangundo, Mbiuni and Mwala.

Cropping pattern

As in most less developed country smallholder farming systems, there is virtually no monocropping, and intercropping of various annuals is more important. Hardly any farmers cultivate all their land, a little over 50 percent being usual, the rest being left fallow or under bush grass for livestock to graze (Collinson and Onchere, 1978). In this area farmers are expected to conserve soil and water by such methods as constructing ditches, terraces and benches (Peberdy, 1958).

Maize (*Zea mays*) has come to be the dominant crop during the last two or three decades; there seem to be production problems with sorghum (*Sorghum vulgare*) and bulrush millet (*Penissetum typhoides*). Birds of *Quelea* spp. cause untold damage to these two crops, and popular taste seems to be turning from these two crops to maize. The major crops interplanted with maize include pigeon pea (*Cajanus cajan*), beans (*Phaseolus vulgaris*) and cow-pea (*Vigna* spp.).

Essentially there are two cropping seasons, dictated by the bimodal rainfall pattern (Fig 1). Actual farming operations start when the short rains set in. This is the most critical farming time as time of planting is known to influence yields of major staples. Thus, in just a matter of weeks, the pigeon pea crop planted the previous year has to be harvested, carried to the homestead and threshed, and the land prepared for the next sowing. Those with oxen and ploughs do this after clearing the pigeon pea plants, except when, occasionally, new land is being opened up, in which case sowing is delayed until after seed-bed preparation.

Maize is the first seed to be sown. Beans are sown later, after the maize has germinated, together with cow-pea and other minor crops. Pigeon pea is the last seed to be sown.

Some cotton and sunflower are grown as a cash crop by about 10

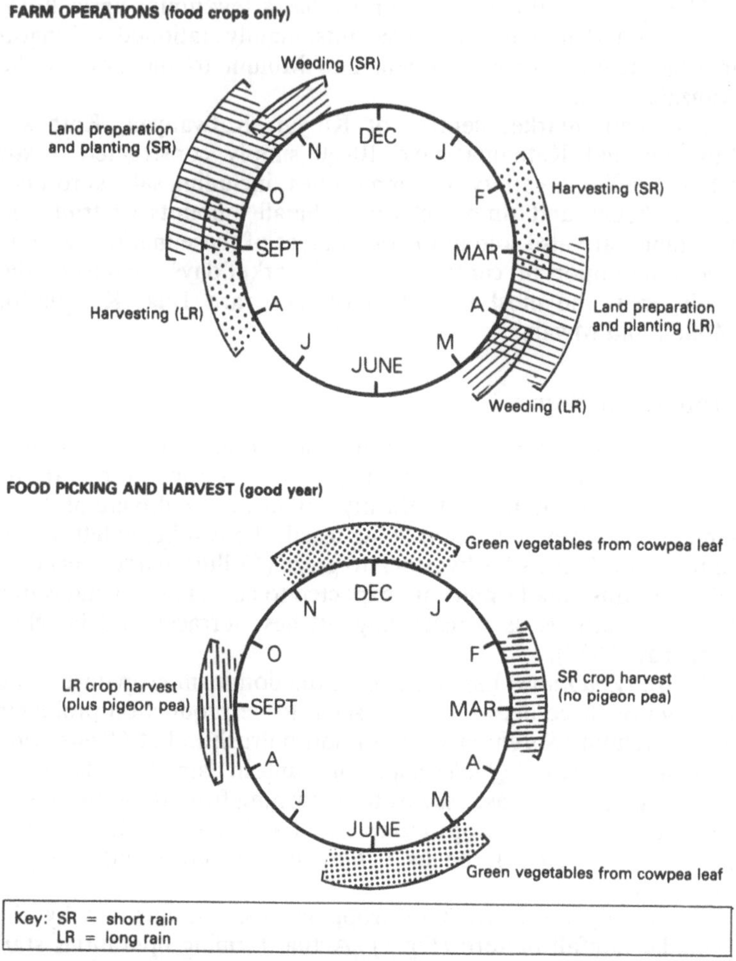

Figure 1. The pattern of farm activities and food availability.

percent of households on the east of Kanzalu ridge. These are sown after the staple crops but there is a good deal of interplanting during the short rains. The relatively inactive period just before the rains end is preferred for the planting of fruits, vegetables and other minor crops and this is usually done simultaneously with the preparation and repair of benches or terraces for soil and water conservation. The cropping pattern of the major staples is more or less the same on the west of Kanzalu ridge, although more minor crops are interplanted there than in the east. On both sides of the ridge maize and other staples are planted between the already

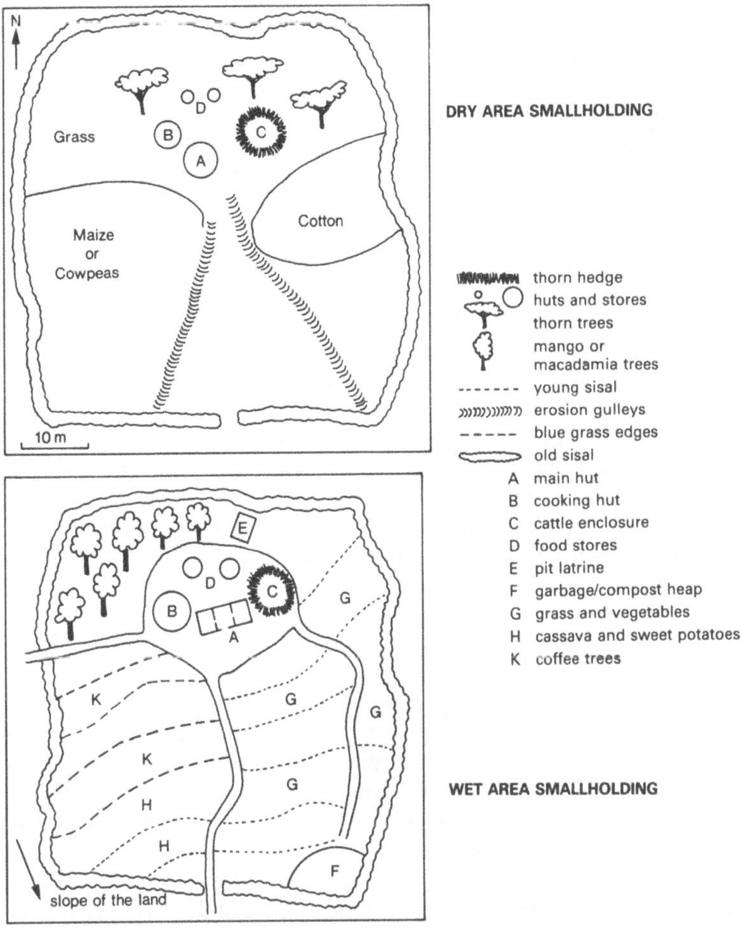

Typical Machakos smallholdings.
(Modified from Fig. 84 in *The Lands and Peoples of East Africa*. Hickman et al. Longman, 1973)

grown pigeon pea during the long rains. For the majority of the year the area west of Kanzalu looks greener than that to the east because coffee—the cash crop in this area—is an evergreen, whereas the cotton and sunflower grown in the east are annuals.

Over 90 percent of the farmers east of Kanzalu use oxen for cultivation, though only about 50 percent of farmers actually own a pair of working oxen. Those who do have oxen and a plough tend to lend or hire them out to others, normally after they have completed their own work. Thus households with no plough and draught oxen of their own tend to plant late.

Work on the farms tends to peak during the critical operations of land preparation, planting, weeding and harvesting. Between these operations, and in particular after the weeding of either the short- or long-rain crops, family labour is diverted to several other farming and non-farming activities (Onchere, 1982). Cash-crop cultivation is generally considered a man's job while food crops are regarded as the women's province, but this attitude may be changing.

Over 80 percent of households keep cattle and goats or sheep. Animal husbandry is more prominent in the eastern part of the area, where the average herd size is 8.94 animals (cattle, sheep and goats) per household. Taking one cow or ox, or five goats or sheep, as one livestock unit, there are about three units per hectare east of Kanzalu which, considering the pattern of pasture growth and in the absence of elaborate supplementary feeding, is rather a high stocking rate. The trend in recent years, however, has been for the cattle and livestock count per household to fall. Collinson and Onchere (1978) estimated that there had been a drop of about 10 percent between 1969 and 1977, possibly owing to the occasional droughts, to population pressure on land, or to some less systematic form of destocking.

Household economy

Agriculture is generally the most important source of household income and thus fundamental to household economic development in the area. Incomes, however, are notoriously difficult to define and measure in rural areas of less developed countries because no farm records are kept and income from other sources is not always accurately recalled.

Between 1973–82 several investigators determined income by different methods of sampling, data collection and analysis (Kolkena, 1975; Wallis and van Waning, 1976; Kuné et al., 1979; Onchere,

Table 2.
Average monthly income and sources of income according to area (approximately 8 Ksh=1 US$).

Income and source of income	*Western part*	*Eastern part*
Total income, Ksh	407	235
Sources of income:		
Non-farm income	60%	55%
Coffee	20%	—
Foodcrops and livestock	20%	45%

1982). In an agro-economic survey based on single visits in 1975 Onchere estimated yearly income at Ksh 4885 to the west of Kanzalu and Ksh 2825 to the east (Ksh 8≃US$1; see Table 2). These figures are higher than those reported by most other studies, possibly because harvests were fairly good in 1975 (Onchere, 1976). All studies found higher incomes to the west of Kanzalu than to the east, but also a more uneven distribution of income on the western side.

Farming income provides 40–70 percent of total income. One economically significant off-farm activity—apart from salaried work outside the study area—is the picking of coffee on the nearby coffee estates of Kayatta and Matungulu. In the 1978–79 coffee harvest Ksh 2.50 was paid per *debe* (18-litre container) of coffee picked: an average day's picking would be five debes, yielding Ksh 12.50, or about Ksh 75 per week or Ksh 300 per month.

About 19 percent of the de jure population is, on average, absent from the study area at any given time (see Chapter 5). Most of these absentees are labour migrants and it is likely that they make an important contribution to the socio-economic well-being of the area. Migrants visit their rural homes regularly and bring home a considerable amount of money and goods (including food) on these visits. Apart from this short-term influence on household resources, migrants (mostly males aged 20–59 years) may also have a long-term development effect on the area through their contact with external sources of education and the spreading of new skills. The fact that most local administrative chiefs or assistant chiefs, and village-level opinion leaders are elderly men who have in the past worked elsewhere in the country supports this view.

The author making a home visit.

2. Patterns of food production, availability and intake

A study was undertaken east of Kanzalu ridge with the major aim of analysing the patterns of food production, availability and intake of about 80 carefully selected households with children of differing nutritional status (Onchere, 1982). Data were collected longitudinally, over a full agricultural calendar in 1978–79, using mainly 48-hour and 24-hour recall techniques. The hypothesis was that households with undernourished and/or low-birth-weight children were, on average, poorer and would show less adequate patterns of food production, availability and intake than households with well-nourished children.

Materials and methods

The nutrition studies described in Chapters 10 and 11 provided an up-to-date sampling framework, since data were available on the nutritional status of all under-5s in the area as well as on birth weights. The households were sampled and analysed according to nutritional status and birth weight of the 'reference child' in the household. Within each nutritional group the sample was drawn at random but with differing sampling fractions. Three household groups can be distinguished:

> *UNC/LBW* households with either one or more UnderNourished Children or one or more Low-Birth-Weight children. (*UNC* = below 75 percent Harvard Standard weight for age and *LBW* = birth weight of 2.5 kg or less);
>
> *NBW* households with well-nourished children with Normal Birth Weights (*NBW* = above 75 percent Harvard Standard weight for age and birth weight over 2.5 kg);
>
> *SPE* households without UNC/LBW children that were considered 'successful' or 'model' (= *SPE*cial) by an agricultural extension officer during the study period.

This means therefore that the three samples can be arranged according to their degree of vulnerability: the UNC/LBW group—a group of 'more vulnerable' households, and the NBW and SPE groups, two groups of 'less vulnerable' households.

Four male and two female field-enumerators collected data during a full agricultural year. The male enumerators visited about 10 households a day, using a 48-hour recall technique. They collected data on such aspects as: farm and off-farm activities of household members; sales, purchases and gifts of any items including food and money; farm structures and equipment; land use and land sizes; crops harvested, sold or stored; livestock numbers and changes; and income and expenditure patterns. They visited each of their assigned households every other day.

Most of the 'agricultural' data were converted in such a way that they could be expressed as 'subsistence units' (SU) per household. One SU is the equivalent of a notional adult male and values for other household members were derived from the FAO/WHO-recommended energy intakes per day (FAO/WHO, 1973).

Sex and age-group	*Conversion factor*
adult male	1.0
adult female, non-pregnant, non-lactating	0.7
lactating woman	0.9
pregnant woman, 1st trimester	0.8
pregnant woman, 2nd and 3rd trimesters	0.9
child <1 yr	0.3
child 1–3 yrs	0.4
child 4–6 yrs	0.6
child 7–9 yrs	0.7
boy 10–12 yrs	0.9
boy 13–19 yrs	1.0
girl 10–19 yrs	0.8

The female enumerators collected data on food preparation and consumption. Using a 24-hour recall technique, they visited 4–5 households daily and thus covered all households once a fortnight. During the interviews they collected information for all household members who had been present the previous day. Only age was taken into account in the analysis, using the following conversion factors to calculate nutritional parameters per 'consumption unit' (CU).

Age group	*Conversion factor*
<7 yrs	0.5
7–13 yrs	0.8
over 13 yrs	1.0

Results

Food availability pattern

There are two cropping seasons in the area, which dictate the farm activities, food production and food availability (see Fig. 1). The significance of the short rains and long rains and how these influence food availability and consumption was established by identification of a clear 'food trough' period (in July–August) and two 'food peak' periods as shown in Figure 2.

During July–August the food supply from the household's own *shamba* (farm) decreased and the average total intake per consumption unit dropped below 10.0 MJ/day; in several households the food intake even approached 4.0 MJ/CU/day. During this food-trough period about a quarter of the energy consumed was derived from bought food. Towards the end of the year the availability of food from the shamba was even lower, but intakes were kept high by what can be described as a 'Christmas purchase' effect, when many relatives from outside the study area return home with foods and/or money.

From Figure 2 it can also be observed that the first food peak follows the short-rains crop harvest, whereas the second follows

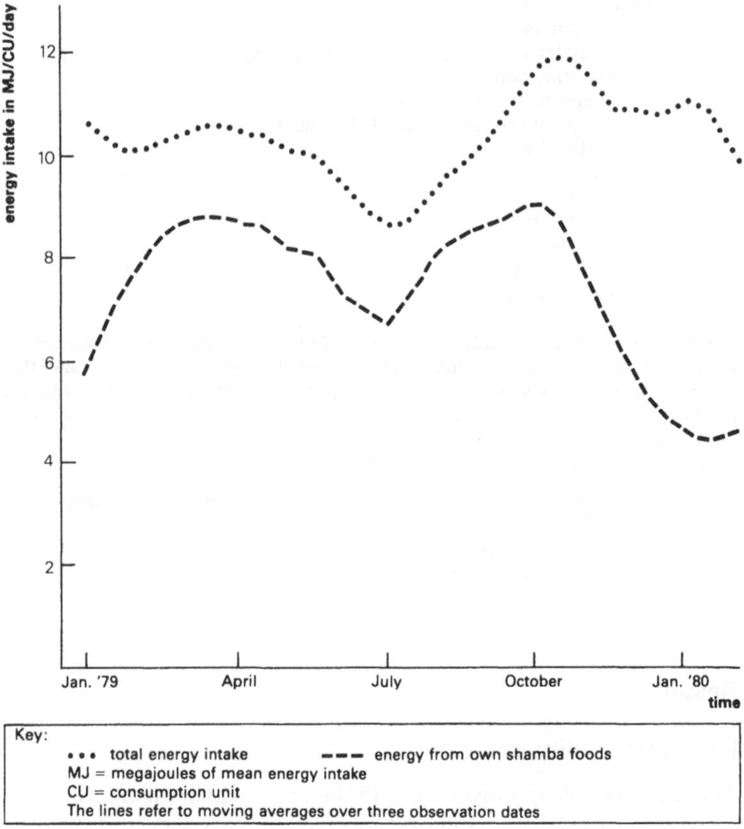

Figure 2. Contribution of own shamba produced foods to total energy intake over a full agricultural cycle (MJ/CU/day) (n = 65; UNC/LBW and NBW households).

the long-rains harvest, particularly the pigeon pea harvest. It is in the period after the pigeon pea harvest that cash crops such as cotton and sunflower are sold, which could explain why there was an apparent increase in disposable income in most households over the study period, as shown in Figure 3. It can also be seen that 'more vulnerable' households had a lower weekly expenditure on food, possibly because they had lower disposable income compared with 'less vulnerable' households.

There appeared to be a significant rise in expenditures in all groups from 1978 to 1979. This was partly because food prices increased somewhat over the study period and partly because

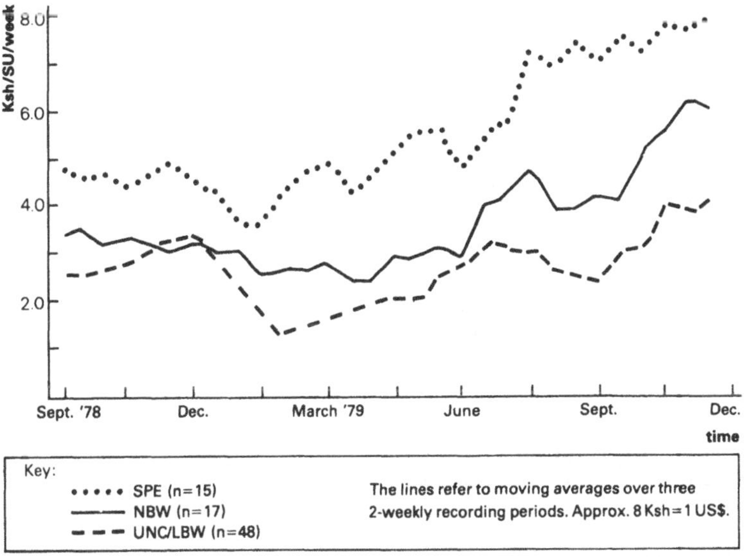

Figure 3. Mean weekly expenditures on purchased foods by various groups of households (Ksh/SU/week).

expenditures were under-reported at the beginning of the study; respondents seemed reluctant to give accurate data on incomes and expenditures initially but once they got used to the field-workers' frequent visits, reporting accuracy improved considerably.

Food storage and production patterns

The apparent lack of foods in store during December, January and February was more than compensated nutritionally by the high food purchases around Christmas-time, followed by early culling of green vegetables (cow pea leaves) and immature young beans, both from the short-rains crop planted in September–October. Soon afterwards the more reliable short-rains maize crop matured and began to be consumed piecemeal from the fields.

The March–April food-storage peak, shown in Figure 4, refers to dry maize only; by this time a lot of green (fresh) maize has been eaten. The pattern in Figure 4 shows marked differences between household groups of differing vulnerability, with the more vulnerable group displaying the poorest storage pattern.

In all households the short-rains crops (maize and beans) were much better than the long-rains crops, although the pigeon pea

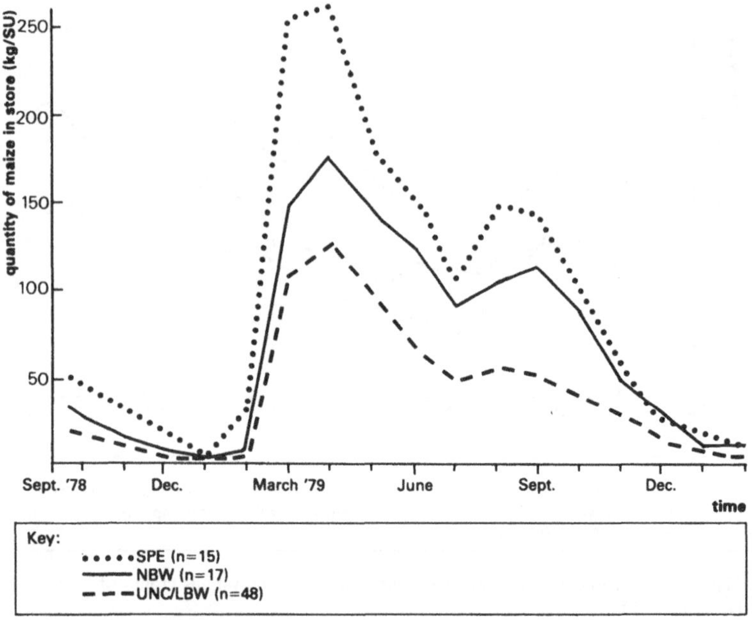

Figure 4. Quantity of maize stored by various groups of households (kg/SU).

crop (planted during the short rains) is not harvested until the end of the long rains.

A significant positive relationship was also found between the quantity of land cultivated per 'subsistence unit' and the quantity of food produced, expressed in Ksh/SU (Fig. 5). Thus, where more land could be cultivated, productivity was higher than in households that for one reason or another had not extended their area of cultivation. The main reason for failing to cultivate more land appeared to be not having draught oxen rather than shortage of land. Those who do not own oxen have to borrow or hire them, and a significant positive relationship can be seen between the ownership (and use) of oxen and ploughs and the quantity of food produced and consumed (Onchere, 1982—details not quoted here).

Generally, farmers tended to cultivate about half their land, using mainly family labour and simple hand tools: clearly use of oxen and ploughs considerably increases the speed with which farming operations can be carried out at critical times of the year.

Maize yields per hectare to the east of Kanzalu ridge were generally lower than yields on the west side; both compared

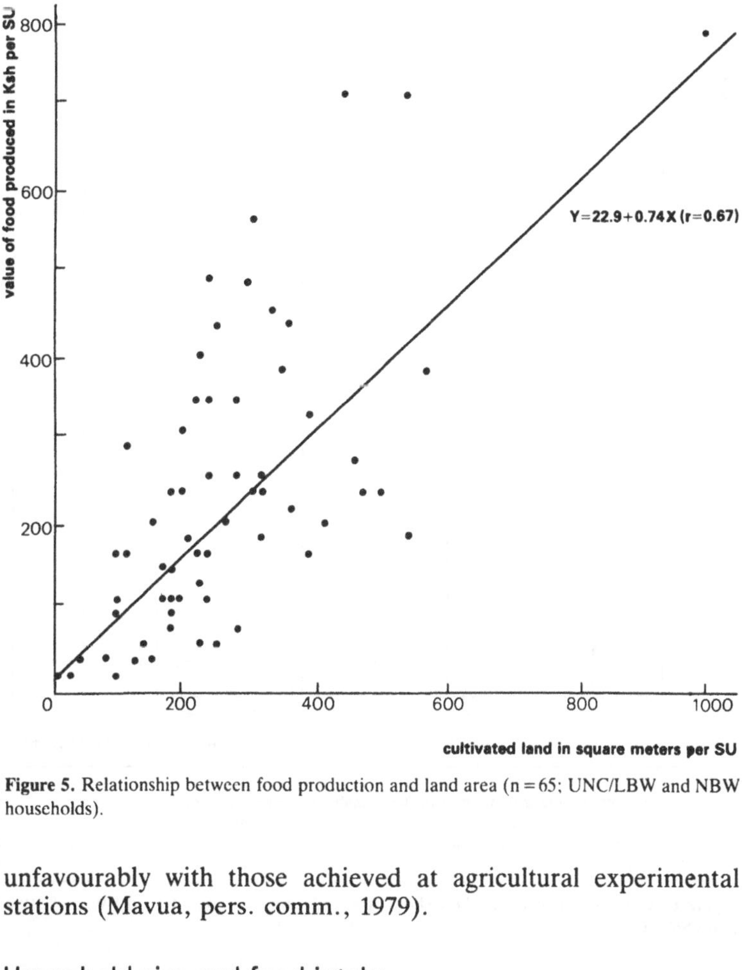

Figure 5. Relationship between food production and land area (n = 65; UNC/LBW and NBW households).

unfavourably with those achieved at agricultural experimental stations (Mavua, pers. comm., 1979).

Household size and food intake

Figure 6 shows a significant negative relationship between household size and food intake, clearly demonstrating that per capita food intake diminishes as family size increases. An analysis of covariance was done to test the null hypothesis that there was no relationship between these two variables. For this analysis 20 measurements were available per household in four periods of observation: the hypothesis was rejected for all periods studied (Onchere, 1982). No clear relationship was found between food intake and other household characteristics such as sex, age, education or religion of head of household.

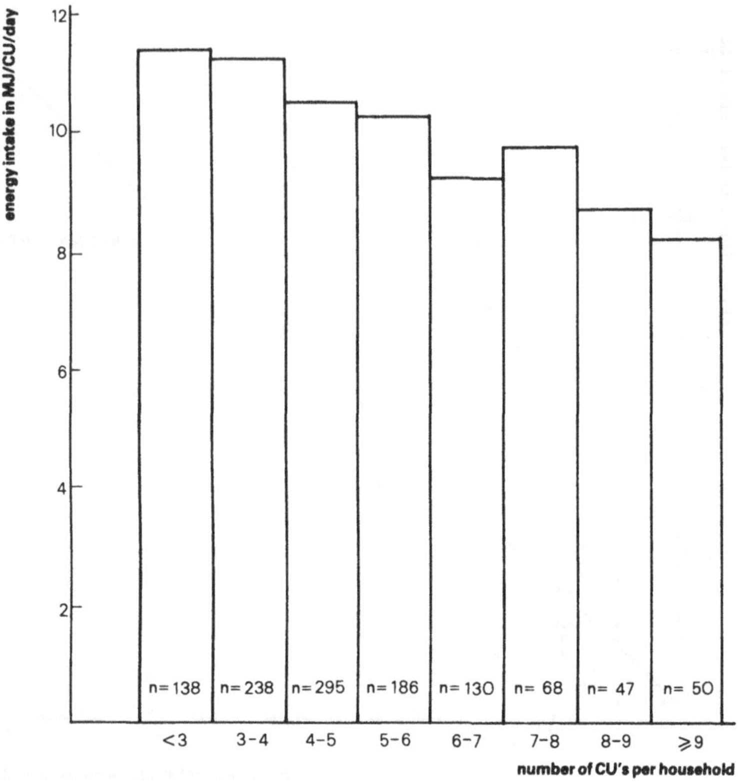

Key:
n = number of measurements in the 65 households; there were about 20 measurements per household in 4 periods of observation
MJ = megajoules of mean energy intake
CU = consumption unit

Figure 6. Relationship between household size and energy intake (UNC/LBW and NBW households).

Discussion

The analysis in the second part of this chapter indicates that households regarded, from the nutritional status of their children, as more vulnerable tended to produce less food, to have less food in store and to have less money to spend on food at any given time than less vulnerable households. The latter, as represented by the NBW and SPE groups, tended to be 'richer' in various respects, such as land size and ownership of oxen and other livestock, though not all these relationships were statistically significant.

Previous research in the Machakos area has shown that the

quality of the habitual diet is favourable but quantitative intakes are below FAO/WHO-recommended intakes (see Chapter 13). Efforts to increase productivity of land and labour are thus bound to have a beneficial impact on nutritional status and health. Such efforts should, however, recognize that farmers in the area are neither purely subsistence farmers nor purely commercially motivated. They are definitely not profit-maximizers in the capitalistic sense. Their primary concern appears to be to produce enough food to feed their families and possibly a little more to sell for cash for such basic necessities as salt, matches and simple clothing.

Research and development programmes should not be based on achievements possible under optimal conditions at experimental stations but should be adapted more to the felt needs and problems of the farmers involved. Inputs that clearly increase productivity in a research setting may fail in practice owing, for instance, to lack of manpower, draught animals, and capital.

Similarly, while it is nutritionally and economically justifiable to promote family planning programmes in the area, it should be realized that the tendency to have large families will persist as long as children—in the minds of the people—are considered as an investment rather than 'consumption units', as a potential source of family labour and possibly of financial support in old age rather than as a liability needing food, clothing and education. The key to eventual success of family planning programmes may well lie in agricultural and economic development of the region and the country as a whole. It is, however, not the concern of this chapter to discuss in any detail the pros and cons of large family size but simply to point out that a significant relationship does exist, in the Machakos study area, between family size and per capita food intake.

In conclusion it may be emphasized that the nature and complexity of agricultural and nutritional problems is far from being understood. In order to progress, an interdisciplinary approach is highly desirable. In this sense the Machakos Project legacy is unique, despite the obvious difficulties of organizing and conducting a heterogeneous group of investigators from different disciplines.

References

Braun HMH, The reliability of the rainy seasons in Machakos and Kitui districts, National Agricultural Laboratories, Nairobi (1977).

Collinson MP and Onchere SR, The JPM/CIMMYT preliminary report: Data presentation for parts of lower drier areas of northern division of Machakos, CIMMYT/Medical Research Centre, Nairobi (1978).

Fairburn WA, Geology of North-Machakos-Thika area, Survey of Kenya, Report No. 59 (1963).
FAO/WHO, Energy and protein requirements, Report of the ad hoc Expert Committee, FAO, Rome (1973).
Gemert W, The weather in Machakos project area from 1975 to 1979, Medical Research Centre, Nairobi (1980).
Kolkena TFM, Report on a socio-economic survey in two rural areas of Machakos district of Kenya, Medical Research Centre, Nairobi/Dept of Geography, University of Utrecht (1975).
Kuné JB et al., The economic setting at household level, Trop Geogr Med 31 (1979) 415–47.
Mbuvi JP et al., A preliminary evaluation of the soils of the North-Western Machakos district, Kenya Soil Survey, Nairobi (1974).
Onchere SR, Structure and performance of agricultural product and factor markets in the northern division of Machakos district, Kenya, thesis, University of Nairobi (1976).
Onchere SR, The pattern of food production, availability and intake of the people of eastern Kenya: The case of north-western Machakos, Thesis, University of Reading, UK (1982).
Peberdy J, The Machakos Gazeteer, Ministry of Agriculture, Nairobi (1958).
Wallis M and van Waning E, Report on a socio-economic survey in two rural areas of Machakos district, Kenya, Medical Research Centre, Nairobi/University of Utrecht (1976).

3

Household activities and dietary patterns

W.M. van Steenbergen
J.A. Kusin
S.R. Onchere

Introduction

Traditional dietary patterns, developed through generations, are based on locally available foods and are deeply rooted in a culture. They change over time as subsistence economy is partly replaced by market economy. They are also influenced by other aspects of 'development', such as education, migration, exposure to commercially advertised foods and so on.

The fundamental question from a nutrition point of view is whether the quality of a traditional diet is conducive to malnutrition and other deficiencies.

To gain an impression of prevailing dietary patterns and sources of foods consumed, observations were made in a random sample of households in two ecologically different but adjacent locations in the study area during two seasons.

Materials and methods

The study was conducted in the months September–December, 1975 (lean season) and June–September, 1976 (harvest period for maize) by one nutritionist and five female field-workers, recruited from the area.

In each of the five sublocations one to three clusters of households were selected at random. Seventy-three households with one or more children under 4 were included. Forty-seven of these households were located in the western (Matungulu) and 26 in the eastern (Mbiuni) part of the area, providing a sample of around 3 percent of the total number of households. They can be considered representative of the population in the area concerned.

A field-worker spent four consecutive days from 7 a.m. to 7 p.m. in one household. All field-workers were supervised daily by the nutritionist.

By observation and interview they recorded the living conditions, food availability and sources, ways of food preparation, meal pattern and activities in every household. A detailed record of every mother's activities was made by the diary method.

Results

Family life

The people lived mostly in fenced-in compounds, scattered throughout the area, consisting of two to four separate huts and a food store. The average household under study had nine members, living in different huts, the head of the household and his wife occupying the best. In the western part of the area more huts had zinc roofs and home-baked brick or stone walls and two to three rooms; in the eastern side grass roofs, mud blocks and one-room houses were more common. Older children as well as newly married couples usually build their own houses, nowadays mainly from home-baked bricks. The interior is simple; a few small stools, one or two home-made wooden or sisal-stringed beds, a table and a folding chair to be unfolded for an important guest constitute all the furniture in the average household.

A little more than half the families under study lived in an extended household. Such a household might include the head, his wife or wives and unmarried children, married sons with family, other relatives and servants, all sharing a common kitchen, having a common foodstore and usually tilling the same land. Many families are incomplete, with one or more members living outside the area, either employed or in search of a salaried job. Generally they come home at least once in a month for a short visit.

Children collecting firewood.

Household and farm management are a combined effort of all household members, starting early in the morning at sunrise and lasting until a few hours after sunset. Within their capacity, all members perform fixed duties, contributing towards the family's well-being. The old people (*wazee*) are respected, fed and cared for. They are regarded as authorities, and act as head of the household. Men who remain at home take their part in cultivating the cash crop, in trading livestock, in building the house, and in food crop production, particularly the ploughing. Weeding and harvesting of both the food and the cash crop (coffee) are done in collaboration with the womenfolk. Milking and grazing cattle is predominantly the responsibility of the women and children. *Shambas* (gardens) are usually near the compounds. Grazing areas and drinking places for cattle may be far distant. In practice women do most of the work.

The 'activity study' carried out among mothers of children under three, showed that the largest part of their time, some 7 hours a day, is spent near home, in food preparation, childcare and resting, and domestic activities (Fig. 1). The latter include collecting water and firewood as well as cleaning the house and washing clothes and household utensils. Mothers are more or less bound to remain near home to look after the youngest children during morning hours when almost all children from 4–15 years old are at school. Children in lower classes do not attend school in the

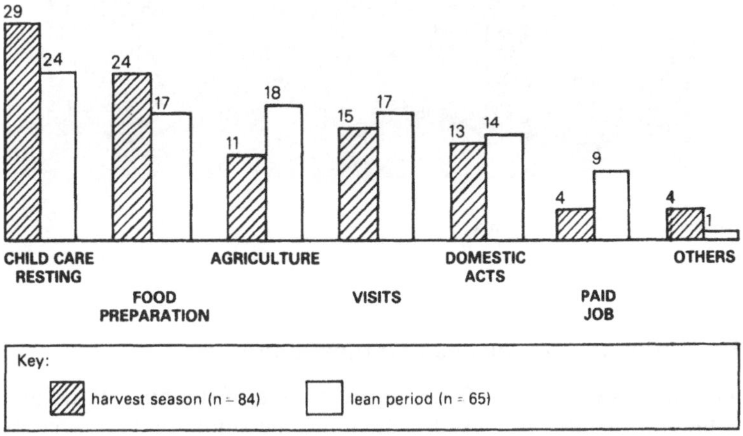

Figure 1. Distribution of maternal activities as percentages of a 12-hour day; both areas combined.

afternoons and they then look after the younger ones in order to give mothers time to collect water and firewood (approximately one hour a day), and to visit the market, church or friends (2 hours a day). Nearly 2 hours a day are spent in the garden or farm or looking after livestock. In general the differences between the western and eastern parts of the area are small. On the other hand, the differences between the two seasons are relatively large. The extra time needed on the farms during the planting and weeding season results in less time being spent on food preparation and child care and resting.

In extended families mothers are less tied down, because grandparents and other relatives are regarded as very suitable caretakers for young children. The pace of daily life is unhurried; even though continuous demands are being made on the mother, she accepts this as long as family members are healthy, everybody is fed adequately and school fees can be paid on time.

Women returning from the market.

Food preparation, dishes and meal patterns

The fireplace is on the floor, in the middle of the hut. Wood and sometimes charcoal is used as fuel and the smoke has to force its way through the thatching of the roof or through an open window or door. Three stones are used as a tripod that holds the cooking pot. The fireplace has no protection and children occasionally accidentally fall into the fire.

The kitchen may also serve as living and sleeping quarters for household members as well as for goats and sheep that sometimes occupy a corner overnight.

Cooking equipment used to cook maize and beans consists of large locally made clay pots with narrow necks, which hold the heat and allow little evaporation. *Sufurias* (aluminium cooking pots) are in use for the preparation of other dishes. Enamel or plastic cups, bowls and plates as well as calabashes and spoons are commonly used for drinking and eating. Gourds are in use for the storage of milk, water, home-made butter, beer, seeds etc. A mortar and pestle is noticed in only some households as maize is only home-pounded for one particular dish (*mothokoi*); otherwise maize, millet and sorghum grains are ground by means of a diesel mill available at market centres.

Preparing a meal in a typical huge cooking pot in which several meals of maize and beans are simmered for hours, usually in a separate cooking hut.

Water needed for food preparation and personal cleanliness is collected by the women and children. Distances to the water points vary considerably. In the eastern part of the area it can take as much as three-quarters of an hour to walk to the nearest hole, dug into a dry river bank or the ever-flowing Athi river. Dug holes provide water at a very slow rate and women often have to queue for it. Lively scenes can be observed at special places along the Athi river; women collecting water for domestic purposes; others washing their laundry with cattle, sheep and goats having their daily drink next to them; and many people using the river as a swimming pool or bath. The western part of the area has fewer water problems; quite a number of wells, scattered throughout the area, provide sufficient good quality water. However, some areas are heavily infected with bilharzia.

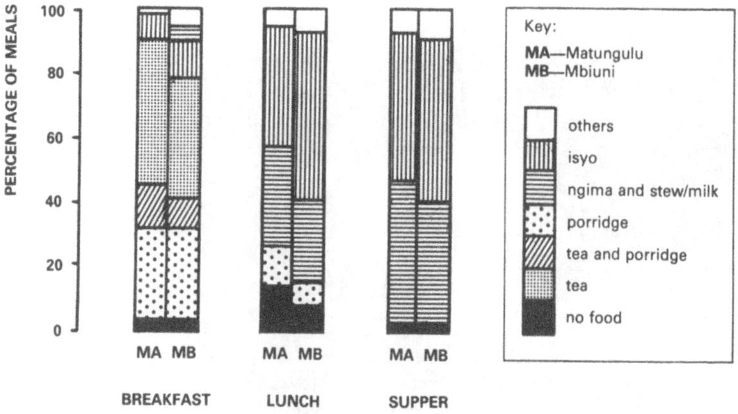

Figure 2. Meal pattern in Matungulu (western) and Mbiuni (eastern) households seasons combined; in percentage.

Food preparation is done by women. The usual Kamba culinary repertoire includes five different maize dishes; two or three tuber dishes are occasionally consumed on the western side. Figure 2 shows the meal pattern of both areas (the two seasons are taken together as no substantial differences between them were observed). Three meals a day, the same as in the old days (Hobley, 1967), is the common pattern.

Breakfast

In general, during morning hours a calabash of porridge and/or a cup of tea is taken. About 10 percent of the families eat some left-over food from the day before; less than 5 percent take no breakfast at all.

Tea for breakfast is becoming increasingly fashionable in many parts of East Africa (Rodrigues, 1972; Keller et al., 1969). The Kamba only prepare tea when sugar and preferably also milk are available. Tea, milk and sugar are added to boiling water and kept simmering for about 10 minutes. An average of 60 g sugar and 150 ml milk are used for each litre of tea.

Porridges are distinguished by their thickness; *mutweku* is a drinking porridge (around 70 g flour per litre); *makamu* is a thicker type eaten with a spoon (100–140 g flour per litre); *ekii* is a fermented type of drinking porridge rarely seen any more nowadays.

Most of the porridges are prepared from maize flour; sugar and milk are added according to taste when available. On average 20 g sugar and 200 ml milk are used for a litre of porridge. Porridges prepared from millet and sorghum flour were once very popular, but nowadays these cereals are very scarce and regarded as particularly suitable for children and for women who have given birth.

Lunch

An evenly distributed approximately 80 percent of all midday meals feature *isyo* or *ngima* with stew; in around 10 percent of consumer days no lunch is eaten; while other meals (less than 10 percent) are porridge, chapatti bread, *nzenga* (see below), or a tuber dish (Fig. 2). *Isyo*, the Kamba national dish since a long way back (Lindblom, 1920), is a mixture of the staple foods maize and beans or peas. It is regarded not only as the most delicious but also the most nutritious dish, and hence is consumed practically every day in large quantities. A saying in the area is: 'A day without *isyo* can never be a good day'. The maize kernel and pulses are cooked for 2–5 hours. Up to 10 kg *isyo* may be cooked at one time and this may serve a family of 10 people for about three meals. At mealtime, enough of the mixture for one serving is fried with fat and onions or is just heated. The proportion of maize to beans or peas varies with the season. During harvest period the proportion of fresh maize to fresh peas is around 2:1. A few months later the ratio is on average 3–4 parts dry maize to one part dry legumes, with wide variations due to stock variability and money available.

The Kikuyu tribe in Kenya has a similar dish named *githeri*. Kikuyu *irio* differs from Kamba *isyo* in that besides the maize and beans or peas it contains vegetables, Irish potatoes, and bananas singly or in combination (Rodriguez, 1972; Keller et al., 1969). Only very few Kamba households add vegetable (*Colocasia* leaves) to the maize-bean mixture. A special type of *isyo* is called *mothokoi*. This consists of the same maize and bean-pea mixture but the maize is wetted and pounded in a wooden mortar to remove the bran before it is cooked with the legumes. This soft and more easily digestible type of *isyo* is prepared on special occasions and for special population groups such as the old people with difficulty in chewing. A similar maize preparation is reported from Tanzania (Schlage, 1969) under the name *pure*.

Ngima (Swahili: *ugali*) served with a stew is a well known dish in eastern and South Africa (Robson, 1974; Rodriguez, 1972; Keller et al., 1969). According to the Kamba it is their second best dish. *Ngima* is a thick paste prepared from (whole) maize flour and water (1 part flour to 3 parts water). It is ready after about 30 minutes' cooking. When flour is short, a thinner type, *kitheke*, is prepared. *Ngima* is sometimes served with fresh or sour milk, but more often with a stew.

Stew is a mixture of tomato, onion, and fat with the addition of one or more of: potatoes, green vegetables, pumpkin, fresh pulses or meat. The average number of ingredients used in a stew is just over three, with tomato, fat and onions ranking highest. *Ngima* and stew is cooked for one meal at a time. A left-over may serve as a snack, particularly for children. *Nzenga* is broken maize grains; the maize is ground in a special *nzenga* mill. The big pieces and flour are separated by a sieve, the coarser *nzenga* is cooked for about one hour and served with milk or with a stew. The flour is used for the preparation of porridge or *ngima*. *Nzenga* resembles rice, which is considered a luxury in the area.

Supper

Evening food is usually served late, towards the end of the day, just before bed. Again, maize dishes are the most usual: over 80 percent of the dinners served are *isyo* or *ngima*, with *isyo* predominating. The other meals are similar to those served at lunch time. The foods people eat between their main meals are difficult to assess: boiled or roasted fresh maize, sweet potato and taro appear the most important. Sugarcane, papaya, mango, bananas and loquats are eaten almost exclusively by children.

Sources of foods and frequency of consumption

The most frequently used foods in both seasons and in both areas are maize, pulses, milk, vegetables, sugar, tea and fat (Fig. 3). Consumption patterns of maize, pulses and milk are very similar in both areas; households in the eastern part of the area, however, obtain these foods proportionally more from their own farms than

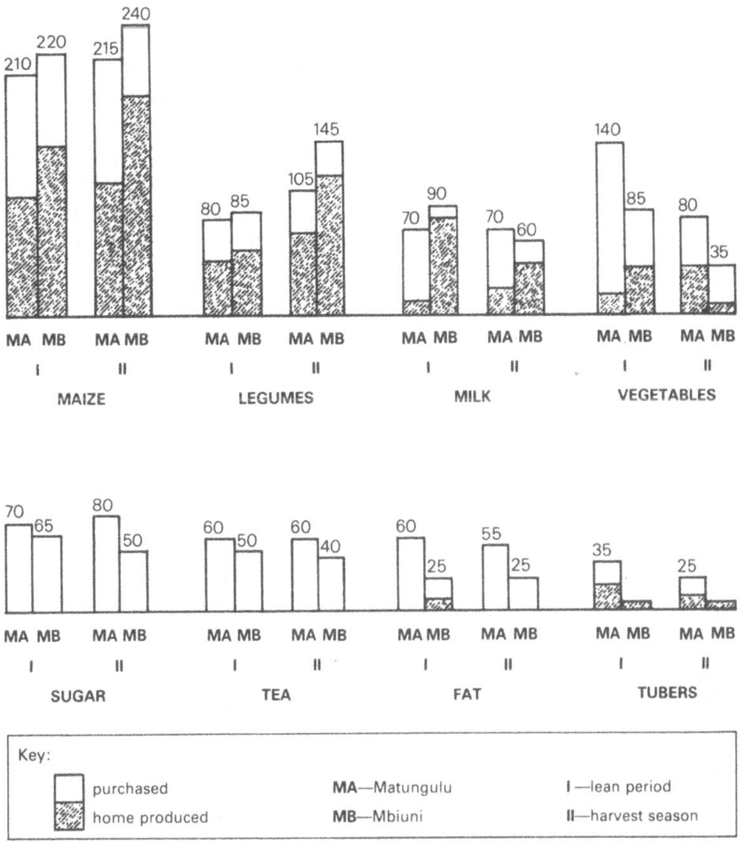

Figure 3. Food consumption frequencies and food sources per 100 days; Matungulu (Western) and Mbiuni (Eastern) households; harvest season and lean period (N=650 consumer days).

do people in the western part. Maize is eaten twice a day and beans or peas once a day.

From the lowest to the highest income groups, Kamba people cannot do without maize and beans. The better-off more and more often add fat and meat and increase the proportion of beans or peas to maize. Even when stocks are finished and food has to be bought, maize and legumes remain their favourite food. The price of the alternative foods (Table 1) may, however, also be an important decisive factor. A few months before the new harvest, maize has to be bought about half the time (Fig. 3). Surprisingly, however, even during the maize harvest time, maize was purchased in 38 percent and 23 percent of the occasions it was eaten in the western and eastern parts of the area respectively. This may have been because fresh maize is not suitable to grind into flour. The purchased flour is the *Jogoo* type, commercial maize meal of 83 percent extraction, or whole maize flour. Beans and pigeon peas are, taking the seasons together, about 66 percent home-produced. Table 1 shows that maize is the cheapest source of both calories and vegetable protein; pulses are the next relatively cheap vegetable protein source.

Table 1.
Food prices in Machakos district, 1975
in Kenyan cents per 100 g food, per 1000 calories and per 10 g protein.

*Food**	*Price in cents for*		
	100 g food	*1000 Kcal*	*10 g protein*
Maize, whole	13	36	14
Wheat flour (70% extraction)	26	74	26
Rice (highly milled)	35	99	50
Bread, white	40	160	50
Legumes (kidney bean)	35	100	15
Sweet potato	13	114	87
Irish potato	17	226	85
Green banana	16	125	160
Cowpea leaf	10	208	20
Cabbage varieties	13	500	65
Tomato	25	1250	250
Packet standardized milk	20	300	61
Humanized milk (powder)	260	520	197
Meat (beef, moderate fat)	55	209	34
Egg	80	506	62
Fat	114	127	—
Sugar	45	113	—

1 Ksh = 100 Kenyan cents is equivalent to approximate 0.12 $ USA.
* B.S. Platt, Tables of representative values of foods commonly used in tropical countries.

Milk is consumed on about 70 out of 100 consumer days (Fig. 3). Calculated over both seasons, milk is bought 81 percent and 21 percent of the time in the coffee-growing and grazing areas respectively. People in the west side of the area buy packets of milk from the shops; in the eastern part one can only buy fresh milk from a neighbouring farm. Milk is relatively more expensive than meat (Table 1), yet the Kamba regard milk as an essential part of their diet. Sugar and tea are used, on average, every other day and are bought from local shops.

Fat—a Kenyan-manufactured vegetable fat—is more frequently part of the daily menu in the west than in the east, on average every other day in the former and once in four days in the latter. In terms of calorie value, fat is only slightly more expensive than sugar (Table 1). Very few households make butter from their own cows' milk.

Vegetable consumption—including leaf vegetables and tomatoes —differs both between the two seasons and between the two areas. During the rainy seasons people in the west part eat some kind of vegetable every day, people in the east about every other day; towards the dry season consumption is reduced in the western part to every other day and in the eastern part to once in 3–4 days (Fig. 3).

The type of vegetable consumed varies with the season: during the rainy periods most households have cow-pea leaf and some pumpkin leaf from the gardens while the markets—in the western area in particular—offer, as well as locally grown greens, white cabbage and *sukuma-wiki* (*Brassica carinata*); in the dry seasons greens are very scarce and tomatoes are the only vegetable available in the gardens; once in 3–4 days people in the western part treat themselves to purchased greens. Figure 3 shows that tubers are almost exclusively eaten (and cultivated) in the western area; these include sweet potato, green banana and taro. Sweet potato, taro and cassava are market crops until scarcity sets in when the rains are late. During extended droughts these tubers replaced the maize and the bean staple *isyo* (Redlich, 1971).

Other foods consumed are sorghum, millet, rice, wheat, meat, bread, fruits, onion and salt. Except for onion and salt, consumed in small quantities almost every day, these foods taken together account for a negligible share in the diet.

Discussion

In the two ecologically and economically different parts of the study area the traditional way of life is still maintained, and so are the dietary patterns. The traditional diet of maize and beans, supplemented by vegetables, with some fat and milk, can be considered qualitatively adequate.

In spite of an overall acceptable food consumption pattern, the subsistence farm households in the eastern part are in a vulnerable situation. Lower income was reflected in a lower frequency of consumption of fat, green leafy vegetables, and meat as compared with the western, coffee-growing part. This trend suggests that the quality of the diet will improve at higher income levels. Similar observations have been made in other developing countries (Perissé et al., 1969).

Improvement of the precarious food situation in the eastern part depends largely on the possibility of increased production, and generation of employment. If this cannot be achieved in the near future, emigration can be expected to occur at a higher rate than at present.

Apart from food availability, per capita food consumption is determined by family size. In view of the limited possibilities of increased agricultural output in a rain-dependent, semi-arid area, and of the high fertility rate in the population (see Chapter 5), it is essential that population growth is limited in the years to come.

Finally, attention should be given to the markedly unhygienic living conditions. It is quite likely that in this area morbidity plays a larger role in the pathogenesis of malnutrition than inadequate food intake.

References

Hobley CW, Bantu beliefs and magic, Frank Coss & Co Ltd., 1967, p. 154.

Keller W, Muskat E and Valder E, Some observations regarding economy, diet and nutritional status of Kikuyu farmers in Kenya, In; Investigations into health and nutrition in East Africa, Kraut H and Cremer HC, Weltforum Verslag, München, 1969, p. 241.

Lindblom G, The Akamba in British East Africa, Archives d'études orientales, Uppsala, 17 (1920) 511.

Perissé J, Sizaret F and François P, Nutrition Newsletter, 7 (1969) 5.

Redlich LC, The role of women in the Kamba household, Department of Sociology, Occasional paper, Nairobi, (1971) No 7.

Robson JRK, Ecol Food Nutrit, 3 (1974) 61.

Rodrigues V, Food production and diet: a case study at Githunguri, Thesis, University of Nairobi, 1972, p. 73.

Schlage C, Analyses of some important foodstuffs of Usambara, In; Investigations into health and nutrition in East Africa, Kraut H and Cremer HC, Weltforum Verslag, München, 1969, p. 55.

4

Temporal changes in economic, social and hygiene conditions

R. Slooff
T.W.J. Schulpen

Introduction

In population-based research, household surveys serve to quantify environmental factors for descriptive or analytical purposes. The data obtained may be used either in their original individual form, as in multivariate analyses, or in arbitrary classes that provide a basis for the stratification of the population under study. Whatever the statistical procedures may be, the conclusions that can be drawn depend on the test-retest reliability of the survey data and, more particularly, on the validity of the variables chosen as indicators of the phenomena under study.

The compromises between survey accuracy and economy are well known. In epidemiological studies, where staff and time needed for relatively intensive enquiries are usually scarce, non-medical household aspects are often investigated by means of quick surveys. These normally concentrate on certain 'proxy' variables which are believed to represent the more fundamental characteristics involved.

In order to identify households with children at risk it was one of the aims of the Machakos Project to determine the relationships between patterns of ill health and the child's home environment. To this end a number of social, hygiene and economic household surveys were carried out in the study area (Slooff and Schulpen, 1978; Kuné et al., 1979). Most of the 'proxy' variables used for these surveys had been selected on the basis of the results of two in-depth sample studies carried out earlier (Kolkena, 1974; Kolkena and Pronk, 1975; Wallis and Van Waning, 1976, internal reports MRCN).

Although the health surveillance information in the project was of a longitudinal nature, the social, hygiene and economic survey data related to only one point in time. To determine whether changes in the study area or in particular households could have affected the validity of the survey material when confronted with longitudinal morbidity and mortality data, a comprehensive re-survey was carried out several years later. In this chapter we shall report on changes that took place between the two surveys. In particular, attention will be paid to the stability of the variables used and to the construction of components from selected variables. Methodological questions will be addressed briefly. Full technical details are to be found in Slooff (1981, internal report KIT) and Slooff and Gemert (in press).

The economic setting

Background information on the economic conditions in the study area may be found in Chapter 2 of this monograph and in the paper by Kuné et al. (1979). The most striking aspect is the distinction between the coffee-growing western part, consisting of sublocations Kingoti and Kambusu (see map in Chapter 1), which is relatively rich and the poorer eastern part, consisting of sublocations Katheka, Katitu and Ulaani, where the coffee-growing potential is almost none and cash incomes are much lower. In both parts farm incomes alone are generally insufficient for subsistence needs. A considerable part of the cash income is derived from non-agricultural activities, many of them carried on outside the study area.

The findings of the economic survey carried out in 1974 and the outcome of the 1978 re-survey in respect of the same variables are summarized in Table 1. The mean values of 12 out of 17 variables had changed significantly over the four-year interval, at least in the 619 households of the re-survey sample.

As four years had elapsed between the two surveys, allowances had to be made for the possible effects of ageing alone. When this was done (Slooff and Gemert, in press), the only overall changes that could be fully attributed to time effects occurred in the variables *beans harvested, produces harvested, possessions inside house, professional possessions* and *granaries*.

Enquiry from the Kenya Meteorological Department, Nairobi, showed that more rain had fallen in the area in the year preceding the 1978 survey than in that preceding the 1974 survey. This may explain the increase in beans harvested and produces harvested. The observed accumulation of possessions inside house and professional possessions agrees with what was known about the improved income position of coffee farmers and the general trend

Table 1.
Summary of comparisons between variable scores of 1978 and scores from 1974 survey on economic household conditions (n=619).

Variable	*Scoring options*	*Mean values* $\bar{x}_1$	$\bar{x}_2$	$\bar{x}_2 - \bar{x}_1$	*Nature of change*	*Stability*
Maize harvested	0–7	3.22	3.14	–.08	W>E	–
Beans harvested	0–4	.98	2.32	1.34*	W>E	–
Produces harvested	0–5	2.10	3.50	1.40*	W>E ↑	–
Fruit trees	0–5	1.17	1.48	.31(*)	W>E	+
Coffee grown	0–1	.49	.58	.09(*)	W>E ↑	–
Coffee harvested	0–9	1.81	1.80	–.01	W>E	+
Macadamia trees	0–6	.70	.73	.03	W>E	+
Co-operatives memberships	0–6	.76	1.01	.25(*)	W>E	–
Granaries	0–7	1.32	1.08	–.24*	W>E	–
Possessions inside house	0–7	4.38	5.37	.99*	W>E ↑	+
Possessions outside house	0–3	.34	.32	–.02	W=E	–
Cattle	0–5	1.32	1.47	.15(*)	W>E	+
Goats, etc.	0–6	1.71	2.24	.53	W>E	–
Professional possessions	0–4	.75	1.09	.34*	W=E	+
Bedrooms**	0–9	1.32	1.62–1.81	.30–.49(*)	W>E	–
Quality of house	0–6	3.31	3.76	.45(*)	W>E	+
Fieldworker's impression	0–2	.77	.94	.17(*)	W=E	–

x_1 = variable score in 1974
x_2 = variable score in 1978
* = significant at p=.01 level
(*) = significant at p=.01 level but difference attributed to ageing
W>E ↑ = differences between the 2 parts significantly aggrevated in both surveys
W>E ↓ = differences between the 2 parts significantly reduced in both surveys
W>E = differences between the 2 parts not significantly altered in both surveys
W<E = differences not significantly altered in both surveys

** = In 1978 a 'bedroom' was defined in a different manner from 1974. Therefore, the comparison had to be two-fold, resulting in higher and lower estimates for $\bar{x}_2$ and $\bar{x}_2 - \bar{x}_1$
W = western part
E = eastern part
W=E = no significant differences between the 2 parts in any of the surveys
\+ = stable) criteria mentioned in the text
– = unstable)

of modernization in the area at the time. The reduction in numbers of granaries may have been caused by an increasing emphasis on larger stores of greater durability that was noticeable in the project area. It is likely that the trend towards the sale of farm surpluses that used to be stored as domestic food reserves (Onchere, pers. comm.) was an additional factor. Further observations on time effects will be found in the discussion below.

The differences observed in 1974 between the western and eastern parts of the study area were confirmed by the 1978 findings. This agreement supports the assumption that the variables selected are valid indicators of economic household status.

Social conditions and hygienic environment

The social and hygiene survey of 1975 (Slooff and Schulpen, 1978) had also shown marked differences between western and eastern parts of the study area. The more traditionally oriented inhabitants of the eastern part appeared to be relatively less educated, had less paid employment, lived in houses of poorer quality, had more difficulty in obtaining proper drinking water and generally showed the signs of a community relatively more isolated from the influences of modern society. This general conclusion largely confirmed the findings of the economic survey carried out the year before.

Compound in Ulaani (eastern part).

Table 2.
Summary of comparisons between variable scores of 1978 and scores from 1975 survey on social and hygienic conditions (n=619).

Variable	*Scoring options*	*Mean values* $\bar{x}_1$	$\bar{x}_2$	$\bar{x}_2 - \bar{x}_1$	*Nature of change*	*Stability*
Church membership	0–2	1.76	1.76	.00	W>E	–
Education of head of household	0–3	1.36	1.51	.15*	W>E	+
Maximum education	1–3	2.20	2.34	.14(*)	W>E	+
Presence of grandmother	0–1	.35	.41	.06(*)	W=E	+
Job level of head of household	0–3	.86	.96	.10(*)	W=E	+
Maximum job level	0–3	1.03	1.27	.24*	W=E	–
Maximum commuting distance	0–2	.87	.93	.06	W=E	+
Drinking water	0–2	1.50	1.58	.08(*)	W>E ↓	+
Latrine	0–1	.57	.61	.04	W>E	+
Cleanliness of latrine	0–2	1.31	1.21	–.10	W<E	–
Education of mother	0–3	1.21	1.32	.11*	W>E	+
Job level of mother	0–3	.08	.09	.01	W=E	–
Marital status of mother	0–2	1.81	1.80	–.01	W=E	+
Presence of father	0–4	2.52	2.54	.02	W=E	+
Inverse sleeping density	0–3	1.69	1.92	.23*	W>E	–
Cooking or fire in bedroom	0–1	.70	.63	–.07*	W>E	–
Cattle or goats in bedroom	0–1	.87	.83	–.04	W>E	–
Inner smoothness of bedroom	0–3	1.43	1.50	.07	W>E	+

x_1 = variable score in 1975
x_2 = variable score in 1978
* = significant at p=.01 level
(*) = significant at p=.01 level but difference attributed to ageing

W>E ↑ = differences between the 2 parts significantly aggrevated in both surveys
W>E ↓ = differences between the 2 parts significantly reduced in both surveys
W>E = differences between the 2 parts not significantly altered in both surveys
W<E = differences not significantly altered in both surveys

W = western part
E = eastern part

W=E = no significant differences between the 2 parts in any of the surveys
\+ = stable) criteria mentioned in the text
– = unstable)

Part of the east-west differences observed are attributable to the topography of the area, in which the Kanzalu range and the poor transport facilities militate against a more equitable distribution of amenities, or access to these. In addition, differences in soil conditions and in the availability of water for irrigation are assumed to have played a role in stagnating agricultural progress in the eastern part.

Table 2 summarizes the findings in respect of social conditions and hygienic environment in the surveys of 1975 and 1978. In the three-year interval 9 of 18 variables appeared to have changed significantly in the 619 re-survey households. Overall changes not due to ageing effects (Slooff and Gemert, in press) took place in the variables *education of head of household, maximum job level, education of mother, inverse sleeping density* and *cooking or fire in bedroom*.

Improvements in the level of education have resulted from the increasing number of young people going to school in the area, and the natural replacement of old heads of household by younger family members raised the scores for education of head of household. A growing participation in non-farming labour activities helped to increase maximum job level scores and the improvement in the inverse sleeping density is consistent with the trend towards better housing standards. The slight decrease in cooking or fire in bedroom scores (meaning that more children slept in rooms heated with charcoal burners or in rooms used for cooking) indicates that some families may have newly adopted the habit of

Compound in Kingoti (western part).

leaving a fire smouldering at night. As with the economic variables, there were differences between the sublocations. These confirmed the picture of a study area divided into a more progressive western part and a more conservative part on the eastern side of the Kanzalu range.

The problem of instability

Turning from the description of changes in levels and their relation to development, the crucial question must be posed how seriously do such changes affect the validity of our cross-sectional data sets when used in a comprehensive analysis against longitudinal data. In this respect a conceptual distinction needs to be made between (a) absolute changes and (b) rank order changes. Absolute changes affect the scores of variables. If they take place in a systematic manner throughout a population they will affect the mean values as well. Rank order changes disturb the rank orders of individuals within the population, irrespective of absolute changes. Rank order changes in themselves do not affect mean values of the population as a whole. It has to be realized that massive changes in rank order may affect the analytical validity of a variable more seriously than a change in its mean value not accompanied by a disturbance of rank order.

When a variable is assessed in a defined population on two different occasions, a comparison between the two measurements will be affected by variance. Some of this variance will be error, some of it will be unstable and the rest will be stable variance. Stable variance tends to conserve rank order in the population. As part of the 1974 surveys each candidate variable had already been screened for error variance by only accepting those variables that would be reproducible with a correlation coefficient (r) of at least 0.6 on intra- and inter-observer checks. Although this ruled out most error variance, the remaining variables are still subject to unstable and stable variance. For analytical purposes it is necessary to select those variables with the lowest degree of unstable variance. For the sake of this discussion such variables will be called 'stable'. Figure 1 depicts the difference between extremely 'stable' and 'unstable' variables.

As an arbitrary measure for stability we used $r = 0.5$ and $r = 0.7$ as cut-off points for respectively the correlation coefficients of first and second variable scores and the correlation coefficient corrected for attenuation (using 1974/75 inter-observer variance). In Tables 1 and 2 stable and unstable variables have been marked with + and – signs in the appropriate columns. Of 17 economic variables, 7 qualified as stable (41.2 percent). The figures for the social and hygiene variables were 8 out of 11 (72.7 percent) and 3 of 7 (42.9 percent) respectively. Although the cut-off points used were arbitrary this suggests that the variables included in the economic survey of Kuné et al., (1979) were comparatively less stable than those studied in the social and hygiene survey of Slooff and Schulpen (1978).

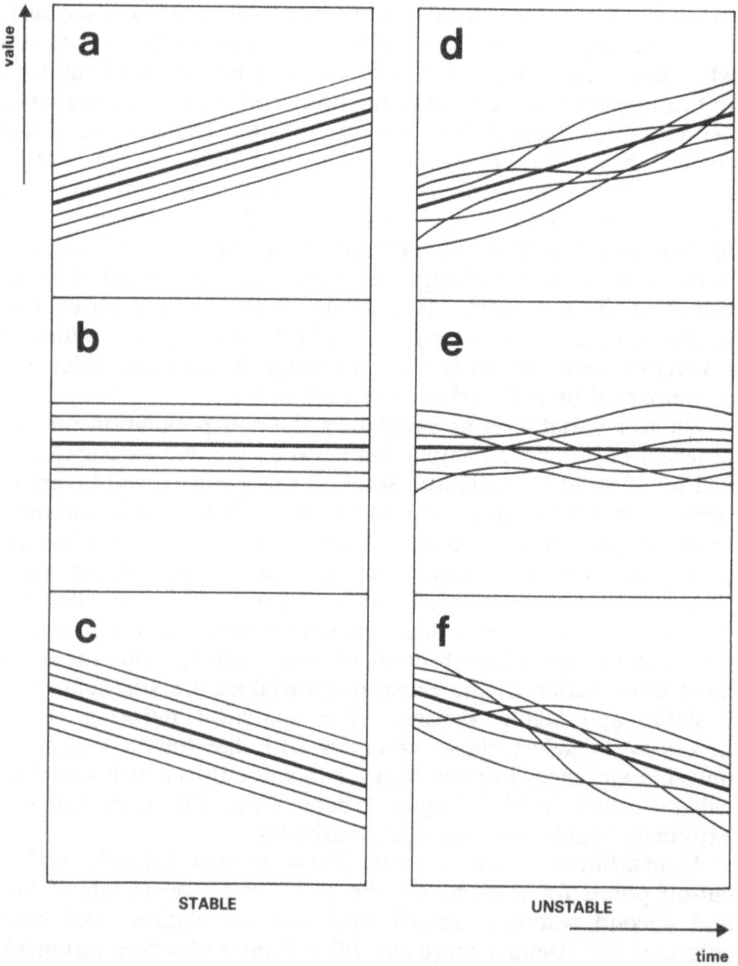

Figure 1. Schematic presentation to demonstrate the effect of instability in relation to the behaviour of the mean value. Thick lines: mean values. Thin lines: values for individuals in the population.

The concept of status and the need for components

The qualification of the 35 variables studied in the various surveys as proxy variables implies the notion of some deeper-rooted processes at the household level that are difficult to observe and quantify but may nevertheless have a bearing on the status of a household relative to other households. Since the effects of such processes are likely to change little over a period of only three or four years the most appropriate variables to serve as proxies for status should be found among the more stable.

It is conceivably possible to test the relationship with ill health for each single variable and then formulate a number of fitting hypotheses. The original objective of the Machakos Project was not, however, to clarify the aetiology of childhood diseases, but to identify classes of households with children at risk. In epidemiological studies dealing with such problems it is common practice to stratify the population by certain criteria of socio-economic status. The criteria applied usually relate to the levels of education and income of adult members of the household. In addition, standards may be used to define the level of interaction of household members with persons and institutions in the community. Various other aspects of the household environment may be quantified as well, e.g. quality of housing (United Nations, 1969). The recognition of risk categories among households is not facilitated by the adoption of many distinctive characteristics unless these are combined into a limited number of status components. These will reflect underlying phenomena more closely than any of the single variables constituting them. An added benefit of analysing patterns of ill health against a limited number of component values is the greater simplicity of testing and interpretation.

On the basis of these considerations it was decided to attempt arranging the stable variables in the survey data into a few components reflecting household status. Three staff members of the Machakos Project who had considerable field experience in the area were invited to examine the survey material independently and to suggest sensible combinations of the 18 stable variables to be used as status components. It was explained that such combinations needed to contain meaningfully related variables but should express relatively independent household qualities. After we had carried out the same exercise ourselves, the whole group met to compare notes and to decide on one common proposal. At this stage three unstable variables, considered to be prima facie of local importance (viz. maize harvested, cooking or fire in bedroom, cattle or goats in bedroom) were added as candidate component elements. Once the choice of variables to be combined had been agreed, further discussions were held to determine the absolute weights to be given to individual variables in computing component scores.

Component characteristics

The resulting components were named: I Agricultural potential, II Wealth, III Modern orientation, IV Hygiene and V Family structure. Table 3 provides details of the composition of these components. An ideal component should form a stable aggregate

Table 3.
Composition of 'components' constructed from 18 stable and three unstable variables. Each 'component' score is the sum of the products of the scores and actual weights of its variables.

'Component'		Variable		Actual weight *
I. *Agricultural potential*	Ec	1	maize harvested	1.6
	Ec	4	fruit trees	2.0
	Ec	6	coffee harvested	.9
	Ec	7	macadamia trees	.7
	Ec	12	cattle	1.5
	Ec	14	professional possessions	1.7
II. *Wealth*	Ec	10	possessions inside house	1.6
	Ec	16	quality of house	1.1
	H	2	latrine	2.0
III. *Modern orientation*	S	2	education of head of household	3.4
	S	4	maximum education	1.6
	S	7	job level of head of household	2.0
	S	9	maximum commuting distance	2.1
	S	10	education of mother	3.0
IV. *Hygiene*	H	1	drinking water	3.6
	H	8	cooking or fire in bedroom	2.1
	H	10	cattle or goats in bedroom	2.7
	H	11	inner smoothness of bedroom	.9
V. *Family structure*	S	6	presence of grandmother	2.0
	S	13	marital status of mother	3.7
	S	14	presence of father	2.0

*the actual weight is equal to the absolute weight attributed to the variable divided by its 1974/75 standard deviation.

Table 4.
Stability of five 'components' as listed in Table 13, expressed as Pearson correlation coefficients for 1974/75 and 1978 component scores, R_{12}.

	R_{12}-value		
'Component'	*Western part (sublocations 1 and 3)*	*Eastern part (sublocations 2, 4 and 5)*	*Whole study area*
I. Agricultural potential	.62	.67	.63
II. Wealth	.70	.78	.74
III. Modern orientation	.72	.77	.74
IV. Hygiene	.49	.63	.58
V. Family structure	.74	.80	.77

of related variables and show little mutual correlation when tested against others. The stability of such a component will be a function of its ability to describe a rank order of socio-economic status amongst households. Lack of mutual correlation should indicate the independent nature of the underlying phenomena represented by the components.

Pearson correlation coefficients for 1974/75 and 1978 component scores are presented in Table 4. These values underestimate the true stability of the components since the test-retest error has not been taken into account. As for practical purposes investigators have to contend with scores affected by all types of variance simultaneously, it is not essential to know about component stability after controlling for test-retest error. It may be borne in mind that the individual variables had already been selected for low test-retest error as part of the 1974/75 survey analyses.

It appears that component V, Family structure, was the most stable, followed by components II, Wealth, and III, Modern orientation. All five were most stable in the eastern, poorer, part of the study area. This confirms the impression that the people there were either more resistant to change or more isolated from outside influences than those in the western part.

Pearson correlation coefficients between the components are summarized in Table 5. The most independent component was V, Family structure, which displayed the lowest correlation coefficients with the remaining components. More closely related to other components was II, Wealth, which scored the highest correlation coefficients with I, Agriculture potential, III, Modern orientation and IV, Hygiene. All other associations between components were moderate. The fact that each component had its own

Table 5.
Pearson correlation matrices for 'components' I to V per area and per year.

Area		*1974/75* II	III	IV	V	*1978* II	III	IV	V
western part (n=360)	I	.42	.09	.30	−.10	.46	.12	.26	−.03
	II		.47	.48	−.23		.47	.48	−.13
	III			.26	−.16			.26	−.14
	IV				−.13				−.01
eastern part (n=259)	I	.48	.13	.31	−.05	.54	.27	.27	−.01
	II		.50	.53	−.12		.51	.48	−.07
	III			.26	−.19			.32	−.09
	IV				−.10				−.02

typical pattern of association with the four others suggests they were validly representative of distinct underlying phenomena.

Component mean scores in the 1974/75 and 1978 surveys can be compared for further support of their usefulness. These values, which are presented in Table 6 with their standard deviations, agree with the broad conclusions drawn from the surveys of 1974/75 and 1978. The components describe the changes in the re-survey sample in a manner that is consistent with the picture presented by the full range of separate variables, including those that are unstable. Components I, Agricultural potential, II, Wealth, and III, Modern orientation have increased more than components IV, Hygiene, and V, Family structure. The differences in mean scores for Agricultural potential and Wealth components between the western and eastern parts were greater in 1978 than in 1974/75.

Table 6.
Means and standard deviations for 'components' I to V per area and per year.

	Western part (n=360) 1974/75	1978	*Eastern part (n=259)* 1974/75	1978	*Whole study area (n=619)* 1974/75	1978
I	14.1±8.3	15.2±8.1	11.2±6.4	12.7±7.2	12.9±7.7	14.2±7.8
II	13.6±4.5	16.0±3.8	9.3±5.3	11.1±5.4	11.8±5.2	14.0±5.1
III	16.5±6.8	17.6±6.6	13.7±7.4	15.4±7.2	15.3±7.2	16.7±6.9
IV	12.5±2.4	12.3±2.9	7.7±3.9	8.2±4.6	10.5±3.9	10.6±4.2
V	12.6±4.1	12.9±4.2	12.2±4.1	12.2±4.2	12.4±4.1	12.6±4.2

Discussion

One of the aims of the 1978 survey was to detect any short-term changes in the household environment of 0–4-year-old children over time. As the baseline had been established in the first few months of 1974 and 1975, the target population for the re-survey had to be limited to those children born between 1 May 1973 and 1 May 1974 for whom baseline data were available.

A number of methodological questions arise which are best illustrated with the aid of Figure 2. One question relates to timing and choice of survey target populations. Although disease surveillance was started in the beginning of 1974 and lasted until the middle of 1981, the timing of the economic, social and hygiene surveys of 1974 and 1975 was such that the utility of the cross-sectional data obtained was mostly restricted to birth cohort A, i.e. children born between 1 May 1970 and 1 May 1974. Additional cohorts were included in the disease surveillance for whom either the social and hygiene data (cohort B) or the economic data were missing (cohort C), or for whom no cross-sectional data were

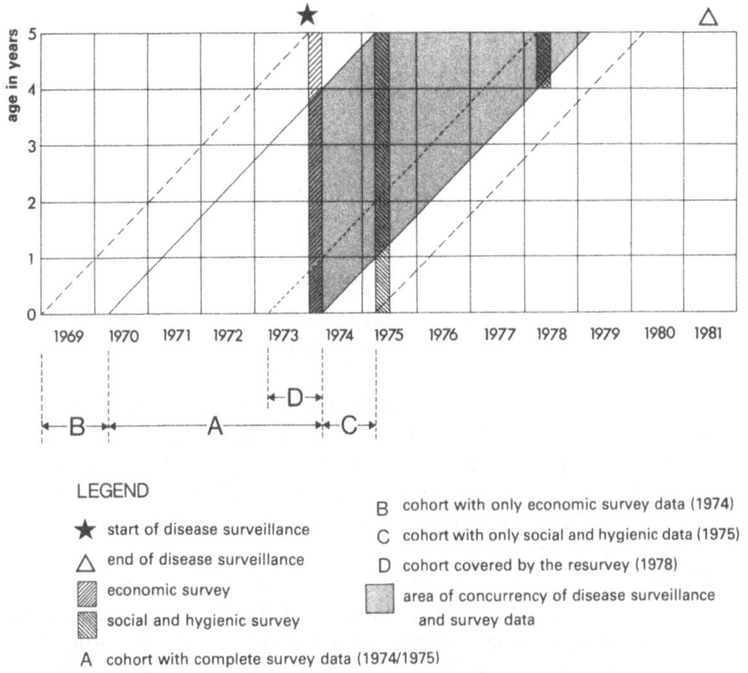

Figure 2. Lexis diagram illustrating the relation between disease surveillance and concurrency with actually accomplished cross-sectional surveys.

available at all (cohorts born after C). Optimal possibilities for a comprehensive analysis of morbidity and mortality against these survey data are therefore limited to occurrences that took place in the shaded area of Figure 2. The total number of person-years in this shaded area was unnecessarily reduced by the poor timing of the household surveys relative to the onset of disease surveillance. A much better mutual adjustment would have been obtained if an initial survey on 0- and 4-year-old children had been carried out in January 1975 and if the full household survey had been undertaken in January 1979 (see Fig. 3).

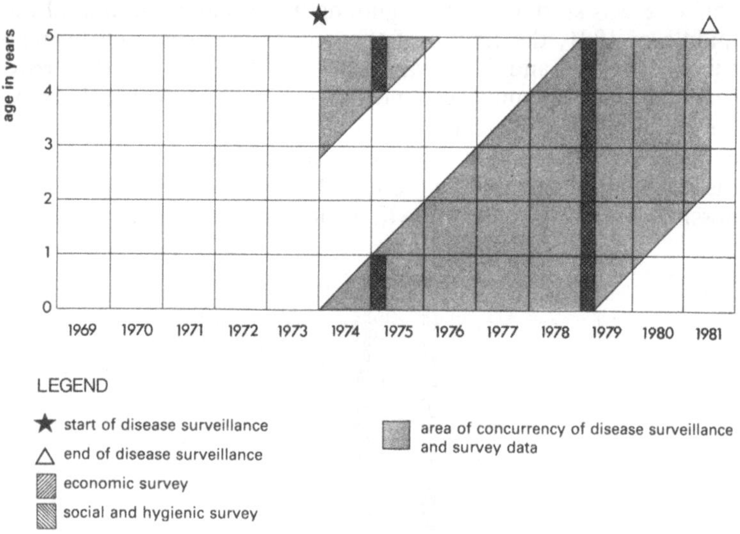

Figure 3. Lexis diagram illustrating the relation between disease surveillance and theoretical concurrency with cross-sectional surveys if they had been carried out as shown.

The study sample for the 1978 re-survey, identical with birth cohort D, traverses the shaded area of Figure 2 over a longer period of time than any of the other birth-year cohorts involved. Even if the re-survey results should only apply to this cohort the conclusions reached still refer to roughly 0.36 of the total number of relevant person-years.

More must be said about the problem that prompted us to undertake the re-survey—the validity of the cross-sectional database in this longitudinal project. In the first place it was shown that most variables included in the cross-sectional surveys in 1974/75 had undergone marked changes in mean value, in rank order, or both. Therefore the validity of most of these data is limited and re-surveys were indeed essential to determine the restrictions for their use. Secondly, it was found that some changes in mean value reflected ageing effects of the household rather than impact of external phenomena (see Tables 1 and 2). Thirdly, it appeared that changes in mean values were quite unrelated to changes in rank order. In some variables changes in scores were mutually related, which suggested the action of patterns of change. The construction of components from related stable variables may be a solution to the limited validity of individual variable scores, but this assumption needs further support from analyses against morbidity and mortality data, as presented in Chapter 21. In an analysis against schistosome egg outputs, components I, Agricultural potential and II, Wealth, were negatively associated with household infectivity scores (Nordbeck et al., 1982).

Generally speaking, the less stable a variable is over time the less accurately it describes the relative position of the household or the child in a dynamic environment. This may be for various reasons. For instance, instability in household variables may be caused by the action of random effects that make certain households move up or down more markedly than others. With subjective variables the random element of judgement may have been largely responsible for their instability. This may explain the instability of *field-worker's impression* (Ec 17) and *cleanliness of latrine* (H 6). A further cause of instability may be found in external factors of which the effects were unevenly distributed over the study area. Such effects may have caused instability in beans harvested (Ec 2) and produces harvested (Ec 3). In addition, climatic effects may have influenced harvests in some sublocations, resulting in much better crops in 1978. A skewed frequency distribution such as in possessions outside house (Ec 11) and job level of mother (S 11) may have promoted instability under the impact of individual shifts in scores.

A variable will be stable if it describes situations possessing a certain 'permanency'. Changes in such variables take the form of cumulative increases or cumulative decreases. Prima facie such an aspect of 'permanency' may be attributed to all stable variables in Tables 1 and 2. Much could have been gained if survey questions on items of a momentary or non-permanent nature had been avoided or if the relatively permanent aspects of the household environment had been given the most attention. More reflection on these aspects and a liberal use of common sense in the design of the surveys would have been worthwhile. It is encouraging that the available survey material still yielded 18 stable variables. The five 'components' constructed appeared to be satisfactorily stable and reasonably independent of each other.

Conclusions

The gathering of meaningful cross-sectional data on economic, social and hygiene aspects of the household environment in Machakos has proved to be a difficult, cumbersome and time-consuming task. A number of problems could have been avoided by better planning. These were: (1) the inappropriate timing of cross-sectional surveys immediately following the implementation of disease surveillance; and (2) the inclusion of some unstable variables that might have been rejected in time if a critical review of permanency characteristics of candidate variables had been attempted.

On the positive side, it is noteworthy that the re-survey approach used has proved to be essentially suitable for the detection of temporal change. It has also been found possible to distinguish reasonably well between changes due to external influences and those attributable to ageing. The changes attributed to external influences can be explained by what is known about developments in the area.

It is remarkable that a relatively short time has proved sufficient to detect economical and social changes in a typical rural tropical African community that too many people simply regard as conservative, traditional or stationary.

References

Kolkena T, Some indication of the economic conditions in the western part of the study area of the JPM project, Internal Report MRCN, Nairobi, 1974.

Kolkena T and Pronk A, Report on a socio-economic survey in two rural areas of Machakos District, Kenya (part 1), Internal Report MRCN, Nairobi, 1975.

Kuné JB, Slooff R and Schulpen TWJ, Machakos Project Studies XV: The economic setting at the household level, Trop Geogr Med, 31 (1979) 441–457.

Nordbeck HJ, Ouma JH and Slooff R, Machakos Project Studies XXII: Schistosomiasis transmission in relation to some socio-economic and other environmental factors, Trop Geogr Med, 34 (1982) 193–203.

Onchere SR, personal communication (1979).

Slooff R and Schulpen TWJ, Machakos Project Studies VI: The social and hygienic environment, Trop Geogr Med, 30 (1978) 257–274.

Slooff R, Machakos Project Studies: Short-term changes and stable components in the household environment, Internal Report KIT, Amsterdam, 8 December 1981.

Slooff R and Gemert W, Machakos Project Studies: The household environment revisited, Trop Geogr Med [in press].

United Nations, Principles and recommendations for the 1970 housing censuses, (1969).

Wallis M and Van Waning EE, Report on a socio-economic survey in two rural areas of Machakos District, Kenya (part 2), Internal Report MRCN, Nairobi, 1976.

5

Population growth, fertility, mortality, and migration

J.K. van Ginneken
A.S. Muller
A.M. Voorhoeve
Omondi-Odhiambo

Introduction

The first objective of the demographic surveillance system was to provide the population data necessary for the various epidemiological and other studies that were being carried out in the study area, in particular accurate denominators of the various rates used in the epidemiological studies. The system also provided accurate data on the population characteristics of subgroups or categories of the population needed by various investigators who wanted to carry out special studies of these subgroups.

The second objective of demographic surveillance was to determine the population characteristics of this rural area in detail, together with birth, death and migration rates. We also wanted to see to what extent changes had occurred over the 7 years during which data collection continued.

Materials and methods

Data collection procedures

The Machakos Project started with a retrospective baseline survey of demographic characteristics of the population carried out by trained field-workers in the middle of 1973. The results of this baseline survey will not be reported here.

Data collection on a fortnightly basis started in November 1973 and continued until September 1978, when the frequency was reduced to monthly; this continued until April 1981. In this chapter the results of demographic surveillance over the 7-year period between the end of 1973 and the end of 1980 will be reported.

Interviews were carried out by about 12 male and female field-workers during the fortnightly surveillance and by 7 during the monthly rounds. They had 1–4 years of secondary schooling and all were permanent residents in the area. A system was designed that enabled the supervisory staff of the project, in particular those based in Nairobi, to check the performance of the field-workers.

Ages were determined for the most part during the baseline survey in 1973, from birth certificates when possible, but in most cases these did not exist so then a calendar of local events that listed all important events known or remembered from hearsay that had taken place in Machakos District since approximately 1880, was used (for details see Chapter 1).

Demographic information was recorded on sheets that contained data on six rounds of visits. These sheets were inserted in a so-called buff card containing basic information on a household (name, sex, date of birth etc.) and then removed when data on six rounds had been filled in.

Definitions

Enumeration of the population took place both on a de facto and a de jure basis. These terms will be defined since our usage of them is non-standard (see, e.g., Shryock and Siegel, 1971; United Nations Commission for Africa, 1974; Marks et al., 1974).

The de facto population of a household consisted of those persons who slept in that household on the night preceding the visit by a field-worker. Visitors were not included when they were found in a household by a field-worker for the first time. If they were still there on a subsequent visit, however, they were then counted.

The de jure population consisted of present and absent household members. Persons were defined as absent when, in the opinion of other members of the household, in particular the head of the household, they belonged to the household and visited it more or less regularly throughout the year, particularly during weekends and holidays. If a household member had been absent continuously for several months and moreover was not expected back, that person became an out-migrant and was removed from the de jure population. Visitors became members of the de jure population when they were found in the study area on a second visit by a field-worker. This de jure population definition as employed here differs from that usually employed in demographic surveys. Normally only those absent members who have their place of usual residence in the study area are included (Shryock and Siegel, 1971, p. 92) and a UN publication defines this for Africa as the place he/she has lived in most during the last 12 months (UNECA, 1974, p. 30). This recommendation was not followed here and heads of households and other household members who worked in Nairobi or other places and returned to their residence in the study area for weekends, holidays, etc, were included in the de jure population.

Also normally in demographic practice a minimum of 6 months of continuous presence in a particular area is required for a visitor to be classified as an in-migrant and to become a member of the de jure population. A person who is present, but has been there for less than 6 months remains a visitor. Likewise, 6 months of continuous absence is the condition for a person to become an out-migrant and to be removed from the de jure population (UNECA, 1974, p. 29). In our case, however, visitors were taken as in-migrants if encountered on a second visit by a field-worker; absentees should, therefore, in theory have been removed from the de jure population when found to be absent for the second consecutive time and reported to have moved away. Many absentees were, in practice, only removed from the de jure population after a period, up to September 1978, of up to 3 months' and, after that time, of up to 6 months' absence. An asymmetry in entrance and exit requirements was thus introduced which inflated the de jure population by 1–2 percent.

There were several reasons why this broader definition of the de jure population was employed. One was that it was necessary for several epidemiological and other studies to include absentees (for instance, children who were temporarily away or women delivering elsewhere). A second reason was that absent male members of households make important economic and social contributions to the study area: it is unrealistic to treat them as if they do not exist. A third reason was that our definition corresponded to the definitions used by the inhabitants of the study area themselves as to who belonged and who did not belong to a household.

Some birth and death rates reported later are presented both on a de jure and a de facto basis because there was reason to believe that the results would be different. With the wide definition of the de jure population we employed, it was possible that births and/or deaths, especially those involving absent members of the study population, would not be enumerated. The de jure rates were calculated according to regular procedure while for the de facto rates we used the 'generally present' approach. (This approach will not be explained here; for details see van Ginneken and Omondi-Odhiambo, 1979.)

A distinction was made between three types of mobility: temporary migration, permanent in- and out-migration, and permanent internal migration (Gold and Prothero, 1975; Shryock and Siegel, 1971). Temporary migration, which is to a large extent labour migration or labour circulation, concerns movement by absent members of a household who work elsewhere but come back at weekends or other times during the year. In- and out-migration have already been explained. Internal migration is a permanent move from one residence to another within the study area. In this chapter figures on internal migration will not be given separately; they are included in the in- and out-migration rates. (For details of these definitions and procedures see van Ginneken and Omondi-Odhiambo, 1979 and van Ginneken 1981.)

Data quality control

In order to check and improve the quality of the data collected, a number of control comparisons of information from different sources were introduced. The presence and absence patterns of a 10 percent sample between 1975 and 1977 were coded separately and compared with results already stored elsewhere. Relatives or neighbours of a sample of 1153 absentees were also interviewed in detail as to whether or not they should be considered as absentees; their patterns of contact with relatives in the area; the reasons for their absence; and whether they were alive or not (Omondi-Odhiambo, 1977). Finally, a survey was done among relatives of about 400 out-migrants who had left their households in 1979, to verify their classification as out-migrants and to find out why they had gone.

Checks were also carried out in order to see that information on births and deaths was as accurate as possible. From 1975 to 1978 a study was also conducted on perinatal and maternal morbidity and mortality in relation to antenatal and delivery care received (see Chapters 18, 19 and 20). In that study, pregnancies identified by field-workers were followed up until delivery. The information about the outcome of these pregnancies was compared with information on births provided by the demographic surveillance system. Discrepancies were identified and reconciled when necessary. In addition, the infants resulting from these pregnancies were followed up for a period of one year after birth, which allowed accurate determination of the number of neonatal and infant deaths after birth. This information on deaths was again compared with information derived from the demographic surveillance. Thus two semi-independent data-collection systems were in operation at the same time between 1975 and 1978.

Results

De facto and de jure population

Information on the de facto and de jure population sizes in different years is provided in Table 1. A large population increase in the de facto population between 1974 and 1978 (45.1 per 1000 population per year on average) and a much smaller increase in 1979 and 1980 (10.9 per 1000 population) are seen. The overall population increase between 1974 and 1980 was 35.2 per 1000. These figures have been calculated by the compound interest formula (Barclay, 1958, p. 30). Accurate figures on the de jure population were only available at the end of 1974, 1975, 1979, and 1980. The percentages of absentees during these years were 19.1, 18.9, 18.2 and 19.0 percent respectively. No accurate figures were available for 1976–1978 because the definition of out-migrants was temporarily changed and at the end of 1979 the reporting of out-migrants had not yet returned to normal. For this reason we estimated the de jure population sizes between 1976 and 1979 on the basis of the de facto population, assuming the percentage of absentees to be 19 percent. This percentage is very close to the figure of 18.7 percent obtained on the basis of re-coding of data on present-absent patterns of 10 percent sample between 1975 and 1977.

Age and sex distribution

Figure 1 and Table 2 contain information on the de jure and de facto populations by age and sex. A distinctive feature of the age pyramid is the large number of children below 15, which is a reflection of high fertility and declining mortality levels prevailing

Table 1.
De facto and de jure population in 1974–1980.

Year	*De facto (present)*	*Absent*	*De jure (total)*
Dec. 1973	18 583	4359	22 942
Dec. 1974	19 369	4579	23 948
Dec. 1975	20 170	4693	24 863
Dec. 1976	21 198	4972	26 170
Dec. 1977	22 102	5183	27 285
Dec. 1978	23 171	5435	28 606
Dec. 1979	23 188	5463	28 751
Dec. 1980	23 680	5555	29 235

in the study area. Figure 1 shows a somewhat irregular pattern of de jure population sizes in the adult age groups. The age groups 30–34, 40–44, and 50–54 tend to be smaller than expected in comparison with the age groups 35–39, 45–49, and 55–59.

Another characteristic of the population pyramid is the relatively high percentage of the population (in particular the female population) over 70. This surplus of older people, which can also be found in several age categories between 45 and 65, is accompanied by a deficit in several age categories between 25 and 45. This is an indication of a tendency to over-estimate ages in the adult population, more pronounced for females than for males. There was a digit preference for ages ending in 0 especially between 1900 and 1940.

The population pyramid of the de facto population has also been presented in Figure 1. Males are more often absent from households than females, particularly in working age groups between 20–59.

Information on sex ratios (number of males per 100 females) can be derived from Table 2. One expects these ratios on a de jure basis to be a little higher than 100 in the younger age groups up to

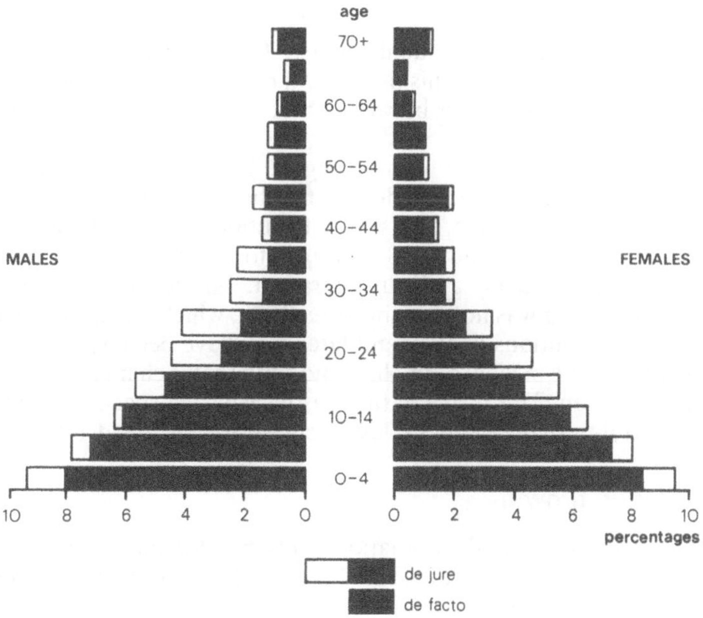

Figure 1. De jure and de facto mid-year population: average 1974–1978.

Table 2.
De jure and de facto population by age and sex: average mid year population in 1974–1978.

Age	*De jure population* *Female*	*Male*	*Total*	*De facto population* *Female*	*Male*	*Total*
0– 4	2447	2403	4850	2146	2052	4198
5– 9	2040	2002	4042	1865	1830	3695
10–14	1675	1639	3314	1516	1536	3052
15–19	1402	1426	2828	1133	1184	2317
20–24	1213	1138	2351	854	685	1539
25–29	835	1050	1885	605	501	1106
30–34	520	646	1166	432	333	765
35–39	521	565	1086	448	287	735
40–44	372	361	733	328	253	581
45–49	511	446	957	455	297	752
50–54	299	302	601	266	230	496
55–59	288	297	585	274	221	495
60–64	169	203	372	153	178	331
65–69	138	143	281	128	112	240
70+	327	248	575	311	212	523
Total	12 757	12 869	25 626	10 914	9911	20 825

30 to 40, followed by a gradual decline. The sex ratios (not shown here) largely conform to this theoretical model in the youngest and oldest age groups, but in between there are fluctuations ranging from 93.8 to 125.7.

The age and sex distribution of Figure 1 and Table 2 is derived from data largely collected during the baseline survey in 1973. Adjustments in the age and sex distribution were made several times between 1974 and 1978, taking into account data on newborns, deaths and in- and out-migration. For technical reasons further updating was not possible after 1978, which means that age and sex distributions in 1979 and later may have become decreasingly unrealistic in view of the high mobility that is characteristic of this population. This is one of the reasons why age-specific fertility and mortality figures may be less accurate for 1979 and 1980.

Population growth

Table 3 shows annual population growth rates and their components. The average annual rate between 1974 and 1980 was 33.9 per 1000 population, calculated as a weighted average for the 7 years. This figure is very close to the population growth rate calculated by the compound interest formula mentioned above

Table 3.
Rate of natural increase, net migration rate and population growth rate per 1000 population in 1974–1980.

Year	*Midyear population*	*Rate of natural increase per 1000*	*Net migration rate per 1000*	*Population growth rate per 1000*
1974	23 484	33.7	9.2	42.8
1975	24 407	37.3	0.2	37.5
1976	25 521	36.1	15.1	51.2
1977	26 729	36.5	5.2	41.7
1978	27 946	38.6	8.7	47.3
1979	28 679	38.6	–33.6	5.1
1980	28 993	39.8	–23.1	16.7
Average 1974–1980		37.4	– 3.5	33.9

and it was thus not necessary to use this more complex approach.

Natural increase, that is the excess of births over deaths, contributed much more to population growth than net migration, which is the difference between in- and out-migration. Natural increase was about 37 per 1000, while net migration out of the study area was 3.5 per 1000 on average per year between 1974 and 1980. The rate of natural increase was fairly constant between 1974 and 1980 but the balance between in- and out-migration fluctuated widely in the same period. Between 1974 and 1978 there was on the whole more in- than out-migration while there was a sharp reversal in 1979 and 1980. As a result there was rapid population growth between 1974 and 1978 and only a small increase in 1979 and 1980. The reasons for these changes in population increase will be given below.

Average population growth rates by sex and geographical area are presented in Table 4. Population growth rates of males and females were similar but there are differences between the two parts of the study area. While the western part was characterized by a balance of in- and out-migration, the eastern part experienced a net out-migration of 8.7 per 1000. This difference is undoubtedly a reflection of the differences in economic conditions prevailing in the two parts. As a result, the western part grew at an average rate of 37 per 1000 per year while growth in the eastern part was only 29 per 1000.

Crude birth and death rates

Table 5 shows crude birth and death rates on a de jure and de facto basis. The de facto rates are only available for the years 1975–

Table 4.
Population growth rate population by sex and geographical area: annual average between 1974 and 1980

Sex and area	*Rate of natural increase per 1000*	*Net migration rate per 1000*	*Population growth rate per 1000*
Female	37.8	-2.6	35.2
Male	36.9	-4.3	32.6
Total	37.4	-3.5	33.9
Western part	37.0	0.2	37.2
Eastern part	37.8	-8.7	29.1
Total	37.4	-3.5	33.9

Table 5.
Crude birth and death rates and rate of natural increase per 1000 population on de jure and de facto basis between 1974 and 1980.

	Crude birth rate		*Crude death rate*		*Rate of natural increase*	
Year	*de facto*	*de jure*	*de facto*	*de jure*	*de facto*	*de jure*
1974	—	42.1	—	8.4	—	33.7
1975	45.8	43.3	6.5	6.1	39.3	37.3
1976	44.4	42.7	7.0	6.6	37.4	36.1
1977	45.4	43.3	6.7	6.7	38.7	36.5
1978	47.0	45.1	6.7	6.5	40.3	38.6
1979	—	44.6	—	6.0	—	38.6
1980	—	44.5	—	4.8	—	39.8
Average 1975–78	45.7	43.6	6.7	6.5	39.0	37.1

1978. De facto birth and death rates and the rate of natural increase averaged 45.7, 6.7 and 39.0 per 1000 population per year respectively and were fairly constant between 1975 and 1978. Corresponding de jure rates were somewhat lower. We believe that the de facto rates are in general of somewhat better quality than the de jure rates. The difference is not large, however, and since de jure data are available for more years we shall present age-specific rates below on a de jure basis only.

Age-specific fertility rates

De jure age-specific fertility rates between 1975 and 1979 are shown in Table 6. Fertility rises steeply after age 15–19 until it reaches a peak in one of the age groups between 20–34 after which there is a gradual decline. This peak was in the 25–29 group in

Table 6.
Age-specific and total fertility rates per 1000 women between 15 and 49 in 1975–1979.

Age group	*1975*	*1976*	*1977*	*1978*	*1979*	*Average*
15–19	93	89	93	110	98	97
20–24	283	300	263	309	300	291
25–29	345	286	330	289	317	312
30–34	295	312	283	308	294	298
35–39	259	218	274	222	248	244
40–44	117	194	153	178	150	158
45–49	66	54	49	44	54	53
Total fertility rate	7.290	7.265	7.225	7.300	7.305	7.265

1975, 1977, and 1979, while there were bimodal distributions in 1976 and 1978. These fluctuations are probably due to the relatively small numbers of births (from about 1060 to 1260) which took place in the study area in each of these five years. The total fertility was 7265 per 1000 women or about 7.3 live births per woman. Table 6 also indicates that the fertility was constant between 1975 and 1979.

Another measure of fertility is the completed family size, which is the mean number of children born to a cohort of women who have reached the end of their childbearing years, usually between 45 and 49. Due to technical problems the only figure available for this was on a de facto basis at the end of 1973. The completed family size at that time was 7.6 children per woman.

Crude and age-specific mortality rates

The crude rates have already been shown in Table 5 and it can be seen that (de jure) crude death rates decline from 8.4 per 1000 in 1974 to 4.8 in 1980.

Mortality rates in the major age groups between 1974 and 1980 are provided in Table 7. Mortality declines sharply after the first year of life and starts rising again in the age group 45–64 until a level is reached ranging from 27 to 46 per 1000 in the age group 65 years and older. Fluctuations that are observed in different years are most likely due to the small number of deaths (ranging from 138 to 181) that were reported. The infant mortality rate averaged 47 between 1974 and 1980 with a variation of 39 to 59.

Age-specific mortality rates by sex, given in Table 8, indicate that male mortality is higher in all age groups than female.

Table 7.
Crude and age-specific mortality rates per 1000 population and infant mortality rates per 1000 live births between 1974 and 1980.

Age groups	*1974*	*1975*	*1976*	*1977*	*1978*	*1979*	*1980*	*Total*
<1	50.1	41.0	61.6	50.8	62.1	40.0	40.4	49.1
1– 4	16.3	6.0	8.7	8.1	5.1	8.4	3.3	7.8
5–14	1.5	1.6	1.2	2.5	1.3	1.8	1.9	1.7
15–44	2.3	2.3	2.4	2.6	3.4	2.5	1.6	2.4
45–64	11.3	7.4	3.6	6.5	5.9	5.7	3.9	6.2
65+	45.8	42.7	34.1	32.9	27.3	28.7	29.5	33.9
Total	8.4	6.1	6.6	6.7	6.5	6.0	4.8	6.4
Infant mortality rate	49.5	38.8	58.7	47.6	55.6	39.1	39.5	46.8

Table 8.
Crude and age- and sex-specific mortality rates per 1000 population: annual average between 1974 and 1980.

Age group	*Female*	*Male*	*Total*
<1	45.9	52.1	49.1
1– 4	7.4	8.3	7.8
5–14	1.2	2.2	1.7
15–44	1.8	3.0	2.4
45–64	4.9	7.5	6.2
65+	30.8	37.6	33.9
Total	5.6	7.1	6.4

Temporary migration

We have already seen that on average an estimated 19 percent of the de jure population were absent when they were visited by the field-workers during their rounds. The prevalence of this 'absenteeism' was higher for males (23 percent) than for females (14 percent). The percentage of absentees peaked (about 50 percent) for males between 20 and 39 years old and for females (about 25 percent) between 20 and 34 years old. The absentees consisted of several different categories of people. People away for a short time visiting relatives, attending wedding and funeral ceremonies, or traders made up a small proportion. The large majority of the absentees, however, were temporary labour migrants. Many absentees (especially heads of households) were gainfully employed in Nairobi and other towns in Kenya; then there were farmers (especially in the western part) who moved seasonally to another farm they owned outside the study area (e.g. on Yatta Plateau); yet others were wives and children who went temporarily to join their husbands in Nairobi or to their farms elsewhere, students in boarding schools, or polygamous men who were temporarily staying with another wife outside the area.

Permanent in- and out-migration

Figures of in- and out-migration between 1974 and 1980 are given in Table 9. All forms of permanent movement to and from the study area as well as within it are included in this table. On average in- and out-migration cancelled each other out in the 7-year period for which data are available. There was a steady population increase due to net in-migration between 1974 and 1978 and a much stronger population decrease due to net out-migration in 1979 and 1980. Corresponding figures on net migration for single years have already been shown in Table 3. Table 9 also shows a decline in the total volume of in- and out-migration (gross migration) in 1979 and 1980 compared with previous years. The major reason for this is probably the reduction in frequency of data-collecting visits from fortnightly to once a month in September 1978. This means that it is possible that both in- and out-migration rates in 1979 and 1980 were actually somewhat higher, and this would mean that the net out-migration rates observed in 1979 and 1980 were due not only to less in-migration but also to more out-migration. The reasons for the substantial change in in- and out-migration between 1979 and 1980 were the unfavourable economic conditions in the study area, as will be explained in the last section.

Table 10 shows in- and out-migration rates by sex and area. The volume of in- and out-migration (gross migration) is substantially

Table 9.
In- and out-migration rates per 1000 population: annual average between 1974 and 1980.

Period	*In-migration rate*	*Out-migration rate*	*Net migration rate*	*Gross migration rate*
1974–1978	102.5	94.6	7.9	197.1
1979–1980	71.1	99.1	–28.0	170.2
1974–1980	92.7	96.0	–3.2	188.7

higher for females than for males. This difference is due to family-related reasons, in particular marriage and divorce, wives joining their husbands after marriage or birth of a child or returning to their parental home after separation or divorce. These movements are thus especially common in the age groups of women between 15 and 29 years old, as can be seen from the age- and sex-specific migration rates (not shown here). Other categories of in- and out-migrants (both male and female) are: families who establish a new farm or business elsewhere; teachers and pastors who are transferred to or from the study area; and farm labourers, housemaids, and servants.

Table 10 also indicates that gross migration in the western part of the area was somewhat less than in the eastern part. In- and out-migration cancel each other in the western part while the eastern part is characterized by net out-migration of about 8 per 1000.

Table 10.
In- and out-migration rates per 1000 population by sex and geographical area: annual average between 1974 and 1980.

Sex and area	*In-migration rate*	*Out-migration rate*	*Net migration rate*	*Gross migration rate*
Female	108.1	110.7	-2.6	218.8
Male	77.5	81.4	-3.9	158.9
Total	92.7	96.0	-3.2	188.7
Western part	88.0	88.1	-0.1	176.1
Eastern part	99.7	107.5	-7.8	207.2
Total	92.7	96.0	-3.2	188.7

Note: The net migration rates in this table do not exactly match those in Table 4 because of errors in the recording of in- and out-migrants.

Discussion

Age and sex composition

Inspection of the population pyramid and the sex ratios indicates that on the whole the distribution of the population by age and sex is acceptable and in line with age distributions reported in African censuses in general (Ominde, 1975) and the 1979 Kenya census (Machakos District) in particular (CBS, 1981). The comparison with the 1979 Machakos district census also shows that age groups between 15 and 44 are somewhat under-represented in the study population, while several age groups in older age brackets are somewhat over-represented. These differences are probably due to over-reporting of age by adults, particularly by women. With respect to sex ratios we found that the largest difference between our data and the 1979 census was the lower ratio in the 70-years-and-older age group.

Population increases

The crude birth rate in the study area (de facto basis) was 45.7 per 1000, while the crude death rate was 6.7 per 1000, leading to a rate of natural increase of 39.0 per 1000 between 1975 and 1978. These rates can be compared with those of two national surveys that were conducted in 1973 and 1977, the first of which estimated the crude birth rate in Kenya at 49–52 and the crude death rate at 13 (CBS, 1975) while the second arrived at rates of 53 and 14 (CBS, 1979) respectively. This shows that fertility, and particularly mortality, were lower in the study area than in Kenya as a whole, while the rate of natural increase was almost the same. The rapidity of the

A fieldworker interviewing one of the mothers.

population increase poses a serious threat to economic and social development in the area. It seems that, other things being equal, the population of the area will double in about 19 years. Part of this growth can be absorbed by the area itself, but since economic opportunities within the study area are limited, out-migration is bound to rise at the same time. There is less potential for economic development in the eastern than the western part of the area and this means that out-migration is likely to continue on a larger scale in this less prosperous part than in the more affluent western part.

The quality of information on births and deaths

The possibility has to be investigated that the low birth and death rates are due to under-reporting of vital events. Such under-reporting is a common phenomenon in demographic studies in developing countries (e.g., Brass et al., 1971; Marks et al., 1974; Myers, 1976; UNECA, 1974; Adlakha et al., 1981). It is more pronounced for deaths (in particular infant deaths) than for births, and under-reporting of vital events is more common in single-visit than in multi-round surveys. Under-reporting of these events does, however, occur in multi-round surveys, as used in our study, but we believe that we have kept under-reporting of births and deaths to a minimum, in particular between 1975 and 1978, for the following reasons.

First, data collection between 1974 and 1978 took place on a fortnightly basis—such a short recall period that it is unlikely that births and deaths would be missed. Secondly, elaborate procedures were used during the stage of data collection in the field to ensure that the quality of information was satisfactory, e.g. the field-workers received adequate training and there was close supervision of field-workers. Thirdly, use was made of supplementary sources of information to check and improve the quality of the collected data. In particular, the operation of two semi-independent data collection systems (the demographic surveillance and the outcome of pregnancy study) helped to make reporting of infant deaths as complete as possible. Fourthly, to ascertain whether deaths had occurred among absentees unknown to the field-workers, relatives of a sample of 1153 absentees were interviewed to check if any unrecorded deaths had occurred in this group. No such deaths were found, confirming that in the large majority of cases contact was maintained with these absentees. Fifthly, there is no tendency in the study area to hide deaths; the dead are customarily buried at the ancestral homesteads. Moreover, the field-workers were acquainted with nearly all the households they visited so they also knew about any deaths.

Nevertheless, in spite of these control measures, it is likely that some births and deaths were missed, particularly among the absentees, and this is probably one of the reasons why the de jure birth and death rates were somewhat lower than the de facto rates.

There may have been more under-reporting of deaths in 1979 and 1980 than in 1975–1978 because the outcome of pregnancy study was discontinued at the end of 1978. In summary, therefore, we accept the crude birth and death rates between 1975 and 1978 as genuine, but we do not completely trust the death rates in 1979 and 1980. For this reason we do not think we can say that we have proved a genuine decline in the crude death rate from 8.4 in 1974 to 4.8 in 1980.

Age-specific fertility

The total fertility rate on a de jure basis in the study area averaged 7265 births per 1000 women (or about 7.3 births per woman) per year between 1975 and 1979. This indicates again that fertility in the area is somewhat lower than in Kenya as a whole, since two recently conducted national surveys arrived at values of 8065 and 8100 births per 1000 women (Henin et al., 1979; CBS, 1980). Comparison of the age-specific rates in the study area with Kenya as a whole indicates that whereas fertility at older ages in the study area is at the same level or even higher, fertility in the study area is lower at younger ages.

The demographer on his motorbike.

Infant and adult mortality

The infant mortality between 1974 and 1980 was 47 per 1000 live births. This rate is lower than those reported in the two recent national surveys mentioned above, one of which gave an infant mortality rate for Kenya of 83 per 1000 live births, the other 96 per 1000 (Henin et al., 1979; CBS, 1980). We think this difference between the study area and Kenya as a whole is genuine and not due to under-reporting of infant deaths, as explained above. The most likely reason for the low infant mortality level in the study area is the favourable economic, social and hygienic conditions in the area compared with other parts of Kenya (see Chapter 17).

The adult mortality rates, particularly for ages 65 and above, are too low. This becomes evident on comparison with Sweden, which is considered to have one of the lowest mortality levels in the world: an apparent rate of 33.9 for age 65+ in the study area contrasts with 55.4 for Sweden (in 1973). The main reason for this is the overestimation of ages, particularly in women and especially in the older age groups; this has led to too large a denominator for the age-specific rates in these age groups.

Temporary and permanent migration

The extent of this type of mobility can be gauged from the finding that most of the absent members of the de jure population consisted of temporary or labour migrants and their families. This labour migration is of considerable economic and social importance in the study area and we agree with Gold and Prothero and with Goldstein that this phenomenon should be studied in more detail (see Gold and Prothero, 1976; Goldstein 1976).

Data on the incidence of permanent in- and out-migration indicate that this type of mobility is also of considerable importance and dependent very much on economic circumstances. Our findings on in- and out-migration cannot be compared with those of censuses and surveys undertaken in Kenya (e.g., as summarized by Ominde, 1975 and by Mbithi and Barnes, 1975), because of differences in methods of data collection and analysis used. A comparison with gross migration figures in a rural area of Ghana shows an even larger volume of in- and out-migration in that area than in rural Machakos (Univ. of Ghana Medical School, 1979).

Between 1974 and 1978 there was an average net in-migration of 8 per 1000 per year, but this was followed in 1979–1980 by a substantial net out-migration of 28 per 1000 per year. Patterns of in- and out-migration were also different in the two parts of the study area. The richer western part was characterized by net in-migration between 1974 and 1978, followed by a much larger exodus in 1979 and 1980, while in the poorer eastern part there has always been net out-migration and this increased in 1979 and 1980 compared with previous years. We suggest that the pattern of in- and out-migration can to a considerable extent be explained by economic factors, particularly shortage of land, which is a chronic problem everywhere in the study area as a result of the rapidly increasing population. The lack of economic opportunities in general, and of land in particular, explains much of the continuous net out-migration between 1974 and 1980, particularly in the eastern part of the area, and it has led to more temporary migration in the western part where many farmers have bought another farm outside the study area (e.g., on Yatta Plateau).

We further suggest that the direct cause of the changes in population increase and in in- and out-migration in 1979 and 1980 compared with 1974–1978 was a change in economic conditions. As long as these remain favourable, and as long as there is enough food, the population tends to remain in the area; this was the case between 1974 and 1978. There may even be net in-migration, as was the case in the western part, where coffee is grown. As soon as economic conditions deteriorate and food shortages occur, as in 1979 and 1980, there is less in-migration and more out-migration. Two factors in particular contributed to the net out-migration in 1979 and 1980: the drop in coffee prices and the unsatisfactory weather conditions leading to bad coffee, maize and bean harvests.

References

Adlakha AJ, Sullivan JM, and Abernathy JR, Recent trends in the methodology of demographic surveys in developing countries, Scientific Report Series No. 26, Univ. of North Carolina at Chapel Hill, USA, Laboratories for Population Statistics, 1980.

Barclay GW, Techniques of population analysis, Wiley, New York, 1958.

Brass W et al., The demography of tropical Africa, Princeton Univ. Press, Princeton NJ, 1968.

Central Bureau of Statistics, Demographic baseline survey report 1973, Nairobi, CBS, Ministry of Finance and Planning, Kenya, 1975.

Central Bureau of Statistics, Economic survey 1979, Nairobi, CBS, Ministry of Finance and Planning, Kenya, 1979.

Central Bureau of Statistics, Kenya Fertility Survey: 1977–1978, Volume 1 (1980) Nairobi, CBS, Ministry of Economic Planning and Development, Kenya, 1980.

Central Bureau of Statistics, Kenya 1979 census, unpublished data, Nairobi, CBS, Ministry of Economic Planning and Development, Kenya, 1981.

Goldstein S, Demography, 13 (1973) 423.

Gold W and Prothero R, Space and time in African population mobility, In; People on the move: studies on internal migration, Kosinski L and Prothero R, Eds, Methuen and Co., London, 1974.

Henin RA, Mott F, and Mott S, Recent demographic trends in Kenya and their implications for economic and social development, Nairobi, Population Studies and Research Centre, Univ. of Nairobi, Kenya, 1979.
Marks ES, Seltzer W and Krotki KJ, Population growth estimation: A handbook of vital statistics measurement, The Population Council, New York, 1974.
Mbithi PM and Barnes C, Spontaneous settlement problem in Kenya, East African Literature Bureau, Nairobi, 1975.
Myers RJ, The dual record system: an overview of experience in five countries, Scientific Report Series No 26, Univ. of North Carolina at Chapel Hill, USA, Laboratories for Population Statistics, 1976.
Ominde S, The population of Kenya, Tanzania and Uganda, Heinemann, Nairobi, 1975.
Omondi-Odhiambo, General characteristics and mortality levels among the registered JPM absentee study population and need for future research: a pilot survey, internal report, Medical Research Centre, Nairobi, 1977.
Shryock HS and Siegel JS, The methods and materials of demography, US Department of Commerce, Washington, DC, 1971.
United Nations Economic Commission for Africa, Manual on demographic sample surveys in Africa, Addis Ababa, Ethiopia, UN Econ. Commission for Africa, 1974.
Univ. of Ghana Medical School and UCLA School of Public Health, The Danfa Comprehensive Rural Health and Family Planning Project, Final Report, Ghana, 1979.
van Ginneken JK and Omondi-Odhiambo, Technical Report on analysis of demographic data of Joint Project Machakos, internal report, Medical Research Centre, Nairobi, 1979.
van Ginneken JK, Second progress report on analysis of demographic data of Joint Project Machakos between 1974 and 1980, internal report, Medical Research Centre, Nairobi, 1981.

Part III
Communicable childhood diseases

6
The epidemiology of measles

J. Leeuwenburg
A.S. Muller
A.M. Voorhoeve
W. Gemert
P.W. Kok

Introduction

Reports and publications from many African countries point to a high mortality from measles (Morley et al., 1963; McGregor, 1964; O'Donovan, 1971). Most of these contain data based on hospital returns, very little being known about what goes on in the susceptible population at large. Hospital statistics generally provide only a fragmentary and biased view of disease patterns because the patients seen are a selection from the hospital catchment area and usually only the seriously ill are admitted.

Accurate population-based figures on age-specific incidence and mortality are essential for proper planning of immunization programmes. In Europe and the United States measles is uncommon in children under one year of age. Measles vaccine is normally given after the first birthday because, in a (small) proportion of children, persisting maternal antibodies may prevent an adequate antibody response to the vaccine. In many African countries it may be necessary, however, to administer the vaccine at an earlier age because of a considerable measles incidence and mortality below age one. The population-based measles surveillance in the Machakos Project Study Area aimed to ascertain these features more precisely.

During the seven years of the study a variety of data related to measles epidemiology were collected. Factors like spatial spread of the disease and secondary attack rates within households were also assessed. The age-specific incidence rates of measles in under-5s, together with seroconversion data, led to a proposal for an optimal age for measles immunization. The longitudinal design of the project enabled us to evaluate further-attenuated measles vaccine under field conditions.

Materials and methods

Surveillance

Information on measles was acquired through the disease surveillance system (see Chapter 1) in the study area. During their visits the field-workers made enquiries apout measles, whooping cough and other symptoms of respiratory and diarrhoeal disease. They also recorded observations on signs of disease. During the same visits accurate data on age at onset of certain diseases such as measles were recorded.

When measles was suspected by either the mother or the field-worker, the child was reported to one of the project physicians for verification of the diagnosis. Signs and symptoms of the disease, history of vaccination and recent contact with other measles cases were all recorded on a standardized check list. Whenever possible a pernasal swab was taken for culture for measles virus and a capillary blood sample was obtained for antibody determination by the haemagglutination inhibition test.

Diagnosis

The clinical diagnosis of measles was established on the basis of the presence of a combination of major and minor criteria as derived from the above standardized check list. Table 1 shows the criteria used to diagnose definite, probable or possible

Table 1.
Criteria for establishing the clinical diagnosis.

Major criteria	*Minor criteria*
Morbilliform rash	History
Desquamation of skin	Contact within 4 was with measles case
Koplik's spots	Fever
	Cough
	Conjunctival inflammation
	Redness of oral mucosa

Definitions	*Grade*	*Class*
1 major + 3 minor criteria or desquamation + history	3	Definite
1 major + 2 minor criteria or 4 minor criteria	2	Probable
3 minor criteria or 1 major + 1 minor criterion or a history of measles alone	1	Possible

measles. These diagnoses were called grades 3, 2, and 1 respectively and assigned probabilities of 1.0, 0.67 and 0.33 to arrive at estimates of incidence and mortality rates. The validities of the major and minor criteria were tested by comparing measles cases (laboratory-confirmed) with control children.

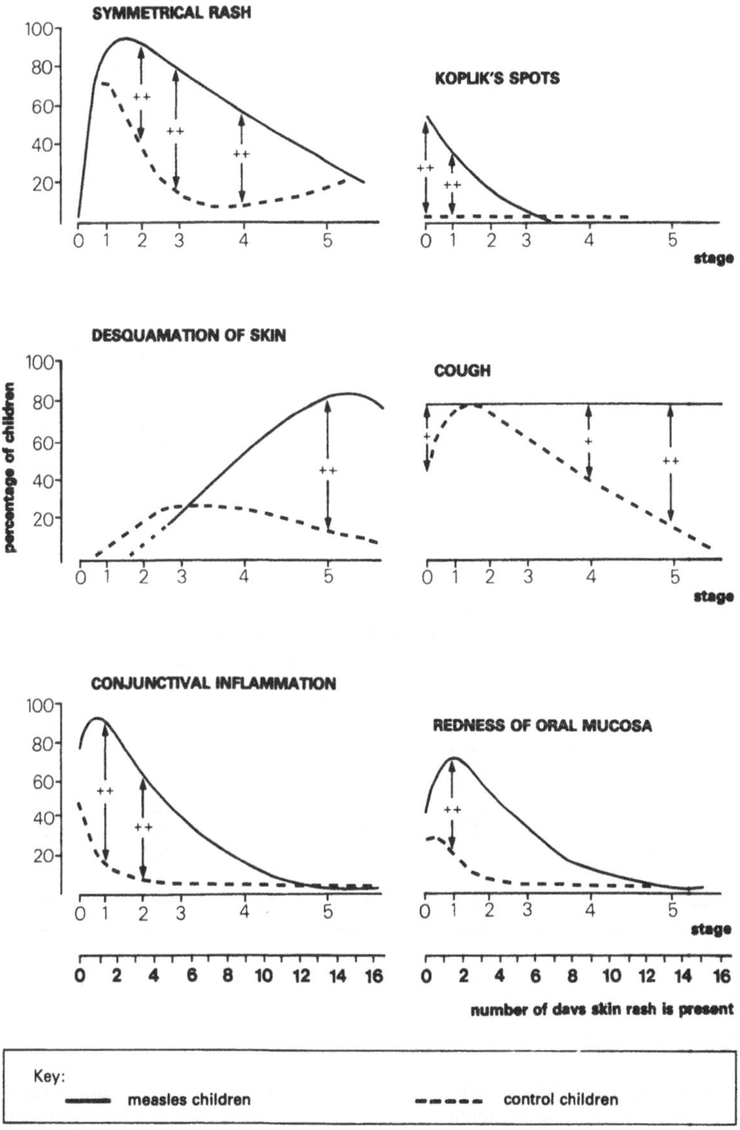

Figure 1. Relation between stage of disease and presence of 3 major and 3 minor criteria for measles (solid line) and control children (broken line) in percent of number of children in each stage.

It appeared that at different stages of the disease a sign or symptom has a different sensitivity and specificity (Fig. 1). The stages of the disease were defined on the basis of the number of days the rash had been present according to the mother. Ninety-six percent of the measles cases showed a symmetrical rash two days after the onset (stage 1). Koplik's spots appeared to be a highly specific sign but of low sensitivity. Desquamation (peeling) of the skin was characteristically a late sign of measles with increasing specificity and sensitivity during the course of the disease. Cough as a sign of measles discriminated only if the skin rash was not yet detectable and nine days or more after the onset of the rash. The shapes of the curves for redness of the oral mucosa and conjunctival inflammation were similar in the measles group; for the control group the curves were only slightly different.

The laboratory diagnosis was based on either virus isolation by culture on primary baboon kidney and Vero cells, by demonstrating at least a four-fold rise in titres in paired sera obtained four weeks apart (haemagglutination inhibition test) or by the detection of measles-specific IgM antibodies by the indirect immunofluorescence technique.

In 556 suspected measles cases a comparison was made between the diagnostic scores obtained from clinical signs and symptoms only, and the scores obtained when additional laboratory data were taken into consideration. A summary of this exercise is given in Table 2. The comparison between the final diagnosis (laboratory evidence included) and the clinical diagnosis (based on major and minor diagnostic criteria) shows agreement between the two methods within one diagnostic grade in over 90 percent of cases. In other words, when describing a measles epidemic the figures will be similar whether the final score or only the clinical score is used.

An elaborate account of the above methodology has been given by Gemert et al. (1977).

Table 2.
Relationship between clinical diagnosis (D) and final diagnosis (F) for children with a completed checklist of clinical measles signs.

		(D) 0	1	2	3	Total
	0	53	35	8	1	97
	1	13	11	13	20	57
(F)	2	5	10	18	62	95
	3		15	30	262	307
Total		71	71	69	345	556

Vaccine trial

One hundred and fifty children (without a history of measles immunization or illness) between 9 and 24 months of age were sequentially allocated to six groups in 1980. Five different methods of vaccine administration were tried; one group served as a control group. The methods employed were: 0.5 ml subcutaneously by needle and syringe; 0.1 ml intradermally by dermojet; 15 applications by bifurcated needle; 27 punctures by needle-bearing cylinder; and vaccine administered as nose drops. The control group received saline by needle-bearing cylinder. The vaccine used was Attenuvax II (MSD) which is a further attenuated, live, more heat-stable vaccine. Antibody titres were determined 4 weeks after the immunization; the titres of the control group served as a baseline. The vaccine was tested for potency immediately after reconstitution and after 7½ hours of exposure to ambient temperatures. Children in the control group and serological non-responders were (re)vaccinated.

Results

Laboratory data

A summary of the laboratory findings in 653 patients reported to have measles is presented in Table 3. Pernasal swabs were only taken in the early stage of the disease and not if the child was clearly in the stage of convalescence with peeling of the skin as the only obvious evidence of measles. Of the 204 swabs obtained, 45 percent yielded measles virus; 96 percent of the isolates were from children on or before the third day of the exanthem. There was no relation between isolation rate and age. Blood was taken at least once from 44 percent of the 653 patients. Measles-specific IgM was looked for in 78 patients and found to be present in 68 percent. This was done either because paired sera did not show a rise in antibody titre or because only a single blood specimen was available. Since there was a high level of agreement between laboratory and clinical diagnosis, it was considered justifiable to discontinue specimen collection for measles in 1978.

Table 3.
Laboratory specimens taken from 653 patients reported to have measles and proportion of confirmatory results.

Laboratory specimen	*Performed* *n*	%	*Positive* *n*	%
Pernasal swab	204	31.2	92	45.1
Paired blood sample	195	29.9	89	45.6*
Pernasal swab + paired blood sample	96	14.7	59	61.5
Positive swab + paired blood sample	33	5.1	30**	90.9*
Negative swab + paired blood sample	63	9.8	29	46.0*
Single blood sample	95	14.5	0	0
Measles IGM antibody determination	78	11.9	53	67.9

* 4-fold antibody titre rise.

**In three patients from whom measles virus was isolated without showing a 4-fold antibody titre rise, a nose swab was taken several days before the first blood sample.

Epidemic pattern between 1974 and 1981

In the course of 7 years of surveillance, three episodes of high incidence were observed (Fig. 2). Measles did not completely fade out between the epidemics, but there was a considerable interval between the epidemic waves. The number of susceptibles gradually built up in this 'low infection' period and a somewhat sudden increase in reported cases then occurred over a period of time. The epidemic did not at all follow the normal pattern and when we

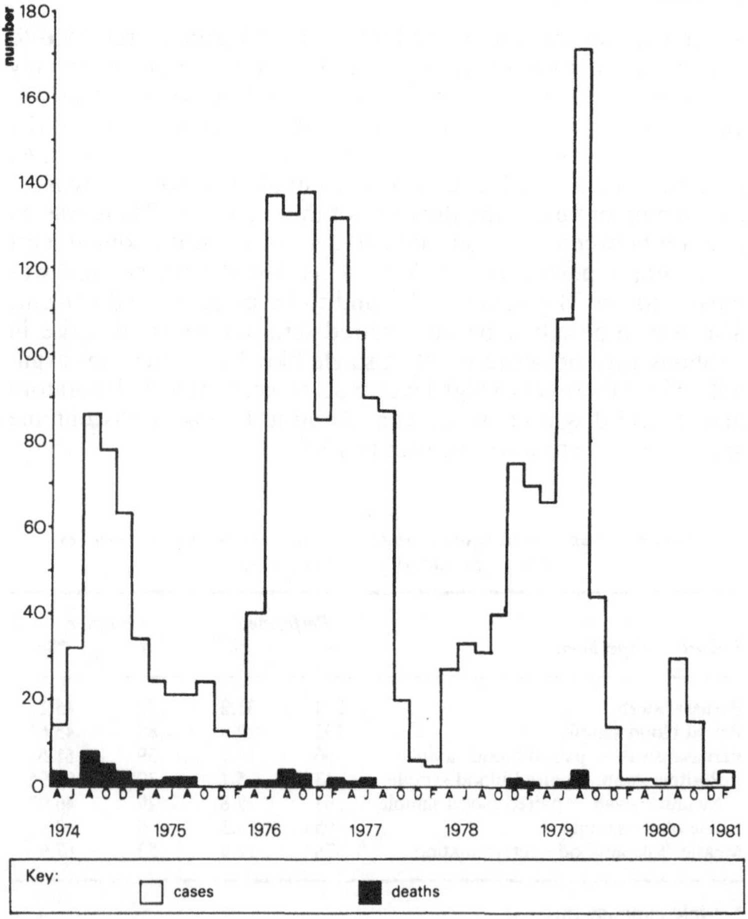

Figure 2. Two-monthly number of measles cases and measles deaths, April 1974–April 1981.

analysed the measles cases according to sublocation level, as was done for the period April 1976 to November 1977 (second epidemic), we noticed that in Kingoti and Kambusu sublocations measles had hardly disappeared at all during this period, though peaks are distinguishable. In contrast, in Ulaani there was only one single distinct peak, resembling a point-source outbreak with a skew profile to the right (Fig. 3).

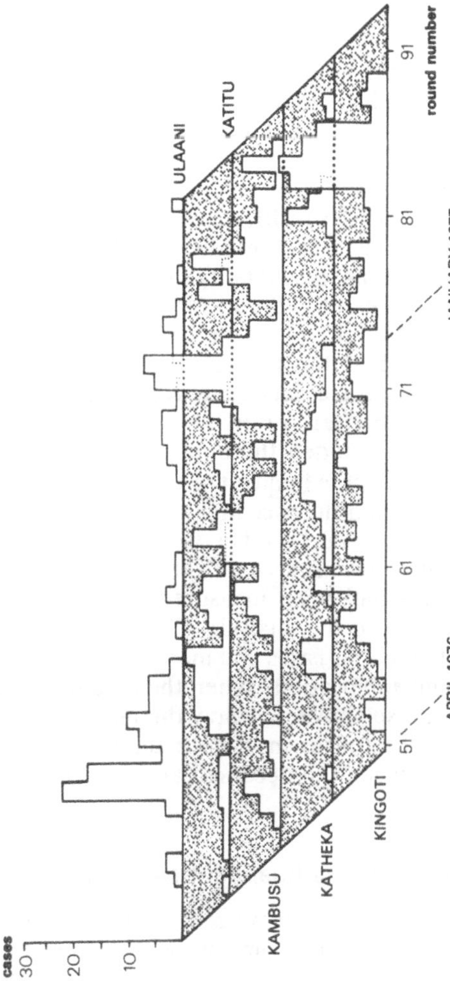

Figure 3. Measles cases April 1976–November 1977, by sublocation.

Table 4.
The mid-upper arm circumference, expressed as percentage of the Harvard standard, prior to measles, in children who died later of measles and in those who survived.

Deaths			Survivors		
Mean	*SD*	*n*	*Mean*	*SD*	*n*
84.0	7.7	31	86.0	8.0	64

$t = 1.15$ $p \approx .25$

At the height of the epidemics, between 80 and 170 cases were reported per 2-month period. When we divided the 7 years into three periods based on the epidemic pattern, we noticed that in the first period, from April 1974 to April 1976, there were 422 cases with 26 deaths (attributed to measles and occurring within 4 weeks of the onset of the measles rash), a case fatality rate of 6.2 percent. The second epidemic, from April 1976 to April 1978, comprised 978 cases with 14 deaths, case fatality rate 1.4 percent. In the third epidemic, up to April 1981, there were 734 measles cases with 8 deaths, a case fatality rate of 1.1 percent.

We also investigated the impact of nutritional status on the outcome of measles, since data were available on mid-upper arm circumference in children prior to contracting measles. The surveillance system included three-monthly routine recording of this measurement and more frequent recordings in cases of illness. No statistically significant difference in nutritional status, as measured by arm circumference, was found between those children who died of measles and those who survived (Table 4). Only children whose arm circumference had been measured within 3 months of the onset were included in the analysis. The survivors were selected from the definite measles cases and matched for age, date of onset of the disease and sublocation. When the data were broken down by sex and into those above or below the median age of contracting measles, no differences in arm circumference measurements were observed between the deceased and the survivors.

Population-based versus hospital-based data

During the first two epidemics we compared the population-based surveillance data with data from the nearby Kangundo hospital, the referral hospital for the study area. Between 1974 and 1976 the proportion of cases from the study area hospitalized at Kangundo was 12 percent, between 1976 and 1978 only 6 percent. In spite of this difference the case fatality rate of admitted measles cases in both periods was 22 percent. This contrasts sharply with the population case fatality rates of 6.2 percent and 1.4 percent, respectively, reported above. In 1974–1978, the median ages of hospitalized cases and of all cases were 18 and 31 months respectively.

Age distribution

The distribution of measles cases and deaths by age in months in the under-5s is illustrated in Figure 4. Twenty-seven percent of all measles cases were aged 5 years or older; half of them were between 5 and 7; and the other half between 7 and 15. Only four cases were seen in older persons, at ages of 17, 19, 23 and 35 years.

The figure shows that there were very few cases between 1974 and 1981 below the age of 6 months, obviously because of maternal antibodies in children in that age group. In the second half of the first year of life the incidence rose considerably to a peak at 9 and 10 months of age. There were more cases betweens 6 and 12

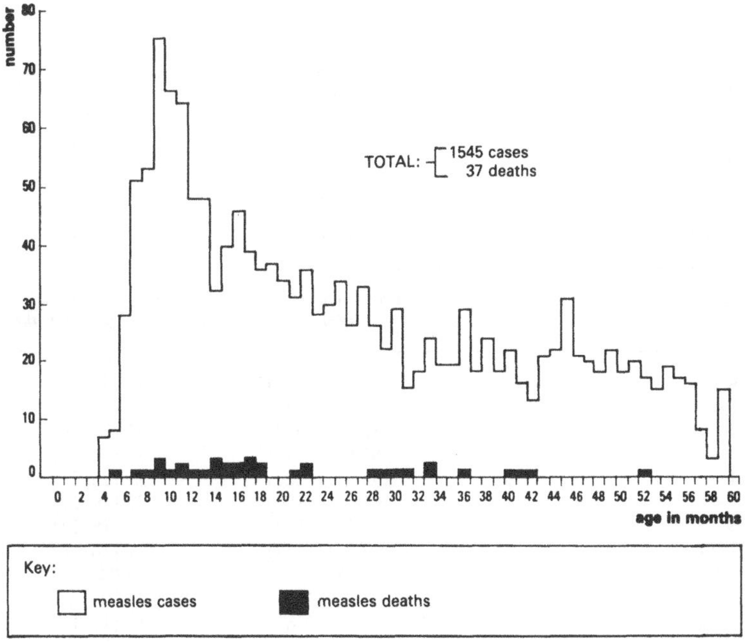

Figure 4. Distribution of measles cases and deaths in under-5s, by age in months, Machakos Project Study Area, Medical Research Centre, Nairobi, Kenya, April 1974–April 1981.

months of age than in any other 6-month age group. The average annual incidence rates by age between 1974 and 1981 are shown in Table 5.

Considering measles deaths, it was obvious that, though numbers were small, the largest proportion of deaths occurred before the second birthday. In the under-5s, the case fatality rate observed over the total 7-year period was 2.4 percent (37 out of 1545); in the over-5s it was 1.9 percent (11 out of 589). We have mentioned earlier that during the first epidemic wave (1974–1976) the overall case fatality rate was higher (6.2 percent) than in the following epidemics (1.4 and 1.1 percent respectively).

A practical application of the above age-specific incidence curve (Fig. 4) has been the combination of these data with data from a 1975 collaborative study on seroconversion after vaccination

Table 5.
Measles incidence rates, April 1974–April 1981.

Age (years)	*Estimated number of cases*	*Average population at risk (end of 1977)*
<1	352	1097
1–	455	1081
2–	295	1030
3–	255	964
4–	188	928
5–	150	928
6–	143	896
7–14	292	5974
>15	4	14 387
Total	2134	27 285

Age (years)	*Incidence per 1000*	*Average annual incidence per 1000*
<1	321 (293–349)*	46 (41–51)*
1–	421 (392–450)	60 (55–65)
2–	286 (258–314)	41 (36–46)
3–	264 (236–292)	38 (33–43)
4–	203 (177–229)	29 (25–33)
5–	162 (138–186)	23 (19–27)
6–	160 (136–184)	23 (19–27)
7–14	49 (44– 54)	7 (6– 8)
>15	0.28	0.04
Total	78 (75– 81)	11 (11–11)

*95% confidence limits

Table 6.
Projected reduction in measles cases with measles immunization at ages four to ten months, Machakos Project Study Area, Medical Research Centre, Nairobi, Kenya, April 1974–April 1981.

Age i of immunization (months)	*No. of measles cases at age ≥i months*	*No. of measles cases at age i*	*Cumulative measles incidence (%)*	*% Sero-conversion*	*Estimated prevented cases**		*Probable vaccine failures*	
					Number	*In % of total*	*Number*	*In % of total*
1	*2*	*3*	*4*	*5*	*6*	*7*	*8*	*9*
4	1545	7	.5	15	231	15	1314	85
5	1538	8	1.0	35	537	35	1001	65
6	1530	28	2.8	52	788	51	742	48
7	1502	51	6.1	72	1063	69	439	28
8	1451	53	9.5	86	1225	79	226	15
9	1398	75	14.4	95	1292	84	106	7
10	1323	66	18.6	98	1264	82	59	4

*assumes that half of the measles cases occurring in the same months of immunization cannot be prevented; the other half is subjected to the age-specific seroconversion rate.

(Kenya Ministry of Health/WHO, 1977), in order to arrive at a recommendation for the optimal age for measles immunization.

Table 6 summarizes the results of combining those two sets of data. Columns 2, 3 and 4 are derived from the observed age distribution up to the age of 10 months. Column 5 gives the age-specific seroconversion rates after vaccination, allowing for the waning pattern of maternal antibodies by age and for the age-influence itself on seroconversion. Columnn 7 shows that the same degree of protection against measles would be available from vaccinating at 8, 9 or 10 months, estimated at 79 percent, 84 percent and 82 percent reduction respectively. Since about 85 percent of the measles deaths occurred in children aged over 9 months, vaccination at 8 or 9 months would also markedly reduce measles deaths.

Column 8 gives the estimated number of vaccine failures. It shows that the number of expected vaccine failures when vaccinating at 8 months was twice that at 9 months (15 percent and 7 percent respectively). Since a high vaccine-failure rate might jeopardize the credibility of a measles vaccination programme in the community, the optimal age for administering measles vaccine in a population of this age disribution of measles cases is 9 months.

Susceptibility and secondary attack rates

The high incidence of measles between 6–11 months of age is a reflection on the one hand of the increasing proportion of susceptible children and on the other hand of the early age at which the rural African child encounters the measles virus.

The percentage of susceptibles was estimated during a serological survey of four different 25 percent systematic random samples of all under-5s who were bled during 1975 and 1976. All children having an antibody titre of 1/40 or less were considered susceptibles. The estimated percentages of susceptibles were 63 percent, 71 percent, 53 percent, 38 percent and 24 percent for the age groups of <1, 1, 2, 3 and 4 years respectively, leading to an overall 51 percent susceptibility in under-5s. In the 0–14 year age group the mean susceptibility was estimated to be 28 percent (Voorhoeve et al., 1977, Muller et al., 1977). This figure was used for the estimation of the secondary attack rate within households, but it is clearly an approximation. In order to define a secondary case subsequent to an index case, the criteria as described by Gordon (1965) were applied: the first day of the measles rash in a secondary case is observed 8–18 days after the first day of the rash in the primary measles case (in the same household). Figure 5 represents this rule in the form of a diagram.

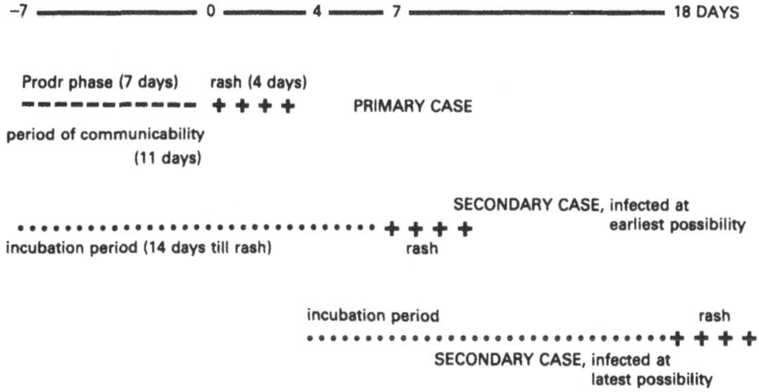

Figure 5. Schematic representation of shortest and longest intervals possible between the onset of the measles rash in the primary case and the secondary case (day 0 is the day of appearance of the rash in the primary case).

In the period April 1974 to October 1977 a total of 216 secondary cases of measles were identified in 783 households with a primary case. The mean number of siblings under 15 years of age was estimated to be 1.8 from demographic information. The secondary attack rate within households was thus estimated to be approximately $216 \times 100/783 \times 1.8 \times 0.28 = 54$ percent. This percentage corresponds with the findings of Gordon et al. (1965): about half the susceptible children in a household develop measles after the introduction of the disease by an index case.

Further studies (Leeuwenburg et al., 1979; Ferguson and Leeuwenburg, 1981) have shown that the spatial spread of measles is a function of the mobility of children, which is age-related. Children below the age of 3 years are mainly confined to the homestead or by the mother's movements. Older children enter nursery schools, where the environment exposes susceptible children more readily to measles. The nursery school child may act as a primary case and infect a younger sibling who no longer has maternal antibodies. This at least partially explains the high incidence of measles in the 6–11-months age group.

Another source of infection is the dispensary, health centre or outpatient department, where mothers may go for treatment for themselves or for their infants. Mothers often reported that measles occurred in their children shortly after having attended a health facility.

Vaccine trial

The results of the Attenuvax II vaccine trial are summarized in Table 7. It shows that only vaccine administered by syringe and needle or by dermojet evokes a significant antibody response when compared with the control group. The other three methods employed (nose drops, needle-bearing cylinder and bifurcated needle) produced titres not significantly different from the control group (Kok, Kenya and Ensering, 1983)

The numbers of morbid signs and symptoms (general malaise, respiratory symptoms, diarrhoea and vomiting, fever, rash and peeling) in the groups receiving vaccine and the control group were compared at weekly intervals. About 14 days after the vaccination there were 15 percent more respiratory symptoms in the vaccine groups; fever, however, was encountered in 22 percent of the control children and in 16 percent of vaccine recipients. One can therefore conclude that the vaccine used in the trial caused few reactions.

With regard to the temperature stability of the vaccine, potency testing showed that the vaccine should not be used for more than about 3 hours after reconstitution when kept at ambient temperature, since its $TCID_{50}$ (tissue culture infective dose) falls substantially after 3–6 hours' handling without cooling.

Discussion

The Machakos Project has generated a number of data that are relevant for understanding of the impact of measles in a rural area. During 7 years of disease surveillance three epidemics were

Table 7.
Geometric mean titre (Hai Method) of measles antibodies 4 weeks after immunization with five different methods.

	Number of children	*GMT (SD)*	*Significance level (p) when compared with control group*
Syringe and needle 0.5 ml	23	36.6 (11.8)	0.001
Dermojet 0.1 ml	21	51.3 (6.4)	0.001
Needle-planted cylinder	20	6.8 (6.7)	N.S.
Bifurcated needle	20	12.0 (13.1)	N.S.
Nose drops	25	8.1 (19.6)	N.S.
Control group	24	6.5 (9.5)	

observed, with declining case fatality rates of 6.2, 1.4 and 1.1 percent. This could not be explained by interference of the research team; nor were there differing prescription policies at the regular clinics in the area. The proportion of measles cases referred to the nearby hospital was twice as high in the first epidemic as in the second, yet the case fatality rate in hospitalized cases was 22 percent during both periods. Morley (1963) found a case fatality rate of 25 percent among hospitalized patients in Western Nigeria, a rate three to four times higher than the figure found in a village survey. Similar figures were reported from Guatemala (Gordon, 1965) and recently also from India (WHO, 1979). We have shown that the outcome of measles in terms of death or survival cannot be attributed to nutritional status (as measured by mid-upper arm circumference) prior to the disease.

Between 1974 and 1977, the median age of hospitalized cases was 18 months, in contrast to the median age of 31 months for all cases. The relative percentage of cases below one year was twice as high among hospitalized patients as it was among all cases. This demonstrates once more that it is not justifiable to make inferences on age distribution and mortality of measles among the general population from hospital data.

To what extent our data would apply to other areas of Kenya cannot be established, though the living conditions, population density and agricultural potential in the study area are comparable with those of many other regions of the country. An intensive population-based study such as we have carried out is expensive and difficult to execute. To find out whether accurate data on measles can also be determined more economically, in 1978 we compared the recall of mothers with respect to measles with our data obtained by two-weekly surveillance. Recall up to 6 months yielded agreement (agreed positive and agreed negative) in 66 percent of cases detected by surveillance. The 7–18 months' recall resulted in only 27 percent agreement. For certain purposes, therefore, a 6-months' recall may be acceptable, but recall for longer than this may yield data of doubtful value.

The diagnosis of measles based on a standardized list of major and minor criteria agreed closely with laboratory-supported diagnosis. We are confident that data obtained after the collection of laboratory data was discontinued were reasonably accurate.

The surveillance system enabled us to determine accurately the age of onset of measles in months, since the demographic surveillance provided birth dates. We were able to obtain an accurate picture of the age distribution in the under-5s, based on over 1500 cases documented during 7 years. This pattern of the age-specific incidence is not likely to shift very rapidly and give incidence peaks at older ages: the age profile between 1974 and 1978 was similar to that between 1978 and 1981.

From available data, measles immunization coverage ranged up to 56 percent for Machakos district in the 12–23-month age group in 1981 (KMRI, 1982). This does not imply that these children were effectively protected against measles: some had been vaccinated between 6–8 months of age and also the cold-chain conditions in the field left much to be desired, though Kenya has embarked on an expanded national immunization programme and vigorous efforts are being made to improve both vaccine coverage and the cold chain.

Seroconversion data from a collaborative Kenya Ministry of Health/WHO Study (1977), together with our age distribution data, provide a rationale for recommending immunization against measles at 9 months, particularly when the reduced number of vaccine failures at this age—half that at 8 months (WHO, 1982), is taken into account. Many recommendations on measles vaccination are either based on age distribution obtained from hospital data, or on seroconversion rates alone (Ogunmekan and Harry, 1981). Though the seroconversion rates after vaccination improve with age, the age distribution of cases makes a compromise necessary, based on the optimal proportion of cases that can be prevented (in our data 84 percent at 9 months) with as few vaccine failures as possible (7 percent at 9 months of age).

The field organization of the Machakos Project made it possible to test a further attenuated measles vaccine under field conditions, evaluating different methods of administration at the same time. It has been shown that the vaccine studied had few side effects, but caution is needed in handling it. The manufacturer's claim of heat stability for 48 hours when reconstituted could not be substantiated. Subcutaneous injection of 0.5 ml of the vaccine or administration of 0.1 ml by dermojet evoked satisfactory antibody responses in a large proportion of recipients.

By vaccinating children at an appropriate age with an efficacious vaccine we can achieve a reduction in measles morbidity and mortality. This is the main objective of the Expanded Programme on Immunization of the World Health Organization, which has been adopted by Kenya.

We have shown that measles immunization at 9 months of age with a heat-stable vaccine can increase the effectiveness of an immunization programme. Measles epidemics such as we observed in the Machakos Project during 1974 to 1981 may thus become a feature of the past.

To conclude this chapter we would like to stress that measles immunization programmes must take account of existing beliefs and practices about measles among populations to be immunized. These beliefs and practices are important because they may affect programme outcome. Several of these beliefs and practices, which are described in Chapter 24, will be summarized here.

In the Kamba culture measles is perceived as one of 'God's diseases'; the origin of such diseases is not known, but they are believed not to result from society or witchcraft, and all children are affected at one time or another. In contrast to 'God's diseases' are 'man's diseases', which are believed to be associated with witchcraft and sorcery; such diseases are caused by an enemy. The treatment of man's diseases is entirely the domain of the herbalist/diviner, who has supernatural powers; modern medicine is generally believed to be ineffective.

The frequency of measles and its usual pattern of occurrence in epidemics associates it with 'wind and weather'. The disease is regarded as part of the normal development of a healthy child. When a mother suspects her child has measles she does all that is considered appropriate to make the rash erupt. Traditionally, certain herbs are given for this purpose. The disease is believed to cause an ulcer in the stomach, as manifested by the sore in the mouth, and because of this milk and water are withheld from the child, which may lead to rapid dehydration, particularly as measles is often accompanied by diarrhoea (50 percent of our cases). Traditional practices in dealing with measles have tended to be replaced by seeking help at dispensary or hospital and they play a lesser role nowadays but they could have contributed to the higher case fatality rates in the first period of surveillance.

References

Benenson AS, Control of communicable diseases in man, American Public Health Association, Washington, 1975.

Collaborative study by the Ministry of Health of Kenya and the World Health Organization, Measles immunity in the first year after birth and the optimum age for vaccination in Kenyan children, Bull Wld Hlth Org, 55 (1977) 21.

Ferguson AG and Leeuwenburg J, Local mobility and the spatial dynamics of measles in a rural area of Kenya, Geo Journal, 5 (1981) 315.

Gemert W, Valkenburg HA and Muller AS, The diagnosis of measles under field conditions, Trop Geogr Med, 29 (1977) 303.

Gordon JE, Jansen AJ and Ascoli W, Measles in rural Guatemala, J Pediatrics, 66 (1965) 779.

Kok, PW, Kenya PR and Ensering H, Measles immunization with further attenuated heatstable vaccine using five different methods of administration, Trans, R Soc Trop Med Hyg, (1983), in press.

Leeuwenburg J, Ferguson AG and Omondi Odhiambo, Spatial contagion in measles epidemics, Trop Geogr Med, 31 (1979) 311.
McGregor IA, Measles and child mortality in the Gambia, W Afr Med J, 13 (1964) 251.
Medical Research Centre, Kenya Medical Research Institute, Report of the Dept of Epidemiology, Jan 1981–June 1982, 6–8, 1982.
Morley D, Woodland M and Martin WJ, Measles in Nigerian children, J Hyg Camb, 61 (1963) 115.
Muller AS, Voorhoeve AM, Mannetje W and Schulpen TW, The impact of measles in a rural area of Kenya, E Afr Med J, 54 (1977) 364.
O'Donovan C, Measles in Kenyan children, E Afr Med J, 48 (1971) 526.
Ogunmekan DA and Harry TD, Optimal age of measles vaccination in different age groups. II. Seroconversion to measles vaccine in different age groups, Trop Geogr Med, 33 (1981) 379.
Voorhoeve AM, Muller AS, Schulpen TWJ, Gemert W, Valkenburg HA and Ensering HE, The epidemiology of measles, Trop Geogr Med, 29 (1977) 428.
World Health Organization, Expanded programme on immunization. Measles, Wkly Epidem Rec, 54 (1979) 345.
World Health Organization, Expanded programme on immunization. The optimal age for measles immunization, Wkly Epidem Rec, 57 (1982) 89.

7

The epidemiology of pertussis and results of a vaccine trial

A.S. Muller
J. Leeuwenburg
A.M. Voorhoeve

Introduction

There is growing concern to improve the efficacy of infant immunization in countries that have not yet achieved a full permanent network of basic health services. Through its Expanded Programme on Immunization, the World Health Organization has embarked on a worldwide effort to control those childhood diseases that are preventable by immunization. Diphtheria, pertussis, and tetanus can be prevented by the administration of a combined vaccine (DPT) on three occasions during the first year of life. An immunization schedule that requires a minimum of contact with the children would greatly help to improve rates of coverage in countries where health resources are limited. In recent years evidence has accumulated that two doses of high-potency inactivated polio vaccine (IPV) are sufficient to protect against paralytic poliomyelitis (Salk et al., 1981). If in addition two injections of DPT vaccine provide sufficient protection, a schedule could be devised whereby all necessary childhood immunizations could be provided at two attendances.

Before schedules involving a reduced number of injections are introduced on a large scale, their effectiveness in protecting the susceptible childhood population against the relevant diseases should be established. The disease surveillance system of the Machakos Project of the Medical Research Centre, Nairobi offered an opportunity to study the epidemiology of diseases before and after the introduction of mass immunization. Also, by randomized controlled vaccine trials, the clinical effectiveness of a reduced number of immunizations could be compared with the effect of established schedules. This chapter describes the epidemiology of pertussis in Machakos as well as a pertussis vaccine trial.

Material and methods

Epidemiological study

The study area and the fortnightly (monthly from September 1978) surveillance system have been described in Chapter 1. Suspected cases of whooping cough were referred to a project physician, who recorded the presence or absence of clinical signs according to a standardized protocol. A pernasal swab was taken for isolation of *Bordetella pertussis* and finger-prick blood for a total and differential white blood cell count. Antibody levels were determined if the child was seen during the first few weeks of the disease and permission for taking blood could be obtained from the mother. Two months later an attempt was made to obtain a second blood sample. The pernasal swabs were inoculated on Bordet-Gengou medium containing 0.25 unit of penicillin per ml and on diamidine-penicillin-fluoride medium. Further streaking of the inoculum was done with a sterile loop in the field laboratory. The plates were then transported to Nairobi and incubated at 37°C for 6–7 days before being discarded if negative. Positive plates were subcultured and the *Bordetella* strains were sent to Amsterdam for serotyping, (Patel et al., 1978). The serum samples were examined for agglutinating antibodies by the microtechnique. The antigen, selected after testing various antigens for specificity and sensitivity, was prepared from *B pertussis* strain no. 3838 by the Netherlands National Institute of Public Health.

In cases where a mother insisted that her child had typical signs of pertussis, but these had not been confirmed by the project staff or by laboratory tests, the mother was re-interviewed 6–12 months later by a specially trained field-worker using a standardized interview protocol, to find whether she still believed her child had had pertussis. The interviewing field-worker did not know what diagnostic score the child had received when it was originally reported.

A scoring system based on a list of clinical and laboratory signs was made up at the onset of the study and used by the physicians for each child reported to have pertussis by the field staff. All clinical signs had to be observed by a project physician except for the whoop, for which the field-workers' observations were equally acceptable. The following criteria were used.

Criteria considered as conclusive (4 points):

— subconjunctival haemorrhage not caused by physical trauma in a child reported to have whooping cough
— isolation of *Bordetella pertussis* from a pernasal swab
— a white blood cell count ≥30 000/cu mm with ≥60 percent lymphocytes.

Major criteria (2 points):

— whoop
— choking and/or vomiting after the paroxysm
— a white count ≥30 000 with lymphocytes between 50 and 60 percent
— a white count ≥15 000 but less than 30 000 with lymphocytes ≥60 percent
— at least a four-fold rise in agglutinating antibody titre or a conversion from negative to positive (≥1/12) between the first and second samples, provided no DPT had been given during that period
— a history obtained half to one year later agreeing with the previous history as to time and duration of the illness, including an unequivocal description of whooping cough signs by the mother.

Minor criteria (1 point):
— paroxysms
— production of sticky stringy mucus
— absence of an inspiration in anticipation of the cough
— periorbital oedema
— close contact with a definite case of whooping cough
— a white count between 15 000 and 30 000/cu mm with lymphocytes between 50 and 60 percent
— an agglutinating antibody titre of 1/12 or more in children born since the start of the surveillance who have not received DPT vaccine and who have not been diagnosed as pertussis previously
— a history obtained half to one year later agreeing with the previous history as far as time and duration of the illness are concerned.

The points obtained on these criteria are converted into a scoring system for cases as follows:

0. No clinical or laboratory evidence; the history makes the diagnosis unlikely but it cannot be ruled out (0 or 1 point)
1. No clinical or laboratory evidence; the history makes the diagnosis possible (2 points)
2. Clinical signs and/or laboratory results make the diagnosis probable but not certain (3 points)
3. Clinical signs and/or laboratory results make the diagnosis definite (4 points or more)

In this report, incidence and mortality figures are estimated with 95 percent confidence limits, assuming probabilities of whooping cough of 0.15, 0.40, 0.75 and 1 for cases with scores 0, 1, 2 and 3 respectively. Therefore, 'estimated cases' of pertussis referred to below in the text and in the figures and tables are in fact cumulative probabilities of pertussis. These probabilities were based on the findings in cases where clinical as well as laboratory data were available. The percentage of cases in each scoring category in which pertussis was confirmed by laboratory results was used to estimate the probability for that score. It appeared that in the case of score 0 the diagnosis was unlikely but could not be entirely excluded. The registered population of December 1977 was used as the denominator for incidence and mortality rates.

Blood taking was discontinued in December 1977. This had an influence on the total number of estimated pertussis cases because the presence of lymphocytosis was occasionally the decisive criterion in scoring a reported case, but as far as antibody levels were concerned it hardly mattered because these contributed very little to the diagnosis (Voorhoeve et al., 1978). As a result the heights of the epidemic curves before and after December 1977 are not entirely comparable. During the 4 years of follow-up for the vaccine trial, however, no changes in the diagnostic criteria occurred.

Vaccine trial

The diphtheria-pertussis-tetanus (DPT) vaccine trial was started in December 1975 (Mahieu et al., 1978). Three-monthly immunization rounds covering those children who had reached the age of 3 months since the previous round, were carried out every 3 months until December 1977, intake of new cases having been stopped in June 1977. The control group (children with uneven project numbers) received BCG, first DPT, and oral polio during their first round; smallpox, and second DPT and polio during the second round; and the third DPT and polio, as well as measles vaccine, during the third round. The study group (children with even numbers) differed from the controls only in respect of the second round, when the second DPT was replaced by Salk polio vaccine. The DPT vaccine used in the trial was prepared by the Netherlands National Institute of Public Health, Bilthoven, Netherlands; the pertussis component contained 16 opacity units of *Bordetella pertussis* cells and 7 international units per dose. Two lots of vaccine were used. Unfortunately, no potency testing of the vaccine was done during the trial. We are satisfied, however, that proper cold-chain conditions were maintained throughout.

There were 2183 children eligible for inclusion in the trial, i.e. registered in the study population and born in the defined months. After excluding all children whose history or vaccination record suggested prior DPT immunization, 1165 children (53 percent) were entered into the trial. Both trial children and non-trial children were followed up by the routine disease surveillance described above. By the end of 1977, 466 children had received three DPT injections 3 months apart and 436 two DPT injections 6 months apart.

Four samples of capillary blood for pertussis agglutinating antibody determination were obtained—at 1 month, and 2, 3¼ and 4¼ years after their second or third DPT injection—from approximately 100 children in the trial.

Determination of a serological baseline before the first DPT injection was deliberately omitted because it was likely to jeopardize the children's participation in the trial. It is reasonable to assume that whatever pertussis antibody was present before the start of the trial was randomly distributed between study and control group.

Results

DPT vaccine coverage

The proportions of children in the Machakos Project area below 5 years of age (excluding the children in the vaccine trial) who received at least two DPT doses from the regular health services were estimated to be 27, 40, 29 and 35 percent at the end of 1976, 1977, 1978 and 1979 respectively.

Laboratory results

Laboratory data have only been analysed for the period April 1974–March 1977 (Patel et al., 1978). Agglutinating antibody levels in 618 paired sera of suspected pertussis patients were of little diagnostic significance; no appreciable difference was apparent between the distribution of titres in first and second samples; 39 percent of bacteriologically proven pertussis cases had no demonstrable antibodies in the second serum sample. Only 20 children out of 618 for whom two blood samples were available had an at least four-fold titre rise or a conversion from negative to positive as the only confirmation of the reported pertussis. The titre distributions in four different 25 percent systematic random samples taken at half-yearly intervals, i.e. before, during and after the first documented epidemic, were essentially the same.

Bordetella pertussis was isolated from 13 percent of 1078 pernasal swabs, isolation rates being somewhat higher in older children. The predominant serotypes in 94 isolates were 1,2,3, (40 percent) and 1,2 (44 percent). Type 1,3, which predominates in well-immunized communities, occurred in 16 percent.

A white count ≥15 000/cu mm with a lymphocytosis ≥50 percent was found in 36 percent of 934 children, of whom 91 (10 percent) had a total count ≥30 000. The presence of lymphocytosis was not related to age, although 12 very high total counts (≥60 000) all occurred in children below 6 years of age. Of 75 bacteriologically proven cases, 71 percent had a white count ≥15 000/cu mm with a lymphocytosis ≥50 percent. The highest white blood cell count in a proven case was 127 000 (78 percent lymphocytes); the lowest was 2500 (72 percent lymphocytes).

Pertussis incidence 1974–1981

Figure 1 represents the estimated number of cases between April 1974 and 1981. There were two epidemic waves; the small number of cases (16) that occurred among children in the vaccine trial coincided with the second epidemic. If the incidence is based on probable (Score 2) and definite (Score 3) cases only, the shape of the epidemic curve remains essentially unchanged although at a level some 10–20 percent lower during the two epidemics and 40

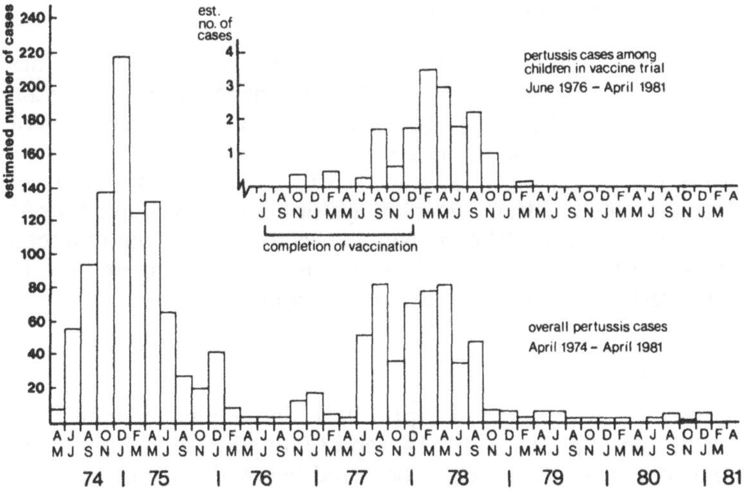

Figure 1. Distribution of pertussis cases among children in vaccine trial and among all children over the period April 1974–April 1981. Number of cases estimated according to scoring system (see text).

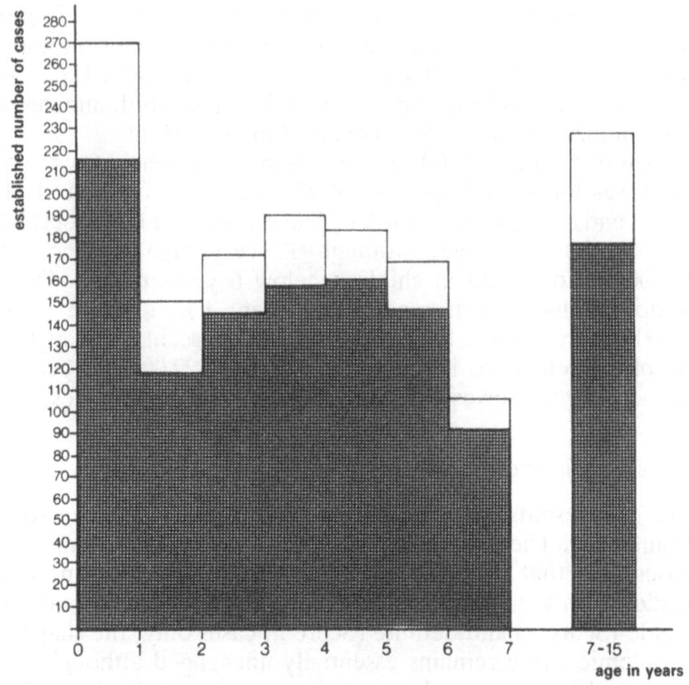

Figure 2. Age distribution of pertussis cases, April 1974–April 1981. Shaded areas represent probable and definite cases (scores 2 and 3).

percent lower at periods of low endemicity. Also, when cases are plotted according to age (Fig. 2), the shape of the histogram remains nearly the same whether based on all estimated cases or only on probable and definite cases.

The largest number of estimated cases occurred below the age of one year, and children 6 years of age or younger accounted for 84 percent of all cases. The median age was 3.5 years. Out of a total of 1465 estimated cases, 758 were female, giving a sex ratio of 0.93. Pertussis incidence rates are given in Table 1.

Mortality

Between April 1974 and April 1981 the estimated number of deaths due to pertussis was 14, representing a case fatality rate of 1 percent. Half these deaths occurred below the age of one year (case fatality rate 2.6 percent); the others were evenly distributed among children aged 1–4 years. There were no fatalities due to pertussis among children included in the vaccine trial.

Table 1.
Pertussis incidence rates, April 1974–April 1981.

Age	*Estimated cases*	*Average population at risk (Dec. '77)*	*7 yrs incidence per 1000*	*Average annual incidence per 1000*
<1	270	1097	246 (221–272)*	35 (31–39)*
1–	150	1081	139 (118–159)	20 (17–23)
2–	171	1030	166 (143–189)	24 (20–27)
3–	189	964	196 (171–221)	28 (24–32)
4–	183	928	197 (172–223)	28 (24–32)
5–	168	928	181 (156–206)	26 (22–29)
6–	106	896	118 (97–139)	17 (14–20)
7–14	228	5974	38 (33– 43)	6 (5– 6)
Total	1465	12 898	114 (108–119)	16 (15–17)
Total population		27 285	54 (51– 56)	8 (7– 8)

*95 percent confidence limits

Vaccine trial

Some children who had entered the trial were reported with pertussis before completing their immunizations: in the study group an estimated 2.5 cases of pertussis developed between first and second dose. In the control group 2.0 cases of pertussis occurred between first and second dose, and 4.2 cases between second and third dose. The above cases have not been considered when comparing the outcome of the two- and three-dose groups. Nine hundred and two children (77 percent of those entered in the trial) completed the three vaccination rounds and were followed up to April 1981.

Figure 3 shows the distribution of agglutinating antibody titres at intervals of 1, 24, 39 and 51 months after administration for children who received two and three doses of DPT vaccine. In Figure 3a a comparison can be made with the titre distribution among children of the same age group not included in the trial. Most of these have no demonstrable antibody titre. Differences between titre distributions of the two- and three-dose groups were tested with the Wilcoxon two samples test. Results are given in Table 2. At 1 month after administration of the last (second or third) dose of DPT vaccine there was no difference in titres. At longer post-vaccination intervals antibodies waned more rapidly in the two-dose group. Differences between the groups were statistically significant after an interval of 2 years ($p<0.01$). Waning of antibodies is reflected in the median titres presented in Table 2.

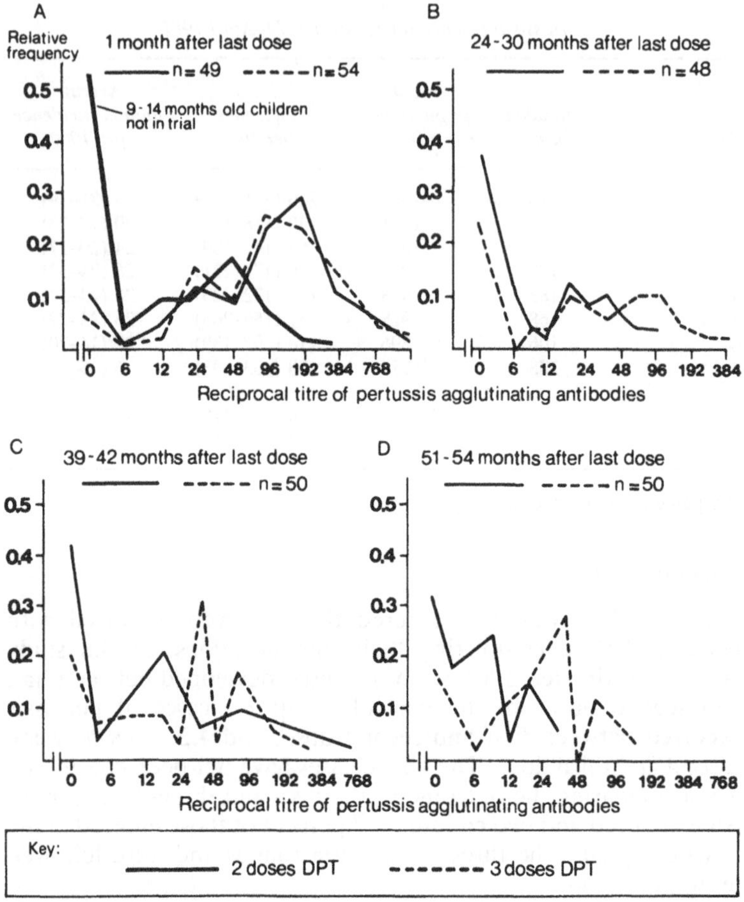

Figure 3. Frequency distribution of pertussis agglutinating antibody titres after two or three doses of DPT vaccine at four different post-vaccination intervals.

The proportion with no demonstrable titre rose in the two-dose group from 10 percent after one month to 38 percent after two years or more. Corresponding percentages for the three-dose group were 6 percent and 23 percent respectively.

Table 3 presents the observed number of pertussis cases in the vaccine trial based on probability of the disease with scores 0 to 3 as well as for scores 2 and 3 only. For all scores the number of cases observed in the two-dose group (8.15) was the same as in the three-dose group (8.55); when only scores 2 and 3 are considered cases occurred more frequently in the two-dose group but the difference was not statistically significant. Compared with the

Table 2.
Differences between agglutinating antibody titre distributions of experimental and control group—Wilcoxon two samples test.

	A *interval* *1 month*	*B* *interval* *2–2¼ years*	*C* *interval* *3¼–3½ years*	*D* *interval* *4¼–4½ years*
2 DPT				
Number	49	48	50	50
Geometric mean titre	1:70	1:6,7	1:5,5	1:4,5
Percentage without demonstrable titre	10	38	42	32
3 DPT				
Number	54	48	50	50
Geometric mean titre	1:96	1:19,2	1:15,2	1:12,5
Percentage without demonstrable titre	6	23	20	18
Wilcoxon two-sample test	$p>0.20$	$p<0.01$	$p<0.01$	$p<0.01$

Table 3.
Pertussis cases per 1000 person-months of observation in trial and non-trial subjects (of same birth cohorts).

	Trial		*Non-trial*
Number of children	902		1281
Person-months of observation	46 173		66 837
Observed number of cases (all scores)	8.55 (3DPT) 8.15 (2DPT)	16.7	52.4
Pertussis cases per 1000 person-months of observation (all scores)	.36 (3DPT) .36 (2DPT)	.36*	.78
Observed number of cases (score 2+3)	4.25 (3DPT) 6.75 (2DPT)	11.0	41.3
Pertussis cases per 1000 person-months of observation (score 2+3)	.18 (3DPT) .30 (2DPT)	.24**	.62

*percentage reduction 54 **percentage reduction 61

observed number of cases in the 1281 children of the same birth cohorts not included in the trial, the reduction among the trial-children was 54 percent (all scores) or 61 percent (scores 2 and 3). Since the non-trial children did not form a randomized control group as some of these children were likely to have received DPT immunizations elsewhere, it is not justified to consider these percentages to express actual vaccine efficacy. The reduction percentages have also been calculated separately for each cohort born in a specified 3-month period. The number of pertussis cases per cohort was of course very small, which might explain why reductions in percentages of trial children as compared with non-trial children varied from 13 to 88 percent.

Discussion

The Machakos Project has provided a unique opportunity to study the epidemiology of pertussis and to assess the protective value of giving only two pertussis immunizations during infancy. In contrast to measles, the diagnosis of whooping cough is difficult under field conditions because the clinical manifestations are often not apparent during a brief period of observation. In addition, absence of agglutinating antibodies in the serum and of lymphocytosis in the peripheral blood does not exclude the diagnosis. Over one-third of patients from whom *B pertussis* was isolated and in whom antibodies were determined were serologically negative. Although 65 percent of the patients were under 5 years of age, a serological baseline survey showed that only 26 percent of children in their fourth year of life had pertussis agglutinins in the serum. Moreover the presence of agglutinating antibody may to some extent have been due to recent immunization instead of recent clinical illness.

Clinically, infants often do not develop a whoop; they usually, however, exhibit the paroxysmal cough with choking and/or vomiting described by Morley as typical for pertussis in infants (Morley and Stephens, 1972). We found the absence of an inspiration in anticipation of the cough, described by Morley as pathognomonic for a whooping cough paroxysm, extraordinarily difficult to observe in the setting of a crowded field office.

Blood taking was regarded as less essential if the diagnosis could be established on clinical grounds alone. Pernasal swabs were taken more readily in young infants than older children because in the former the diagnosis can be more easily missed if they do not whoop. The resulting selection of children subjected to these procedures might explain why the results in this study do not correspond with those of the combined Scottish study, which found a higher isolation rate of *Bordetella pertussis* and a lower seroconversion rate in infants under the age of 6 months than in older children (Combined Scottish Study, 1970).

The scoring system for the diagnosis of pertussis, assigning certain probabilities of the disease being present according to the score, is unavoidably a little arbitrary. The consistency of the findings, however, whether based on all scores or only on probable and definite disease (scores 2 and 3) gives a reasonable assurance that conclusions drawn from the figures are justified.

In spite of the above-mentioned diagnostic difficulties we are confident that we have been able to document the epidemic pattern of the disease with reasonable accuracy. We observed two pertussis outbreaks 3 years apart and consequently expected a third one in 1980; this, however, did not occur. The decrease in frequency of pertussis outbreaks may have been due to a vaccine-induced increase in herd immunity.

Our finding that more girls are affected than boys is consistent with other studies (Gordon and Hood, 1951). The median age of 3.5 years found in our study comes close to that found in industrial countries among families living under poor economic conditions in overcrowded homes, resulting in intra-household spread (Bassili and Stewart, 1976), which is probably the major mode of spread in Machakos. In Western Nigeria inter-household spread seems to be more common, which might explain, in addition to differences in immunization coverage, the lower median age found by Morley, Woodland and Martin (1966).

The case fatality rate of 1 percent is lower than most reports from developing countries suggest, but it still is formidable as compared with fatality rates from the developed countries and much higher than the incidence of serious adverse reactions to the vaccine reported from, for example, the Netherlands (Hannik and Cohen, 1979) and England (Miller et al., 1981). According to Cook more than 95 percent of all pertussis deaths occur in developing countries (Cook, 1979). The hotly debated issue in some West European countries as to whether the benefit of routine pertussis immunization of infants outweighs the risks is therefore of no relevance for most developing countries. In such countries the value of increasing immunization coverage in order dramatically to reduce morbidity and mortality from immunizable diseases is fully recognized and supported by the World Health Organization through its Expanded Programme on Immunization. Simplification of vaccination schedules is one way to improve coverage.

In the present vaccine study two pertussis immunizations showed encouraging results in comparison with three doses. Initially antibody response was the same in the two- and three-dose groups. Later in the trial, waning of antibody was more pronounced in the two-dose group (Fig. 3 and Table 2). The actual clinical protection during, on average, 4 years of observation, was not significantly different in both groups (Table 3).

The study confirms the findings of Mangay-Angara et al. (1978) in the Philippines which, however, were confined to one serological evaluation. We were able to determine post-vaccination agglutinating antibody levels on four occasions, the last 4¼ years (51 months) after completion of the immunization during infancy. The objection may be raised that no antibody determinations were carried out before the start of the trial. These were deliberately omitted, because we had reason to believe that many mothers would refuse to participate in the trial if it were to start with bleeding their children and we think it reasonable to assume that the distribution of baseline titres in both groups was similar. Owing to the small amounts of serum available, it was not possible to titrate sera after absorption of nonspecific antibodies. This may have led to a number of nonspecific reactions (Preston, 1979); their effect can be expected, however, to have been randomly distributed between the two- and three-dose groups and a difference in antibody titre distribution between the two groups is likely to be largely related to the number of vaccine doses received. In addition, it is difficult to conceive how the large difference in titre distribution between trial and non-trial children one month after the last DPT dose could be entirely explained by such nonspecific reactions.

The potency of the vaccine used was somewhat above average. No adverse reactions were noted. News of any major adverse reactions would certainly have reached us through the field-workers, who were members of the communities they were observing. On the other hand, only 902 children were included in the trial, while the incidence of shock and convulsions up to 3 days after injection of a 16-opacity-unit DPT-polio vaccine in the Netherlands is about 1 in 2700 children (Hannik and Cohen, 1979). The estimated attributable risk of serious neurological disorder occurring within 7 days after immunization in Great Britain is one in 110 000 injections (Miller et al., 1981). All we can therefore conclude from our data is that such adverse reactions did not occur among 900 children.

From the point of view of study design it would have been preferable to have included a randomized control group of children not receiving any pertussis vaccine at all, but this would have been clearly unethical and not feasible. Under the circumstances the best we could do was to compare the trial children with children not included—for reasons beyond our control—in the trial but of the same birth cohorts as the trial children. These children were not randomly selected and some of them had probably been immunized elsewhere. Nevertheless we found an appreciable difference in attack rates between trial and non-trial children, follow-up being equally intensive in both groups.

A pertussis outbreak expected to occur in the second half of 1980 did not materialize, probably because of increased herd immunity due to immunization. It is conceivable that more vaccine failures among the trial children would have occurred if pertussis transmission had resumed in the last part of the follow-up period but even if this had happened, the affected children would by then have reached an age at which pertussis injection is responsible for relatively mild disease with a low mortality.

The present study was primarily designed to demonstrate that half-yearly mass immunization campaigns may be a suitable instrument to protect the childhood population in remote areas without access to continuous mother and child health services. For this reason a 6-month interval was chosen between the two DPT doses of the study group. The BCG scar would serve as a marker for the first dose, the smallpox scar as a marker for the second dose. Children having both scars would be adequately protected.

With the eradication of smallpox and the discontinuation of smallpox vaccination, cohorts born since 1980 no longer have smallpox scars even though they may have been fully immunized. There are of course many parts of the world where DPT is available either on a continuous basis from regular mother and child health clinics or at intervals considerably shorter than 6 months. A three-DPT schedule is preferable in such situations because it obviates the problem of children contracting whooping cough during the 6-month interval between the first, non-protecting DPT dose and the second one, i.e. below the age of 9 months, which is a vulnerable age both in terms of incidence and mortality.

The present vaccine trial indicates that two DPT doses provide adequate protection against pertussis when given 6 months apart. It is important to know whether this will also be the case when shorter intervals are used. The effect on the incidence of diphtheria and tetanus could not be studied, since neither disease was observed among the study population during the entire period of surveillance.

References

Bassili WR and Stewart GT, Epidemiological evaluation of immunisation and other factors in the control of whooping-cough, Lancet, i (1976) 471–3.

Combined Scottish Study, Diagnosis of whooping cough: Comparison of sero-ogical tests with isolation of Bordetella pertussis, Br Med J, 4 (1970) 637–9.

Cook R, Pertussis in developing countries: possibilities and problems of control through immunization, In; Third International Symposium on Pertussis, DHEW publication, no. (NIH) 79-1830, 1979, p. 283.

Gordon JE and Hood RI, Whooping-cough and its epidemiological abnormalities, Am J Med Sci, 222 (1951) 333.

Hannik CA and Cohen H, Pertussis vaccine experience in the Netherlands, In; Third International Symposium on Pertussis, DHEW publication, no. (NIH) 79-1830, 1979, p. 279.

Mahieu, JM, Muller AS, Voorhoeve, AM and Dikken H, Pertussis in a rural area of Kenya: epidemiology and preliminary report on a vaccine trial, Bull Wld Hlth Org, 56 (1978) 773–80.

Mangay-Angara H, et al., Dev Biol Stand, 41 (1978) 15–22.

Miller DL, Ross EM, Alderslade R, Belleman MH and Rawson NS, Pertussis immunisation and serious acute neurological illness in children, Br Med J, 282 (1981) 1595.

Morley DC, Woodland M and Martin WJ, Whooping cough in Nigerian children, Trop Geogr Med, 18 (1966) 169.

Morley DC and Stephens AJH, Whooping cough in the developing world, Trop Doct, 2 (1972) 16.

Patel S, Schoone G, Lighthart GS, Dikken H and Preston NW, Agents affecting health of mother and child in a rural area of Kenya. V. Pertussis serotypes in Kenyan children 1974–1975, Trop Geogr Med, 30 (1978) 141–6.

Preston NW, Abstract 2928, Trop Dis Bull, 76 (1979) 1087.

Salk J, van Wezel AL, Stoeckel P, et al., International Symposium on Reassessment of Inactivated Poliomyelitis Vaccine, Bilthoven 1980, Dev Biol Stand, (1981) 181–98.

Voorhoeve AM, Muller AS, Schulpen TWJ, 't Mannetje W and van Rens M, Agents affecting health of mother and child in a rural area of Kenya. IV. The epidemiology of pertussis, Trop Geogr Med, 30 (1978) 125–39.

8

The incidence of diarrhoeal disease

J. Leeuwenburg
W. Gemert
A.S. Muller
S.C. Patel

Introduction

Diarrhoea is generally considered to be one of the major causes of childhood morbidity and mortality in developing countries. Quite an amount of information on diarrhoea in childhood, however, is obtained from hospital-based studies, while population-based studies are relatively rare. The results to be reported in this chapter are population-based data on morbidity and mortality of acute diarrhoeal disease in children 0–4 years of age. The longitudinal nature of the project allowed assessment of the magnitude and impact of diarrhoea among children in this age group. Surveillance data from April 1974 to the middle of 1977 are presented here.

Methods

Between June 1974 and June 1977 all mothers were asked by 12 field-workers in the course of fortnightly home visits to 4000 households whether any of their children below 5 years of age had been ill since the previous visit. If the answer was affirmative, information on the occurrence of diarrhoea during the same period was sought; no enquiry was made about the number of diarrhoeal spells per fortnight. From April 1976 onwards data on the occurrence of diarrhoea were obtained from all children irrespective whether the mother had reported them ill or not.

Reliability tests

In order to estimate the reliability of mothers' answers, two small studies were carried out: first two field-workers who had been given permission by 10 families consisting of 57 people made observations of the stools produced and kept between 7 a.m. and 7 p.m. for a period of 2 weeks. Each morning the respondents were asked about bowel movements during the night. At the end of this period a third field-worker questioned every respondent about the occurrence of diarrhoea during the past 2 weeks. The answers were compared with the observations made in the preceding fortnight.

In a second attempt to validate the answers of mothers to questions on diarrhoea among their children under 5 years of age, the field-worker asked the mothers to keep a stool specimen of any child having diarrhoea on the day of his visit. If no stool specimen was kept, a revisit was made on the same day. The field-worker described the consistency of the stool and decided whether or not it constituted diarrhoea. Several training sessions with the entire staff resulted in a fair degree of agreement among field-workers and supervisory staff as to whether a stool specimen represented diarrhoea or not. Out of a total of nearly 1000 reports of 'diarrhoea today' the field-workers managed to observe a stool specimen in 63 percent. Both studies suggested 15–40 percent over-reporting of diarrhoea by mothers.

Stool specimens

A systematic random sample (1:16) was obtained from the under-5s in the course of three house-to-house surveys conducted in April–September 1974, in January–April 1975 and in March–April 1976. Rectal swabs were collected for the isolation of Enterobacteriaceae. It was not feasible to revisit children in the sample who were not at home when the laboratory team called; and a small number of mothers refused to let a swab be taken. As a result the completion rate for the three surveys ranged between 64 and 76 percent. Each swab was immediately inoculated on the following agar plates: MacConkey, desoxycholate citrate, brilliant green and mannitol salt. Subsequently the swab was dipped in selenite broth as an enrichment medium for salmonellae and after overnight incubation inoculated on all the above agar plates, except mannitol salt.

Climatological data

A climatological index was composed from data on temperature, humidity and rainfall obtained from weekly observations at five weather stations in the study area. No significant differences in these measurements were observed between the stations. Because temperature, humidity and rainfall are interrelated a principal component analysis was performed on mean minimum and mean maximum temperature, mean minimum humidity, rainfall in mm precipitation and number of rainy days per week. Two important components could be identified: rain and temperature. The rain component accounted for 50 percent of all variation in the variables measured and is used in this paper as an indicator of 'wetness'. Unlike rainfall, the rain component can have a negative value.

Mortality data

Information on mortality and on causes of death was routinely obtained during the fortnightly visits by field-workers to all the households in the study area.

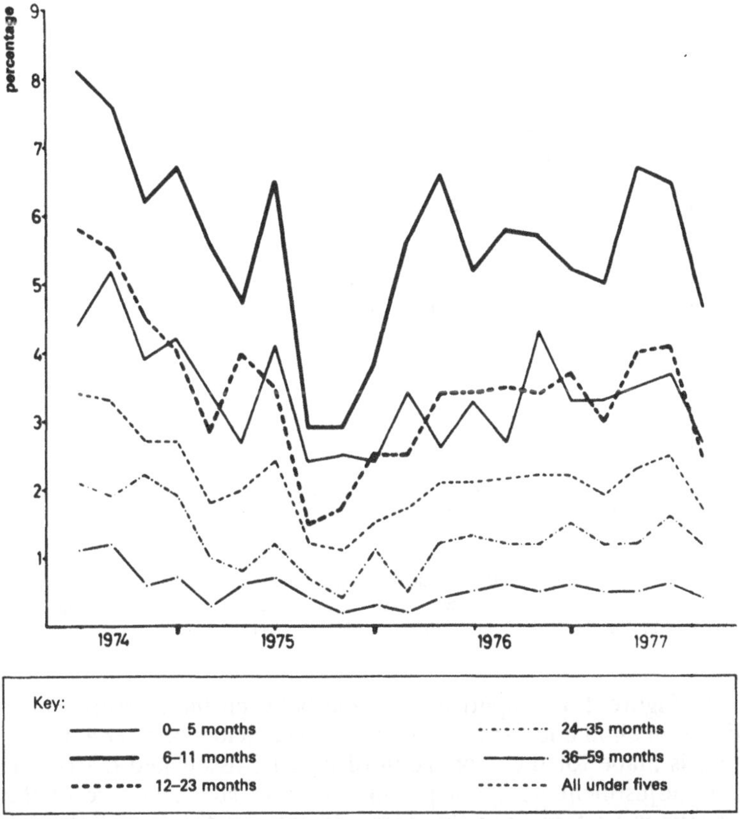

Figure 1. Two-weekly percentage of children reported and/or observed to be ill with diarrhoea, 1974–1977.

Results

Age-specific incidence rates of episodes of diarrhoea in children who were reported and/or observed to be ill are given in Figure 1. On the vertical axis the percentages by age group per round of all children under surveillance who were ill with diarrhoea are plotted against time (horizontal axis). One can observe striking differences between the various age groups: children 0–5 months of age had virtually the same diarrhoea incidence as children 12–23 months of age, whilst the children 6–11 months had a consistently and statistically significantly ($p<0.001$) higher percentage of diarrhoea than younger or older children. A marked decline in diarrhoea incidence in all age groups is noticeable in the second half of 1975.

Figure 2. A: Two-weekly incidence of diarrhoea in ill under-5s; B: Two-weekly incidence of diarrhoea associated with measles cases under 5 years of age; C: Two-weekly incidence of diarrhoea in ill under-5s not suffering from measles. (C=A–B).

In Figure 2 a comparison is made between the diarrhoea incidence in all ill under-5s and the diarrhoea incidence after a deduction is made for the proportion of measles-associated diarrhoea. The adjustment does not produce a more stable picture of the diarrhoea pattern over the years. It appears that the decline in

Table 1.
Average 2-weekly incidence of diarrhoea in children under 5 years of age.

	Age in months					
	0–5	*6–11*	*12–23*	*24–35*	*36–59*	*Total*
Diarrhoea, incidence in ill children (%), June 1974–June 1977	3.4	5.6	3.4	1.3	0.5	2.2
Diarrhoea incidence in all children (%), April 1976–June 1977	15.8	24.5	15.9	7.4	3.7	10.5
Average no. of children present per round of 2 weeks June 1974–June 1977	394	422	832	797	1454	3899

diarrhoea incidence was not caused by the absence of measles cases during that period. Data on reported measles cases are provided in Chapter 6.

During the period April 1976–June 1977 when diarrhoea information was obtained from all children irrespective of whether the mothers considered them ill or not, we found a four- to seven-fold higher incidence of diarrhoea when compared with ill children for the different age groups, as can be seen in Table 1.

From April 1974–December 1977, out of a total of 306 deaths under 5, 46 children (22 males, 24 females) were reported to have died of diarrhoea and vomiting. Thirty-three children were under one year of age; 13 children were 0–5 months of age; the median age of the diarrhoea deaths was 7½ months, the mode was 6 months and the mean age was 13 months. The age range was 2–57 months. About half the children died in the nearby sub-district hospital at Kangundo. The numbers for the different years are given in Table 2, compared with the number of measles deaths and the total number of deaths in under-5s. Most diarrhoea deaths (80 percent) were reported to have occurred in March–July, whilst the overall mortality pattern in under-5s was fairly homogeneous over the months (see Chapter 17).

Table 2.
Number of deaths from diarrhoea and vomiting, from measles, and from all causes in the under-5 population, April 1974–1977.

	Diarrhoea and vomiting	*Measles*	*All causes*
1974 (April–Dec only)	5	18	78
1975	12	8	67
1976	15	9	90
1977	14	5	71
Total	46	40	306

The results of the bacteriological surveys are given in Table 3. The isolation rate for the three surveys combined was 12 percent. During the first survey this rate was roughly three times higher than during the next two surveys ($p<0.01$). Of the total of 47 isolates, 26 were shigellae (mostly *Shigella boydii* and *Sh. flexneri*), 15 were pathogenic *Escherichia coli* and 6 were salmonellae. No particular age pattern could be observed for the three pathogens but the numbers are small. There was no significant difference in isolation rate of enteropathogens from stool specimens of children

Table 3.
Isolation rates of three bacteriological surveys.

Period of survey	*No of specimens*	*No of isolations*	*Percentage of isolations*
April–Sept 1974	130	28	20
Jan–April 1975	95	6	6
March–April 1976	157	13	8
Total	382	47	12

with and without diarrhoea. Seven isolates originated from 35 children with diarrhoea; 347 children in the sample had no diarrhoea yet in 40 cases an isolation of enteropathogens was obtained. This finding may to a large extent, however, be due to a bias in the samples as a result of the low completion rate.

In Figure 3 the rain component of the climatology data is presented for 1975 and 1976, as well as the diarrhoea incidence in the under-5 population. Though the pattern of the rain component shows a bimodal seasonality, the diarrhoea morbidity does not follow a seasonal trend.

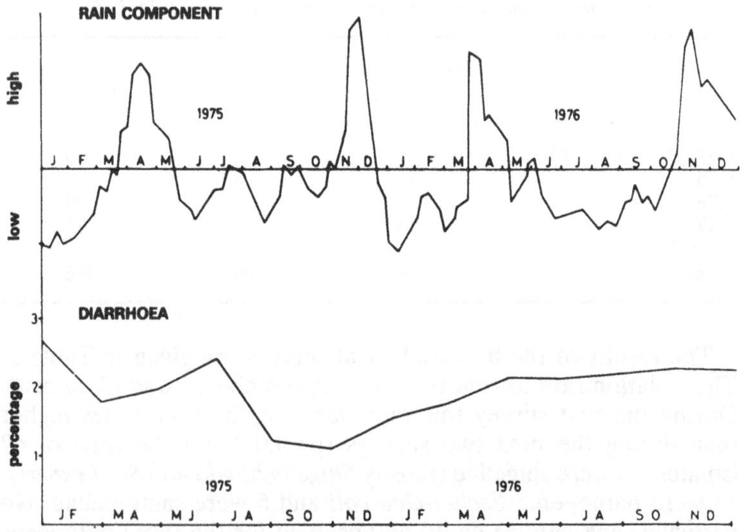

Figure 3. A comparison of the rain component obtained from five weather stations in the study area with the 2-weekly incidence of diarrhoea in ill under-5s, 1975 and 1976.

Discussion

The age-specific pattern of diarrhoea shows marked differences: the age group 6–11 months old has the highest percentage of diarrhoea. This can be explained by the phenomenon of weanling diarrhoea, as first described by Gordon et al. (1963). The weaning period varies in different cultures; in the Machakos Project study area, van Steenbergen found in a cluster sample of 183 children under 3 years of age, that weaning—gradually accustoming the child to solid foods—took place between 7 and 18 months (see Chapter 12). The weight-for-age of these children, expressed as a percentage of the Harvard Standard, dropped after 6 months of age, started to rise again after the age of 1½ years and remained fairly constant (84 percent) up to the age of three. The age incidence of diarrhoeal disease thus parallels the observed deviation from the normal growth curve.

The diarrhoea surveillance system used in the Machakos Project only yielded a minimum estimate of diarrhoea attacks, because no information about the number of spells of diarrhoea per fortnight was obtained. On the other hand, we have evidence that mothers tend to over-report diarrhoel episodes by 15–40 percent. Van Zijl (1966) reported a diarrhoea incidence of 35 percent per month among children 0–6 years of age in Venezuela as well as Iran, while we observed an attack rate of at least 10.5 percent per two weeks (=21 percent per month) in all under-5s. In Guatemala Gordon et al. (1964) found attack rates from 46 per 100 children per year in the first half-year of life to 120 in the second year of life.

The mortality due to diarrhoea and vomiting was considerable. Over the entire period of observation the proportional mortality rates were approximately the same for measles (13 percent) and diarrhoea (15 percent); only in the first half-year of the study did measles outrank diarrhoea as a cause of death. During that period a high measles case fatality rate was observed (see Chapter 6). In view of our experience that the mothers tend to over-report diarrhoea in their children, the proportion of deaths due to diarrhoea and vomiting may as well be an overestimate. It was seldom possible to verify the diagnosis in children who died in the nearby Kangundo hospital, since their hospital records could only occasionally be traced.

No clustering of diarrhoea deaths by village of residence was detected; the clustering in the months of March–July, fairly consistent over the different years of observation, is difficult to explain.

The isolation rates in the bacteriological surveys are comparable with those in other studies (Cruickshank, 1963). In Kenya, Kalya and Oduori (1972) reported on a series of 180 children (age range 2 months to 7 years) admitted to Kenyatta National Hospital for diarrhoea. They found that 16 percent of them harboured enteropathogenic *E. coli*, shigellae, or salmonellae. No data, however, were given on controls.

Recently there has been more emphasis on the viral aetiology of acute diarrhoea in young children. In India, Maiya et al. (1977) demonstrated that rotavirus was a significant cause of morbidity in 13 of 50 children under 2 years of age with acute gastroenteritis; no rotavirus was found in 30 matched controls. Also Ryder and Sack (1976) stressed the role of rotavirus as a common cause of childhood diarrhoea. In Kenya, rotavirus is being isolated in at least 30 percent of young children admitted to the paediatric ward of Kenyatta National Hospital for acute diarrhoea. The majority of cases in whom rotavirus was demonstrated were under 2 years of age (Mutanda, 1978). Metselaar (1978), in a sample of 207 sera from children in Machakos district, found antibodies against rotavirus in virtually all sera from children over 30 months of age. Rotavirus may thus play a significant role in diarrhoeal morbidity in this rural area.

Maina (see Chapter 24) examined socio-cultural factors related to diarrhoea among the study population. She points out traditional practices that may aggravate the effect of diarrhoea on the health of the child, like cutting the gums and banning foods and fluids. Such practices may well extend the duration and severity of diarrhoea spells in individual children, since proper rehydration is often ignored.

The decline in diarrhoea incidence in all age groups in the second half of 1975 is difficult to explain. It coincided with the lower frequency of reported measles cases, as well as with the drop

Child feeding child.

in the frequency of malnutrition (<80 percent weight for age, Harvard Standard), also observed in the second half of 1975 and in early 1976 (Jansen, unpublished data).

It is well known that diarrhoea plays a role in the measles syndrome; we found that the incidence of diarrhoea in measles cases less than 5 years old was nine-fold that for children without measles. Scrimshaw et al. (1966) reported an eight-fold incidence of diarrhoea in children with measles. We recorded diarrhoea as a concomitant symptom in 50 percent of measles cases. Morley et al. (1967) reported diarrhoea in 51 percent of measles inpatients. In the under-5 population, measles and malnutrition cases represent only quite a small proportion of children; the decline in diarrhoea incidence should be explained by other factors. It is often suggested (e.g. McGregor et al., 1970) that there is a relationship between diarrhoea incidence and the rainy season(s), but this was not demonstrated in our study.

Initially diarrhoea information was only obtained from children who were reported and/or observed to be ill; later on, all mothers were questioned about their children's diarrhoea experience at the time of the field-worker's visit or in the preceding two weeks. This yielded a four- to seven-fold increase in diarrhoea incidence. Diarrhoea thus appears to be a common condition among under-5s, not necessarily considered by mothers to be an illness.

References

Cruickshank R, Diarrhoeal diseases in the United Kingdom, In; Epidemiology, Pemberton J, Ed, Oxford University Press, 1963, p. 62.

Gordon JE, Chitkara ID and Wyon JN, Amer J Med Sci, 245 (1963) 345.

Gordon JE, Guzman MA, Ascoli W and Scrimshaw NS, Bull Wld Hlth Org, 31 (1964) 9.

Kalya R and Oduori ML, E Afr Med J, 49 (1972) 949.

McGregor IA, Rahman K, Thomson AM, Billewicz and Thompson B, Trans R Soc Trop Med Hyg, 64 (1970) 48.

Maina B, Modern and indigenous medical care utilization patterns with respect to measles and acute diarrhoea among the Akamba, MA Thesis, University of Nairobi (1977).

Maiya PP, Pereira SM, Mathan M, Bath P, Albert MJ and Baker SJ, Arch Dis Childh, 52 (1977) 482.

Metselaar D, Sack DA, Kapikian AZ and Muller AS, Trop Geogr Med, 30 (1978) 531.

Morley DC, Martin WJ and Allen J, E Afr Med J, 44 (1967) 496.

Mutanda LN, Epidemiology of acute gastro enteritis in early childhood in Kenya, PhD Thesis, Univ. of Nairobi (1978).

Ryder RW, Sack DA and Kapikian AZ, Lancet, i (1976) 659.

Scrimshaw NS, Salomon JB, Bruch HA and Gordon JE, Amer J Trop Med Hyg, 15 (1966) 625.

Zijl WJ van, Bull Wld Hlth Org, 35 (1966) 249.

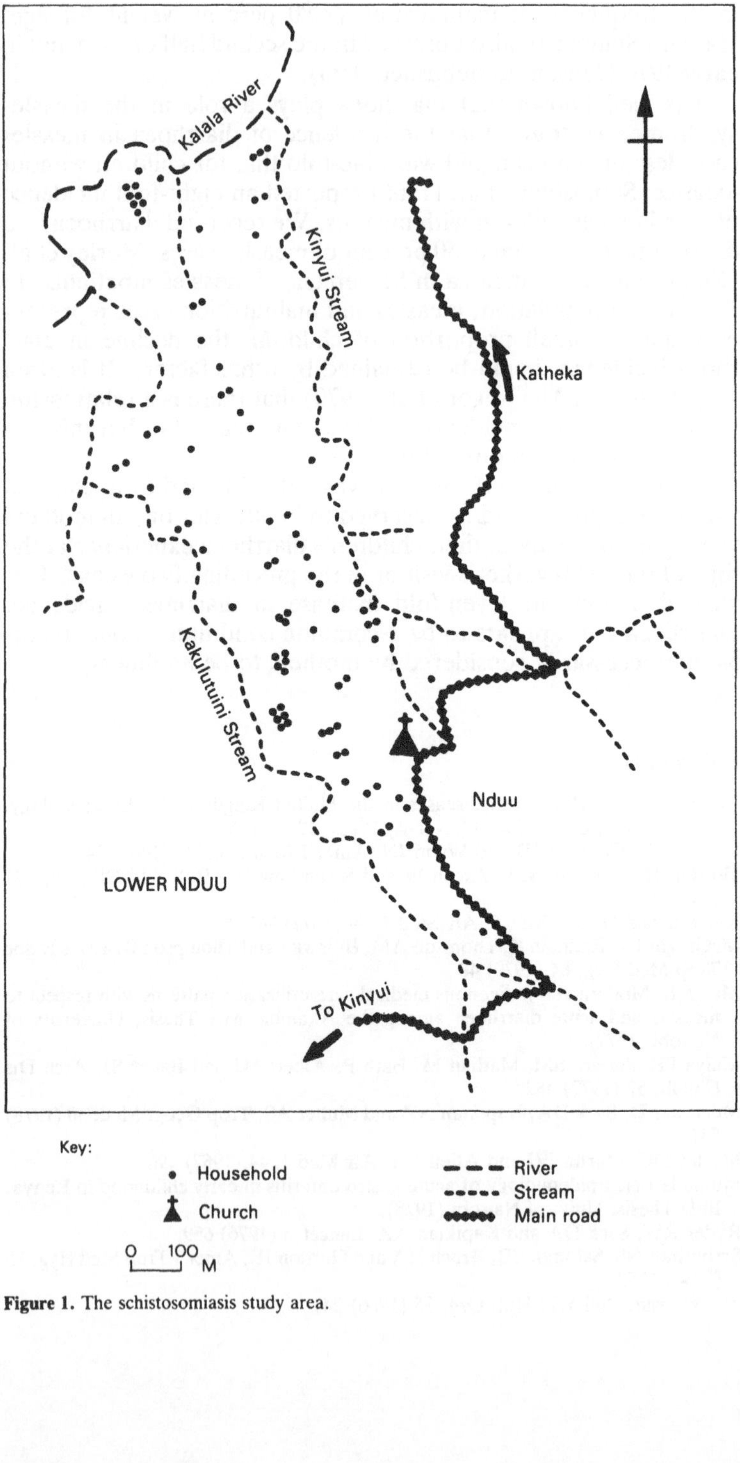

Figure 1. The schistosomiasis study area.

9

The human ecology of schistosomiasis and its cost-effective control

K.S. Warren
A.A.F. Mahmoud
J.H. Ouma
T.K. Arap Siongok

Introduction

After completing a study of morbidity in schistosomiasis mansoni relative to intensity of infection in schoolchildren on the island of St Lucia (Cook et al., 1974), the Division of Geographic Medicine of the Department of Medicine at Case Western Reserve University in Cleveland, Ohio, USA wished to expand its studies of human schistosomiasis to examination of entire communities. A collaborative research programme was arranged with the Division of Vector-Borne Diseases, Ministry of Health, Nairobi, Kenya and the Medical Research Centre of the Royal Tropical Institute of Amsterdam, The Netherlands.

In the Machakos Project study area morbidity in relation to intensity of infection of schistosomiasis mansoni in an entire community was investigated over a two-year period. A rapid and simple variant of a standard diagnostic test was developed and studies were performed on a low-dose, low-toxicity drug regimen. Treatment was then provided for the heavily infected proportion of the population only, follow-up being continued over the subsequent four years. The project also broadened out into similar studies of schistosomiasis mansoni in Nyanza Province, an area holoendemic for malaria, and of schistosomiasis haematobia in Coast Province. The latter also included the development of a new diagnostic test and a shorter, simpler drug regimen. The results of these studies were then gathered into a comprehensive, cost-conscious control plan for schistosomiasis throughout Kenya.

Materials and methods

Our primary studies were performed in the village of Lower Nduu in the Kingoti sublocation of the study area (Arap Siongok et al., 1976). This is bounded on the south by a main road, on the north by the Kalala River and on the east and west by the Kinyui and Kakulutuini streams (Fig. 1). At the time of the initial studies it had a population of 499 individuals over one year of age who lived in scattered households and were members of the Kamba tribe. Basic demographic data were collected as described in Chapter 1. Stool examinations were performed by a variant of the Kato thick smear technique. A questionnaire about the major symptoms or signs attributable to *S mansoni* infection was translated into the Kamba language and administered by local health workers. The physical examination included measurement of weight, height, liver size both in the mid-clavicular and mid-sternal lines while the patient was recumbent, and splenic size graded on the Hackett scale.

All 90 households in the village of Lower Nduu were included in the study. Eighty-three percent of the 499 individuals in the village completed all the parasitological and clinical examinations. More than 50 percent of the population fell into the age group 1–19 and the male-female ratio was 44:56. Previous studies had shown that malaria has a very low endemicity in the study area, and the prevalence of intestinal helminth infections was also low.

Results

S mansoni eggs were detected in the stools of 82 percent of the 416 individuals in the study. Peak prevalence (98 percent) was found in the 10–19 age group, and prevalence in the age groups 40 and above fluctuated between 71 percent and 75 percent. Eighteen percent of the population were uninfected; 28 percent were lightly infected (10–100 eggs/g); 21 percent were moderately infected (101–400 eggs/g); 33 percent were heavily infected (more than 401 eggs/g); and 16 percent of the population had egg counts over 1000/g. The mean egg counts of the entire population were 515 for females, 478 for males, and 499 eggs/g faeces for both. The intensity of infection in females peaked (1026 eggs/g) at ages 10–14, in males (1019 eggs/g) at 20–24 years. Both sexes showed a marked decline in the intensity of infection from age 25 on.

In response to the questionnaire, approximately 85 percent of the population claimed that they had been able to do their usual work both in the last 24 hours and in the last two weeks regardless of the presence and intensity of infection; approximately 15 percent, however, said they had felt weak during those periods. On the other hand while 8 percent and 11 percent of the uninfected population complained of abdominal pain over the last 24 hours and two weeks respectively, the percentages reporting this symptom in the heavily infected group (1000+ eggs/g) rose to 21 percent and 28 percent*. Diarrhoea, as defined by more than three

*Using the chi-square test these changes were statistically significant ($p<.025$).

watery stools per 24 hours, occurred somewhat more frequently in the most heavily infected groups, but this result was not statistically significant.

On physical examination hepatomegaly was very common. The liver was palpable 3 cm or more below the mid-sternal line in 22 percent of the uninfected group, but the prevalence of liver enlargement increased with intensity of infection up to 52 percent in the most heavily infected group. Livers palpable 7 cm or more below the mid-sternal line were observed in only 3 percent of the uninfected population, but were found in 21 percent of the most heavily infected individuals. Similar correlations with intensity of infection were seen with liver enlargement in the mid-clavicular line. Splenomegaly (Hackett scale 2 or greater) did not occur in the uninfected population but it was seen in somewhat over 2 percent of the lightly and moderately infected and in 7 percent of the heavily infected groups.

Most of the stool samples were formed but soft; only a small proportion of watery stools were seen and these bore no relation to intensity of infection.

Twelve individuals with hepatosplenomegaly were extensively studied in hospital. Oesophageal varices were found in two patients.

The conclusions reached on the basis of this study are as follows. Morbidity due to schistosomiasis mansoni tended to correlate with intensity of infection as manifested by quantity of eggs excreted. The majority of the infected population, even in a hyperendemic area such as Lower Nduu, had only light or moderate infections and these were rarely associated with significant morbidity. Disease manifestations were seen largely in those with heavy infections. The results were in agreement with previous studies in schoolchildren in St Lucia.

These studies were followed by the development of a low-cost, efficient system for the control of schistosomiasis mansoni called 'targeted mass treatment' (Warren and Mahmoud, 1976). It was based on the following premises:

1. disease is related to intensity of infection;
2. heavy infections can be identified rapidly;
3. low-dose therapy will reduce heavy to light infections with minimal side effects from treatment.

One year after the initial survey in Lower Nduu the entire village was re-surveyed. During the second survey a rapid method for the detection of individuals with heavy infections was developed and was called the 'Quick Kato' technique. Using this technique those with moderate and heavy egg counts could be detected in less than two minutes per subject.

For treatment, patients were given half the recommended dose of hycanthone (1.5 mg/kg i.m.). No side effects were observed (vomiting is seen in 40 percent of patients with the recommended dose of 3 mg/kg). This was confirmed in a later dose-response study also carried out in Machakos District (Warren et al., 1978). Following these results 118 individuals with egg counts higher than 400/g (30 percent of the population examined) were treated (Mahmoud and Warren, 1980). Their mean age was 14.8 years and mean egg count was 1250 eggs/g. Follow-up egg counts four months later revealed a 97.1 percent reduction in output to 36 eggs/g. No eggs were detected in the stools of 33 percent of the treated individuals; 65 percent had egg counts of 10–100/g, two individuals had egg counts of 170/g and only a single person remained with an egg count of 450/g.

At the third annual survey, one year after treatment of the heavily infected individuals, the whole community was re-examined, and 116 of the 118 treated individuals were available for follow-up. Their egg counts averaged 115/g or 9 percent of the pre-treatment level, but 9 of 116 (7 percent) had attained egg excretion levels of over 400/g.

When the entire community was considered, the changes related to treatment of less than one-third of the studied population were of interest (Mahmoud et al., 1983). The prevalences of infection at the three annual surveys were respectively 83 percent, 88 percent and 75 percent. The major change detected, however, was in intensity of the infection. While at the first and second surveys there was a mean of 33 percent of the population excreting more than 400 eggs/g, this proportion decreased significantly to 8 percent at the third survey. At the second survey the intensity of infection in the 10–14 age group was 1056 eggs/g; it was only 100 eggs/g at the third survey, one year after treatment. Mean liver enlargement of the 118 heavily infected individuals prior to treatment was 6.3±1.0 cm in the mid-sternal line and 2.4±0.6 cm in the mid-clavicular line. One year following treatment these corresponding measurements were 3.5±0.4 and 1.0±.3 cm ($p<0.01$) The population has been followed up over the subsequent three years and the results are undergoing analysis.

Other studies in Kenya

In order to broaden our concepts of the prevalence, intensity and morbidity due to schistosomiasis in Kenya further studies of schistosomiasis mansoni were carried out in the far west of the country in Nyanza Province near Kisumu on the shores of Lake Victoria (Smith et al., 1979) and of schistosomiasis haematobia in the east of the country in Coast Province near Mombasa (Peters et al., 1976; Warren et al., 1979; Arap Siongok et al., 1979).

The Kisumu study involved a 30 percent random household sample of a community of 40 fishermen in an area holoendemic for malaria (Smith et al., 1979). Prevalence and intensity of *S mansoni* infection were somewhat lower than in the Machakos study and peak prevalence and intensity occurred at a higher age. The association between the presence of hepatomegaly and splenomegaly and intensity of infection found in Machakos, was not apparent in the Kisumu study, probably related to the confounding effect of malaria.

Schoolchildren between 5 and 18 years of age in the Coast Province near Mombasa were examined for the presence of *S haematobium* eggs by Nuclepore filtration of urine, a method that proved to be sensitive, reproducible and rapid (Peters et al., 1976). Prevalence was 84 percent and the urine of 26 percent of the children contained 400 eggs/10 ml or more. Dysuria and haematuria were more common in the infected population, and hydronephrosis and hydroureter, as determined by intravenous pyelography, were common, in particular among those heavily infected (Warren et al., 1979). Treatment with metrifonate in a single oral dose of 10mg/kg resulted in a marked reduction in egg output (Arap Siongok et al., 1979).

Conclusion

The data gathered in all the above studies were particularly useful when the senior author (KSW) was asked by a major bilateral aid agency to be a consultant for the development of a major control programme for schistosomiasis in Kenya. With the aid of the Ministry of Health a plan was developed based on data gathered in the above series of epidemiological, diagnostic and therapeutic field studies. The basic goal of the programme was not to attempt to eradicate schistosomiasis in Kenya, which would be very costly to attempt and unlikely to be successful, but to develop a simple and relatively low-cost scheme of control of disease based on chemotherapy alone.

Two factors were of great importance with respect to the prevalence of schistosomiasis: the rapid growth of the population in the country, and the spread of the infection as a result of irrigation. In 1969 it was estimated that approximately one million of Kenya's population of 11 million had schistosomiasis, but in 1979 it was calculated that approximately 2 million of the estimated popu-

Multiple opportunities to acquire schistosomiasis.

lation of 17 million were infected. Epidemiological investigations of *S mansoni* infection in the central area of the country (Machakos District) and in Nyanza Province along the shores of Lake Victoria revealed that from a half to three-quarters of the infected population had light to moderate infections with relatively few signs of liver disease. Another important fact was that, except for populations engaged in specific water-related occupations (e.g. fishing), the highest prevalence and intensity of infection occurred in schoolchildren. Studies of schistosomiasis haematobia in schoolchildren in Coast Province showed an overall prevalence of 84 percent with a moderately high intensity of infection. Again, renal, ureteral, and bladder abnormalities clustered in heavy infections, but disease was also seen in children with low egg counts at the time of diagnosis.

On the basis of these results, it was recommended that a major campaign to control schistosomiasis by chemotherapy be directed largely towards schoolchildren aged 5–19 years in endemic areas (Warren KS, 1982), treating only those with 50 or more *S mansoni* eggs/g faeces and all those infected with *S haematobium*. For diagnosis of schistosomiasis mansoni the 'Quick Kato' technique would be used, and for *S haematobium* infection the Nuclepore filtration. Both of these can be read almost immediately in the field with no staining. The regimens for mass chemotherapy established in Kenya were hycanthone at 1.5 mg/kg for *S mansoni* infections resulting in an average 97 percent reduction in egg burdens four months after treatment, with virtually no toxicity, and metrifonate for *S haematobium* infections at 10 mg/kg in a single dose providing a 96 percent reduction in egg burdens (Arap Siongok TK et al., 1979). Both drugs were very inexpensive at less than $1 per regimen.

It was estimated that, using these systems targeted at schoolchildren in areas where the heaviest rates of infection occurred, a six-year programme involving complete coverage of all endemic areas twice would cost less than $10 million.

Based on the findings of the Kenyan studies it is anticipated that this approach will keep the levels of infection below those necessary to cause disease in the great majority of individuals in the country. It is also possible that it will have an effect in decreasing transmission by reducing egg output into the environment.

In conclusion it should be acknowledged that it was the direct collaboration with the Medical Research Centre that made the longitudinal schistosomiasis study in Machakos possible and led to the broader range of studies that resulted in the development of a control scheme for all of Kenya.

Acknowledgement

Support for these studies came from the Edna McConnell Clark Foundation.

References

Arap Siongok TK, Mahmoud AAF, Ouma JH and Houser HB, Morbidity in schistosomiasis mansoni in relation to intensity of infection: study of a community in Machakos, Kenya, Am J Trop Med Hyg, 25 (1976) 273–84.

Arap Siongok TK, Ouma JH, Houser HB, Warren KS, Quantification of infection with *Schistosoma haematobium* in relation to epidemiology and selective population chemotherapy. II. Mass treatment with a single oral dose of metrifonate, J Infect Dis] 138 (1979) 856–8.

Cook JA, Baker ST, Warren KS, Jordan PA, Controlled study of morbidity of schistosomiasis mansoni in St Lucian children, based on quantitative egg excretion, Am J Trop Med Hyg, 23 (1974) 625–33.

Mahmoud AAF, Warren KS, Control of infection and disease in schistosomiasis mansoni by targeted chemotherapy, Clin Res, 28 (1980) 474A.

Mahmoud AAF, Arap Siongok TK, Ouma J, Houser AB and Warren KS, Effect of targeted treatment on intensity of infection and morbidity in schistosomiasis mansoni, Lancet, i (1983) 849–51.

Peters PA, Mahmoud AAF, Warren KS, Ouma JH, Arap Siongok TK, Field studies of a rapid, accurate means of quantifying *Schistosoma haematobium* eggs in urine samples, Bull WHO, 54 (1976) 159–162.

Smith DH, Warren KS, Mahmoud AAF, Morbidity in schistosomiasis mansoni in relation to intensity of infection: study of a community in Kisumu, Kenya, Am J Trop Med Hyg, 28 (1979) 220–9.

Warren KS, The present impossibility of eradicating the omnipresent worm, Rev Infect Dis, 4 (1982) 955–9.
Warren KS, Mahmoud AAF, Targeted mass treatment: a new approach to the control of schistosomiasis, Trans Assoc Am Physicians, 89 (1976) 195–204.
Warren KS, Mahmoud AAF, Muruka JF, Whittaker LR, Ouma JH, Arap Siongok TK, Schistosomiasis haematobia in Coast Province, Kenya: relationship between egg output and morbidity, Am J Trop Med Hyg, 28 (1979) 864–70.
Warren KS, Ouma JH, Arap Siongok TK, Houser HB, Hycanthone dose-response in *Schistosoma mansoni* infection in Kenya, Lancet, i (1978) 352–4.

A family from the study area.

Part IV
Nutritional status of mothers and children

10

Food consumption in pregnancy and lactation

J.A. Kusin
W.M. van Steenbergen
S.A. Lakhani
A.A.J. Jansen
U. Renqvist

Introduction

In the last decade maternal nutrition during pregnancy and lactation has received increasing attention (Klein et al., 1976, Aebi and Whitehead, 1979; Lechtig et al., 1979; Metcoff et al., 1981; Hamilton et al., 1981). Obviously, it is essential for good reproductive performance and maintenance of her own health (WHO, 1965) that a mother's diet is adequate: the question is what should be considered 'adequate'. From the evidence available, there is a large discrepancy between observed and recommended dietary intakes of pregnant and lactating women in developing countries. In such populations fetal growth seems to be reasonably protected, while lactation continues for about 2 years without apparent difficulty. Recent data indicate, however, that in the same populations low birth weight is quite common (Sterky and Mellander, 1978) and breast milk yield is considerably less than in better nourished women (Whitehead et al., 1978; Hennart et al., 1981).

There is clearly a great need for more information on maternal nutrition and reproductive performance in different parts of the Third World. The studies conducted in Machakos area in the last 4 years should be interpreted against this background.

In October 1977 a prospective study was started to assess the relationship between maternal nutrition during pregnancy and birth weight, subsequent lactation performance and infant growth. This study is a continuation of the study of outcome of pregnancy in relation to antenatal and delivery care (see Chapter 18).

This chapter presents cross-sectional data on food consumption of pregnant women (cohort 1 October 1977–31 December 1978) and lactating women (cohort 1 January 1978–31 December 1979).

Materials and methods

It was planned to follow as many women throughout pregnancy as could be notified. Field-workers made home visits for case-finding at 2-weekly intervals until September 1978 and at 4-weekly intervals after that time. Anthropometric examinations and dietary interviews were scheduled in each trimester of pregnancy, i.e. at 3–4 months, 5–6 months and 7–9 months. Both were done at the field station; defaulters were visited at home.

Anthropometric and dietary data were collected from each low-birth-weight infant and its mother and a matched normal-birth-weight infant-mother pair at 6-weekly intervals in the first year postpartum and at 3-monthly intervals in the second year. A group of non-pregnant, non-lactating women were included for comparison.

Dietary intakes for one day were recorded by a semi-quantitative 24-hour-recall method. The woman was asked to describe what she had eaten the previous day in chronological sequence. Then she was asked to demonstrate the amounts she had eaten, using household utensils. In the case of liquids, the amounts were measured with water. Volumes of solid dishes were measured with dry maize or beans. The weights of cooked dishes and their raw ingredients were calculated from these volumes, either by means of the average recipe or from the actual proportions indicated by the respondent. Food tables were used to calculate energy and nutrient intake (Platt, 1975; FAO, 1968).

The validity of the semi-quantitative recall method was tested on the food intake of 47 and 113 women in 1977 and 1979 respectively. Individual intake over one day was calculated by both the recall and weighing methods. The paired tests showed no significant differences except for energy and iron in the 1979 study (Table 1). Mean energy values obtained by the weighing method were 5.7–5.8 percent higher than the recall results.

Recommended daily intakes (RDI) suggested by WHO (1974) have been used as a reference. For women lactating over 6 months, RDI have been adjusted on the basis of breast milk production by Kamba women, viz. about 500 ml at 7–12 months and about 350 ml at 13–24 months (see Chapter 12). The RDI used for pregnant and lactating women are presented in Table 2.

Results

Sample

Around 1000 pregnancies are to be expected annually in the whole of the study area. About 30 percent of the pregnant women are not included in the study, because they were not reported pregnant.

Table 1.
Comparison of weighing and recall methods for energy and nutrient intake (n=113; 1979).

		Weighing (W) method		Recall (R) method		Absolute difference W-R	Percentage difference W-R	S.D. difference	p value paired t-test
		mean	S.D.	mean	S.D.				
Energy	kcal	2405	783	2269	721	136	5.7	713	p<00.5
Protein	g	77.2	31	73.1	30	4.1	5.2	25.7	N.S.
Calcium	mg	523	213	524	237	–1.5	–0.3	197	N.S.
Iron	mg	24.7	9.8	22.6	9.2	2.1	8.6	8.9	p<00.5
Retinol equiv.	μg	459	673	481	678	–22	–4.8	405	N.S.
Thiamine	mg	2.49	1.14	2.34	1.11	0.15	6.0	0.94	N.S.
Riboflavine	mg	1.03	0.39	0.98	0.42	0.05	4.3	0.35	N.S.
Ascorbic acid	mg	90	96	89	81	1	1.8	83	N.S.

Table 2.
Recommended daily intakes, adapted from WHO.

Nutrients	*Pregnant women*[1] *1–4 m (1st trimester)*	*Pregnant women*[1] *5–9 m (2nd + 3rd trimester)*	*Lactating women*[2] *0–5 months*	*Lactating women*[2] *6–11 months*	*Lactating women*[2] *12–23 months*
Energy, kcal/kg BW	kg×40+150	kg×40+350	kg×40+550	kg×40+440	kg×40+300
Protein*, g/kg BW	kg×0.75+0	kg×0.75+13	kg×0.75+24	kg×0.75+14	kg×0.75+10
Calcium, mg	450	1100	1100	830	730
Iron, mg	28	28	28	28	28
Vit. A, mg	0.75	0.75	1.20	1.02	0.94
Thiamine, mg	0.90	1.00	1.10	1.02	0.98
Riboflavine, mg	1.30	1.50	1.70	1.54	1.46
Ascorbic acid, mg	30	30	50	42	38

*protein intake: estimated chemical score 70
[1] for pregnant women the pregravid weight was used, taking 90 percent of Harvard standard as pregravid weight
[2] for lactating women the actual body weight was used to calculate energy and protein requirements

Of the other 70 percent, half were seen two or three times, the rest only once. In this chapter only the food consumption of the latter group is reported.

In the period October 1977–December 1978, 366 pregnant women were interviewed, 109 in the first trimester, 165 in the second and 92 in the third trimester of pregnancy. Between January 1978 and December 1979, a total of 244 lactating women were interviewed, 113 with low-birth-weight infants (≤2500 g) and 131 mothers with normal-birth-weight children. The cross-sectional interviews selected for analysis were equally distributed over the three lactation periods, 0–5, 6–11 and 12–23 months.

Meal pattern and type of diet

Kamba women generally take tea with milk and sugar as breakfast and full meals around midday and late in the evening. There are two main dishes throughout the year. The most preferred is *isyo*, a whole maize-legume mixture, cooked with salt and sometimes fried after cooking. The other is *ngima*, a stiff maize-flour paste served with a vegetable stew. On special occasions a rice dish or *chapatis* (wheat-flour pancakes) are prepared. No change in meal pattern or type of dishes was observed during pregnancy and lactation.

Food consumption

Maize, legumes, milk, fat and sugar were the foods eaten most regularly. Other cereals, tubers, vegetables and animal products other than milk were included in the diet occasionally (Table 3). No particular food was omitted from the habitual diet during pregnancy or lactation, but in pregnancy there was a tendency towards a lower consumption in the third trimester. Lactating women consumed significantly more maize and legumes than pregnant women, even in the first and second trimester, but their consumption of milk was less.

No differences were found in food consumption during the course of lactation or between mothers with low- or normal-birth-weight infants, so all the data for lactating women were pooled.

Energy and nutrient intake

Owing to a lower consumption of, especially, maize and pulses, energy and nutrient intakes of pregnant women were considerably lower than those of lactating women. Table 4 shows that in all groups median intakes were always lower than mean intakes, the

Table 3.
Food consumption in grammes per day.

Food, g	*Statistics*	*NP/NL*	*Pregnant women, trimester*			*Lactating women*
			I	*II*	*III*	*0–23 months*
		n=50	*n=109*	*n=165*	*n=92*	*n=244*
Maize flour	mean	130	150	161	118*	196**
	SD	130	161	132	128	167
	P_{50}	114	125	150	94	188
	% none	30	28	22	35	24
Maize kernel	mean	130	117	92	87	138**
	SD	141	154	108	113	162
	P_{50}	105	73	75	67	100
	% none	34	39	38	39	33
Cereals (excl. maize)	mean	30	16	21	14	16
	SD	62	46	59	41	58
	P_{50}	0	0	0	0	0
	% none	76	88	84	86	90
Tubers	mean	36	48	70	49	62
	SD	156	224	276	146	243
	P_{50}	0	0	0	0	0
	% none	84	90	86	80	88
Legumes	mean	126	103	98	91	137**
	SD	147	120	106	114	156
	P_{50}	89	65	86	68	110
	% none	34	38	37	37	32
Leafy vegetables	mean	30	21	38	29	51
	SD	61	41	67	57	74
	P_{50}	0	0	0	0	0
	% none	76	74	67	71	61

Other vegetables	mean	52	76	85	78	97
	SD	118	141	158	134	219
	P_{50}	0	0	0	0	0
	% none	56	58	54	49	55
Fruit	mean	30	54	33	64	22
	SD	77	110	147	154	93
	P_{50}	0	0	0	0	0
	% none	82	77	86	76	88
Fat	mean	7	9	7	6	8
	SD	8	8	8	7	10
	P_{50}	4	5	4	4	6
	% none	36	32	31	37	25
Sugar/sugarcane	mean	39	25	34	30	32
	SD	33	22	45	45	34
	P_{50}	33	25	26	26	29
	% none	6	17	16	16	11
Milk	mean	124	112	123	94*	97**
	SD	98	135	149	112	97
	P_{50}	100	70	68	66	70
	% none	12	20	17	23	16
Animal products (excl. milk)	mean	24	21	14	20	21
	SD	61	40	41	55	57
	P_{50}	0	0	0	0	0
	% none	78	79	82	79	77

* Trimester III versus I + II: $p<0.05$ by student-T-test
**Lactating women versus pregnant I + II: $p<0.05$
SD = standard deviation
P_{50} = median values
NP/NL = non pregnant/non lactating

Table 4.
Energy and nutrient intakes per day.

Nutrients	Statistics	NP/NL	Pregnant women, trimester			Lactating women
			I	II	III	0–23 months
		n=50	n=109	n=165	n=92	n=244
Energy, Kcal	mean	1765	1602	1623	1406*	1978**
	SD	575	612	636	543	694
	P_{50}	1751	1560	1570	1376	1872
Energy, KJ	mean	7387	6728	6794	5886	8275
	SD	2410	2570	2664	2275	2904
	P_{50}	7332	6552	6589	5760	7832
Protein, g	mean	59	51	50	45*	63*
	SD	29	21	21	21	26
	P_{50}	53	50	48	41	60
Fat, g	mean	26	24	23	20*	26
	SD	14	15	14	12	16
	P_{50}	22	20	20	17	22
Carbohydrates, g	mean	332	303	310	268*	381**
	SD	110	124	129	107	141
	P_{50}	322	288	292	269	359
Calcium, mg	mean	431	379	417	347	460
	SD	195	191	226	172	215
	P_{50}	372	343	385	335	438

Iron, mg	mean	16.9	13.8	15.2	13.0	19.6**
	SD	9.6	8.2	7.7	7.7	8.9
	P_{50}	14.5	12.6	14.9	11.9	18.4
Vit. A, mg	mean	0.64	0.44	0.54	0.44	0.64
	SD	1.23	0.51	0.66	0.51	0.83
	P_{50}	0.15	0.23	0.25	0.20	0.29
Thiamine, mg	mean	1.58	1.30	1.37	1.16*	1.72**
	SD	1.06	0.67	0.71	0.63	0.83
	P_{50}	1.47	1.27	1.34	1.11	1.62
Riboflavin, mg	mean	0.88	0.72	0.76	0.65*	0.87**
	SD	0.57	0.32	0.35	0.29	0.34
	P_{50}	0.74	0.68	0.72	0.61	0.81
Ascorbic acid, mg	mean	66	78	84	96	88
	SD	87	118	167	175	122
	P_{50}	21	43	42	58	62
Prot. Kcal %	mean	13.4	12.7	12.3	12.8	12.8
Fat Kcal %	mean	13.2	13.5	12.8	12.8	11.6
Carb. Kcal %	mean	73.4	73.8	74.9	74.4	75.6

* Trimester III versus I + II: $p<0.05$ by student-T-test
**Lactating women versus pregnant I + II: $p<0.05$
SD = standard deviation
P_{50} = median values
NP/NL = non pregnant/non lactating

differences being largest for retinol equivalents and ascorbic acid. In the first and second trimester of pregnancy approximately the same amounts of energy (1600 kcal), protein (50 g), fat (24 g), thiamine (1.3 mg) and riboflavine (0.75 mg) were consumed.

Significantly lower intakes were recorded in the third trimester, although iron (range 13.0–15.0 mg), retinol equivalents (range 0.44–0.54 mg), ascorbic acid (range 78–96 mg) and calcium (range 345–415 mg) did not show any trend according to duration of pregnancy. In the course of lactation, on average the intakes of energy (1980 kcal), protein (63 g), iron (19.6 mg), thiamine (1.7 mg) and riboflavine (0.87 mg) were significantly higher than during pregnancy (see Table 4). Due to the large day-to-day variation in the intakes of retinol equivalents, ascorbic acid and calcium, no differences in these were found between pregnant and lactating women.

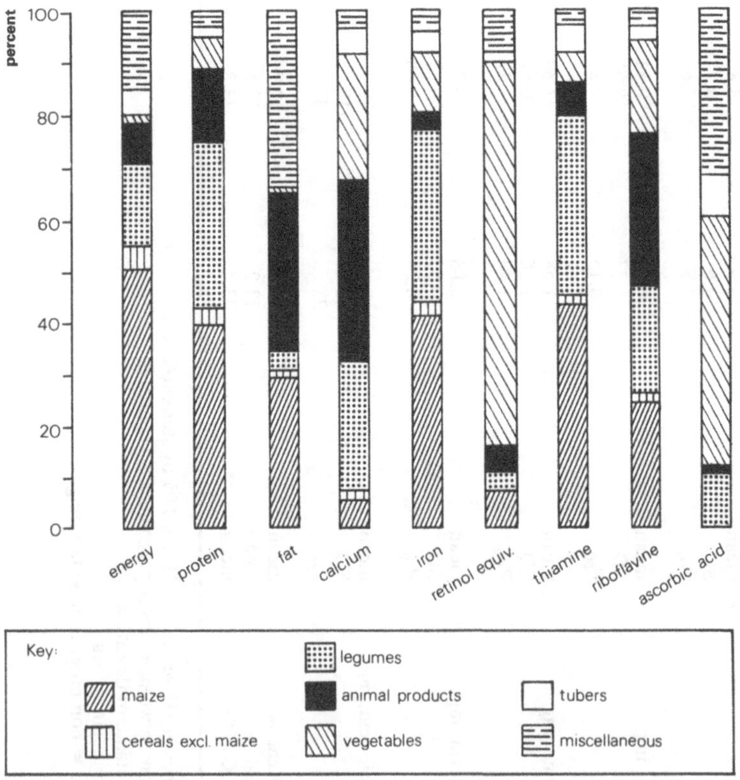

Figure 1. Percentage contribution of food groups to mean energy and nutrient intakes. n=1271 intakes.

The relative contributions of carbohydrates (74–76 percent), proteins (12–13 percent) and fats (12–13 percent) to the energy intakes were similar in all groups. Carbohydrates consisted of 19 percent mono- and disaccharides and 81 percent polysaccharides. Fifteen percent of the proteins were of animal origin. Fat intake was composed of nearly equal proportions of saturated, mono-unsaturated and polyunsaturated fats. Mean cholesterol intake was 34–40 mg and fibre 12–14 g per woman per day.

Since no differences in the relative contributions of the major food groups to average intakes were recorded, the data from the total sample of pregnant women (e.g. irrespective of numbers of records per woman) are given as illustration of the sources of energy and nutrients in Figure 1.

Adequacy of the diet

The energy and nutrient intakes of all the subgroups of women fell short of WHO-recommended dietary intakes, except for thiamine and ascorbic acid. Protein was below RDI in the second and third trimester of pregnancy only. The largest deficits were recorded during pregnancy as shown in Figure 2.

Seasonal variation in dietary intakes

In the Machakos area two harvests of maize, beans (*Phaseolus vulgaris*) and cow-peas (*Vigna ungiculata*) and one harvest of pigeon peas (*Cajanus cajan*) are common. The most frequently used vegetables are grown by a large number of families in their own gardens. Tomatoes are abundantly available in the dry season. *Sukuma-wiki* (*Brassica carinata*), cow-pea and pumpkin (*Cucurbita moschata*) leaves are picked during and shortly after the rainy season. Banana and papaya are available throughout the year, mango in March–April, yellow pumpkin in May–July. To assess the seasonal pattern of dietary intakes, the data have been analysed by month of dietary interview. All dietary records of pregnant women in the second trimester and of the total sample of lactating women were used, irrespective of the number of interviews per woman.

Figure 3 indicates that seasonality in dietary intake was most pronounced for retinol equivalents and ascorbic acid. Peaks coincide with the availability of leafy vegetables and yellow pumpkins.

As far as energy and protein are concerned, an intake peak can be observed at the end of the year and a trough in May and June. While the latter is related to the lean months, before the harvest of maize and legumes, the peak cannot be explained by the agricultural calendar.

Discussion

Pregnant Kamba women consumed less than lactating mothers. It is not clear why food intake was reduced in the last trimester of pregnancy. As staple food availability was not a major constraint it

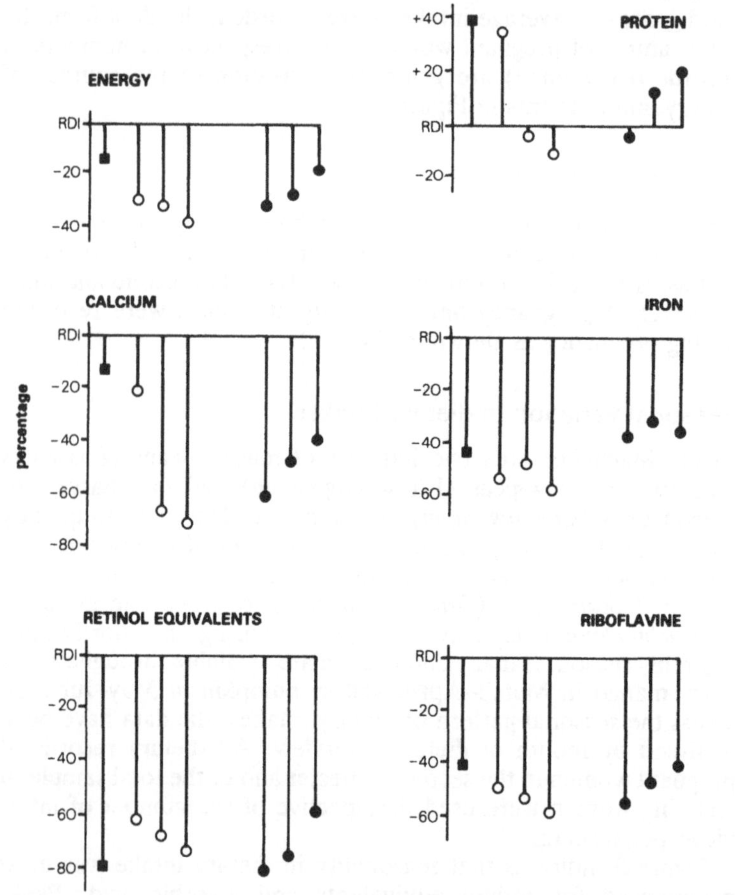

Figure 2. Adequacy of the diet by physiological state: median intake as percentage of recommended intake.

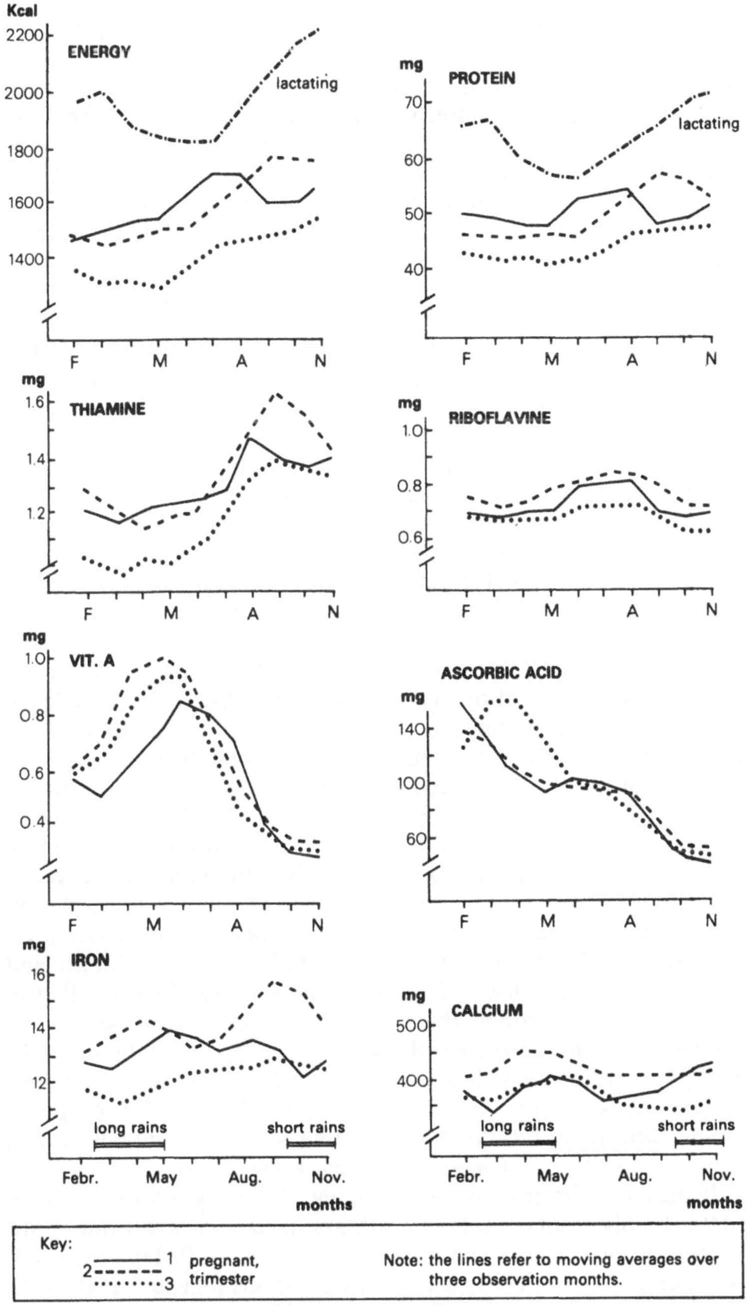

Figure 3. Mean energy and nutrients intakes by months of survey.

is likely that the restriction is related to cultural habit (to prevent a difficult labour) and to the nature of the habitual diet. A typical Kamba diet of 1600 kcal weighs about 1.8 kg while a typical UK diet of similar energy quantity would weigh only about 1.1 kg (Paul and Muller, 1980). In other words, the Kenyan diet is very voluminous, composed of a relatively large amount of carbohydrates (and fibre), little fat and much protein of acceptable quality. Towards the end of pregnancy, uterine size may interfere with the consumption of large quantities of a maize-bean diet.

The few studies of food consumption during pregnancy and lactation in African countries that are available indicate that energy intakes range from 1400–2000 kcal and protein intakes from 25–40 g per day, while vitamin and mineral intakes are marginal (Maletnlema and Bavu, 1974; Gebre Medhin and Gobezie, 1975; Edozien et al., 1979; Prentice, 1980). Dietary intakes are much higher, however, among lactating women in the Ibadan area of Nigeria (Abakada and Hussain, 1980). The energy intakes of Kamba women were in the upper range of published data while their protein intakes were considerably higher.

Compared with WHO-recommended daily intakes, energy and nutrient intakes during pregnancy and lactation were marginal to low except for protein, thiamine and ascorbic acid. Energy intake was least adequate in the last trimester of pregnancy and in the first half-year of lactation. The former results from the coincidence of a decline in consumption and a rise in RDI. The increase in energy intake, expressed as percent RDI, with advancing duration of lactation can be explained by a lower RDI due to a decline in breast milk yield. Ideally, dietary adequacy should be assessed in relation to functional performance and maternal nutritional health, apart from being compared with recommended intake.

Repercussions of poor nutrition during pregnancy and lactation on birth weight and breast milk yield have been reported (Bergner and Susser, 1970; Lechtig et al., 1975; Bellavady, 1976; Jelliffe and Jelliffe, 1978; Prentice, 1980). In the most recent investigation in the Gambia, seasonal fluctuations in breast milk yield and prevalence of low birth weight were observed (Whitehead et al., 1978; Prentice, 1980). It should be noted that in the lean (rainy) season daily energy intake was 1350–1450 kcal for pregnant women and 1200–1300 kcal for lactating women. Gambian women were also leaner than Kamba women in Machakos.

It may well be that at higher levels of dietary intake and with better bodily reserves fetal growth and lactation performance are efficiently protected (Thomson and Hytten, 1979; Hytten, 1980; Rush et al., 1980). There are good indications that such is the case in this study population (Chapters 11–12).

References

Abakada AO and Hussain MA, Nutritional status and dietary intake of lactating Yoruba mothers in Nigeria, Ecol Food Nutr, 10 (1980) 105.
Aebi H and Whitehead R, Eds, Maternal nutrition during pregnancy and lactation, Nestlé Foundation Publ Series No 1, Verlag Hans Huber, Bern-Liebfeld, Langdruck AG, 1980.
Bellavady B, Nutrition in pregnancy and lactation, Ann Indian Med Sci, 12 (1976) 1.
Bergner L and Susser M, Low birth weight and prenatal nutrition: an interpretative review, Pediat, 46 (1970) 946.
Edozien JC, Dietary influences on human lactation performance, In; Maternal nutrition during pregnancy and lactation, Aebi H and Whitehead R, Eds, Hans Huber Publishers, 1979.
Food consumption table for use in Africa, FAO, 1968.
Gebre Medhin M and Gobezie A, Dietary intake in the third trimester of pregnancy and birthweight of offspring among privileged and non-privileged women, Am J Clin Nutr, 28 (1975) 1322.
Hamilton S, Popkin BM, Spicer D, Nutrition of women of childbearing age in low income countries: significance, patterns and determinants, Carolina Population Center, Univ of North Carolina, USA, 1981.
Hennart P et al., Influence of pregnancy, breast-feeding and mother/child inter-relationship on the nutritional status of the child in Central Africa, Medizin in Entwickelungsländer, 11 (1981) 165.
Hytten FE, Nutritional aspects of human pregnancy, Nestlé Found Publ Ser No 1 (1980) 27.
Jelliffe DB and Jelliffe EFP, Maternal nutrition, In; Human milk in the modern world, Oxford Univ Press, Oxford, 1978, p. 59.
Klein RE, Arenales P, Delgado H et al., Effects of maternal nutrition of fetal growth and infant development, PAHO Bull, X (1976) 301.
Lechtig A et al., Maternal nutrition and fetal growth in developing societies, Am J Dis Child, 129 (1975) 434.
Lechtig A et al., Report of an international workshop, Effects of maternal nutrition on infant health: implications for action, Panajachel, Guatemala March 1979, Arch Latinoamer Nutr, suppl 1 (1979).
Maletnlema TN and Bavu JL, Nutrition studies in pregnancy, Part I: Energy, protein and iron intake of pregnant women in Kisaraw, Tanzania, East African Med J, 51 (1974) 515.
Metcoff J, Klein EM and Nichols BL, Eds, Proc of a workshop on nutrition of the child: maternal nutritional status and fetal outcome, October 1979, Houston, USA, Am J Clin Nutr, 34 (1981) 653–817.
Nutrition in pregnancy and lactation, WHO Technical Report Series No 302, WHO, Genève, 1965.
Paul AA and Muller EM, Seasonal variations in dietary intake in pregnant and lactating women in a rural Gambian village, Nestlé Found Publ Ser No 1 (1980) 114.
Platt BS, Tables of representative values of foods commonly used in the tropical countries, Medical Research Council, Special Report Series No 302, Her Majesty's Stationery Office, 1975.
Prentice AM, Variations in maternal dietary intake, birth weight and breast-milk output in the Gambia, Nestlé Found Publ Ser No 1 (1980) 167.
Rush D, Stein Z and Susser M, A randomized controlled trial of prenatal nutritional supplementation in New York City, Pediat, 65 (1980) 683.
Sterky G, Mellander L, Eds, Birth-weight distribution—an indicator of social development, Uppsala, Offset Center AB, 1978.

Thomson AM and Hytten FE, Nutrition during pregnancy, In; Nutrition and the world food problem, Rechcigl M Jr, Ed, Karger, Basel, 1979, p. 63.
Whitehead RG, Hutton M, Muller E et al., Factors influencing lactation performance in rural Gambian mothers, Lancet, ii (1978) 178.
WHO/FAO, Handbook on human nutritional requirements, WHO/FAO, Rome, 1974.

The young soon start to carry the younger.

11

Anthropometric results in pregnancy and lactation

A.A.J. Jansen
J.A. Kusin
B. Thiuri
S.A. Lakhani
W.'t Mannetje

Introduction

Our knowledge of the role of nutrition in human reproduction and lactation performance in populations of developing countries is still extremely meagre. Little is known about minimum adequate weight gain during pregnancy. Well-nourished, healthy women in industrialized countries, eating to appetite, gain on average 15–25 percent of their pregravid weight or 11–14 kg, but a wide range in weight gain seems compatible with normal fetal growth (Winick, 1968; Hytten and Leitch, 1971; Thomson and Hytten, 1973).

In 'normal' pregnant women about 3–4 kg are laid down as fat (Naismith, 1980). These fat stores are supposed to be the energy reserves needed to subsidize lactation during the first 6 months (WHO, 1973). Data from Guatemala suggest that the minimum adequate weight gain during the whole duration of pregnancy should be of the order of 8 kg for women with a mean height of 149 cm (Beteta, 1963). Bailey (1975) wrote that a gain of less than 5 kg may be an indication of protein-energy malnutrition.

To throw more light on the interrelationship between maternal nutrition during pregnancy, lactation and the reproductive performance of mothers in the Machakos programme, a longitudinal study of anthropometric measurements of pregnant and lactating women was conducted over the period 1 May 1978 to 31 December 1980 and the results are presented here.

Materials and methods

Male field-workers taking part in the programme's disease and demographic surveillance system were instructed to assist in identifying pregnancies. Once identified, the mothers were invited to attend 'pregnancy meetings'. Defaulters were visited at home. Examinations, by trained female field-workers, were scheduled in each trimester at 3–4, 5–6 and 7–9 months; the routine schedule included an external obstetric examination, measurement of height, weight, upper arm circumference, and triceps and subscapular skin fold thicknesses, as well as a semi-quantitative 24-hour recall of food intake according to the method described in Chapter 10. Birth weight was measured within 48 hours of birth.

No local standards for weight for height by month of pregnancy being available, these were calculated, based on the assumptions that (i) 90 percent weight for height of Caucasian non-pregnant women is acceptable (Jelliffe, 1966); (ii) weight gain during 40 weeks of pregnancy is 20 percent of pre-gravid weight, and (iii) weight gain per month follows the same curve as for British pregnant women (Hytten and Leitch, 1971).

In the same period it was planned to follow all low-birth-weight (LBW) infant-mother pairs and a matched control group of normal-birth-weight (NBW) infant-mother pairs. Data were collected at 6-weekly intervals during the first year postpartum in a similar way to the pregnancy study.

Constraints

Longitudinal studies under field conditions are notoriously difficult. Even with good logistics and regular supervision of field-workers, only a small number of women were seen according to schedule.

Many factors were responsible for this failure to attain a high coverage of pregnant women, particularly in the first trimester. Male field-workers were either culturally reluctant to enquire about pregnancies or they were not attentive enough to report them. Consequently mothers were often not enrolled until the pregnancy was already visible. Regular follow-up was hampered by the mobility of the population. Many mothers went intermittently to stay with relatives or their husbands residing outside the study areas, and quite a number delivered in their village of origin, instead of in the study area. During the lactation period, maternal mobility was again the main reason for defaulting.

Results

Pregnant women

During the period 1 May 1978–30 June 1980 a total of 2874 women were pregnant. Of these 1739 (61 percent) were enrolled in the study and followed until 31 December 1980 when the last delivery took place. The majority were examined in the third trimester only, followed by those examined in both second and third trimesters. Only 190 mothers were seen in all three trimesters.

Mean age in the total sample enrolled was 26.3 years (SD 6.6) and mean parity 3.3 (SD 3.0). About 15 percent were primiparae. On average, rural Kamba women in the sample had their first child when they were 19.6 years old (SD 2.4). At ages 25, 30, 35 and 40

Table 1.
Selected measurements according to duration of pregnancy (Means and standard deviations) (n=190).

Months pregnant	3.1±0.7	5.3±0.7	7.6±1.0	—
Weight (kg)	52.5±7.0 (50.2)	54.7±7.3 (54.3)	56.7±7.0 (57.3)	$p<0.01$
Upper arm circumference (cm)	24.8±3.1	25.0±3.4	24.5±2.1	n.s.
Triceps skin fold (mm)	14.2±5.4 (15.9)	14.6±5.0 (16.0)	14.6±8.5 (15.7)	n.s.
Subscapular skin fold (mm)	12.2±4.6 (12.2)	12.7±4.8 (13.3)	12.9±5.6 (13.7)	$0.01<p<0.05$
Muscle area (cm^2)	33.4±9.6	34.0±12.1	32.2±5.6	n.s.
Fat area (cm^2)	16.3±7.6	16.8±7.4	15.9±6.9	n.s.

In parentheses: data for reference women: weight: Hytten and Leitch, 1971; Kusin et al. 1979; skinfolds: Taggart et al., 1967.

mean parities were 2.7, 4.4, 6.6 and 8.7 respectively. Mean height was 157.1 cm (SD 5.0); a height of 150 cm or less was recorded in 181 women (10.4 percent).

Anthropometric measurements of the 190 mothers who were seen in all three trimesters are presented in Table 1. In early pregnancy the mean weight of the women was higher than the calculated standard; towards the end of pregnancy it was slightly less. Average weight gain between 3.1 and 7.6 months was modest: 4.1 kg, i.e. 57.8 percent of the reference value for women of the same height. When compared with an estimated pre-gravid weight of 52.2 kg for Kamba women of the same height (Jansen, unpubl. data) average weight gain was 4.5 kg in 7.6 months. As far as the other anthropometric measurements are concerned, it was observed that the mean upper arm circumference remained below 90 percent of the standard for non-pregnant women (Jelliffe, 1966).

The mean triceps skinfold was 89.3 percent of a British 'standard' (Taggart et al., 1967) at 3.1 months; and 93.0 percent at 7.6 months. As in British women, the subscapular skin fold increased with advancing pregnancy; at 7.6 months it was 94.2 percent of the 'standard'. Mean muscle and fat areas decreased slightly. Two-way analysis of variance shows that only the changes in weight and subscapular skin fold are significant.

Table 2.
Mean weight for height as percentage of local standard according to duration of pregnancy and parity. (n=3371)

Month of pregnancy	*Weight/height*	*Parity*	*W/H*
2–3	107.0 (37)	0	101.7 (579)
3–4	104.6 (223)	1–2	99.0 (1114)
4–5	102.2 (354)	3–4	98.4 (699)
5–6	101.2 (611)	5–6	101.1 (466)
6–7	100.2 (652)	7–9	101.8 (384)
7–8	99.1 (775)	≥10	104.3 (129)
8–9	98.0 (638)	—	—
9–10	95.7 (81)	—	—

In parentheses: number of women examined.

Average weights for height (W/H) per month of pregnancy as percentages of the calculated standard are presented in Table 2. The measurements of all women seen at different times were used (n = 3371). There was a gradual fall in mean W/H with advancing duration of pregnancy; in other words, women became leaner towards the end of pregnancy. The data grouped by parity showed that no deterioration in weight for height occurred in the high parity groups. The percentage distribution in 10 percent class intervals is shown in Figure 1. The trend to lower weight for height towards the end of the pregnancy is clearly illustrated.

Lactating women

In the same observation period a total of 267 LBW newborns were recorded, among which were 20 pairs of twins and one set of triplets; 200 LBW and 200 NBW mothers were followed up. The data presented refer to the sample of mothers seen at least six times during the first year postpartum. They were all lactating throughout the period of observation.

It is interesting to note that the profile of LBW mothers was significantly different from that of NBW mothers. The first group of LBW mothers was younger and shorter; more of them than of

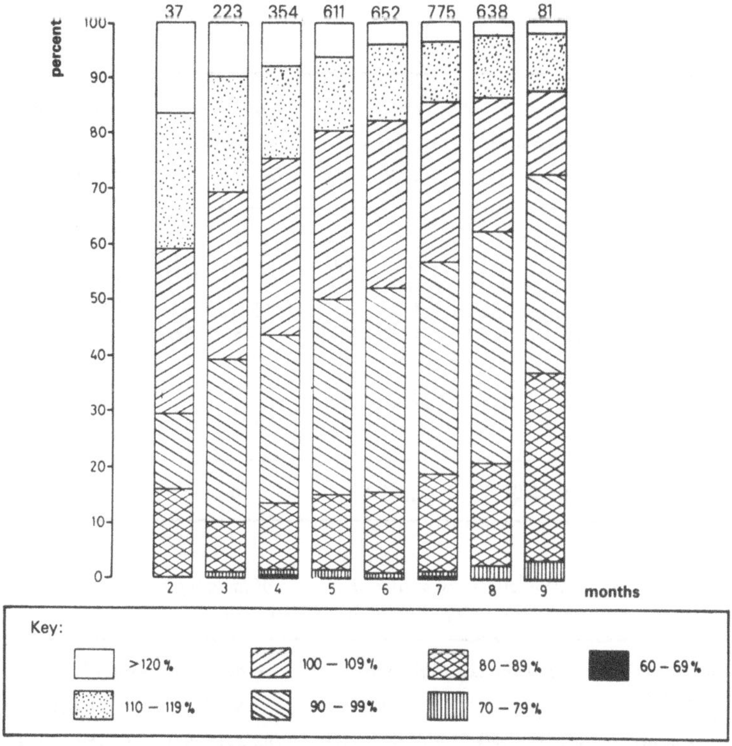

Figure 1. Weight for height as percentages of local reference by month of pregnancy.

the NBW group were primigravidae (Table 3).

The longitudinal changes in anthropometric measurements during the first year postpartum are shown in Tables 4–6 and Figure 2. The pattern of weight changes was similar for LBW and NBW mothers. The weight of NBW mothers decreased from

Table 3.
Characteristics of mothers of NBW and LBW children (means and standard deviations).

Characteristic	*NBW*	*LBW*	*Significance*
Age, years	28.5±7.3	26.1±7.0	p<0.05
Parity	3.3±2.2	2.2±2.1	p<0.05
Parity 0	6.8%	15.9%	
Height, cm	158.2±5.7	154.9±6.0	p<0.01

Table 4.
Mean weights and upper arm circumferences of lactating women according to time of measurement.

Time of measurement (weeks postpartum)	*Weight (kg)*				*Upper arm circumference (cm)*			
	NBW		*LBW*		*NBW*		*LBW*	
	(n=43)	*SD*	*(n=58)*	*SD*	*(n=59)*	*SD*	*(n=69)*	*SD*
0	54.8	7.7	51.1	7.4	25.1	2.3	24.1	2.6
6	54.3	7.7	50.7	7.6	25.1	2.5	24.1	2.4
12	54.3	8.2	50.0	7.8	25.5	2.6	24.2	2.3
18	53.7	8.2	50.3	7.9	25.6	2.4	24.3	2.5
24	53.3	8.2	50.2	7.7	25.5	2.6	24.3	2.5
30	52.6	7.9	49.7	7.6	25.6	2.6	24.3	2.4
36	52.6	8.7	49.3	7.6	25.4	2.4	24.3	2.4
42	52.2	8.1	49.3	7.7	25.5	2.6	24.3	2.3
48–52	52.2	8.5	48.7	7.6	25.7	2.5	24.2	2.3
	$p<0.01$		$p<0.01$		n.s.		n.s.	

Table 5.
Mean triceps and subscapular skin folds of lactating women according to time of measurement.

Time of measurement (weeks postpartum)	*Triceps skinfold (mm)*				*Subscapular skinfold (mm)*			
	NBW		*LBW*		*NBW*		*LBW*	
	(n=53)	*SD*	*(n=66)*	*SD*	*(n=44)*	*SD*	*(n=54)*	*SD*
0	15.2	5.0	13.4	6.1	7.1	2.3	6.2	2.6
6	15.8	5.2	14.0	6.0	7.4	3.1	6.4	2.6
12	16.4	6.2	14.2	6.2	7.3	2.9	6.3	2.5
18	16.2	5.6	14.6	6.4	7.0	2.7	6.1	2.4
24	16.6	6.0	14.4	6.0	7.1	3.2	5.9	2.6
30	16.2	6.2	14.2	6.0	7.0	3.4	6.0	2.5
36	16.0	5.8	14.0	5.8	7.2	3.5	5.7	2.4
42	16.0	6.2	14.2	5.8	6.6	2.8	5.6	2.3
48–52	16.0	5.8	14.0	6.0	6.8	3.5	5.3	2.3
	n.s.		n.s.		n.s.		$p<0.01$	

54.8 kg (SD7.7) soon after birth to 52.2 kg (SD8.5) after one year while a similar decline took place in LBW mothers: from 51.1 kg (SD7.4) to 48.7 kg (SD7.6). This corresponds to a loss in weight of 4.7 percent in one year for both groups.

The patterns of change in mean upper arm circumference, skin folds and calculated fat and muscle area were not consistent. A

Table 6.
Mean muscle and fat areas of lactating women according to time of measurement.

Time of measurement (weeks postpartum)	*Muscle area (cm²)*				*Fat area (cm²)*			
	NBW		*LBW*		*NBW*		*LBW*	
	(n=48)	*SD*	*(n=57)*	*SD*	*(n=48)*	*SD*	*(n=57)*	*SD*
0	34.0	6.1	32.0	5.7	17.8	6.1	14.3	6.3
6	33.4	6.1	31.5	5.4	18.4	6.6	15.1	6.0
12	34.0	5.4	31.4	5.2	19.4	6.3	15.2	6.2
18	34.7	6.2	31.2	5.9	19.0	7.3	15.9	6.8
24	34.0	5.4	31.3	5.7	18.6	8.4	15.8	6.6
30	34.4	6.0	31.8	5.7	18.0	8.3	15.7	6.6
36	34.0	5.1	31.8	5.8	18.7	7.9	15.4	6.0
42	34.4	6.0	31.9	5.3	18.8	8.4	15.7	6.2
48–52	34.9	5.4	31.8	5.0	18.9	8.1	15.2	6.3
	n.s.		n.s.		n.s.		n.s.	

tendency could be observed towards a loss of fat in the subscapular area over time: in NBW mothers this changed from 7.1 mm (SD2.3) to 6.8 mm (SD3.5) after one year and in LBW mothers from 6.2 mm (SD2.6) to 5.3 mm (SD2.3). The difference was only statistically significant in the group of LBW mothers. The observation that LBW mothers had at all times lower values for anthropometric measurements than NBW mothers is important.

Birth weight

The relationship between birth weight and maternal variables is still being analysed, but to give an idea of the pattern of birth weight in the study area, mean birth weight is about 3100 g (SD 500 g), and the percentage of infants with a birth weight of 2500 g or less varies from 8–12 percent per year (singletons only). These figures are based on 50 percent of infants born in the study area in the period 1977–1980 whose weight could be measured within 48 hours. These figures are very close to those reported by Voorhoeve in Chapter 20.

Discussion

The mean weight of non-pregnant, non-lactating women in the study area was about 52 kg, which is close to local reference weight. From the cross-sectional data, calculated mean weight gain during the whole period of pregnancy was about 5.8 kg or 11 percent of pre-gravid weight. The weight gain observed between

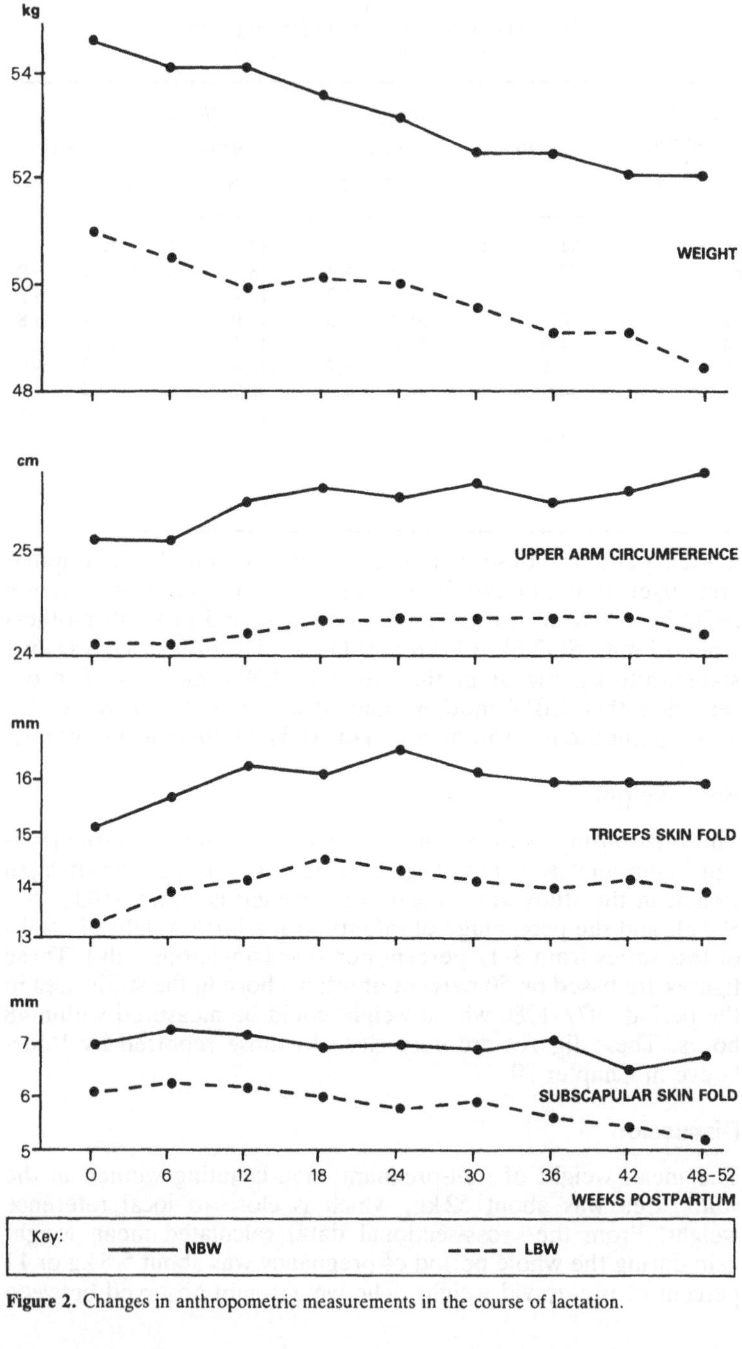

Figure 2. Changes in anthropometric measurements in the course of lactation.

3–8 months of pregnancy in the longitudinal sample (4.1 kg) tallies with the low weight gain calculated above. It is dangerously close to the 'malnutrition borderline' mentioned by Bailey (1975) and in agreement with the low energy intakes reported in Chapter 10.

Under such circumstances adequate fetal growth can only be safeguarded at the expense of maternal reserves. Apparently this occurs in the study population. Assuming a placental weight of 500 g, amniotic fluid 1500 g and 1000 g (20 percent) extra water in the maternal circulation, a mean birth weight of 3100 g can be achieved with a maternal weight loss of about 300 g (6100 g–5800 g). The falling trend in weight for height in the course of pregnancy supports this view.

The weight of NBW mothers in the first month postpartum (54.8 kg) seems to contradict the above hypothesis, but this need not necessarily be so, as the data pertain to two different groups. The NBW mothers may represent the better-off group in the study population. Analysis of the data from women followed during pregnancy as well as lactation will give a better insight into the process involved.

Although in general the maternal body can compensate for the low energy intake during pregnancy and low weight gain does not result in poor fetal growth, the fact that LBW mothers were leaner than NBW mothers indicates that there is a limit in maternal weight for height that can support adequate fetal growth. Moreover, the percentage of LBW in the study population—though low for a developing country—is higher than among affluent Kenyan women of the same tribe (unpubl. data). It may well be that energy intakes above 1500 kcal per day during the last months of pregnancy—a critical level according to Stein et al. (1975)—will be accompanied by a reduction in the number of LBW infants.

Considering stature as a measure of maternal nutritional health during childhood, the lower height of LBW mothers supports the view that it will take generations for a population to achieve optimal reproduction performance. The observation that weight for height during pregnancy was not negatively associated with parity is important, suggesting that recovery takes place during lactation, since one of the main reasons for stopping breast-feeding is a new pregnancy. One can only speculate on how this is accomplished. Some authors mention that fertility is related to maternal nutritional status (Frisch, 1975; Delgado et al., 1978; Bongaarts, 1980; Prentice, 1980). It may be that the chance of a new pregnancy is higher in women who have regained weight.

Another important observation is that mothers lose 2.4 and 2.6 kg in weight respectively to subsidize milk production and successfully so (see Chapter 12). At energy intakes marginal according to recommended levels, preference is given to milk production instead of maintenance or recovery of maternal body composition. This is in contrast with findings among well-nourished British women (Wichelow, 1975; 1976), which showed that mothers who failed to lactate successfully had not increased their energy intake compared with their non-pregnant, non-lactating level, whereas mothers who lactated successfully had, and that lactating mothers who dieted to lose weight immediately produced less milk. Apparently, as Naismith (1980) showed, populations accustomed for generations to a low level of dietary intake undergo a metabolic adaptation.

References

Bailey KV, Manual Public Health Nutrition, WHO, Brazzaville, 1975.

Beteta C, Embarazo y Nutricion, Thesis Universidad San Carlos, Guatemala, 1963.

Bongaarts J, Does malnutrition affect fecundity—a summary of evidence, Science, 208 (1980) 564.

Delgado H, Lechtig A, Brineman E et al., Nutrition and birth interval components: the Guatemalan experiences, In; Nutrition and Human Reproduction, Mosley H (ed), Plenum Press, New York, 1978, p. 385.

Frisch RE, Social Biology, 22 (1975) 17.

Hytten FE, Leitch I, The physiology of human pregnancy, Blackwell Scientific Publications, Oxford, 1971.

Jelliffe DB, The assessment of the nutritional status of the community, WHO Monogr Ser No 53, Geneva, 1966.

Kusin JA, Voorhoeve AM, Jansen AAJ, Lakhani S and 't Mannetje W, A longitudinal study of pregnant women in relation to outcome of pregnancy in Kenya, The Ind J Nutr Dietet, 16 (1979) 195.

Lunn PG, Watkinson M, Prentice AM, Maternal nutrition and lactational amenorrhoea, Lancet, i (1981) 1428.

Naismith DJ, In; Maternal Nutrition during Pregnancy and Lactating, Aebi H and Whitehead R (eds), Nestlé Foundation Workshop, 1979, Hans Huber Publ. Bern Stuttgart, Vienna, 1980, p. 17.

Stein ZA, Susser M, The Dutch Famine, 1944–1945, and the Reproductive Process. I. Effects on six indices at birth, Pediat Res, 9 (1975) 70.

Taggert NR, Holliday RM, Billowicz WZ, Hytten FE, Thomson AM, Changes in skinfolds during pregnancy, Br J Nutr, 21 (1967) 439.

Thomson AM, Hytten FE, Nutrition during pregnancy, World Review of Nutrition and Dietetics, 16 (1973) 22.

WHO/FAO. Joint Expert Committee, Energy and protein requirements, WHO Techn Rep Ser No 522, Geneva, 1973.

Wichelow MJ, Caloric requirement for successful breastfeeding, Arch Dis Child, 50 (1975) 669.

Wichelow MJ, Success and failure of breastfeeding in relation to energy intake, Proc Nutr Soc, 35 (1976) 62A.

Winick M, Food Technology, 32 (1968) 42.

12

Lactation performance

W.M. van Steenbergen
J.A. Kusin
M. van Rens
K. de With
A.A.J. Jansen

Introduction

The importance of breast-feeding for healthy child growth and development is now widely recognized (Jelliffe and Jelliffe, 1979). Differences in opinion exist concerning the time during which exclusive breast-feeding is sufficient to maintain adequate growth during infancy. It varies from about 6 months (Jelliffe and Jelliffe, 1979; Lauber and Reinhardt, 1979; Rajalakshmi, 1980; Das et al., 1982) to less than 4 months (Whitehead, 1979; Villar and Belizan, 1981; Waterlow et al., 1980; Waterlow, 1981). There is clearly a need for quantitative data on breast milk yield and composition, particularly concerning factors influencing them (Whitehead et al., 1978; Prentice, 1980). This study on the breast-feeding behaviour and breast milk yield and composition of Kamba mothers aims to contribute to knowledge in this area.

Materials and methods

The results of two separate studies will be reported.

The objective of the first study, carried out in the months September–December 1975 (lean season after the long rains) and in June–September 1976 (harvest season for maize) was to assess breast milk yield by lactation month and season as well as breast milk composition.

A sample of 85 infants and toddlers under 3 years of age was chosen at random from the corresponding age group in the study area and their breast milk intake during four consecutive days and one night was measured.

In the second study breast milk yield was assessed in relation to maternal nutritional status, in the months August–September and November–December, 1979. Two groups of mothers were selected according to their nutritional status in the third trimester of pregnancy: a 'W/H plus group' with a weight for height of 100 percent or more of the local standard (see Chapter 11), and a 'W/H minus group'

Table 1.
Numbers of mothers according to lactation period.

Lactation period	Study I, Number of mothers: *Total*	*Sept–Dec 1975*	*June–Sept 1976*	Study II (W/H+)[1], Number of mothers: *Total*	*Aug–Sept 1979*	*Nov–Dec 1979*	Study II (W/H–)[2], Number of mothers: *Total*	*Aug–Sept 1979*	*Nov–Dec 1979*
0– 1	7	0	7	17	8	9	15	10	5
2– 3	13	7	6	17	7	10	16	13	3
4– 5	9	4	5	18	9	9	15	5	10
6–11	22	8	14						
12–17	22	10	12						
18–23	12	5	7						
Total	85	34	51	52	24	28	46	28	18

1) WH+: weight for height in third trimester over 90 percent of international standard
2) WH–: weight for height in third trimester 70–80 percent of international standard

who had a weight for height of less than 90 percent. They were matched for age, sex and birth weight of the infants as well as location of the household. Mothers with a low-birth-weight infant (≤2500 g) or twins were excluded. The WH+ group consisted of 52 mothers with infants of 0–5 months inclusive, the WH– group of 46 such mother-infant pairs. They were observed during two consecutive days and nights (48 hours).

Details on the composition of the sample in both studies are provided in Table 1.

Female field-workers with a few years' secondary education who lived in the study area were recruited for the investigations. These field-workers were trained, and the methodology was standardized and pre-tested before the study started. During the investigations each field-worker stayed with the household for the full study period. She was supervised daily by the first author.

Assessment of breast milk yield

Yields of mothers' milk were assessed by the test-weighing technique described elsewhere (van Steenbergen et al., 1981). Test weighings were done at home; there was no interference with the routine daily activities of the mothers nor with the habitual unscheduled feeding practices.

Breast milk composition

Samples of breast milk were collected in the first study. On the third day mothers were asked not to breast-feed their children between 0700–1100 hours. The last preceding feed was commonly between 0500–0700 hours. Around 11 o'clock the mother expressed her milk manually under the supervision of a field-worker. The whole sample (25–100 ml) was put in a bottle, covered with aluminium paper and placed in dry ice within half-an-hour of collection. The samples were transported to Nairobi on the same day and stored at -20°C. Part of each sample was then sent to the Netherlands by air in containers with dry ice for analysis of fat, retinol, carotene, thiamine and riboflavin. The other analyses were done at the laboratory of the Medical Research Centre in Nairobi. The analytical procedures used have been reported elsewhere (van Steenbergen et al., 1981).

Other measurements

The age and parity of the mother, child mortality and breast-feeding habits were recorded by interview, socio-economic variables of the household by interview and observation. The weight and height of mother and infant were measured according to standardized techniques (Jelliffe, 1966).

Results

Breast-feeding habits

Breast-feeding was started within a few hours after birth; very few mothers waited till the next day. The majority of mothers (56 percent) nursed their children for a period of 1½–2 years; 34 percent said they continued to lactate till about 18 months. The remaining 10 percent of the mothers fed their infants for less than a year. They stopped because of a subsequent pregnancy or because the obligations of salaried jobs or (boarding) school attendance did not allow them to continue longer. Occasionally nursing was temporarily interrupted for one to three days because of illness and/or travelling. During sickness of the baby, mothers continued to breast-feed their children.

In the first 2–3 months of lactation, nursing was mainly governed by the demand of the infant. Frequency of suckling, both by day and night, was high, approximately one feed every two hours. Each feed lasted around 10 minutes. In this period of early lactation, mothers spent most of the day and evening at home. During short but frequent trips away from home for farming, shopping, collecting firewood and water, the young infant was carried on mother's back if no suitable caretaker was available. At night mother and child slept together.

In the third month, most mothers started supplementing breast milk with some cow's milk, commonly given by feeding bottle.

When the infant was older, about 6 months, its demands were less frequently heeded. The breast-feeding pattern was adjusted by the mother to her activity pattern, resulting in about nine feeds per 24 hours. If, for various reasons, the mother was out for several hours, cow's milk and/or porridge was left for the infant, who was fed by a caretaker. Beyond 6 months, children continued to be nursed five to seven times per 24 hours.

Milk volumes according to month and season

The breast milk yield per 24 hours according to the stage of lactation and season is shown in Table 2. Average yield decreased in the course of lactation. At 0–1 month yields averaged 780 ml and at 18–23 months 300 ml. In the harvest season (June–September)

Table 2.
Breast milk yield per stage of lactation according to season, in ml/24 h.

		ml/24h		
Age (months)	*n*	*Lean season (Sept–Dec)*	*n*	*Harvest season (Jun–Sept)*
0– 1	0	—	7	778 (180)
2– 3	7	540 (85)*	6	710 (157)*
4– 5	4	404 (118)*	5	708 (157)*
6–11	8	407 (79)	14	543 (178)
12–17	10	405 (122)	12	470 (148)
18–23	5	210 (62)	7	366 (156)

*p<0.01

170–300 ml more was produced per 24 hours in the first 6 months of lactation ($p<0.01$). A similar trend was observed at later stages of lactation, but the differences were not significant.

Figures 1 and 2 show wide variations in breast milk yields between mothers as well as between each mother's observation days. The within-individual variation was of a similar magnitude to the between-individual variation at all stages of lactation.

As mentioned before, true demand-feeding was practised, particularly for very young infants. Frequency of feeding fell with age as additional foods were introduced. Between 0–4 months, the frequency of nursing during the day and at night were comparable. After this age, children were breast-fed more often during the night, as can be seen from Figure 3. The same figure shows that the milk yield during the night beyond the fourth month was

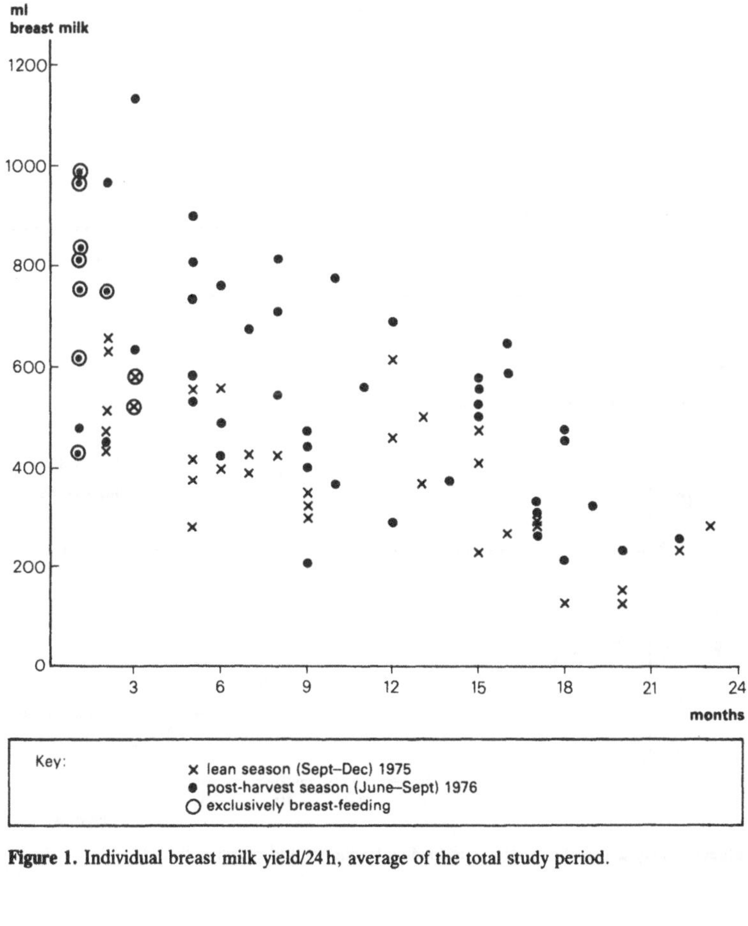

Figure 1. Individual breast milk yield/24 h, average of the total study period.

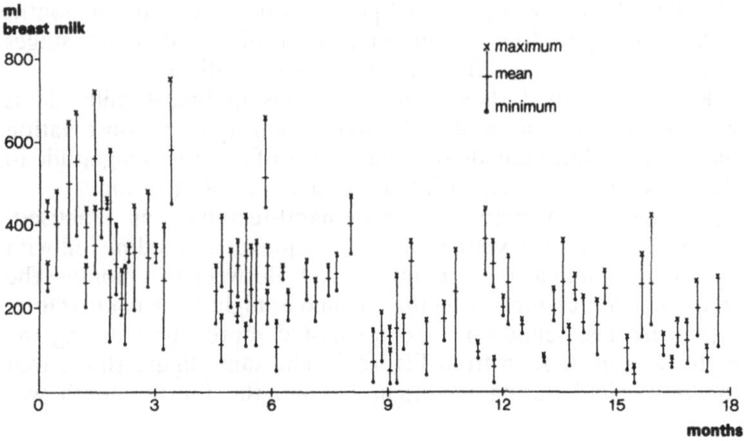

Figure 2. Minimum, maximum and mean individual breast milk yield/12 h over a period of 4 days.

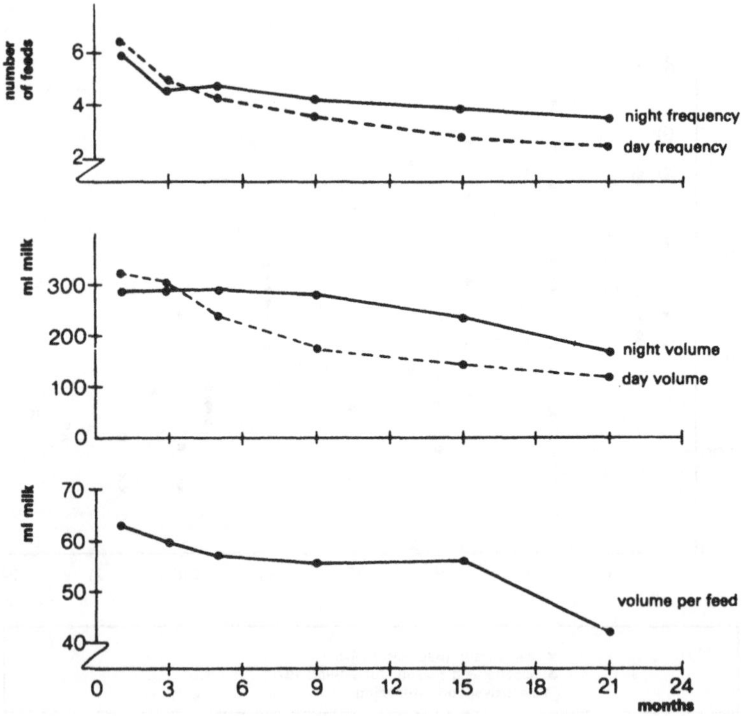

Figure 3. Day and night variations in feeding frequency and breast milk yield.

related to the higher nursing frequency at this time. The amount of milk delivered per feed was similar from 0–17 months, i.e. about 60 ml (Table 3).

Table 3.
Breast milk yield per feed, number of feeds and nursing time per 12 hours according to season.

Age (months)	*n*	*ml milk per feed*	*No. of feeds/12 h*	*Minutes nursing time/12 h*
		Lean season		
0– 5	11	55*	4.7*	51
6–11	8	48	4.4	50
12–17	10	51	3.1	33
18–23	5	34	2.3	26
		Harvest season		
0– 5	18	67*	6.0*	83
6–11	14	63	3.9	47
12–17	12	67	3.0	33
18–23	7	48	3.4	51

*p=<0.01

Breast milk composition (Study I)

Differences in milk composition between the two seasons studied were not consistent. Therefore, in Table 4 the means and standard deviations for the two seasons have been combined. Compared with values from western countries (Jelliffe and Jelliffe, 1978), total and true protein concentrations were in the same range; fat concentrations correspond with the lower values of the range, while all the other nutrients, except thiamine and ascorbic acid, were available in much lower concentrations.

Characteristics of mothers and infants (0–5 months) in Study II

As mentioned before, two groups of mothers were selected in such a way that they contrasted in weight for height in the third trimester of pregnancy. Table 5 indicates that the two groups had comparable height but the difference in weight between the WH+

Table 4.
Chemical composition of breast milk.

Constituents	*n*	*Mean*	*SD*
Total protein, g/100 ml	78	1.07	0.21
True protein, g/100 ml	80	0.86	0.18
Fat, g/100 ml	44	3.07	1.53
Calcium, mg/100 ml	62	20.5	4.00
Retinol equivalents, μg/100 ml	59	34	26
Betacarotene, μg/100 ml	40	30	20
Thiamine, μg/100 ml	28	23	1
Riboflavine, μg/100 ml	28	14	5
Ascorbic acid, mg/100 ml	61	6.0	2.1

Table 5.
Mother's characteristics (mean and standard deviation).

Characteristic	*WH+*	*Number*	*WH–*
	52		*46*
Age, years	28 ± 8.0		27 ± 7.0
Parity	4.8 ± 3.3		4.3 ± 2.8
Height, cm	156 ± 5.0		157 ± 5.0
Weight in third trimester, kg	63.5 ± 5.2		50.2 ± 3.5
Weight during lactation, kg	57.4 ± 6.0		46.0 ± 4.7
Energy intake, kcal	2450 ± 540		2250 ± 515
Protein intake, g	83 ± 24		74 ± 21
Family size	8.9 ± 3.0		7.2 ± 2.5
Child mortality*	10%		9%
Socio-economic status:			
poor	14		20
intermediate	22		25
affluent	16		1

*number of dead children as percentage of number born to each mother (mean)

and WH– group persisted in the first 6 months of lactation and was about 11 kg at the midpoint (3 months). The two groups did not differ in age, parity and child mortality but the socio-economic background turned out to be far better in the WH+ group. The infant characteristics in the two groups were comparable except for the preponderance of females in the WH+ group (see Table 6).

Table 6.
Infant's characteristics (numbers).

Characteristics	*WH+*	*WH–*
Sex: male	27	29
female	25	17
Birth order: first	7	6
2–6	28	28
7+	17	12
Exclusively breast-fed	21	23
Mixed-fed	31	23
Birth interval, months (mean/SD)	26.5±10.1	29.1±12.2
Birth weight, g (mean/SD)	3200±290	3140±330

Table 7.
Breast milk yield, seasons combined: g/24 h.

	WH+			*WH–*		
Lactation month	*n*	*Mean*	*SD*	*n*	*Mean*	*SD*
0	9	861	316	4	637	121
1	8	742	167	11	675	173
2	9	741	219	7	827	219
3	8	830	135	9	669	118
4	10	719	283	9	673	217
5	8	746	186	6	676	268

Milk volumes by maternal nutritional status

Table 7 again shows the large individual variations in breast milk yield. WH+ mothers produced on average about 720–860 g in the first 6 months. The corresponding figures for WH– mothers were about 640–825 g. If a yield of 800 g and over per 24 hours is considered good, more WH+ mothers (38 percent) produced such amounts than WH– mothers (24 percent). A sex difference was observed, with male infants dominating in the group of good producers, mainly in the WH+ group (Kusin et al., 1982).

Factors influencing yield

Many factors influence breast milk yield. Before the null hypothesis that there was no difference in yield between the WH+ and

WH– group was tested, a stepwise regression analysis was performed, using the following variables:

mother: age
parity (P)
season (SS)
weight for height during lactation as percentage of standard (M.WH)
energy intake during lactation (M.EN)

infant: age
sex
birth weight
feeding frequency (FF)
energy intake from additional foods
weight for age as percentage of standard (C.WA)

The regression equation with a minimal residual variance for each group was as follows:

WH+ group: yield = 500+52×(FF)–109×(sex)–12×(P)
WH– group: yield = 549+62×(FF)+111×(SS)+5×(M.WH)–0.16×(M.EN)+4×(C.WA)

It is interesting to note that different variables were found to affect yield in the two groups and, equally remarkably, that in both groups neither lactation months nor whether the infant was exclusively breast-fed or not influenced yields. Only feeding frequency was an important factor in both groups. In the WH+ group, male infants consumed more than female infants, while parity played a minor role. In the WH– group, season was an important factor; maternal weight for height and energy intake, and child's weight for age were of less significance.

It was therefore decided to do a one-way analysis of co-variance with feeding frequency, sex of the infant and season as co-variables and maternal groups as co-factor. The results, presented below, indicate that WH+ mothers produced significantly larger amounts of milk per day than WH– mothers ($p=0.028$).

factor	*df*	*mean square*	*F*	*P*
WH group	1	151422	4.98	.028
regression	3	365322	12.00	.000
error	93	30436		

However, the difference in average yield per day between groups was only 80 ml.

Discussion

Measurement of 24 h breast milk yields is notoriously difficult to undertake because of interference with the emotionally labile let-down reflexes and the inconvenience it causes to the mother, but we got the impression that our study group felt at ease; in fact quite a few mothers showed keen interest to know the amount of milk they produced. Results of this study show that Kamba mothers nursed their infants for a prolonged period and were able to produce amounts of milk comparable to those reported from western countries (Lönnerdal et al., 1977; Whitehead and Paul, 1981). The far higher yields reported, for instance from Australia, may represent the lactation performance of a positively selected group of women (Nutr. Rev. 1982).

The energy intake of Kamba women was far less than recommended (see Chapter 10) and fat reserves built up during pregnancy were low to negligible (see Chapter 11). Whitehead et al. (1978) suggested that the energy requirement for lactation calculated by the FAO/WHO Expert Group (1973) may be too

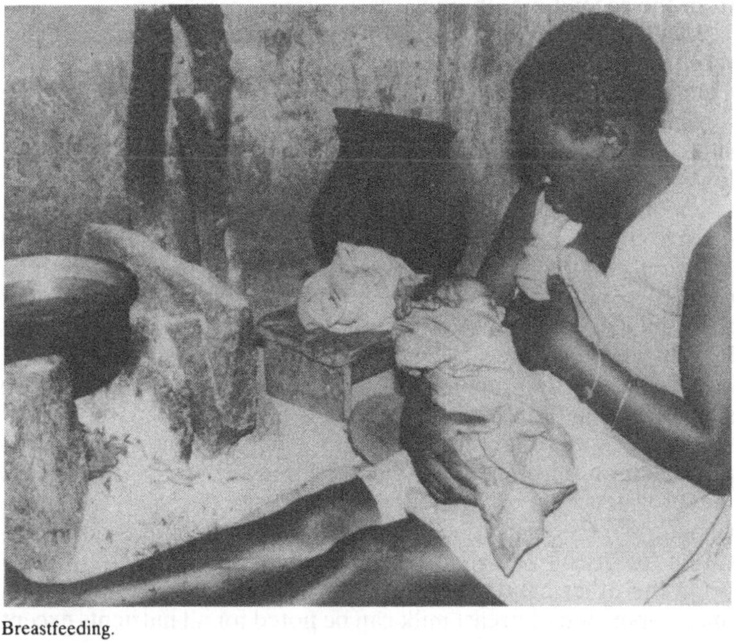

Breastfeeding.

high. Durnin (1980) postulated that the discrepancy between measured energy intake and calculated requirements may be explained by a reduction in physical activity. As energy balance and metabolic studies were not done, no explanation can be given for the observed successful lactation performance of Kamba women subsisting on diets marginal by recommended standards.

Even more difficult to understand is the small though significant difference in yield of about 80 ml per day between WH+ and WH– mothers. Energy intake during lactation was similar for both groups but the weight difference between women of similar heights was about 11 kg. The general opinion that lactation performance in undernourished women is efficiently protected is thus confirmed by our results. However, the fact that season and maternal weight for height influenced yield only in the WH– group suggests a relationship between yield and nutritional factors. The effect of season, more pronounced in the first than in the second study, can partly be explained by the fact that the months June–July (the 'trough' in energy consumption over the year) was not included in the second study.

The ultimate test of lactation performance is infant growth. Exclusively breast-fed infants were able to maintain adequate growth for the first 6 months (Kusin et al., 1982), but such cases were exceptions as traditionally mothers supplemented their milk from the second month onwards.

The reason for this early supplementation is not clear. From recently published data of breast milk intake and infant growth in Cambridge, England (Whitehead and Paul, 1981), it can be assumed that the breast milk volumes of around 800 g would be sufficient for adequate growth for 3–4 months. Indeed, somewhat lower volumes would be acceptable for our infants if account is taken of birth weight, which is about 300 g less than that of British infants. In the groups studied, only 39 out of 127 women produced 800 g milk or more in the first six months of lactation. Kamba women, from experience, may probably be right to supplement their milk so early, since one cannot exclude the explanation that by self-selection only successful breast-feeders continue exclusive breast-feeding for longer periods. In any case, if mothers are supplementing they generally say their milk is too scarce.

The statistical analysis showed no adverse effect of early supplementation on breast milk yield. Moreover, at age 0–6 months the prevalence of diarrhoeal diseases was extremely low (see Chapter 8). One can conclude that in our area there is no justification for discouraging early supplementation.

On the other hand, the effect of a marginal nutrient intake on the composition of breast milk can be noted for all nutrients except protein and ascorbic acid. Nutrition education in this area should therefore stress the importance of mothers regularly taking sufficient quantities of beans and leafy vegetables, as well as support the existing favourable breast-feeding pattern. Increase in energy intake, in the form of visible fats, will presumably follow when the purchasing power of these subsistence households improves (see Chapter 3).

References

Das D, Dhanoa J and Cowan B, Exclusive breast-feeding for six months—an attainable goal for poor communities, Bulletin of the Nutrition Foundation of India, New Delhi, April 1982, p. 3.

Durnin JVGA, Maternal nutrition during pregnancy and lactation, Aebi H and Whitehead RG, Eds, Hans Huber Publ, Bern, 1980, pp. 86–95.

Jelliffe DB, The assessment of the nutritional status of the community, WHO Monograph Series No 53, Geneva, 1966.

Jelliffe DB and Jelliffe EFP, Human milk in the modern world, Oxford University Press, Oxford, 1978, p. 28.

Jelliffe DB and Jelliffe EFP, Improving the nutrition of mothers and young children, Contact, 50 (1979) 2.

Kusin JA, Voorhoeve AM, Jansen AAJ, Lakhani S and Mannetje W, Lactation performance of Kamba mothers, Kenya: Breast milk yield in the first 6 months in relation to maternal nutrition during pregnancy and lactation, International Workshop on Nutrition and the development of the child, Baroda, India, 1982.

Lauber E and Reinhardt M, Studies on the quality of breast milk during 23 months of lactation in a rural community of the Ivory Coast, Am J Clin Nutr, 32 (1979) 1159.

Lönnerdal B, Forsum E and Hambraeus L, In: Food and Immunology, Hambraeus L, Hanson LA and McFarlan H, Eds, Almqvist & Wiksell Intern, Uppsala, 1977.

Adequacy of lactation in well nourished mothers, Nutr Rev, 40 (1982) 136.

Prentice AM, Variations in maternal dietary intake, birth-weight and breast milk output in the Gambia, In: Maternal nutrition during pregnancy and lactation, Aebi H and Whitehead R, Eds, Hans Huber Publ, Bern, 1980, p. 167.

Rajalakshmi R, Gestation and lactation performance in relation to the plane of nutrition, In: Maternal nutrition during pregnancy and lactation, Aebi H and Whitehead R, Eds, Hans Huber Publ, Bern, 1980, p. 184.

Steenbergen WM van et al., Lactation performance of Kamba mothers, Kenya: Breast-feeding behaviour, breast milk yield and composition, J of Trop Pead, 27 (1981) 3.

Villar J and Belizan JM, Breast-feeding in developing countries, Lancet, ii (1981) 621.

Waterlow JC, Ashworth A and Griffith M, Faltering in infant growth in less-developed countries, Lancet, ii (1980) 1176.

Waterlow JC, Observations on the suckling's dilemma—a personal view, J Hum Nutr, 35 (1981) 85.

Whitehead RG, Hutton M and Müller E, Factors influencing lactation performance in rural Gambian mothers, Lancet, ii (1978) 178.

Whitehead RG and Paul AA, Infant growth and human milk requirements—A fresh approach, Lancet, i (1981) 162–165.

Whitehead RG, Infant feeding practices and the development of malnutrition in rural Gambia, UN Univ Food Nutr Bull, 1 (1979) 36.

WHO/FAO, Protein and energy requirements (1973), Geneva, 1974.

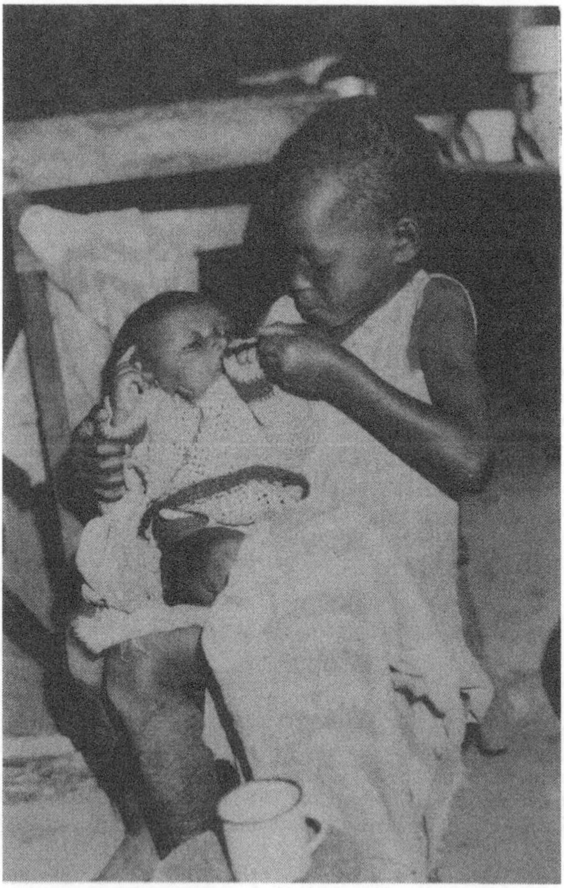

Child helping with the feeding of a baby.

13

Food consumption of pre-school children

W.M. van Steenbergen
J.A. Kusin
A.A.J. Jansen

Introduction

During the first months of life, growth and development in Third World countries correspond well with those of infants in industrialized countries (Waterlow et al., 1980; WHO, 1981). Growth retardation and overt malnutrition are generally observed in the period of transition from exclusive breast-feeding to the family diet (Habicht et al., 1974; Waterlow et al., 1980; Rutishauser, 1975). Inappropriate weaning foods and the frequent occurrence of infectious diseases are mainly responsible for such a situation. This chapter deals with food consumption of infants and toddlers aged 1–3 years and factors expected to influence it.

Materials and methods

The children belonged to a random sample of 73 households of which family food resources and eating habits (see Chapter 3), mothers' lactation performance (see Chapter 12) and young children's food intake and nutritional state, reported in this chapter, were studied. The selection of households is described in Chapter 3; all children under 4 who belonged to the 73 households were included.

The sample consisted of 183 children aged 0–36 months. Precise birth dates were available because they were recorded as part of the fortnightly demographic surveillance since 1973 (see Chapter 5). Seventy-six children were studied in the lean season. September–December, 1975. Of these, 41 children were also included in the second study period in June–September, 1976, making a total of 107 infants and toddlers. The remaining 35 children were left out because they were over 36 months of age at the time or they had temporarily left the area. The age distribution of the children is shown in Table 1.

Each child was observed for 4 consecutive days, during which a trained female

Table 1.
Number of children observed by age group and season.

Age in months	*Lean season* *Sept–Dec*	*Harvest season* *June–Sept*
0– 6	15	19
7–12	11	19
13–18	18	17
19–24	11	17
25–30	13	14
31–36	8	21
Total	76	107

(41 observed in both seasons)

field-worker stayed in the household from 0700–2000 hours. The field-workers were supervised daily by the first author.

All foods to be consumed by the family on that particular day were weighed before preparation. Corrections were made for non-edible parts. After cooking, the total dish was measured. The food consumed by the child was weighed. From this, the equivalent raw ingredients were calculated. To calculate energy and nutrient intake the Food Composition Table of Platt (1977) was used. For some food items not listed by Platt, the Food Composition Table for Africa (FAO, 1968) and the Dutch Food Composition Table (1975) were used as references. To assess adequacy of diets in the various age groups, recorded energy and nutrient intakes were compared with the recommended intakes (FAO/WHO, 1974).

The children were examined clinically by a physician of the Medical Research Centre. Particular attention was paid to signs suggestive of nutritional deficiency as proposed by Jelliffe (1966). Anthropometric measurements were made by the first author. Nude weight was taken, using the Avery Baby Weigher 2412. The child's length was measured with a steel tape and a head-board, while the child was lying on the floor. The anthropometric data were evaluated by comparing the results with the Harvard Standards (Jelliffe, 1966).

A number of variables were selected to assess their influence on the child's energy intakes. The geographical location reflected the living standard and hygiene environment of the household, the western part being more prosperous than the eastern part (see Chapter 4). Variables relating to food availability included: season, source of some foods, type of child feeding and number of meals per study period. The size of the household, presence of father and mother, marital status of the mother and sex of the child were chosen as household variables. The Student t-test was applied to test the significance of differences.

Results

In Chapter 3 we reported that qualitatively good diets were observed in the two ecologically different western and eastern parts of the study area during the lean and the harvest season. Since children's food intake in the two areas and in both seasons did not differ significantly, the results were pooled.

Breast-feeding pattern

Detailed results on breast-feeding habits, individual breast milk consumption and average breast milk intake by season and by nutritional state of the mother have been presented in Chapter 12. Breast-feeding was practised for about 16–24 months. On the other hand, exclusive breast-feeding was only noted during the first 5 months (Fig. 1).

Only 5 out of 64 infants were completely weaned before the age of one year, a further pregnancy being the usual reason. Apart from this, the lure of a salaried job is one of the main incentives to cease breast-feeding. Mothers who stopped feeding around 18 months said that: 'the child refused the milk' or, 'it can eat other food' or, 'it is big enough'.

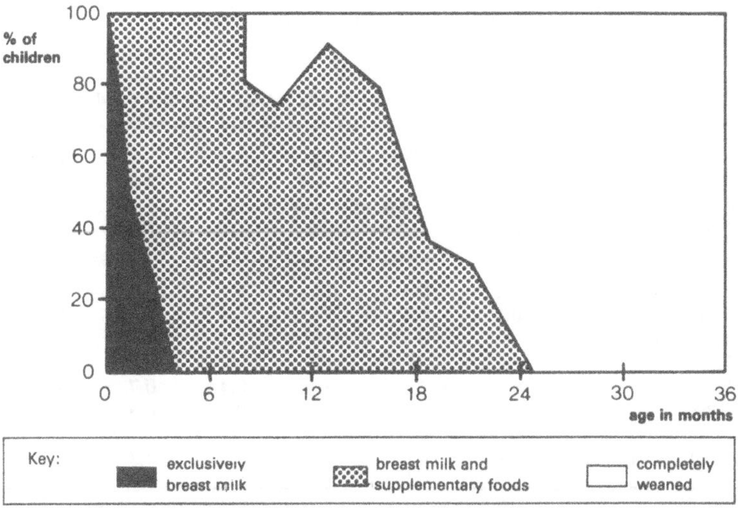

Figure 1. Sequence of breast-feeding and mixed feeding in Akamba children.

Meal pattern

Table 2 shows the average number of times per day that meals were taken by various age groups. Weaning—implying that breast milk was not the sole food any more—started between 1–4 months with cow's milk, and occasionally goat's milk. From 4–5 months onwards milk as a drink was gradually replaced by thin maize-flour porridge. Porridge, given two or three times a day, remained the major dish until around age 2. *Ngima* (Swahili: *ugali*, stiff maize-flour paste, a common family dish) served with milk, or in combination with a tomato stew was eaten by around three-quarters of the infants by the end of their first year. These dishes were given about once a day which is a little more often than adults consume them.

Tea, with milk and sugar, became part of the child's diet after 2 years of age and was drunk about once in 2 days. *Isyo* (whole maize in combination with whole beans or pigeon peas, the dish most frequently served in every household) was consumed by only few children under 2, because it was regarded as unsuitable. Even in their third year, children ate *isyo* less frequently (score 0.7—see Table 2) than adults (1.1). Other dishes such as rice and home-made chapati were taken less often (0.3).

By the age of 2–3, the majority of the toddlers shared the family pot with the understanding that most of them were given an extra meal in between: toddlers had around four servings per day, adults three. Children's appetite was good. The food offered to them was usually finished completely, except during illness.

Table 2.
Consumption frequencies of various foods in age groups of children and in adults.

	Children's age (months)					*Adults*
	0–6	*7–12*	*13–18*	*19–24*	*25–36*	
	No. of observations					
Type of food	*142*	*113*	*123*	*100*	*195*	*600*
Cow's milk	1.1	0.4	0.1	0.1	0	–
Porridge	0.5	2.6	2.3	2.1	1.6	0.5
Ngima+stew or milk	–	0.7	0.9	1.1	1.1	0.6
Tea	–	0	0.2	0.2	0.5	0.5
Isyo	–	0	0	0.4	0.7	1.1
Other	–	0.3	0.3	0.2	0.3	0.3
Total servings/day	1.6	4.0	3.8	4.1	4.3	3.0

Notes: Score is total no. of servings per age group divided by total no. of observation days; the score is 1 when a food is taken once a day
Ngima is a stiff maize-flour paste; 'tea' includes milk and sugar; *isyo* is maize and beans
0 = less than 0.1 – = none.

Food preparation

For detailed information on food intake and preparation in general see Chapter 3. As far as the preparation of children's food was concerned, it was observed that milk when given to infants of 0–3 months was diluted with a little water and heated. Older infants were given milk undiluted.

Maize porridge was prepared from whole flour or from manufactured flour of 83 percent extraction rate. A few older mothers preferred to serve millet- or sorghum porridge; wheat flour (70 percent extraction) or instant flour mixtures were only used by younger mothers. Instant flours were added to hot water whereas home-made porridges were cooked for 15–30 minutes. Porridge as well as fresh milk was cooked in the morning but served the whole day. The portions of milk needed were commonly reheated at each serving. An average porridge consisted of water, milk (200 ml per litre), sugar (20 g per litre) and cereal flour (60–150 g per litre). *Ngima* was prepared from 350 g maize flour per kg mixture, without added salt or spices, taking 20–30 minutes to prepare. It was served with plain cow's milk, buttermilk (left over from butter preparation) or with a 'stew'. At an early age very watery stews (400 g tomatoes per litre stew) were usually given. For children over 1½ years of age a stew prepared from leaf vegetables (African cabbage, cow-pea leaf, heading cabbage) and Irish potatoes (800 g per kg stew) was included.

The ratio of maize to legumes in *isyo* varied with the season from 3:1 to 4:1. Because ripe maize is hard to chew even when cooked and difficult for young children to digest, many mothers mashed the legumes and added only a little maize to the isyo dish for the child.

Method of feeding

For feeding milk and thin porridges at an early age, feeding bottles were preferred. Some mothers used to clean the bottle and nipple by simmering them over a slow fire in a cooking pot; others just rinsed them with cold water.

At over 6 months of age, porridge was commonly fed by spoon or was drunk from a cup, bowl or calabash. *Ngima* was consumed by hand and *isyo* was eaten with a spoon, although some preferred to use fingers. Toddlers were given the food in their own bowl or plate, or shared it with a sibling. Children, particularly the younger ones, for whom many dishes were specially prepared, usually ate at different times from adults.

Food intake

The mean food intake per day per age group is presented in Table 3. Around 100–140 ml cow's milk was taken daily by all age groups. Maize consumption increased from 70 g in the second half-year to 190 g in the third year of life. Tubers were seldom eaten: from the age of 18 months onwards, an average of 50 g per day was

Table 3.
Composition of average food intake by age group in grams per day.

	Age in months				
	0–6	*7–12*	*13–18*	*19–24*	*25–36*
	No. of observations				
Type of food	*142*	*113*	*123*	*100*	*195*
Cow's milk	120	120	75	140	130
Maize	5	70	100	160	190
Tubers	–	15	15	60	60
Legumes	–	0	5	20	30
Vegetables	–	20	30	45	50
Fruits	0	10	15	30	25
Fat	–	1	2	2	2
Sugar	1	4	7	7	10

Notes: Average is total quantity of food divided by total number of observation days, rounded to the nearest 5 g.
0 = less than 0.6 g — = none.

Table 4.
Daily energy and protein intake by age group, including breast milk, mean and per kg body weight, with SD.

		Energy (kcal)		*Protein (g)*	
Age (months)	*n*	*Mean*	*per kg*	*Mean*	*per kg*
0– 3	18	485 (136)	107 (29)	9.5 (3.3)	2.1 (0.7)
4– 6	14	576 (137)	91 (20)	13.7 (5.2)	2.1 (0.9)
0– 6	32	532 (137)	100 (26)	11.6 (4.8)	2.1 (0.8)
7–12	28	712 (178)	93 (24)	15.7 (6.7)	2.1 (0.8)
13–18	32	799 (228)	92 (29)	19.6 (7.2)	2.2 (0.7)
19–24	28	984 (212)	98 (23)	27.4 (6.0)	2.7 (0.7)
25–30	28	1018 (230)	93 (17)	29.4 (7.7)	2.7 (0.7)
31–36	21	1138 (253)	97 (21)	33.4 (9.0)	2.8 (0.7)

consumed. Sweet potato was the most common tuber, followed by taro (*Colocasia esculenta*), cassava, green banana and Irish potato.

After 2 years of age, pigeon peas (*Cajanus cajan*), cow-peas (*Vigna unguiculata*) and beans (*Phaseolus vulgaris*) became an important part of the daily menu, the average consumption being about 30 g per child per day.

Vegetable consumption was influenced by season; in the dry season the mean intake for the group as a whole was less (23 g) than in the rainy season (38 g). In both seasons, taken together, the intake of vegetables increased from 20 g at age 6–12 months to 50 g at age 25–36 months. Heading cabbage (*Brassica capitata*) accounted for 25 percent of the total vegetable consumption in both seasons; tomatoes predominated in the dry season; African cabbage (*Brassica carinata*) and cow-pea leaves contributed some 30 percent of the total vegetable intake in the rainy season.

Fruits eaten by children were usually papaya and bananas, amounting to 25 g per child per day. The mango season fell outside the two study periods.

Fat was not often added. The average intake was 2 g, mainly of a locally manufactured vegetable fat. The amount of sugar increased with age: 4 g at age 7–12 months to 10 g at age 25–36 months were taken in porridge, milk and tea.

Adequacy of diet (including breast milk)

Energy

Table 4 shows the average energy and protein intake per child per day and per kg body weight in the 6-month age groups. Energy intakes increased with age; in the first half-year the average intake was 532 kcal, and in the second half 712 kcal. However, from the second to the third half-year the increase in energy intake was more moderate, from 712 kcal to 779 kcal. The corresponding figures for age 19–24 months and the third year of life were 984 kcal and about 1100 kcal. Calculated per kg actual bodyweight, average energy intakes were 100 kcal in the first 6 months; 93 kcal at age 7–18 months; and around 96 kcal at age 19–36 months respectively.

Protein

The average protein intakes per child per day followed the same pattern as energy intakes: 12 g at age 1–6 months; 16 g at age 7–12 months; 20–27 g at age 13–24 months; and 29–33 g at age 25–36 months. When calculated per kg actual bodyweight the range was from 2.1 g at 1–6 months to 2.8 g at 31–36 months. In Fig. 2, daily intakes of calories and of various nutrients are presented as percentages of recommended intakes (RI) for three age groups, 0–6 months (diet predominantly mother's milk), 7–18 months (breast milk and additional foods, 'weaning period') and 19–36 months (most children being completely weaned), respectively. In the sequence mentioned above, daily energy intakes calculated per kg actual bodyweight were 86 percent, 90 percent and 96 percent of RI respectively.

The same figure illustrates that milk (breast milk and cow's milk) and cereals (mainly maize) accounted for some 90 percent, 80 percent and 70 percent of the energy intake in the age groups mentioned. Protein intake calculated per kg actual body weight as a percentage of RI was 96 percent at age 0–6 months (estimated chemical score of 100) and 118 percent and 160 percent in the age groups 7–18 and 19–36 months (estimated chemical score of 70) respectively. In the first half-year the percentage of the total daily protein consumption derived from milk was 89 percent; during the weaning period 35 percent; and at age 19–36 months 14 percent. Milk was almost the only source of animal protein.

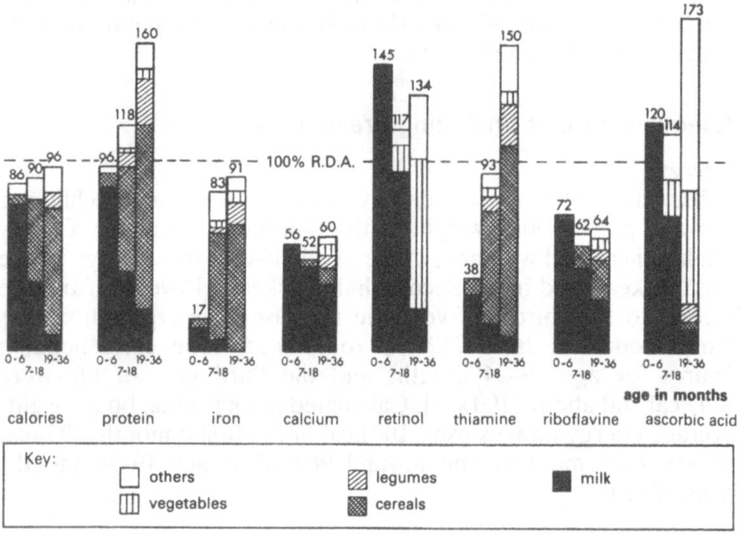

Figure 2. Mean intake of energy and nutrients as percentages of Recommended Intakes, and percentage contribution of single food groups to the total energy and nutrient intakes.

Other nutrients

Iron intake in the first half-year was very low as milk is poor in iron. The iron intake for older infants and children was 83 percent of RI at 7–18 months and 91 percent of RI at age 19–36 months. Cereals contributed 78 percent and 72 percent and vegetables only 3 percent and 6 percent of the total iron intake in these age groups; legumes were responsible for 13 percent of the total iron consumption after 18 months of age.

Calcium intake was between 52–56 percent and 60 percent of the recommended level at the ages of less than 18 months and 19–36 months respectively; 60 percent of the total calcium intake (more in the youngest age group) was derived from milk.

Thiamine intakes showed a trend similar to that of iron: at an early age the consumption was 37 percent of the RI and increased with age to well above 100 percent at age 19–36 months. After 6 months the main thiamine source was cereals (66 percent); legumes were a second important source only in the older age group.

Riboflavine intakes were also low: 72 percent, 62 percent and 64 percent of the RI at 1–6 months, 7–18 months, and 19–36 months respectively. As for calcium, milk was the major source in all age groups, but from 19 months onwards cereals became an important source of riboflavine.

The ascorbic acid recommendations were amply met in all age groups. Most of the ascorbic acid intake came from milk, 98 percent and 62 percent in the two youngest age groups. Tubers and vegetables contributed some 75 percent of the total intake at age 19–36 months.

Distribution of energy from protein, fat and carbohydrates is presented in Table 5. In the first half-year nearly half the total energy intake was supplied by milk fat. After 18 months of age energy from fat decreased to only 12 percent owing to the reduced intake of breast milk and the low intake of visible fats. Consequently, the relative contribution of protein (12 percent) and carbohydrates (76 percent) to energy intake increased sharply.

Table 5.
Percentage distribution of energy from protein, carbohydrate and fat.

Age (months)	*Protein* %	*Carbohydrate* %	*Fat* %
0– 6	9	43	48
7–18	10	63	27
19–36	12	76	12

Factors associated with energy intake

The food intake results indicate that the mean protein intake was sufficient in all age groups; the overall limiting factor in the children's diet appeared to be the energy intake. Individual daily energy intake, expressed as a percentage of RI, was therefore chosen as an independent variable in the analysis of factors that may influence food consumption. The results are presented in Table 6.

In the category of 'food availability', the number of meals ($p<0.05$) and the fact whether children were breast-fed or not ($p<0.01$) showed a significant association with the child's energy

Table 6.
Analysis of factors that may influence energy intake.

		Energy intake in % of R.I.			*Significance*
		n	*Mean*	*SD*	
Food availability					
Season (age group 18–35 m)	harvest	50	93	18	p=0.333
	lean	30	98	28	
Source of major foods	milk-purchased	77	91	20	p=0.19
	—own cows	48	97	31	
(age group 0–35 m)	maize-purchased	92	91	22	p=0.202
	—garden	42	97	24	
Number of meals per four days (age group 0–35 m)	<16	36	86	25	p=0.006
	≥16	76	99	21	
Breast-feeding (age group 18–23 m)	non-breast-fed	16	84	18	p=0.0139
	breast-fed and supplementary food	12	108	30	
Current family setting					
Size of household	<10 persons	92	91	22	p=0.54
	≥10 persons	74	93	24	
Sex	female	89	92	23	p=0.91
	male	74	92	23	
Presence of father	lives at home	65	92	23	p=0.31
	lives elsewhere	63	89	22	
Marital status of mother	single	34	99	24	p=0.059
	married	130	91	22	
Presence of mother	>60% of day-time	66	90	23	p=0.19
	<40% of day-time	35	96	24	
Level of living					
Hygienic environment and income	relatively poor (eastern part)	59	91	21	p=0.1885
	relatively good (western part)	108	92	24	

intake. Children who had 16 or more meals during the 4 days of observation had higher energy intakes (99 percent of the RI) than those who had less than 16 meals (86 percent). In comparing breast-fed and non-breast-fed children, only the 18–23-months age group was considered, as younger children were nearly all breast-fed and older children were completely weaned. Breast-fed children had a higher energy intake (108 percent) than non-breast-fed (84 percent).

Season had no influence on the energy intake in the 18–35-month age group, at which age breast milk was not the main food. Nor did distinguishing the source of the major foods consumed, maize and milk, by whether they were bought or derived from individual farms/cows, show any significant differences in energy intake.

In the category of 'current family setting', none of the variables —size of the household, sex of the child, presence/absence of father, marital status of the mother and percentage of time mothers spent at home—showed any clear association with the children's energy intake.

Although hygiene (housing, water supply), and economic conditions in the western part of the study area were noticeably better than in the eastern part, mean intakes in the two areas were similar (92 percent and 91 percent of the RI respectively).

The correlation coefficient matrix confirmed the reported findings, and no additional significant associations could be proved.

Nutritional status

On clinical examination about 71 percent of the total sample could be considered healthy and acceptably fed; about 22 percent were in less satisfactory physical condition; and about 7 percent were in poor condition. Commonly observed signs more or less suggestive of nutritional deficiency included: pallor (19 percent), dyspigmentation of the hair (22 percent), pot-belly (25 percent), poor muscle development (14 percent) and liver enlargement (31 percent). Splenomegaly was diagnosed in only 3 percent; malaria is not endemic in the area but schistosomiasis is. Skin infections such as scabies, impetigo and ringworm were seldom observed.

The results of weight and height measurements are presented in Table 7, which gives mean weights and heights according to age groups, with their corresponding standard deviations and mean values expressed as percentages of the Harvard Standard. The gradual increase in absolute mean weight and height values with age is obvious and both were 'acceptable' (weight >80 percent and

Table 7.
Weight and height by age group; mean (and SD) and percentage of standard.

Age (months)	*n*	*Weight/g* *Mean*	*% Std*	*Height/cm* *Mean*	*% Std*
0– 6	34	5593 (1188)	96	57.4 (4.7)	95
7–12	30	7873 (1353)	86	68.2 (5.2)	95
13–18	35	8870 (1108)	82	72.2 (4.4)	91
19–24	28	10 145 (1239)	84	77.6 (6.9)	91
25–30	27	10 961 (1514)	84	82.5 (5.2)	91
31–36	22	11 781 (1138)	84	84.9 (4.0)	91

height >90 percent of the Harvard Standard) in all age groups. However, the same table shows a deviation from the standard as the child grows older; mean weight in the age group 0–6 months was 96 percent of the standard, whereas at 7–12 months it was 86 percent and at 13–18 months only 82 percent. After age 18 months there was no further reduction in mean weight, but no catch-up either.

Mean height values followed the same trend as weight, but the figures for height were less affected than weight. A better impression of nutritional status according to weight and height of the child population concerned is obtained when children are grouped according to levels below standard (Table 8). The number of children with a growth deficit was particularly conspicuous with regard to weight, less so when height and weight for height were considered.

It seems, therefore, that weight as well as height increments were somewhat reduced in the first 3 years of life when compared with 1959 USA cohorts, resulting in children who were small for their age, but proportionately well fed.

Discussion

The dietary pattern of young children observed in the research area of Machakos District can in general be considered acceptable. Foods which were consumed besides breast milk included cow's milk and maize and, at a later age, beans and vegetables.

Energy, not protein, appears to be the limiting factor in the diet. From a dietary point of view children between the age of 3 months and 12–18 months are the most vulnerable. A mean energy intake of 79–87 percent RI is on the low side. Similar relatively low intakes during the period of mixed feeding were observed in

Table 8.
Weight and height levels according to percent of standard (numbers).

Age		*Weight for age*			*Height for age*			*Weight for height*		
(months)	*n*	*>80%*	*71–80%*	*<70%*	*>90%*	*81–90%*	*<80%*	*>90%*	*81–90%*	*<80%*
0– 6	34	32	2	0	30	4	0	32	2	0
7–12	30	18	10	2	26	4	0	22	7	1
13–18	35	19	12	4	23	11	1	29	6	0
19–24	28	18	9	1	16	12	0	24	4	0
25–30	27	15	7	5	16	11	0	21	6	0
31–36	22	15	6	1	15	7	0	20	2	0
Total	176	117	46	13	126	49	1	148	27	1

Uganda (Rutishauser, 1975), Southern Ethiopia (Selinus et al., 1971) and Nigeria (McFie, 1967). After 12–18 months Kamba toddlers had energy intakes near recommended levels. This contrasts favourably with the dietary intakes of toddlers studied in the above-mentioned African countries and is in line with results from Kikuyu children in the Muranga District of Kenya (Hoorweg et al., 1981).

As far as protein intakes are concerned, our results confirm other observations, indicating that protein intakes of pre-school children on cereal-based diets are near the recommended levels (Keller, 1973).

The habitual intake of vitamin A and β-carotene is difficult to assess from a 4-day food consumption study. Toddlers consumed dark green leafy vegetables irregularly but, when they did so, ate good quantities. It should be stressed that the study was conducted outside the mango and yellow pumpkin season. It is known that these two food items are given to young children in good quantities when available. It should be mentioned that corneal stages of xerophthalmia were never diagnosed in the years 1975–1980.

The main sources of riboflavine in the area are milk and beans. Seasonal fluctuations in consumption of these food items are less obvious. The marginal intakes of riboflavine recorded are thus likely to reflect the habitual intakes. This is in agreement with the frequent signs of riboflavine deficiency observed. Iron intakes were low among infants but acceptable among toddlers; no information is available on haemoglobin values of these age groups in our study area.

Contrary to expectation, season and location (richer coffee-growing area versus subsistence-farming area) did not affect the child's energy intake. This may be due to the fact that the households studied were not solely dependent on their own food production. Apart from farming, one or more household members had a paid job and so an additional income (see Chapter 2). The difference between seasons was not reflected in amounts of foods consumed but in the source, whether purchased or home-produced.

That the number of meals did show a significant association with the child's energy intake was not surprising. In areas such as ours, where the child's diet is bulky and of low caloric density, the child can only consume the large amounts needed to fulfil its requirements when it eats frequently (Rutishauser, 1974).

The finding that breast-fed children aged 18–23 months had significantly higher energy intakes than those not breast-fed is interesting. It does not support the suggestion, derived from the Rural Kenyan Nutrition Survey (1977), that the prolonged nursing pattern in the Eastern Province (including Machakos District) reflected a relative scarcity of food. Also their finding, that stunting (height for age less than 90 percent of Harvard Standard) was more frequently found among children weaned after 18 months, cannot be explained by our observations on food intake.

Assessment of adequacy of diets should take into consideration the limitations of a short period of recording. Moreover, comparison of recorded intakes with recommended intakes cannot by itself indicate whether a diet is adequate or not. Such conclusions should be supported by clinical and anthropometric evidence. Furthermore, the nutritional status of pre-school children is not only conditioned by food consumption but also by morbidity (see Chapters 6–9 in Part III).

Although growth of pre-school children will be dealt with in Chapter 14, it is interesting to consider the nutritional status of this particular group as well. On average, weight and height for age of infants aged 0–6 months corresponded well with that of the reference group. Faltering of growth did occur, especially in the second half-year of life, but few were malnourished at the time of observation as judged by weight for height. None the less, there is room for improvement. From the data available, it can reasonably be assumed that the reduced weight for age observed in the second half-year of infancy has partly a nutritional basis. The data on growth presented in the next chapter even indicate that weight and height started to falter from as early as 3–4 months of age. Energy intake was most limited at age 3–12 months.

The toddler diet is on the whole acceptable, qualitatively and quantitatively, for maintaining a proper growth rate but not for reducing the deficit imposed earlier in life.

To maintain adequate growth and a good nutritional status in the child population concerned, the favourable habit of prolonged breast-feeding should be encouraged and the good practices of some mothers in the area emphasized.

The following recommendations are feasible for the households concerned and should be given attention in planning nutrition education:

i) modification of the watery gruels fed to infants into porridges of higher caloric density: more flour, fat, milk, and sugar per unit of water;

(ii) introduction of *ngima* with milk or stew from 9 months of age onwards;

(iii) four or more feeds a day.

References

Dutch Food Composition Table, Voorlichtingsburo voor de Voeding, den Haag, 1975.

FAO, Food composition table for use in Africa, Rome, 1968.

FAO/WHO, Handbook on human nutritional requirements, Rome, 1974.

Habicht JP, Martorell R, Yarbrough C, Malina RM and Klein RE, Height and weight standards for pre-school children. How relevant are ethnic differences in growth potential?, Lancet, i (1974) 611.

Hoorweg J, Niemeyer R and van Steenbergen WM, Findings of the nutrition intervention research project, African Studies Centre, Leiden, 1981.

Jelliffe DB, The assessment of the nutritional status of the community, WHO Monograph Series No 53, Geneva, 1966.

Keller WD, Caloric and protein intakes of preschool children, Envir Chld Hlth, 19 (1973) 376.

McFie J, Nutrient intakes of urban dwellers in Lagos, Nigeria, Brit J Nutr, 21 (1967) 257.

Platt BS, Tables of representative values of foods commonly used in tropical countries, Medical Research Council, Special Report Series No 302, Her Majesty's Stationery Office, London, 1975.

Rutishauser IHE, Factors affecting the intake of energy and protein by Ugandan pre-school children, Ecology of Food Nutrition, 3 (1974) 213.

Rutishauser IHE, The dietary background to protein-energy malnutrition in West Mengo District, Uganda, In; The child in the African Environment, Owor R, Ongom VL and Kinya BG, Eds, East African Literature Bureau, Nairobi, 1975, p. 197.

Rutishauser IHE, Ibid. 203.

Rural Kenyan Nutrition Survey, Social Perspectives, Central Bureau of Statistics, Nairobi, Vol 2 No 14, 1977.

Selinus R, Gobezie A and Vahlquist B, Dietary Studies in Ethiopia, Acta Soc Med Upsal, 76 (1971) 158.

Waterlow JC, Ashworth A and Griffiths M, Faltering in infant growth in less-developed countries, Lancet, ii (1980) 1176.

Waterlow JC, Nutrition for the world's children: What do we need to know?, In; Topics in Paediatrics 2, Wharton BA, Ed, Pitman Medical, 1980, p. 210.

Whitehead RG, Infant feeding practices and the development of malnutrition in rural Gambia, UN Univ Nutr Bull, 1 (1979) 36.

WHO Collaborative Study on breast-feeding, WHO, Geneva, 1981, p. 79.

14

Growth pattern of pre-school children

H.A.P.C. Oomen
D.M. Blankhart
W. 't Mannetje

Introduction

The planning, in 1972, for a longitudinal growth study as part of the Machakos Project, was a rather audacious enterprise. It would require much time, trained staff and co-operation of the mothers in scattered homesteads in rough, partly cultivated, hilly terrain without convenient access roads. The obvious choice was between collecting the subjects periodically in a fixed, suitable locality with adequate means for measuring, weighing and registration and home-visiting. This implied resorting to locally available means, makeshift adaptations and necessarily less precise results. Both methods had considerable advantages and disadvantages. The principal investigator at the time, Dr Blankhart, chose the second option. This was deemed necessary because in these unfavourable surroundings for field work there was no acceptable alternative that would ensure inclusion of every infant and toddler in the sample. It excluded intensive supervision and the use of sophisticated equipment; it put a heavy burden on perseverance of field-workers; but it was much more expedient for mother and child.

Unfortunately a major setback occurred when, in the middle of the study period, in 1976, Dr Blankhart died and his part had to be taken over a few months later by his successor, Dr Jansen. Despite this setback, it should be emphasized that this approach, as an in-situ survey, was unique. As a method it was incomparably better than working with only incidental samples or special staff collecting subjects and mothers laboriously at ad-hoc observation points.

Materials and methods

A systematic sample of 1:8 was selected from about 4000 households in the Matunguli and Mbiuni locations for inclusion in the growth study. Children below 48 months were admitted but excluded on reaching age 60 months. Children aged below 48 months migrating into these households were also admitted. Regular assessments were continued from June 1, 1974 to February 1, 1977.

The birth dates were taken from the 'buff cards' of the demographic surveillance system, and are considered accurate to within 2 weeks. A total of 918 children were registered in the 32-month survey; 98 had to be rejected because of administrative discrepancies, and 6 died. Of the remaining 814, only those who were measured and weighed at least five times were included. This resulted in 568 subjects providing 5264 monthly data, an average of 9.3 per subject.

Infants below one year were checked monthly in the first half-year, bi-monthly in the second, and quarterly in the third to fifth years. This provided an average of 145 monthly observations in the first year and 86, 77, 74 and 58 respectively in the second to fifth years. The period in which an individual child was included averaged 22 months, with a minimum of 4 and a maximum of 31 months.

Portable equipment was kept to a minimum. It consisted of a Salter circular 20 kg spring scale, a flexible tape measure, a small stiff 10×20 cm board to serve as a footrest, a plastic sheet to lie on and specially made hanging breeches in which even the smallest child could hang safely. The accuracy of the procedures and of scales were tested regularly.

Home visiting by male and female field-workers was similar to that described in other chapters. They were briefed in detail at the start and briefing was repeated during the survey. Forms were provided, checked and kept at one of the four field offices. Most visits had to be on foot. Parents were informed beforehand and co-operation was satisfactory. The subjects themselves, except the very youngest, soon accepted the weighing and measuring sessions.

Children were weighed with the scales suspended from a bar supported by two people, the field-worker reading the oscillating figure. To avoid discomfort, the child was only lifted a few inches. Two-year-olds gave some trouble by wriggling, but this was less with passive babies and co-operative older children. On checking variability it was concluded that accuracy to ±200 g was acceptable.

Measuring was done on any horizontal area found near the homestead that permitted the use of a vertical head rest. The child was put on a plastic sheet, and while one person, usually the mother, fixed its head to the head rest, the field-worker adjusted the movable foot rest. The latter was then held in place while the child was removed, and then replaced by the measuring tape. Most determinations were done in the open air outside the dwellings. Intra- and inter-observer variations were found acceptable within ±1 cm.

As a framework for comparison the standards derived from the Harvard longitudinal studies (Stuart and Stevenson, 1959) were used. Results were uniformly expressed as percentages, either negative or positive, in relation to those standards. The 'Harvard Standards' employed include weight for age (W/A), height for age (H/A) and weight for height (W/H), using the lists provided by Jelliffe (1966). The figures were screened for differences between the Mbiuni and Matungulu locations, but as these on the whole proved not to be significant, the results were pooled.

Successive age groups were screened for differences between the sexes, using 90 percent W/H as a cut-off point. For the first year the differences were not significant and for the period 13–60 months 14 percent of the measurements in males were under 90 percent W/H as against 17.3 percent in females. This was considered irrelevant for judging differences in growth and the sexes were pooled.

A seasonal trend during the course of the 32-month survey was looked for. A significant difference was found between the average W/A percentage of 83.1

percent in October 1974 and 86.3 percent in April 1976. Such an effect was also demonstrable between the Mbiuni and Matungulu locations. No effect on the incidence of cases below 70 percent W/A in the 13–48-month cohorts was demonstrable. It was concluded that the effect on the incidence of malnutrition was negligible.

Results

General trends of growth indicators

Averages of height in cm and weight in kg in various months, with standard deviations, are presented in Table 1. Figures 1 and 2 show height and weight increases, with 2 SD, and compare the growth curves with the 100 percent and 90 percent of the Harvard standards for height, and the 100 percent and 80 percent standards for weight.

On comparing the average growth indicators with the respective height-for-age and weight-for-age standards we note nearly ident-

Table I.
Average height and weight of the Machakos Project child from 1–60 months (as registered).

Age (months)	*Height (cm)*	*SD*	*Weight (kg)*	*SD*	*No. (entries)*
1	51.4	2.7	4.0	0.7	102
2	54.8	2.7	4.9	0.6	123
3	57.6	2.8	5.6	0.7	142
4	59.7	2.6	6.1	0.7	173
5	61.5	3.5	6.7	0.9	156
6	63.4	2.7	7.1	0.9	164
9	67.1	2.8	7.9	1.0	93
12	69.5	2.6	8.5	1.0	180
15	72.5	3.4	9.0	1.2	83
18	74.4	3.6	9.4	1.0	87
21	76.8	3.7	9.9	1.1	78
24	79.3	3.9	10.3	1.2	76
27	81.8	3.5	10.9	1.2	62
30	83.3	4.2	11.1	1.2	79
33	85.5	4.5	11.7	1.3	71
36	87.7	4.7	12.1	1.3	70
39	89.7	5.2	12.5	1.2	65
42	91.5	5.2	12.8	1.3	70
45	93.5	5.0	13.4	1.3	61
48	94.7	4.5	13.7	1.4	58
51	96.2	4.7	14.2	1.4	60
54	96.9	5.1	14.2	1.5	56
57	99.1	5.3	14.5	1.6	42
60	100	5.8	14.8	1.6	34

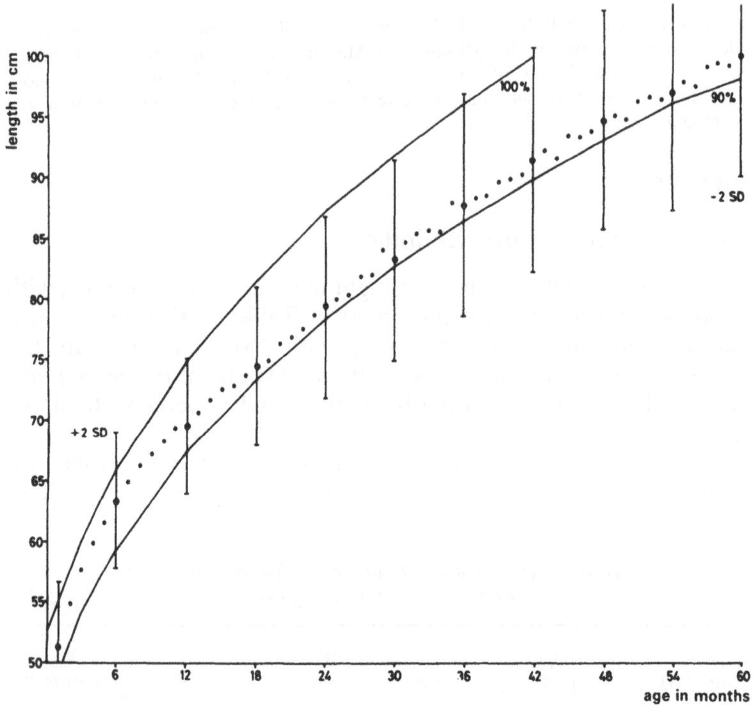

Figure 1. Height increase in the Kamba child population, based on mean values, ±2SD compared to Harvard Standard levels 100 percent and 90 percent.

ical values in the first 6 months. In the subsequent 6–9-month period there was a hardly noticeable drop in H/A but a rather striking drop from 96 percent to 89 percent in W/A. In the following 10–12 months both these declining trends became more marked. In the period between 18–24 months H/A reached a level of 91–92 percent and W/A 82–83 percent, then remained constant until age 60 months. The plumpness of the baby, as expressed in weight-for-height figures, was near 100 percent of the standard in the first months, declined to 94 percent at age 6 months and to 92 percent at age 9 months, and then remained constant at this level. The lesser growing potential of the Kamba child, as compared with its Harvard counterpart, is apparently determined between 15–18 months.

Differentiation of growth indicators in age cohorts

We chose the age cohorts recommended by Waterlow et al. (1977) but added a subdivision in the second year, in which important

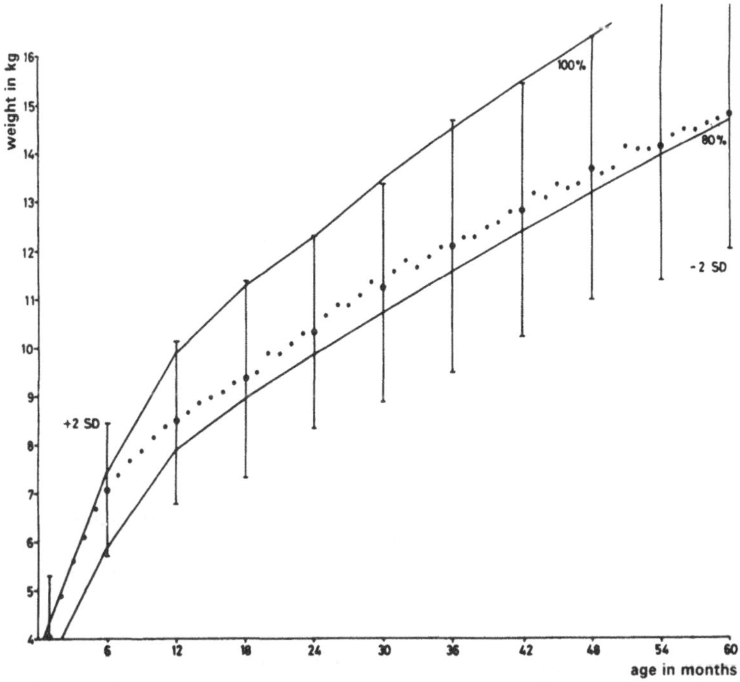

Figure 2. Weight increase in the Kamba child population based on mean values, ±2SD, compared to Harvard Standard levels 100 percent and 80 percent.

changes may be suspected. For each of the eight cohorts the positive and negative deviations from the 100 percent standards for W/A, H/A and W/H were calculated and expressed in 10 percent steps for weight and in 5 percent steps for height. The figures for each of the three growth indicators, W/A, H/A and W/H, are shown in Tables 2–4. They are visualized as histograms in Figure 3 in relation to the 100 percent standards for W/A, H/A and W/H. Subdivision of the bars permits distinction of the degree of deviation in each cohort, either positive (+10 percent becomes 110 percent), or negative (−10 percent becomes 90 percent, etc.). Growth processes occurring in each successive cohort can be compared at a glance and so also can the relative behaviour of the three indicators W/A, H/A and W/H. It is suggested that this presentation is clearer and more comprehensive than the procedures proposed by WHO (1979) for the comparison of the distribution of growth indicators.

In all the cohorts the distributions of weight and height figures

Table 2.
Weight for age. Deviation in 10-percent steps of Harvard Standards in percent of total cohort.

Age, months	*1–3*	*4–6*	*7–9*	*10–12*	*13–18*	*19–24*	*25–36*	*37–60*
No. subjects	*181*	*225*	*242*	*269*	*359**		*337*	*305*
No. entries	*367*	*493*	*405*	*474*	*524*	*505*	*921*	*1518*
>+20%	3.8	3.0	0.2	0.2	0	0	0	0
+10 to +19%	14.2	10.1	4.4	1.1	0.2	0.2	0.4	0.4
0 to + 9%	27.5	28.0	17.5	6.8	5.7	3.2	4.1	1.6
− 1 to −10%	28.3	28.3	34.1	30.8	21.6	17.6	20.0	15.7
−11 to −20%	15.0	21.9	31.1	38.4	44.5	46.3	45.6	42.0
−21 to −30%	7.4	7.5	10.6	16.7	21.6	26.5	25.0	35.0
−31 to −40%	3.8	0.6	1.5	5.1	6.3	5.9	4.5	5.0
<−41%	0	0	0.2	1.1	0.1	0.2	0.4	0.2

*13–24 months

Table 3.
Height for age. Deviation in 5-percent steps of Harvard Standards in percent of total cohort.

Age, months	*1–3*	*4–6*	*7–9*	*10–12*	*13–18*	*19–24*	*25–36*	*37–60*
>+ 5%	1.6	1.6	0.5	0.4	0	0	0	0
0 to + 4%	12.3	12.8	7.7	3.6	2.9	1.8	2.2	2.2
− 1 to − 5%	35.3	43.4	50.0	34.7	20.0	13.4	16.2	18.8
− 6 to −10%	34.0	35.6	35.8	48.4	45.6	44.5	45.4	42.8
−11 to −15%	14.5	5.9	5.4	11.8	28.2	34.6	28.1	26.7
−16 to −20%	2.2	0.6	0.4	1.1	2.7	5.4	6.6	8.3
<−21%	0	0	0.2	0	0.6	0.3	1.5	1.2

Table 4.
Weight for height. Deviation in 10-percent steps of Harvard Standards in percent of total cohort.

Age, months	*1–3*	*4–6*	*7–9*	*10–12*	*13–18*	*19–24*	*25–36*	*37–60*
>+30%	5.1	4.7	2.0	0	0	0	0	0
+20 to +29%	13.1	12.2	4.9	3.4	1.5	0	0.7	0.6
+10 to +19%	29.3	24.7	21.0	10.4	7.2	4.2	4.5	2.9
0 to + 9%	26.9	32.4	36.3	40.4	34.5	32.3	29.3	25.4
− 1 to −10%	16.2	18.6	26.7	32.6	30.3	44.0	49.3	55.4
−11 to −20%	8.4	5.9	8.1	12.1	17.0	17.6	15.8	15.3
<−21%	0.3	0.4	1.0	1.5	1.5	0.9	0.4	0.4

Note: Number of subjects in Tables 3 and 4 are similar to those of Table 2 with minor variations.

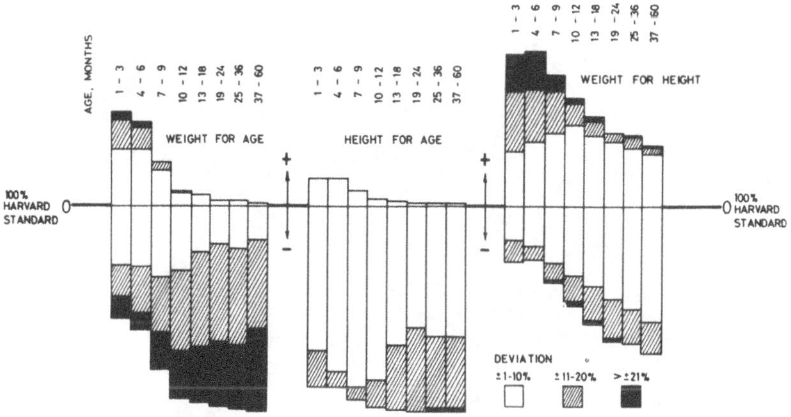

Figure 3. Comparison of age cohorts 1–60 months to the Harvard Standards for weight for age, height for age and weight for height.

were regular, including the 13–24-month period, in which malnutrition is reputedly most liable to appear.

In the two youngest cohorts the W/A reference standard was nearly identical to the values observed for the Kamba baby; in fact at ages 1–3 and 4–6 months 45 percent and 41 percent of infants, respectively, were over 100 percent of the standard. After 6 months that proportion dropped to 22 percent in the 7–9 months cohort and 8 percent in the 10–12-month cohort, hovered around 4 percent in the second and third years and never exceeded 2 percent in the fourth and the fifth years. The moiety exhibiting 90 percent or less of the W/A standard, however, grew rapidly in every initial cohort, and soon reached about 80 percent of all older cohort subjects. This suggests that, once acquired, a weight deficit is not compensated for later but settles at a predetermined compromise. There is no apparent pick-up in growth in the under-90 percent groups in the third to fifth year.

Height-for-age figures in the first half-year showed a quite different pattern from weight-for-age. The Kamba baby is apparently better at increasing its weight than its height, as compared with the Harvard Standards. Only 14 percent exceeded the H/A standard in the 1–3- and 4–6-month cohorts, and this dropped to 8 percent in the 7–9-month and to 4 percent in the 10–12-month age groups. The rate of increase in height was much more steady and well defined than that for weight. A notable retardation at 90 percent and less of H/A affected about one-third of the cohorts in the

Determining length by field-worker and local aid. Laying the child on the plastic sheet and fixing the head to any available vertical surface, the foot rest is applied and held in place. Then the child is removed and the distance measured.

second year and tended to continue in the older child. There was again no tendency for catch-up growth.

Weight for height in a developing child is a changing parameter of growth: the chubby baby differs from the 5-year-old, who is more linearly built. This we see reflected in the W/H presentation of the age cohorts. In the first year there was a preponderance of relatively fat Kamba babies compared with the Harvard Standard. Later on the trend to leanness continued until towards the third to fifth years it hovered around 95 percent of the Standard. About 15 percent did not reach 90 percent of the standard, though only 1–2 percent were below 80 percent.

Growth of persistent deviators after age 12 months

To study growth differences in children over one year old a distinction was made between those who had achieved the highest weights and those with the lowest weights. There were 433 subjects in this group of more than one-year-olds. They had been checked an average 9.1 times, covering an individual growth period of an average 22.2 months. Being consistently over 88 percent of the W/A standard was taken as an arbitrary cut-off point for the fastest growers, and persistently under 75 percent of W/A as the cut-off point for slow-growers. The low-weight group comprised 40 subjects, the heavy-weight group 47.

In both the persistently light and heavy deviators a clustering in families that could not be demonstrated in intermediate groups was noticed. The low-weight group contained four sets of siblings (total 9) the heavy-weight three (total 8). In addition several subjects had siblings just beyond the cut-off points equally showing a relatively poor or relatively excessive weight increment. This concentration in households suggested a common factor, genetic or otherwise, leading either to good or inferior performance.

The heavy-weight group not only achieved a high score for weight (average 91.5 percent of W/A) but also for height (average 94.8 percent of H/A.) They may have been endowed with the greatest growth potential; they may have continuously escaped the health hazards experienced by their less successful counterparts; or they may have been the best fed. If maximal growth is considered a desirable health target, they showed the upper levels that the present Kamba child can achieve.

The figures for sustained growth in the low-weight group showed an average of 71.1 percent of W/A and of 85.9 percent of H/A. Since the latter is close to the overall average it could be concluded that height was less affected than weight. Such a child is lean but has attained the same stature as its fellows.

Indicators of malnutrition

On analysing the low-weight group of 40, three categories could be distinguished. A subgroup of 13 had persisted at a W/A of under

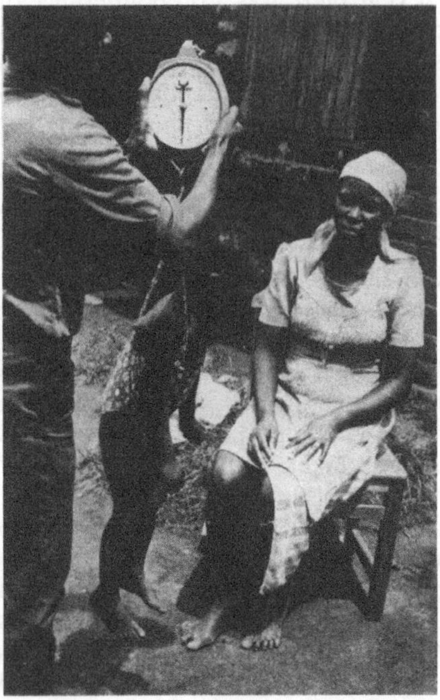

Field-worker weighing a toddler at home in his natural surroundings.

70 percent and clearly had to be labelled malnutrition. A second subgroup of 18 consisted mainly of individuals who had been under 70 percent W/A at intervals but recovered to reach averages of over 70 percent. The remaining 9 proved to be small subjects but regular growers.

Of those falling consistently below 70 percent of W/A, six had entered the survey above age 14 months. The cause of their growth deficit could not be found out but it was suspected to be due to low birth weight. The remaining six were considered to be cases of malnutrition originating during the survey period.

This implied that over the whole survey period of 32 months there had been at any point 8.3 (1.9 percent) lasting and 12.4 (2.9 percent) transient cases of malnutrition. Cross-sectionally, in the successive year groups, the percentage below 70 percent W/A varied from 4.9–6.4 percent.

There were 28 subjects having an average W/A percentage between 70–75 percent. The weight increment of the majority was slow but regular and their weight for height was about 85 percent. They were not considered malnourished and there is no good reason to designate them as 'nutritional dwarfs' (FAO/WHO,

1971). Among all entries above one year the percentage of subjects not reaching 85 percent of W/H were 7.7 percent, 5.2 percent, 2.9 percent and 3.2 percent, respectively, in the second to fifth years. This again suggests that in the lowest-weight subjects stature tended to improve with age.

Discussion

Interpretation of results

In the growth of children in the population concerned three distinct periods can be distinguished in the curves for weight and height (Figs. 1 and 2).

The first covers the first 6 months. In that period nearly half the subjects exceed the standard of weight for age and about 15 percent that of height for age. In view of the lower birth weight of the Kamba child (mean 3100 g, see Chapter 11), this must rate as a good achievement. On considering the negative variations the incidence of 26–30 percent of deviators under W/H 90 percent must include the about 10 percent of low birth weights (2500 g and less) reported in the same population by Jansen et al.

The second period, 7–12 months specifically, shows a rather sudden drop in weight increment and a less striking one in height. Average increments are 620 g/month in the first-half year as against 300 g/month in the second. For the Harvard population these were 670 and 420 g. This compares with the 340 g/month and 225 g/month respectively put forward by Jelliffe (1966) as the limits of adequacy. It implies that the cherubic young baby changes rapidly to a leaner habitus. A smaller decrease in weight and height increments continues into the third half-year but after that the levels remain remarkably constant.

In the third period, growth parameters seem to have reached a lasting compromise. On closer inspection, however, it appears that there are large intra-cohort variations. On the whole the trend to leanness continues at a faster rate than in the standard population as witnessed by the diagram of weight for height (Fig. 3).

The interpretation of these processes seems to be easiest for the first period. This is the hallowed period for breast-feeding in which van Steenbergen et al. found that intake was 100 kcal/kg/day, or 86 percent of recommended daily allowances (see Chapter 13). It may be questionable whether, with a larger intake of breast milk in a child whose birth weight was substandard, higher figures could have been achieved.

An explanation of the fact that the subsequent drop in increments sets in with the 7–9-month cohort is less obvious. Still, the 10–12-month cohort seems to set the pace for the further parameters of growth. Lacking convincing evidence of external factors we have to consider the influence of internal factors. In this period the child's ecology is altered. The mother-and-child 'dyad', the breast-feeding complex and the close proximity of the mother changes to coping with 'alien' food and a more hostile environment. Weight, apparently, is more affected than height. Most probably a lesser amount of available calories is responsible. In the van Steenbergen survey this proved to be 93 kcal/kg/day, or 90 percent of the RDA, which hardly seems sufficient to cause a drop of some 25 percent in average weight increment and of some 6 percent in height increment.

The third period starts in the 13–18-month cohort, setting constant levels for the years to come. We know from van Steenbergen's studies that in the period of 19–36 months the calorie intake rose a little to about 96 kcal/kg/day, satisfying 96 percent of the RDA. In the meantime the relative contribution of breast milk declined steadily. It should be noted that at all times the protein intake was satisfactory (2.1–2.8 g/kg), implying that at least this factor could not be held responsible for the decrease in height increments. This leaves us with the question why the change in parameters occurs exactly in the second half-year whereas no further lowering is discernible in the period of 18–60 months.

The prevalence of serious malnutrition or morbidity from other causes is on the whole fairly low in this period. The rather crude notes that were available on incidence and duration of infectious diseases in our survey did not produce statistically significant differences between high and low scores for weight, nor was there any discernible catch-up in growth.

In the third period the Kamba child is small for age by the Harvard Standard, and leaner than its Caucasian counterpart. Its linearity may be due to its longer legs and arms, a subject that perhaps requires closer study.

This constant lower level at ages 13–60 months affects a fraction of some 20–35 percent, who show a deficit of 20 percent and above in weight for age, and 10 percent and above in height for age (Fig. 3). Weight for height appears satisfactory in the majority, however, and only some 10 percent of the children are really thin, leaving a few percent who really cause concern.

To visualize the situation better, we may compare the average 36-month-old Kamba toddler with his Harvard Standard counterpart. At this stage, the average subject is 96 percent of the standard for weight for height. He measures 88 cm, or 92 percent of height for age, and 12.1 kg, or 83 percent of weight for age. This height and weight are achieved by his Boston counterpart at 23 and 25 months and the latter at age 36 months weighs 14.5 kg and measures 96 cm. The Kamba child reaches 14.5 kg at 60 months, and 96 cm at 51 months. His relative weight for height is still 92 percent, compared with 91 percent at the time of birth.

Local growth standards

The results of the longitudinal survey lead us to the question whether the Harvard Standards should be applied when judging the nutritional status of this population, the alternative being to judge it according to its own local standards. The Harvard Standards as used in a number of publications dealing with developing countries are not, in our view, applicable to this and probably many other African populations, because they lead to an overrating of the significance of below-standard levels.

Categories of children defined as 'stunted'—low H/A and W/A but 'normal' in proportions—and 'wasted'—normal height but low W/H and W/A—by Waterlow (1976) tend to be unnecessarily large in less well-off countries and therefore pessimistic from a health viewpoint. Using even a tentative local standard would largely reduce the proportions diagnosed as low W/A, H/A and W/H.

Similar comments can be made with regard to the 1977 Rural Kenya Nutrition Survey, which brought together an impressive mass of cross-sectional data on growth in 1–4-year-olds (CBS, 1977). Overall parameters for W/A, H/A and W/H in the six regions surveyed were similar or somewhat higher than those in the Machakos area survey. However useful such data may be from a documentary and comparative point of view, they are not a 'baseline assessment of nutritional status'. When compared with the standards of a well-to-do Caucasian population, they are liable to create an anthropometric concept of malnutrition that overlooks the pathological and biochemical changes inherent in clinical malnutrition. The modal Machakos child at 80 percent of W/A or 90 percent of W/H is not halfway to malnutrition but a reasonably healthy child. Unnecessarily high cut-off points cause clinics to spread their efforts over large numbers of children instead of concentrating on the relatively small percentage who really need attention.

After due consideration we have the same objection to the interpretation of parts of our Machakos study material by Stephenson et al. (1979). The 90 percent of W/A that they propose to indicate 'malnutrition' in accordance with the Gomez classification, which calls for 90–75 percent of the standard to be classified as first-degree malnutrition (Gomez et al., 1956), would include nearly 80 percent of the Machakos child population, which is against common sense. Our complete data, taking into account periods of growth and spontaneous catch-up, deny such a concept. In our material protein-energy malnutrition cases were exceptions.

We have thus come to the conclusion that the Harvard Standard should not be applied to our study population and to most other populations in Kenya. We therefore propose a local growth standard, to be expressed as a percentage of the Harvard Standards. Before we do so it is necessary to recall how the Harvard Standards were constructed. They are based 'upon repeated measurements at the ages given of a group of white children of North European descent living in or near Boston. These children were considered free from important defects or chronic diseases. They belonged for the most part to families in the lower economic brackets and had the advantage of regular health supervision' (Stuart and Stevenson, 1959).

The results of this longitudinal survey allow us to establish growth standards for reasonably healthy children by considering the data for the fastest-growing subjects as described above. We propose, therefore, as a local health target 91 percent of the Harvard Standard for weight for age and 95 percent of that for height for age. The cut-off point for the diagnosis of malnutrition should in principle be put at 70 percent of the Harvard Standard of weight for age, but in view of the variation in weight increments, it is recommended that for preventive purposes the cut-off point be put at 75 percent of weight for age. This means that 12 percent of the children in the second half of the first year and 16 percent in the 1–5-year period are considered to be at special risk for malnutrition and should receive extra attention and care.

References

CBS, Rural Kenyan Nutrition Survey, Social Perspectives, 2, No 4, Central Bureau of Statistics, Nairobi, 1977.

FAO/WHO Exp Comm Nutrition, 8th Rep, WHO Techn Rep Ser No 477, Geneva, 1971.

Gomez F, Galvan RR, Frenk S, Cravioto I, Chavez R and Vazquez I, J Trop Pediat, 2 (1956) 77.

Janes DJ, McFarlane SBJ and Moody BM, Lancet ii (1979) 101.

Jelliffe DB, WHO Monogr Ser No 53, Geneva, 1966.

Stephenson LS, Latham MC, Crompton DWT, Schulpen TWJ and Jansen AAJ, E Afr Med J, 56 (1979) 1.

Stuart HC and Stevenson SS, Physical growth and development, In; Textbook of Pediatrics, 7th ed, Saunders, Philadelphia, 1959, p. 12.

Waterlow JC, Busina R, Keller W, Lane JM, Nichaman MZ and Tanner JM, Wld Hlth Org Bull, 55 (1977) 489.

Waterlow JC, In; Nutrition in Preventive Medicine, WHO Monogr Ser No 62 (Annex 5), Geneva, 1976, p. 548.

WHO, Measurement of Nutritional Impact, FAP/79.1, Geneva, 1979.

15

Growth of infants of low and normal birth weight

A.A.J. Jansen
W. Gemert
B. Thiuri
S.A. Lakhani

Introduction

In 1978 a longitudinal study of the nutritional status of pregnant and lactating women was started. Results dealing with food intake and anthropometry during pregnancy and lactation period were reported in Chapters 10 and 11. As a continuation of the pregnancy study, children of low birth weight (LBW) and normal (NBW) counterparts were followed up. The rationale for this part of the investigation was, first, to study growth of LBW and NBW children and its determinants and, secondly, to determine any factors in pregnancy that could explain or lead to low birth weight. Results of serial measurements in terms of weight and length up to a year after birth for both groups will be reported in this chapter.

Materials and methods

During the period from 1 May 1978 to 30 June 1980 a total of 2874 women were reported pregnant; 1739 (61 percent) of these were enrolled in the study; 946 (54 percent) were seen at least twice, i.e. in different trimesters, while 793 (46 percent) were examined only once, mostly in the third trimester.

Efforts were made to weigh and measure the infants as soon as possible after birth, at 6-week intervals during the first year and 3-monthly therafter. Weights were taken with a Salter scale, and length was measured with a locally made measuring board according to established procedures (Jelliffe, 1966). Trained, regularly supervised, female field-workers were in charge of these measurements.

All low-birth-weight infants (defined as 2500 g or less) reported in time were included in the sample. For comparison, a NBW newborn, matched as far as possible for time of birth, sex and location of household was selected for every LBW infant.

From May 1978 to 31 December 1981, a total of 267 LBW newborns were registered, including 20 pairs of twins and one set of triplets. It proved possible to match 200 LBW children with another 200 NBW children. Ultimately, however, only 352 children were included in the analysis (Table 1). There were various reasons for the 48 exclusions: i) it was not possible to find controls for the twins or triplets; ii) some children were born elsewhere, and while the mother might know the birth weight if the child was born in a hospital or health centre, length at birth is rarely recorded; iii) some children born in the study area were reported too late—due to the rains, distance from the field office, birth at the weekend, etc.—or, rarely, the mother refused to collaborate; iv) 26 LBW children died (against 4 NBW children); v) 23 LBW and 13 NBW children migrated soon after birth; and vi) the data on a few children did not seem reliable.

The total number of children seen and measured at specific times varied, for reasons such as absence of the child; absence of the mother at the time of the visit, in which case it was not always proper to examine the child; or illness of the child. As mentioned in the following section, estimates were calculated for missing observations.

Table 1.
Number of children included in analysis.

	Boys	*Girls*	*Total*
LBW	80	113	193
NBW	62	97	159
Total	142	210	352

Statistical analysis

Weights and heights obtained at specific times of measurement were included in the analysis:

Order of measurement	1	2	3	4	5	6	7	8	9	10
Age of child (weeks)	0	6	12	18	24	30	36	42	48	52
Variation in days	+3	±5	±7	±7	±7	±7	±7	±7	±7	±7

Overall, 20 percent of the measurements were missed, including 60 percent of the birth lengths. In order to incorporate missing observations and to estimate mean weights and heights at specific ages the data were treated as follows.

The differences between measurements for a particular child were determined. Suppose we had 5 children with measurements as in the following table:

	Point in time									
Child	*1*	*2*	*3*	*4*	*5*	*6*	*7*	*8*	*9*	*10*
1	$x_{1,1}$	—	$x_{1,3}$	$x_{1,4}$	—	—	$x_{1,7}$	$x_{1,8}$	—	$x_{1,10}$
2	—	$x_{2,2}$	$x_{2,3}$	—	$x_{2,5}$	$x_{2,6}$	$x_{2,7}$	—	—	$x_{2,10}$
3	—	—	$x_{3,3}$	$x_{3,4}$	$x_{3,5}$	—	—	$x_{3,8}$	$x_{3,9}$	—
4	$x_{4,1}$	$x_{4,2}$	—	$x_{4,4}$	—	$x_{4,6}$	$x_{4,7}$	—	$x_{4,9}$	—
5	—	$x_{5,2}$	—	$x_{5,4}$	$x_{5,5}$	$x_{5,6}$	$x_{5,7}$	$x_{5,8}$	—	$x_{5,10}$
	$\bar{x}_{.1}$	$\bar{x}_{.2}$	$\bar{x}_{.3}$	$\bar{x}_{.4}$	$\bar{x}_{.5}$	$\bar{x}_{.6}$	$\bar{x}_{.7}$	$\bar{x}_{.8}$	$\bar{x}_{.9}$	$\bar{x}_{.10}$
n_i	(2)	(3)	(3)	(4)	(3)	(3)	(4)	(3)	(2)	(3)

The means of these measurements ($\bar{x}_{.j}$; $j = 1,...10$) are based on a variable number of observations (n_i). Because of missing information there could be a bias in these means. In order to obtain unbiased means ($M_{.j}$), the differences between any known measurements were determined for each child. Thus for child 1:

$x_{1,1}-x_{1,3}$	$x_{1,1}-x_{1,4}$	$x_{1,1}-x_{1,7}$	$x_{1,1}-x_{1,8}$	$x_{1,1}-x_{1,10}$
$x_{1,3}-x_{1,4}$	$x_{1,3}-x_{1,7}$	$x_{1,3}-x_{1,8}$	$x_{1,3}-x_{1,10}$	
$x_{1,4}-x_{1,7}$	$x_{1,4}-x_{1,8}$	$x_{1,4}-x_{1,10}$		
$x_{1,7}-x_{1,8}$	$x_{1,7}-x_{1,10}$			
$x_{1,8}-x_{1,10}$				

are calculated, and the same for children 2, 3, 4 and 5.

Each difference (e.g. $x_{1,1}-x_{1,3}$= difference between points 1 and 3 [for child 1]) between two points is added together for all children who have measurements for these points, and divided by the number of cases. Thus we obtain: $\bar{x}_1$; $\bar{x}_{.2}-\bar{x}_{.1}$; $\bar{x}_{.3}-\bar{x}_{.1}$;...$\bar{x}_{.10}-\bar{x}_{.1}$, and $\bar{x}_2$; $\bar{x}_{.3}-\bar{x}_{.2}$; $\bar{x}_{.4}-\bar{x}_{.2}$;...$\bar{x}_{.10}-\bar{x}_{.2}$, and ...$\bar{x}_9$; $\bar{x}_{.10}-\bar{x}_{.9}$, and $\bar{x}_{10}$. With these mean values between two points it is now possible to calculate adjusted means. The mean of point 1 (M_1) is the weighted mean of $\bar{x}_1$; $\bar{x}_2-(\bar{x}_2-\bar{x}_1)$; $\bar{x}_3-(\bar{x}_3-\bar{x}_1)$;...$\bar{x}_{10}-(\bar{x}_{10}-\bar{x}_1)$. The weighting occurs according to the number of measurements between two points. The same procedure is then repeated to obtain unbiased means of point 2 (M_2), and so on.

Results

Figure 1 shows the distribution of birth weights according to category. The histograms of the LBW newborns are skewed towards the 'normal' side; the median values of children with normal birth weights are comparable with the mean birth weight in the population, estimated to be 3100 g. Figure 2 shows histograms of birth lengths. The median birth length of LBW children is 46 cm; that of NBW children is 50 cm, irrespective of sex.

Tables 2 and 3 provide information on mean weights and lengths at 10 points in time during the first year of life. The ratios (LBW/NBW)×100 for mean weights and lengths are also shown. The mean weights of NBW boys are persistently greater than those of

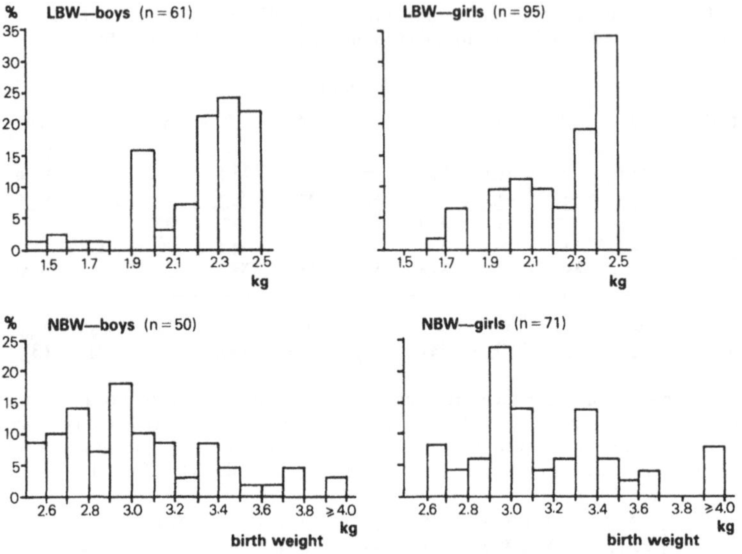

Figure 1. Frequency distribution of LBW and NBW infants according to birth weight.

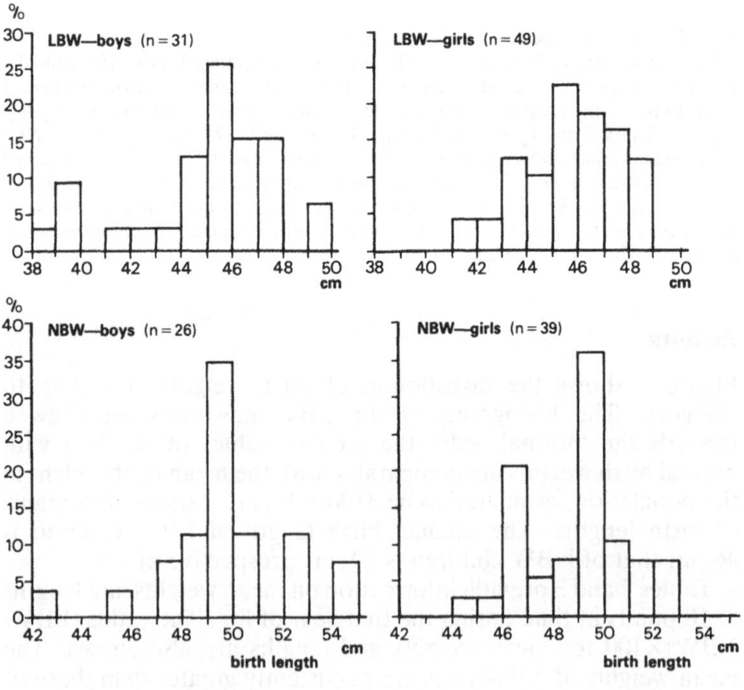

Figure 2. Frequency distribution of LBW and NBW infants according to birth length.

NBW girls. Although the mean weights of male LBW newborns are also greater than those of female LBW newborns, the mean ratios for boys are less than those for girls; towards the end of the first year of life the mean ratios converge. The same applies to length.

In Figures 3–6 growth is compared with international standards (WHO, 1979). Both weight and length curves for LBW children run parallel to those of NBW children, albeit clearly at a lower level. During the first 12 weeks NBW boys follow the standard; afterwards the curve deviates. The curve for NBW girls deviates at 18 weeks. The weight curves for LBW children show some degree of catch-up growth during the first months of life, more pronounced in girls than in boys; later both curves run a course below the 80 percent line.

Mean birth length of NBW children is equal or close to standard length; at all other times mean lengths of NBW infants are below standard values. Both boys and girls deviate to a lower level at about 18 weeks. The curve for LBW boys follows the 90 percent line; LBW girls grow at a slightly higher level.

Table 4 shows mean weights and lengths at 52 weeks, as percentages of standards.

The figures show that mean weights of both LBW and NBW boys lag slightly behind those of girls (as percentages of standards) at 52 weeks. Mean length (as percentage of standard) of LBW and NBW males is comparable to that of females.

No differences in weight and length increments per 6-week period (except from 48 to 52 weeks) were found between boys and girls nor between NBW and LBW children. This can be deduced from Figures 3–6, which show that the curves for NBW and LBW infants run a more or less parallel course. Mean weight increments are slightly above the standard (WHO, 1979) from 0–6 and from 6–12 weeks, similar from 12–18 weeks and persistently below thereafter. The picture for length is similar, except that from 0–6 weeks mean length increments are below the standard.

Discussion

Referring once more to Tables 2–4 and Figures 3–6, it is obvious that there are persistent differences in growth; on the other hand, there is no difference in growth velocity between NBW and LBW infants.

As reported earlier, in Chapter 14, weight and length curves of Kamba children start deviating from the standard at about 4 months after birth. Our study shows that both LBW and NBW boys and girls behave in a similar way with respect to weight, but

Table 2.
Estimated mean weights of LBW and NBW infants.

	Boys		
Age (weeks)	*LBW (n=80) Mean (kg)*	*NBW (n=62) Mean (kg)*	$\frac{LBW}{NBW} \times 100$
0	2.26 (0.24)	3.22 (0.36)	70.2
6	3.52 (0.56)	4.57 (0.60)	77.0
12	4.68 (0.78)	5.78 (0.67)	81.0
18	5.51 (0.90)	6.56 (0.91)	84.0
24	6.08 (0.90)	7.29 (0.97)	83.4
30	6.56 (1.00)	7.71 (1.02)	85.1
36	6.84 (1.12)	7.94 (1.11)	86.1
42	7.12 (1.12)	8.16 (1.01)	87.2
48	7.57 (1.09)	8.56 (1.08)	88.4
52	7.71 (0.96)	8.70 (1.01)	88.6

Standard deviations in parentheses.

Table 3.
Estimated mean lengths of LBW and NBW infants.

	Boys		
Age (weeks)	*LBW (n=80) Mean (cm)*	*NBW (n=62) Mean (cm)*	$\frac{LBW}{NBW} \times 100$
0	45.6 (2.8)	50.9 (2.9)	89.6
6	50.1 (2.4)	54.2 (2.6)	92.4
12	54.2 (2.8)	58.6 (2.6)	92.5
18	58.0 (2.9)	61.7 (2.5)	94.0
24	60.7 (3.2)	64.0 (2.4)	94.8
30	62.4 (3.3)	65.7 (2.7)	95.0
36	64.2 (3.0)	67.5 (2.7)	95.1
42	65.9 (3.3)	68.7 (2.7)	95.9
48	67.6 (3.1)	70.5 (2.6)	95.9
52	68.1 (2.9)	71.0 (2.9)	95.9

Standard deviations in parentheses.

where length is concerned, only NBW children deviate, and LBW infants follow the 90 percent line, at least until they are 12 months old. As it cannot be assumed that LBW children suffer less from disease than their counterparts, it is probable that their regular growth is the result of adequate food intake, i.e. adequate for their size and growth rate. On the other hand, in Chapter 13 it was concluded that the reduction in growth rate observed in the second half-year of infancy has a nutritional basis. Energy was the most

Girls		
LBW (n=113) Mean (kg)	NBW (n=97) Mean (kg)	$\frac{LBW}{NBW} \times 100$
2.21 (0.28)	3.08 (0.36)	71.8
3.46 (0.59)	4.26 (0.45)	81.2
4.49 (0.83)	5.29 (0.67)	84.9
5.29 (0.87)	6.15 (0.73)	86.0
5.86 (0.89)	6.74 (0.83)	86.9
6.28 (1.04)	7.20 (0.95)	87.2
6.68 (0.95)	7.55 (0.93)	88.5
7.01 (0.95)	7.89 (1.00)	88.8
7.23 (1.00)	8.12 (1.06)	89.0
7.44 (0.92)	8.32 (1.06)	89.4

Girls		
LBW (n=113) Mean (cm)	NBW (n=97) Mean (cm)	$\frac{LBW}{NBW} \times 100$
45.9 (1.9)	49.1 (3.1)	93.5
50.2 (2.6)	53.2 (2.1)	94.4
53.8 (3.0)	56.7 (2.0)	94.9
57.2 (2.9)	60.2 (2.1)	95.0
59.5 (2.6)	62.3 (1.8)	95.5
61.8 (2.6)	64.3 (2.1)	96.1
63.3 (3.6)	65.8 (2.2)	96.2
65.3 (2.9)	67.3 (2.1)	97.0
66.6 (2.7)	68.9 (2.3)	96.7
67.4 (2.8)	69.8 (2.2)	96.6

Table 4.
Mean weights and lengths as percentages of standards at 52 weeks.

	Boys		Girls	
	Weight (%)	Length (%)	Weight (%)	Length (%)
LBW	75.6	89.5	78.3	90.7
NBW	85.3	93.2	87.6	93.9

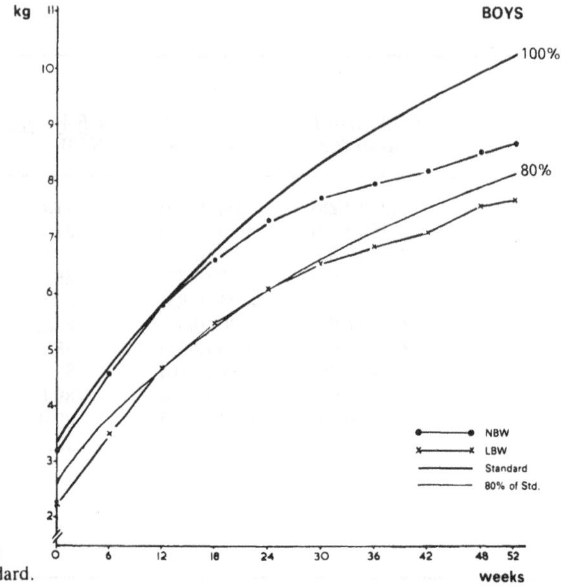

Figure 3. Mean weights of LBW and NBW boys compared with the standard.

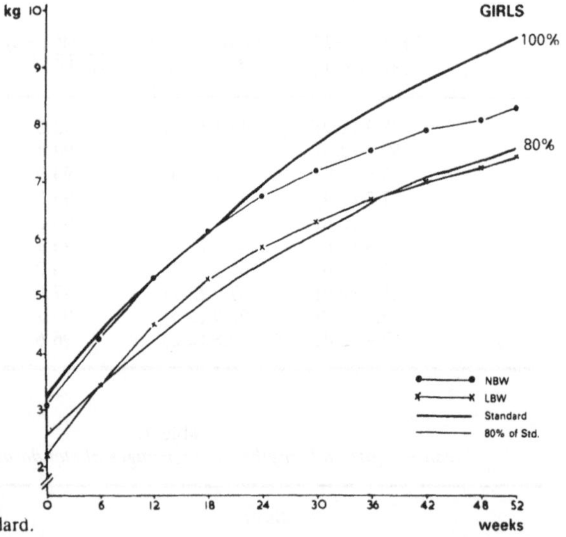

Figure 4. Mean weights of LBW and NBW girls compared with the standard.

limiting factor at age 3–8 months. We also assume that (repeated) infectious disease plays a role, although we do not have hard data to prove (or disprove) that assumption.

It is also possible that our LBW sample is to some extent biased. As mentioned before, 26 LBW children died against only 4 NBW

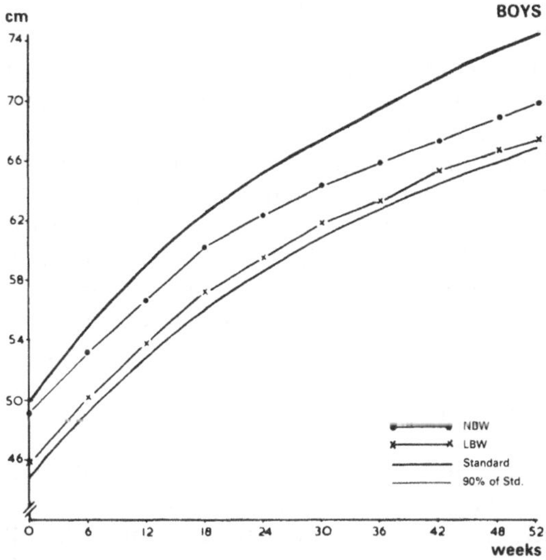

Figure 5. Mean lengths of LBW and NBW boys compared with the standard.

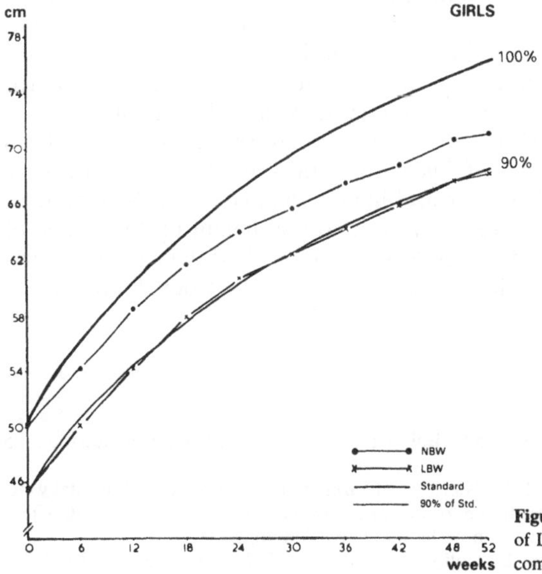

Figure 6. Mean lengths of LBW and NBW girls compared with the standard.

children. It is likely that the strongest and best-growing infants survived.

Ideally, we should have separated premature from small-for-dates infants. For reasons already mentioned—a number of children were born elsewhere or were reported too late when born in the study area—this was not possible. Efforts to teach the female field-workers to distinguish between pre-term and small-for-dates babies met with little success, and the dates of last menstrual periods provided by mothers were not always reliable either. Consequently all LBW babies were pooled.

There was no evidence of catch-up growth in length but LBW infants initially show some degree of catch-up growth in weight. Ultimately NBW children will approach the 80 percent line for weight and the 90 percent line for length (Chapter 14). The LBW children's weight curve crosses the 80 percent line at about 24 weeks in boys and about 36 weeks in girls. To what extent these children are candidates for more severe forms of protein-energy malnutrition remains to be studied. In this respect it is important to note that LBW infants were born to mothers of shorter average stature (Chapter 11).

Differences in physical growth between LBW and NBW children have been reported by others. How long it takes the former to catch up apparently depends on a number of factors. Martell and colleagues (1981) found that differences in weight and length between prematures, small-for-dates and 'normal' children disappeared when the children were on average 18 months old. Toth et al. (1978) found that, 'a significant retardation in weight, stature, head circumference and osseous development of small for gestational age children was observed even at the age of 3 years.'. Neligan et al. (1976) found that premature and small-for-dates children at mean ages of 5 years 8 months, 6½ and 7½ years were 'very significantly' shorter and lighter than controls. Masarone et al. (1977) found differences in weight and height up to the age of 12 years. As some of our children have reached the age of 4 years, further analysis should give an idea about their development.

References

Brooke OG, Butter F, Wood C, Bailey P and Tukmachi FJ, Human Nutrition, 35 (1981) 415.

Martell M, Bertolini LA, Nieto F, Tenzer SM, Ruggia R and Belitzky R, Crecimiento y Desarrollo en los dos primeros años de vida posnatal, Publ Cient No 406, Org Panamericana de la Salud, Washington, 1981.

Masarone M, Amirante E, Collo G and Pessina E, Minerva Pediatr, 29 (1977) 1815.

Neligan GA, Kolvin I, Scott DMcI and Garside RF, Born too soon or born too small, Clinics in Developmental Medicine No 61, Heinemann Ltd, London and Lippincott Co, Philadelphia, 1976.

Toth P, Pecsi S, Szelid Zs, Horvath I, Ferencz B and Mehes K, Acta Paediatr Acad Sci Hung, 19 (1978) 99.

WHO, Measurement of Nutritional Impact, Geneva, 1979.

16

Overview of the nutrition studies

J.A. Kusin
A.A.J. Jansen

It is estimated that in Africa an appreciable proportion of the population continues to live at subsistence levels, well below internationally accepted nutritional requirements. In such populations growth retardation and malnutrition are prevalent among young children; reproductive performance of women is impaired; and continued growth retardation up to adolescence results in stunted physical stature of adults and poor productivity. On the other hand, large segments of the population in poor countries are able to adapt to different environmental circumstances with the preservation of normal functional performance. Taking both aspects into consideration, the basic question to be answered is whether the observed level of nutrition in a given population is detrimental to growth, development and well-being.

The nutrition studies carried out in the period 1974–1981 were non-interventional in nature. Their main object was to record the habitual dietary practices and food intake of biologically vulnerable population groups, as well as their nutritional status and some measures of bodily functions. Such information is of scientific interest, as population-based data available about the interrelationship between maternal and child nutrition are scanty. It also has policy implications for maternal and child health services and nutrition-oriented programmes.

In line with the epidemiological studies of childhood diseases that were carried out in the study area, in 1974–1977 specific attention was paid to the pre-school child. Growth in weight and height were followed longitudinally in a large sample (see Chapter 14); the food consumption (Chapter 13) and breast milk intake of a randomly selected cross-sectional sample were measured; and the chemical composition of mother's milk was analysed (Chapter 12). These studies gave us the opportunity to observe dietary patterns of other household members, the sources of food, and food preparation (Chapter 3).

In 1977 a start was made with the longitudinal study of pregnant women and their offspring as a continuing part of the pregnancy study in relation to outcome of pregnancy and delivery care (Chapter 18). It was terminated in June 1981. During pregnancy serial anthropometric and food-consumption measurements were made at monthly intervals. Birth weight was recorded within 48 hours. Low-birth-weight infants and their (lactating) mothers were followed longitudinally and serial anthropometric and food-consumption measurements were made. A matched group of normal-birth-weight infants and their mothers were followed in a similar manner.

The data are still being analysed. Part of the results on food consumption of pregnant and lactating women are presented in Chapter 10; the pattern of anthropometric measurements in the course of pregnancy and lactation in Chapter 11; growth of low- and normal-birth-weight infants in Chapter 15. It should be noted that the findings of the various investigations are not reported in chronological order.

Salient features

Availability of food

The availability of food is generally governed by individual production and income. In the western part as well as the eastern part of the study area off-farm income contributes significantly to total household income and thus to food availability. Although real famine was not observed during the study period, the eastern part particularly, with less income to spend on food, is vulnerable in periods of crop failure. Due to the marginal potential for agriculture, to uncontrolled fertility, and to relatively low mortality rates, it can be anticipated that food will be short in years to come.

At present the habitual diet is of good quality but low in quantity when compared with recommended intakes. From a policy point of view, a deterioration of the current dietary situation can only be prevented by an increase in off-farm income, improvement of agriculture production, and curtailing of population growth. From the dietary behaviour observed, one can expect that diets will be improved and diversified if incomes rise.

Nutrition during pregnancy and lactation

The discrepancies recorded between the low level of nutrition during pregnancy and lactation and the mothers' remarkable reproductive performance are scientifically intriguing and of great importance as regards policy-making.

As food was not in short supply, mothers can be considered to have been eating to appetite and according to their physiological needs. At energy intakes 20–40 percent below recommended dietary intakes (RDI), fetal growth was efficiently protected as shown by mean birth weights and the relatively low percentage of low birth weights. Breast milk yield during the first 6 months was comparable with that of women in industrialized countries. The fluctuations in maternal weight during pregnancy and lactation illustrate the capacity of the maternal body to compensate for the dietary deficit. Yet, even taking into account these changes in weight, the total energy available is still below that considered necessary to maintain maternal body composition and to support adequate fetal growth and lactation. We were not in a position to conduct energy balance studies under field conditions nor to assess pathways of metabolic adaptation. No answer can thus be given to the question how mothers were able to function in such an efficient way.

As far as other nutrients are concerned, low intakes were recorded for calcium (25–85 percent RDI), iron (40–70 percent RDI), retinol equivalents (20–40 percent RDI) and riboflavine (40–60 percent RDI). As food intakes were measured for 3 years on a monthly basis and results remained consistent, one can reasonably accept that the above figures adequately reflect habitual intakes. Judging from the nutrient concentrations in breast milk, which were lower than the range reported for women in industrialized countries, one can conclude that nutrient intake of Kamba women was indeed less than that of the reference group. However, unpublished data on haemoglobin and serum vitamin A levels in a subsample of women in different physiological states were normal according to international standards. Moreover, clinical signs of nutrient deficiency were seldom diagnosed, except for angular stomatitis which is suggestive of riboflavine deficiency. It is reasonable to assume that peaks in consumption in times of plenty were sufficient to build up reserves to overcome lean seasons, particularly in the case of retinol equivalents.

From the public health point of view these observations justify the conclusion that in this population energy intake from habitual diets is sufficient to support adequate fetal growth and lactation performance with maintenance of maternal health throughout the reproductive cycle. It should be noted that protein intake was at or above RDI. This does not mean that their genetic potential has been achieved: the fact that low-birth-weight infants were on average born to mothers of short stature suggests, however, that it will take a generation or more of good health among girls before their genetic potential can be reached.

In view of the fact that low-birth-weight mothers were leaner than normal-birth-weight mothers, nutrition education should be pursued, stressing the importance of higher energy intakes during the last trimester of pregnancy. It would also be prudent to aim at an improvement of the daily intake of other nutrients, particularly iron and retinol equivalents. This can be achieved by regular consumption of a handful of leafy vegetables per person per day, a measure that can be followed at little or no extra expense.

Nutrition of pre-school children

Apart from pregnant and lactating women, young children are the most affected group in populations with marginal nutrition. Malnutrition is widely prevalent among them due to the interaction of inadequate diet and high morbidity. The main defects are the short duration of breast-feeding and the late introduction of good weaning foods.

In our study population severe malnutrition was rare and occurred mainly in socially deprived households. Growth during the first 6 months of life on average followed Harvard Standards of weight and height for age (W/A and H/A). In the course of the next 6 months W/A dropped to 83 percent and H/A to 92 percent and remained at these levels until the age of 6.

It is interesting to note that infants studied in the project showed good growth performance during the first 6 months, on breast milk supplemented with cow's milk and maize-milk gruels, and also that the breast milk yield of mothers who gave their infants additional food did not fall.

Why did mothers introduce additional food so early when breast milk alone would have been sufficient to maintain adequate growth for 4–6 months? Why was their breast milk yield not negatively influenced by the supplementary feeding? Why was supplementation not followed by a peak in diarrhoea?

Apparently infant-feeding practices are governed by socio-cultural factors as well as the infant's requirements. It is reasonable to assume that the high frequency of suckling was the reason why milk yields remained high. Likewise, it is quite probable that colostrum and mother's milk protected infants against diarrhoea at

Market scenes in Tala and Kinyui.

this age, as Kamba mothers do not follow the WHO recommendation, which is based on the likelihood that earlier supplementation will cause diarrhoea. This practice is not detrimental to the health of their infants. The most vulnerable period appears to be at age 7–12 months, as far as W/A and H/A are concerned. No further deterioration but also no catch-up in growth was observed at age 1–5 years. Weight for height, however, was good at any age suggesting an adaptation to adverse environmental conditions.

Energy intake at age 0–18 months was less than the WHO/FAO recommended intakes but in agreement with intakes of healthy British children. Protein intakes were at or even above recommended levels. It seems, therefore, that only a weak nutritional basis can be found for the observed growth retardation.

No data are available relating growth simultaneously to nutrition and morbidity. As childhood diseases and diarrhoea peak at age 7–18 months, it seems that infectious diseases play a larger role in the process than nutritional inadequacy per se. This aspect should be further explored. From a policy point of view, it can be expected that in this area vaccination programmes and prevention of diarrhoea will be more effective in improving nutritional status of pre-school children than will nutrition programmes. As far as the latter are concerned, emphasis should be put on the type of feeding. The young child, in particular, can only obtain its nutritional needs from local foods when energy in the form of fats is added and when it is allowed to 'nibble' throughout the day instead of eating only at two or three fixed times.

Part V
Perinatal, infant and childhood mortality

17

Age-specific infant and childhood mortality and causes of death

Omondi-Odhiambo
A.M. Voorhoeve
J.K. van Ginneken

Introduction

The study of mortality levels and trends has long occupied demographers and physicians alike. Records of mortality are scanty and unreliable for more than one-third of the world's population in general and Africa in particular. As a result, much of the demographic analysis needed in order to formulate plans for social and economic development is seriously hampered (United Nations, 1955).

In this chapter data on mortality between 1975 and 1978 in the framework of Machakos Project studies are examined. In view of the very close relation between age and risk of death, age is seen in this chapter as the most important demographic variable in the analysis of mortality. The chapter mainly discusses infant and child mortality conditions within the study area and revolves around their age-sex patterns. In particular, neonatal and post-neonatal infant and child mortality rates, which are often considered as significant health indicators of a community, are analysed with respect to their geographical distribution, seasonal variations and, finally, their causes.

Methods and materials

The objectives, design and methodology of the Machakos Project have been outlined in Chapter 1. The first source of information was the demographic surveillance system, which operated in such a manner that whenever a field-worker discovered that someone had died in a household within his assigned cluster, he recorded information on date, place and cause of death in the demographic sheet.

Perinatal and maternal deaths were a subject of a special study. From this second source of information, women who had experienced a stillbirth or had a child that died within the first week of life were visited by one of the doctors in the team and carefully interviewed to determine the most likely cause of death. Likewise, the relatives of a few women who died from complications of pregnancy and/or delivery were interviewed in depth (see Chapter 18).

Causes of death for infants and children between 1 and 5 years of age were also recorded as accurately as possible since this group was the subject of several studies on the epidemiology of communicable childhood diseases such as measles, pertussis and acute diarrhoea (see Chapters 6, 7 and 8). These studies formed the third source of mortality data in the project.

Results

Infant and child mortality rates

Between 1975 and 1978 inclusive, 4768 births were registered. Of these 4627 were live births (2356 males and 2271 females). Within this period a total of 141 stillbirths (85 males and 56 females), 221 perinatal deaths (138 males and 83 females) and 227 infant deaths (125 males and 102 females) were also registered. Table 1 provides data on several types of infant and childhood mortality rates.

While the overall death rate for the 1–4 year age group remained 7.0 per 1000, mortality in the second, third, fourth and fifth years was 10.6, 7.3, 3.8 and 2.5 per 1000 mid-year de jure population respectively. In general, mortality patterns remained remarkably constant in each year of the 4-year period.

Table 1.
Age specific death rates between 1975 and 1978.

	1975	*1976*	*1977*	*1978*	*Total*
Stillbirth rate	29.0	30.6	33.7	25.3	29.6
Perinatal death rate	39.0	48.1	46.9	45.9	46.4
Neonatal death rate	16.4	26.0	22.8	25.9	23.1
Infant mortality rate	38.8	58.7	47.6	55.6	49.1
Child mortality rate (1–4)	6.0	8.7	8.1	5.1	7.0

Note: Stillbirth and perinatal death rates were computed per 1000 births while neonatal and infant mortality rates were computed per 1000 live births. Child death rate (1–4 years) was computed per 1000 mid-year de jure population.

Infant mortality rates by sex for different age intervals up to 3 months after birth for the 1975 to 1978 birth cohorts are shown in Table 2. Mortality was highest within the first 24 hours of life at 9.3 per 1000 followed by a steady decline. This is an indication that there was little if any under-reporting of deaths at specific ages of early infancy. Further evidence will be provided later in the chapter.

Infant mortality rates at 3-monthly intervals are presented in Table 3. Both tables (Tables 2 and 3) indicate that mortality levels were comparatively low and that the rates within most intervals after birth were higher for males than for females, especially in the early neonatal period. No allowance was made in Tables 2 and 3 for the effect of out-migration from the project area. We estimate, however, that between 3 and 6 percent of the infants had already left the study area one year after birth. This means that the denominators for the rates in Tables 2 and 3 are somewhat too large.

The reliability of the data and age pattern of infant mortality

The relationship between neonatal (NN) and post-neonatal (PNN) mortality is known to vary with the level of mortality. At levels of infant mortality in excess of 100 per 1000 about one-third of the infant deaths normally occur in the neonatal period. This finding is based on historical data from Western Europe and on the rationale that infectious diseases, which cause infant deaths primarily in the post-neonatal period, are primarily responsible for high infant mortality rates. The applicability of such an age pattern of mortality in infancy to high-mortality populations in developing areas is now questioned. Recent studies in Bangladesh and Taiwan have found data which differ markedly from those recorded in Western populations. For the period from 1967 to 1969, when the infant mortality rate was 125 per 1000, Stoeckel and Chowdhury (1972) found that 60 percent of infant deaths in Bangladesh occurred in the neonatal period. For Taiwan in the period between 1905 and 1945, at infant mortality levels in excess of 100 per 1000, approximately 45 percent of infant deaths occurred in the neonatal period (Sullivan, 1975).

At infant mortality levels well below 100, it is usually found that neonatal mortality becomes the most important component of infant mortality. This can be seen in data from European countries, and from Taiwan and Sri Lanka. In Taiwan, for instance, at infant mortality levels of 60 to 40 about 65 percent of infant deaths are in the neonatal period. This change in proportion of neonatal to post-neonatal mortality occurs because the post-neonatal rate declines faster than the neonatal rate (Sullivan, 1975). Likewise in Sri

Table 2.
Infant mortality rates (IMR) per 1000 survivors, by sex, for different age intervals up to 3 months after birth, birth cohorts: 1975–1978.

	Male			*Female*			*Total*		
Age interval (in months)	*Deaths*	*n*	*Rate*	*Deaths*	*n*	*Rate*	*Deaths*	*n*	*Rate*
Within 24 hours	28	2356	11.0	15	2271	6.6	43	4627	9.3
2nd to 7th day	25	2328	10.7	12	2256	5.3	37	4584	8.1
2nd, 3rd, 4th week	14	2303	6.1	13	2244	5.8	27	4547	5.9
2nd, 3rd month	11	2289	4.8	13	2231	5.8	24	4520	5.3
Total	78	2356	33.1	53	2271	23.3	131	4627	28.3

Table 3.
Infant mortality rates (IMR) per 1000 survivors, by sex, for different age intervals up to 1 year after birth, birth cohorts 1975–1978.

	Male			*Female*			*Total*		
Age interval (in months)	*Deaths*	*n*	*Rate*	*Deaths*	*n*	*Rate*	*Deaths*	*n*	*Rate*
0 to 3	78	2356	33.1	53	2271	23.3	131	4627	28.3
3 to 6	14	2278	6.1	12	2218	5.4	26	4496	5.8
6 to 9	18	2264	8.0	24	2206	10.9	42	4470	9.4
9 to 12	15	2246	6.7	13	2182	6.0	28	4428	6.3
Total	125	2356	53.1	102	2271	49.9	227	4627	49.1

Table 4.
Infant mortality rates, by age (Machakos Project and selected countries).*

Country	*Period*	*Infant mortality rate*	*Neonatal** mortality rate*	*Post-neonatal mortality rate*	*Percentage of deaths in the neonatal period*
Machakos Project	1975–78	49.1	23.1	25.9	47
Taiwan	1930	151.1	69.2	81.9	46
Taiwan	1966–68	40.4	26.7	13.7	66
United States	1943	37.5	23.7	13.8	63
Scotland	1952	35.2	21.7	13.5	62
England & Wales	1948	33.9	19.7	14.2	58
Norway	1946–50	31.1	16.0	15.1	51

* Per 1000 live births
**Neonatal period defined as 0–27 days
Source: Adapted from Sullivan (1975), pp. 42 and 68

Lanka, at a level of infant mortality of 50 per 1000 live births, neonatal mortality constitutes 57 percent of infant mortality (a neonatal rate of 29.1 and a post-neonatal rate of 21.9 in 1974) (Meegama, 1980).

In the study area we found a neonatal rate of 23.1 per 1000 live births and a post-neonatal rate of 25.9 per 1000. Forty-seven percent of the infant mortality was neonatal at an overall infant mortality level of 49.1 per 1000. This figure of 47 percent is lower than that found in studies in Western and Asian countries, as Table 4 shows.

There are two possible explanations: the low neonatal rates could be an indication of under-reporting of neonatal deaths (this is usually commoner than under-reporting of post-neonatal deaths); alternatively, experience in Machakos could be different from that in other developing areas of the world. We do not have firm grounds on which to decide between these two possibilities but in our opinion the chances that neonatal deaths were under-reported are small, in view of the data-collection procedures, described earlier, that were used.

Mortality rates by sublocations

Mortality rates up to the age of 2 years in the five sublocations of the project area, are given in Table 5. This indicates that there are geographical variations in mortality in the project area. Although

Table 5.
Age-specific death rates by sublocation, 1975–1978.

	Kingoti	*Kambusu*	*Katheka*	*Ulaani*	*Katitu*	*Total*
Stillbirth rate	27.8	35.3	31.1	29.1	23.4	29.6
Neonatal death rate	16.3	29.3	35.5	25.3	17.4	23.1
Infant mortality rate	36.9	53.1	68.8	61.3	43.7	49.1
Second-year death rate	8.9	12.8	22.9	6.1	8.5	10.6

Note: The stillbirth death rate was computed per 1000 births; neonatal and infant mortality rates per 1000 live births; and second-year death rate per 1000 mid-year de jure population.

Table 6.
Infant and child mortality by season: 1975–1978.

	Total deaths		*Deaths between 1–11 months*		*Deaths between 1–4 years*	
Season	*n*	*Deaths per month*	*n*	*Deaths per month*	*n*	*Deaths per month*
Dry Feb.–March	54	27	23	12	17	8.5
Wet (long rains) April–June	102	34	38	13	31	10
Dry July–Oct.	95	24	30	8	34	8.5
Wet (short rains) Nov.–Jan.	79	26	29	10	21	7
Total	330	111	120	43	103	34

Note: Figures in the third and fifth columns do not add up to those in the first column because neonatal deaths were excluded from this table.

the results are not always consistent, rates tended to be lower in the western part (Kingoti and Kambusu) than in the eastern part (Katheka, Ulaani and Katitu). This is in particular true for mortality rates in the post-neonatal period.

The stillbirth rate was highest in Kambusu, a relatively prosperous area, while the other sublocations all had virtually the same rate. Neonatal, infant and child mortality rates on the other hand were somewhat higher in the less prosperous sublocations—Katheka, Ulaani and Katitu—than in more prosperous Kingoti and Kambusu, although the differences were not consistent.

Mortality rates by season

Four seasons can be distinguished in Machakos District. These are the dry season, which comes between the middle of January and the middle of March; a wet season from the middle of March to the end of June, marked by the long rains; a dry season falling between July and the middle of October; and a wet season starting from the middle of October and ending in the middle of January, marked by the short rains.

Unlike in other African countries, where death rates change profoundly with season (see McGregor et al., 1979), analysis of mortality data in Table 6 indicates that mortality did not vary seasonally in the study area. Differences in the number of deaths in the four seasons distinguished above were not statistically significant using the chi-square test.

Causes of death among infants and children

Table 7 lists the percentage distribution of infant and child mortality for the 330 cases recorded between 1975 and 1978, by cause and by age, subdivided into neonatal, post-neonatal and childhood deaths.

Table 7 shows that birth injuries (asphyxia) and prematurity (low birth weight) were the leading causes of death in the first 28 days of life. The table further shows a general shift in the causes of death with advancing age. Gastroenteritis and pneumonia were the most common causes of death among infants during the post-neonatal period. Pneumonia was a prominent cause of death between 1 and 5 months, while the peak for gastroenteritis appeared between 6 and 11 months.

At childhood ages 1–4 years, a strikingly high percentage of deaths was caused by measles. Malnutrition was also found to be a leading cause of death between 1 and 4 years. The figures of Table 7 differ slightly from those reported in Chapters 6–8. We based our diagnosis almost entirely on the history as obtained from the family and this procedure was not the same as that described for the diagnosis of measles, whooping cough and diarrhoea in Chapters 6, 7 and 8.

Table 7.
Percentage distribution of infant and child mortality by cause and age, 1975–1978.

Causes of death	*Neonatal deaths 0–28 days (n=107)*	*Post-neonatal deaths 1–11 months (n=120)*	*Childhood deaths 1–4 years (n=103)*	*Total (n=330)*
Asphyxia	26.2	—	—	8.2
Prematurity (low birth weight)	23.3	0.8	—	7.6
Infection (in neonatal period)	8.7	—	—	2.7
Congenital anomalies	5.8	1.6	—	2.4
Pneumonia	17.5	28.2	12.6	20.0
Gastroenteritis	2.9	39.6	13.6	20.0
Measles	—	13.7	32.1	15.2
Pertussis	—	3.2	2.9	2.1
Malnutrition	1.0	2.4	16.5	6.4
Malaria (fever)	—	3.2	9.7	4.2
Accidents (burns)	—	0.8	2.9	1.2
Tuberculosis	—	—	5.8	1.8
Unknown	14.6	6.5	3.9	8.2
Total	100.0	100.0	100.0	100.0

Discussion and conclusions

The infant mortality rate of 49 per 1000 live births found in the study area is lower than those found in two recent Kenya national sample surveys (which found rates of 83 and 96 per 1000 respectively). (CBS, Kenya, 1979; Henin et al., 1979). Further, the ratio of neonatal to post-neonatal deaths in the first year after birth was also unusually low. We believe these figures are correct for several reasons: first, the 2-week recall period used in this longitudinal study was short; secondly the field-workers were closely supervised; and thirdly, the results of the demographic surveillance were cross-checked whenever necessary with those of the outcome of pregnancy study.

Overall, there are various possible reasons for these findings. First, the ecology and environment: normally, environmental conditions have an important effect on mortality rates, depending on whether or not the environment is favourable to various disease organisms and their vectors. The study area is at an altitude of 1200–1700 m, which provides a fairly healthy climate in which many of the tropical diseases such as malaria and cholera are uncommon, although others such as bilharzia and tuberculosis may be common. The two rainy seasons a year in the area mean that food is probably in better supply than in otherwise similar areas of Kenya. This partly explains the reasonably good nutritional status of infants, children and women. Breast-feeding is universal in the area and the majority of children are suckled for at least a year (see Chapters 12 and 14).

Birth weights and obstetric practices in the area are a second reason. Infants of 2500 g or less at birth have normally a much higher mortality than those of higher birth weights. In the Project area the mean birth weight was 3100 g, and only 10 percent of newborns were 2500 g or below.

A third possible reason was the fact that modern medical facilities, although not immediately available, are not far away. In the event of obstruction of labour occurring at home, it is possible for a woman to be carried the maximum of 20-odd kilometres to the nearest hospital. Furthermore, pregnancy and childbirth are regarded as natural events and the attendants interfere very little. Neonatal tetanus, notably, did not occur at all in the area during the study period (see Chapter 18).

The favourable economic, social and hygiene conditions in the area, compared with other parts of Kenya with similar topography and ecological environment, provide another reason (see Chapters 2 and 4). Furthermore, a considerable number of households enjoyed a substantial non-agricultural contribution to their income from remittances from husbands or relatives working in Nairobi or elsewhere in Kenya (see Chapter 2).

Finally, the medical activities of the Machakos Project in the area probably helped to lower infant and child mortality, though this definitely did not happen to any great extent, as any interventions by the project staff were on a modest scale. Moreover, infant and child mortality were already low when the project started (see Chapter 5).

In summary, we believe that the low infant and child mortality rates recorded in this rural area of Kenya are true and the explanation for them must be sought in a combination of favourable conditions that outweighs co-existent adverse factors.

References

Central Bureau of Statistics, Kenya Fertility Survey: major highlights, Ministry of Economic Planning and Community Affairs, Kenya, 1979.

Henin RA, Mott F and Mott S, Recent demographic trends in Kenya and their implication for economic and social environment, unpublished manuscript, Population Studies and Research Institute, University of Nairobi, Kenya, 1979.

McGregory IA, Williams K, Billewicz WZ and Holliday R, Mortality in a rural west African village (Keneba) with special reference to deaths occurring in the first five years of life, a paper presented at the Conference of Medical Aspects of African Demography, Cambridge, UK, September 17–18, 1979.

Stoeckel J and Chowdhury AKM, Neonatal and postneonatal mortality in a rural area of Bangladesh, Population Studies, 26 (1972) 113–120.

Sullivan JM, The influence of demographic and socio-economic factors on infant mortality in Taiwan, 1966–68, Academia Economic Paper, Vol. 3, No. 1, 1975, pp. 35–69.

United Nations, Age and sex patterns of mortality: model life-tables for underdeveloped countries, ST/SOA/Series A/22, United Nations, New York, 1955.

18

The outcome of pregnancy

A.M. Voorhoeve
A.S. Muller
H. W'Oigo

Introduction

Little is known about the fate of pregnant women in rural Africa who deliver at home. Hospital statistics tend to exaggerate perinatal and maternal mortality figures owing to an excess of patients arriving late with complications. Only about 20 percent of women in rural areas in Kenya, however, deliver in hospital (WHO, 1975) and it is not clear whether the remaining 80 percent are better or worse off. It is important for the planning of maternal and child health services in rural areas to know exactly what the specific problem is in terms of maternal, perinatal and infant mortality. Trained health personnel and resources are scarce in rural areas in Africa and for that reason it is expedient to concentrate available facilities on women at special risk of complications of pregnancy and delivery.

This chapter deals with the outcome of pregnancy of women in the 25 000 population of the Machakos project area, 60 km east of Nairobi, Kenya, who delivered in the 4-year period 1975 to 1978.

Materials and methods

The basis of the present study was the surveillance system comprising fortnightly home visits to 4000 households by 12 field-workers who collected demographic data on all household members and disease information on all children under the age of 5 years. Few adults among the study population knew their precise age and this often had to be estimated by use of a calendar of local events; for adult women the age of the eldest child was often the best guide to age.

When a woman was observed to be pregnant the field-worker was instructed to fill out a questionnaire covering previous pregnancies and deliveries, intentions as to where to deliver and any complaints related to the pregnancy. Height was measured standing against a straight wall or doorpost, by headboard and tape measure. As a digit preference was found for 0 and 5 the height groups for the analysis were chosen in such a way that figures ending with 0 and 5 fell in the middle of each group.

Women considered by the field-worker to be seriously ill were reported to the project's medical staff. They were then either visited at home or seen at one of the weekly referral clinics and advised and treated on the spot, or if necessary referred to the nearest hospital for further investigation and treatment.

Most women who gave birth at home were assisted by one of some 30 traditional midwives in the area. These were usually elderly women known for their special skill and experience. Some of them were also herbalists. None of them had any medical training. Other women were assisted during home delivery by a relative, usually the mother or mother-in-law, sometimes by the husband or a neighbour. Many women gave birth completely on their own.

Formally trained midwives and doctors were only to be found in health centres and hospital. Uncomplicated deliveries in hospital were normally attended by a midwife, a doctor or medical assistant only being called in when difficulties arose.

When a delivery had taken place the field-worker filled out another form with questions about the recent delivery and the care received. If a field-worker had failed to observe the pregnancy of a woman both questionnaires were filled out after delivery. In cases of hospital delivery the birth weight of the child was copied from the hospital files. During the last 2 years of the study the field-workers weighed babies born at home as soon as possible after birth, using a portable Salter scale and basket.

The majority of women, irrespective of whether they delivered at home or in hospital, went at least once during their pregnancy to the antenatal clinic at the nearest hospital.

Women whose pregnancy ended in a stillbirth or a child that died within the first week of life were interviewed and examined by the first author in order to try to establish the most likely cause of the perinatal death. An attempt was made to trace the hospital files relating to perinatal deaths in hospital, but usually these files gave little additional information, as no post mortems were done. Histories obtained from mothers never differed from those obtained from the hospital except in minor details, and they gave a more complete picture of what had really happened. Information on the four maternal deaths was obtained from the family and the hospitals where they occurred.

The majority of the field staff were male. They were instructed to ask whether a woman was willing to answer the questions to them or whether she would rather be interviewed by a female colleague; only occasionally was this requested.

Women can be married according to Kamba custom, with an exchange of bride price, or in church, or by a combination of the two; marriages may be either monogamous or polygamous. Many young women conceive and give birth before marriage: although this is frowned upon by the older generation it does not diminish their chances of making a good marriage. The unmarried mother usually remains with her parents and the child is brought up as one of her siblings. A considerable number of women whose husbands had jobs in Nairobi, Thika or Machakos Town joined their husbands near the time of delivery, gave birth to their baby in one of the hospitals in these towns and returned to the study area after a couple of weeks.

The present study included all women who delivered between 1 January 1975 and 31 December 1978 after a gestation of at least 28 weeks and who belonged to the study population at the time of delivery, regardless of whether delivery took place in or outside the study area, but those who delivered outside the study area and did not return within a year after delivery were excluded.

Results

The total number of children born was 4768, including 52 pairs of twins (one per 91 deliveries). The crude birth rate was 43.6 per 1000 population per year. The total fertility rate for women 15–49 years of age was 7.3 children per woman. The sex ratio was 1.04 (2356 live-born males/2271 live-born females). Table 1 summarizes a number of relevant rates.

Seasonal differences

The months with the highest number of births were September and October, followed by November and March. No systematic differences in stillbirths or neonatal and infant death rates were discernible between the monthly birth cohorts for successive years. When the 4 years are taken together a significantly higher infant death rate is found, however, for children born in January compared with other months ($p<0.001$). There was no difference in outcome between deliveries following the lean months preceding the harvest of maize and beans (January, June) and the deliveries following the harvest period when staple food is plentiful.

Age and parity of the mother

Table 2 provides data on stillbirth, neonatal death and infant death rates per 5-year age group of the mother. The age group 25–34 years had the lowest stillbirth rate; the difference from the younger age groups was not significant at the 5 percent level, but the difference from the older age groups was highly significant

Table 1.
Outcome of pregnancy for 1975–1978.

Totals	*n*		*Rates*
Total children born	4768		
Number of live births	4627	Crude birth rate	43.6/1000 population/year
Late foetal deaths*	141	Stillbirth rate	29.6/1000 total births
Perinatal deaths**	221	Perinatal mortality	46.4/1000 total births
Neonatal deaths***	107	Neonatal mortality	23.1/1000 live births
Infant deaths****	227	Infant mortality	49.1/1000 live births
Maternal deaths	4	Maternal mortality	0.8/1000 deliveries

* stillbirths
** first-week deaths + stillbirths
*** first-month deaths
****first-year deaths

Table 2.
Stillbirths, neonatal deaths and infant deaths by age group of the mother.

Age group	*Total no. of births*	*Live births n*	*Still-births per 1000**	*Neonatal deaths per 1000***	*1–11 months deaths per 1000***	*Survival to 1 year per 1000**
10–14	11	11	—	91	91	818
15–19	575	557	31	27	25	918
20–24	1497	1453	29	24	27	921
25–29	1129	1107	19	23	24	934
30–34	645	630	23	22	33	922
35–39	554	526	51	21	23	908
40–44	239	231	33	26	13	929
45–49	118	112	51	—	27	924
Total	4768	4627	30	23	26	923

* of total births
**of live births

($p<0.001$). No significant differences were found for neonatal and infant death rates.

Stillbirth, neonatal death and infant death rates are given by parity in Table 3. The ultimate outcome was least favourable for nulliparae ($p<0.05$). The differences among the parous women were not significant.

Tables 4 and 5 give the perinatal death rate and the ultimate survival to the age of one respectively, by maternal age and parity.

Table 3.
Stillbirths, neonatal deaths and infant deaths by parity of the mother.

Parity	*Total no. of births*	*Live births n*	*Still-births per 1000**	*Neonatal deaths per 1000***	*1–11 months deaths per 1000***	*Survival to 1 year per 1000**
0	990	957	33	32	33	903
1–2	1440	1403	26	19	21	935
3–5	1229	1201	23	22	30	926
6–9	938	903	37	21	32	920
10+	171	163	47	25	12	918
Total	4768	4627	30	23	26	923

* of total births
**of live births

Table 4.
Perinatal death rates by age and parity of the mother (number of births in brackets).

	Perinatal deaths				
Age group	*Parity 0 per 1000**	*Parity 1–2 per 1000**	*Parity 3–5 per 1000**	*Parity 6–9 per 1000**	*Parity 10+ per 1000**
<20	49 (487)	61 (98)	1000 (1)	—	—
20–24	66 (454)	40 (894)	41 (148)	— (1)	—
25–29	77 (39)	42 (408)	33 (629)	38 (52)	1000 (1)
30–34	250 (8)	— (32)	28 (316)	39 (283)	— (6)
35–39	— (1)	— (5)	70 (115)	58 (380)	75 (53)
40+	— (1)	— (3)	50 (20)	54 (222)	45 (111)
Total	60 (990)	41 (1440)	37 (1229)	50 (938)	58 (171)

*of total births

Table 5.
Survival to age one by age and parity of the mother.

	Survival till the age of 1 year				
Age group	*Parity 0 per 1000**	*Parity 1–2 per 1000**	*Parity 3–5 per 1000**	*Parity 6–9 per 1000**	*Parity 10+ per 1000**
<20	918	918	—	—	—
20–24	892	937	912	1000	—
25–29	897	931	941	923	—
30–34	750	1000	924	919	833
35–39	1000	800	887	916	906
40+	—	1000	900	928	937
Total	903	935	926	920	918

*of total births

The numbers for the separate parities in each age group are small but it is interesting to note that the perinatal death rate for first births is lowest for women under the age of 20, while for subsequent births the age group 20–34 has the lowest perinatal death rate. A sharp increase occurs after the age of 34 years. Among those with the highest survival rate to the age of one were the children from mothers aged 40 years and over with at least 10 children.

High parity family.

Maternal height

Among 4429 women who were measured (93 percent) the mean height was 157.3 cm (standard deviation 6.1 cm, range 136–176 cm with the exception of two crippled women measuring 129 and 130 cm). The mean height for women who experienced a stillbirth, or neonatal or infant death was 157.2 cm (standard deviation 4.8 cm). Table 6 summarizes the perinatal deaths, survival to the age of one, and the number of caesarean sections among women, by height.

The perinatal death rate among women with a height of 163 cm and above was lower than among women with a height less than 163 cm ($p<0.05$). Women with heights less than 148 cm had similar perinatal and infant death rates to those of 148–162 cm but needed a caesarean section more often ($p<0.001$). Women over 162 cm were about the same age as the whole study group. There was no indication that the girls today in the study area are taller than their mothers.

Marital status

Nineteen percent of the women were unmarried and 4 percent were widowed, divorced or separated. The perinatal death rate among unmarried women was significantly higher (62 per 1000)

Table 6.
Perinatal deaths, survival to age one and prevalence of caesarean section by height of the mother.

Height in cm.	*Total no. of births*	*Perinatal deaths per 1000**	*Survival to 1 year per 1000**	*Caesarean section per 1000**
≤142	42	24	929	71
143–147	124	89	887	40
148–152	748	59	922	23
153–157	1327	52	916	11
158–162	1377	46	923	4
163–167	631	32	929	3
168–172	149	34	946	—
173+	31	32	935	—
Unknown	339	21	941	12
Total	4768	46	923	11

*of total births

than among the married (42 per 1000) ($p<0.05$). The rate for widowed, divorced and separated women (49 per 1000) did not differ significantly from that of married women. The infant death rate after the first week of life showed no differences between these categories.

Previous obstetric experience

Table 7 summarizes the outcome of pregnancy in terms of perinatal deaths and survival to age one, by parity, for women who had and had not experienced a pevious perinatal death. The proportion of women who had previously lost a child in the perinatal period increased from 7.1 percent among those who were para-1 to 63.2 percent among those who were para-10+.

The perinatal death rate was significantly lower and the survival rate to one year significantly higher among the children of mothers who had not experienced a previous perinatal death ($p<0.01$). This difference was present only among the lower parities (1–4), however. Whether or not previous children had died after the first week of life did not influence the outcome of the present pregnancy.

Only one perinatal death occurred among 71 women who had had one or more caesarean sections previously; 19 of them (27 percent) had a caesarean section again in the present pregnancy. Among women who had had only previous vaginal deliveries, 0.6

Table 7.
Perinatal deaths and survival to age one for women with and without previous perinatal deaths.

		Women without previous perinatal deaths			*Women with previous perinatal deaths*		
Parity	*Total no. of births*	*No. of births n*	*Perinatal deaths per 1000*	*Survival to 1 yr per 1000*	*No. of births n*	*Perinatal deaths per 1000*	*Survival till 1 yr per 1000*
1	791	735	31	946	56	71	911
2	649	578	43	933	71	99	873
3	501	426	33	927	75	67	893
4	394	314	38	936	80	100	863
5	334	262	19	939	72	28	944
6	294	229	61	904	65	15	923
7	294	222	27	964	72	28	931
8	216	141	57	922	75	40	867
9	134	66	106	894	68	88	882
10+	171	63	48	953	108	65	907
Totals	3778	3036	39	935	742	61	899

percent had a caesarean section in the present pregnancy, as did 1.2 percent of primigravidae. Previous vacuum extraction or forceps delivery did not influence either the outcome of the present pregnancy or the mode of delivery. No symphysiotomies were performed.

Complaints during pregnancy

Table 8 lists the various complaints during pregnancy and associated perinatal deaths. Abdominal pain was by far the most common complaint, but this had no predictive value as to the outcome of pregnancy, nor did any of the other complaints. Table 9 lists the various diagnoses made by either project or hospital medical staff in women referred by field-workers because of more serious illness. Anaemia and malaria were usually diagnosed on clinical grounds by the project staff and treated with iron, folic acid and chloroquine. The other diagnoses were made by hospital-based staff. Urinary tract infection and tuberculosis carried a considerably raised perinatal mortality, but the numbers were small. It should be stressed that Tables 8 and 9 only include complaints and diseases that came to field-workers' attention; only once during pregnancy, when filling out the questionnaire, did the field-workers specifically ask for complaints. Many more complaints

Table 8.
Perinatal deaths of children from mothers with various complaints.

Complaint	*No. of births* *n*	*Perinatal deaths* *n*	*per 1000**
Abdominal pain	553	30	54
Backache	61	4	66
Weakness	58	2	34
Vomiting	21	—	
Swollen legs	15	1	67
Varicose veins	7	—	
Fever	39	3	77
Vaginal bleeding	9	—	
Others	66	2	30
No complaints	3939	179	45
Total	4768	221	46

*of those with the respective complaint

Table 9.
Perinatal deaths of children by disease of the mother.

	No. of births *n*	*Perinatal deaths* *n*	*per 1000**
Toxaemia of pregnancy	5	—	
Urinary tract infection	9	2	222
Anaemia	52	3	58
Malaria	6	—	
Tuberculosis	7	2	286
Heart disease	3	—	
Others	49	2	41
No disease diagnosed	4637	212	46
Total	4768	221	46

*of those with the respective disease

would undoubtedly have been found if they had been regularly and systematically sought.

Birth interval

By birth interval is meant the number of months between the previous live or stillbirth, after a pregnancy of at least 28 weeks, and the present delivery. Figure 1 gives the outcome of pregnancy by

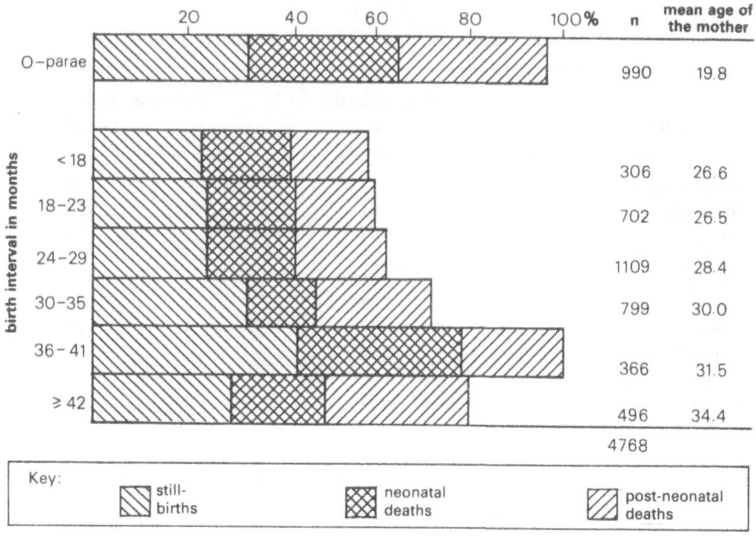

Figure 1. Outcome of pregnancy for successive birth-interval groups.

birth interval. A relatively high proportion of mothers with a birth interval less than 18 months had had a previous stillbirth or death of a child in the first few months of life, and consequently had a higher chance of another perinatal death. Nevertheless, as a group, these women had the same perinatal and infant death rates as those with a longer birth interval. The increase in death rate with birth interval is probably mainly an effect of age: pregnancies among older women were on the whole more widely spaced.

Place of delivery

There were 3459 home confinements (72.5 percent), with a still-birth rate of 23 per 1000; and 1290 (27.1 percent) in hospital, with a stillbirth rate of 44 per 1000. Neonatal and infant death rates were slightly less among the children born at home. Nineteen women gave birth on the way to or from a hospital, with four stillbirths and one first-week death.

Attendants at birth

Figure 2 shows the outcome of pregnancy according to who helped at the delivery. No statistically significant differences were found between stillbirth or neonatal death rates for deliveries attended by a modern trained midwife, a traditional midwife or a relative, or those which took place without any help. The high mortality

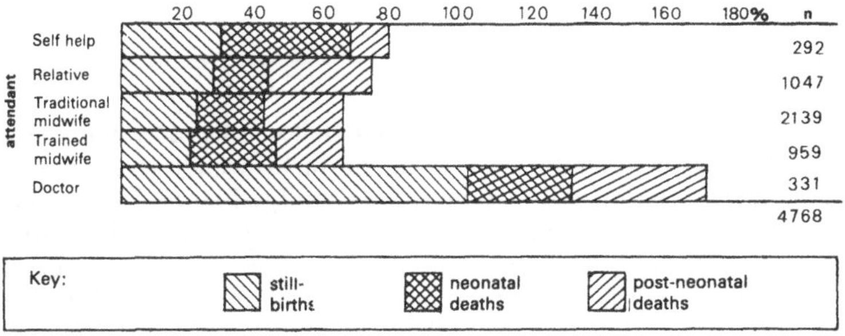

Figure 2. Outcome of pregnancy according to the attendant at birth.

accompanying deliveries attended by doctors is understandable considering the fact that these were complicated cases referred by either trained or traditional midwives.

Mode of birth

Among 58 breech deliveries, 29 babies were stillborn and 4 died during the first week of life. The resulting perinatal death rate of 569 per 1000 was 14 times the rate of 40 per 1000 for vertex deliveries. Caesarean section, forceps and vacuum extraction also carried high perinatal death rates but were often performed on an already compromised fetus. Of the 33 breech deliveries who died perinatally, 27 died due to delay in delivery of the head. Breech deliveries had a better chance of survival when delivery was in hospital.

Length of gestation

The length of gestation was known with reasonable accuracy in 1049 pregnancies. This was not an unbiased sample because women who gave birth to a low-birth-weight infant or experienced a perinatal death had a higher chance of being questioned more closely about the length of gestation. Among 27 children with a gestational age of less than 34 weeks, 18 (667 per 1000) died, all before the end of the first month. Among 122 children with a gestational age of 34–37 weeks 13 (107 per 1000) died before the end of the first month and 4 more during the first year. A gestational age of 38–41 weeks resulted in a combined stillbirth and neonatal death rate of 57 per 1000. Among 93 children with a gestation of 42 weeks or more 13 (140 per 1000) died, all during the first week of life.

Birth weight

Birth weights measured within the first 48 hours were available for 1091 live-born singletons. The mean birth weight was 3133 g (standard deviation 467 g, range 1000–5100 g. Figure 3 gives the neonatal and infant death rates by 500 g weight intervals. Three children weighed less than 1500 g: all three were alive at the age of one year. The difference between the first three groups is significant at the 5 percent level. Only 17 stillbirths were weighed, all born in hospital: their mean birth weight was 3024 g. The mean birth weight of 34 twins was 2309 g; there were six neonatal and four infant deaths among them.

Sex of the child

Stillbirth and neonatal death rates were higher for males than for females. The post-neonatal death rate was the same for males and females.

Causes of death

Table 10 lists the causes and associated circumstances of stillbirths, neonatal and infant deaths. Five groups can be discerned. The first is a group with mechanical obstruction during the second stage of labour; it includes the largest group of stillbirths and is, moreover, the one most accessible to obstetric intervention. The second

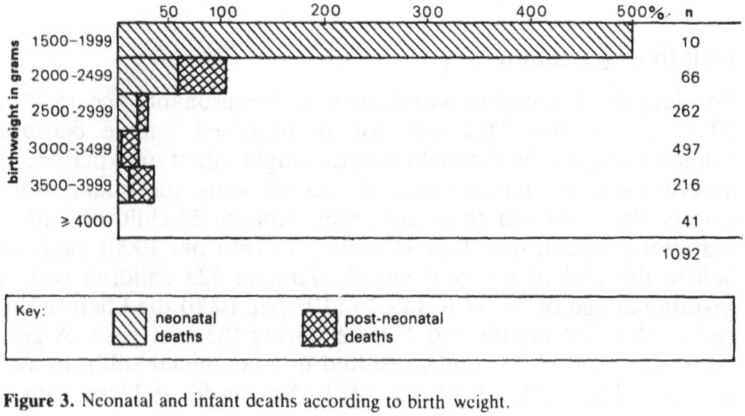

Figure 3. Neonatal and infant deaths according to birth weight.

Table 10.
Causes and associated circumstances of stillbirths, neonatal and infant deaths.

		SB	*ND*	*PND*
I	Complications of labour in mature infants:	65	20	—
	Prolonged labour	35	14	—
	Breech delivery	23	2	—
	Cord prolapse	7	—	—
	Aspiration	—	4	—
II	Low birthweight, APH, maternal illness:	35	30	1
	Low birthweight eci	10	10	—
	Prematurity eci	4	4	1
	Twin pregnancy	2	10	—
	Ante partum haemorrhage	11	2	—
	Maternal illness*	8	4	—
III	Infection and malnutrition:	—	31	91
	Pneumonia	—	16	31
	Gastro-enteritis	—	2	40
	Meningitis/sepsis	—	12	—
	Measles	—	—	11
	Pertussis	—	—	3
	Malaria	—	—	4
	Malnutrition	—	1	2
IV	Congenital malformations:	11	7	2
	Anencephaly	3	—	—
	Hydrocephalus	5	5	—
	Spina bifida	2	—	—
	Cardiac anomalies	—	—	2
	Others**	1	2	—
V	Unknown and accidental:	30	19	26
	Unknown	30	16	25
	Accidental***	—	3	1
Totals		141	107	120

* toxaemia of pregnancy, schistosomiasis mansoni, malaria, tuberculosis, pyelocystitis.
** Siamese twins, oesophageal atresia
***cold exposure, cord bleeding, suffocation, burns

group is a group of ill-defined, often interrelated, causes and symptoms originating from either placental insufficiency or maternal infection. Even with the most sophisticated antenatal screening and treatment the majority of these children would probably have died.

The third group, infection and malnutrition, was responsible for the largest number of infant deaths after the first month. Respiratory infections caused by far the majority of deaths among very young infants, gastroenteritis becoming commoner after the second month. The fourth group, congenital anomalies, consisted only of gross abnormalities, mostly of central nervous system development. It should be emphasized that no post-mortem examinations were performed and some malformations of internal organs are probably included in the fifth group of unknown and accidental causes.

Maternal deaths

There were four maternal deaths: an 18-year-old primipara who had an uncomplicated delivery of a healthy male child in hospital died 2 weeks later, presumably from puerperal sepsis; a woman who had had two previous uncomplicated pregnancies died from a cerebrovascular accident suddenly when 7 months pregnant; an 8-month-pregnant mother of six died in shock after a chloroquine injection; and a 21-year-old primipara was operated on for obstructed labour but died a week later from renal complications.

Discussion

Accurate and comprehensive information on fetal and infant mortality is only available for a minority of the world population. Information on mortality in African countries is usually obtained from retrospective surveys and tends to underrate fetal and infant mortality owing to the tendency to suppress unpleasant memories. There is often confusion over definitions, stillbirths being confused with abortions as well as with early neonatal deaths. In the present study we are confident that we have recorded the outcome of pregnancy in registered women who reached a gestation of at least 28 weeks with a great degree of accuracy.

A few women may have left the study area without anybody knowing that they were pregnant, delivered a stillbirth or a baby who subsequently died and returned to the area without telling anyone, but the field-workers, living in the area and visiting all households every fortnight, would usually have heard some rumour of such an event.

While the birth and fertility rates found in the present study are well within the range found in other tropical African countries, the death rates are surprisingly low. The estimated infant mortality for the whole of Kenya declined from 114 per 1000 live births in 1969 to 104 in 1973 (CBS, 1973) and most surveys between 1950 and 1972 in tropical African countries reported infant death rates between 100 and 200 per 1000 live births, though Gabon, Guinea and Niger reported rates under 100 (WHO, 1976). In European countries the infant death rate ranges from 12.6 per 1000 live births in Sweden to 64.7 in Portugal, half of all infant deaths occurring in the first week of life. Perinatal deaths in 1966 in Europe ranged from 19 per 1000 live births in Sweden to 43.6 in Portugal and were made up in most countries of equal numbers of stillbirths and first-week deaths (WHO, 1969). Non-abortional maternal mortality in Europe in 1974 ranged from 3.2 per 100 000 live births in Finland to 40.1 in Portugal; for Egypt the figure was 92.3 and for Thailand 163.6 (WHO, 1977).

The rates of 49.1 per 1000 live births and 46.4 per 1000 total births found in the present study for infant and perinatal mortality respectively are about half those calculated for the whole of Kenya and even compare favourably with some European countries. To compare figures on maternal mortality a much larger series would be needed, but it is unlikely that extension of the study would show as alarmingly high a figure as that for Thailand.

At first sight, knowing the area with its poor hygiene, housing and transport conditions, one is inclined to doubt the reliability of the low mortality rates found. When looking into this more closely, however, one can discern that a number of adverse conditions encountered in other parts of the developing world are virtually absent in the study area. Most important among these is probably the comparatively good nutrition of women and children (see Chapters 10–16). Breast-feeding is universal and the majority of the children are breast-fed for at least a year. Malaria is not endemic although occasional epidemics occur and it is not a major cause of pematurity or dysmaturity as in other tropical countries (Canon, 1958). Modern medical facilities, although not readily available, are certainly not completely out of reach. When obstructed labour occurs at home it is possible to carry a woman the maximum of 20-odd kilometres to the nearest hospital.

Last but not least, pregnancy and child birth are still considered as normal natural events and there is very little interference by those who attend home deliveries. Neonatal tetanus did not occur at all during the period under study.

Variations in monthly numbers of births reflect the migratory labour patterns of a large proportion of the adult men. December is the month in which most men who are formally employed take their annual leave and for many of them this is the only time of the year they spend more than just a weekend with their wife and family, thus readily explaining the peak of births in September and October; there is no obvious explanation for the peak in November and March.

Why children born in January have a higher chance of dying during their first year than children born in other months is also something we have not been able to explain. January is one of the best months in terms of availability of food and it is a hot dry month in which transport is not a great problem. The absence of seasonal variations in perinatal mortality, even in the eastern part of the study area where food is often scarce in the pre-harvest season, probably reflects the absence of real famine periods of any extent or duration during the period of observation. Temporary scarcity of food can obviously be overcome by a sensible use of what little is available and by purchase.

Poorer survival chances of infants of very young and elderly mothers have been observed in both developed and underdeveloped countries. The influence of parity, however, is inconclusive (Butler et al., 1963, 1969; Gebre-Medhin et al., 1976; WHO, 1970). In the present study a slightly higher stillbirth rate was found for first and the seventh and above children than for second to sixth. The difference is, however, except for first children, eliminated by lower infant death rates. The favourable outcome of pregnancy in women of 40 years and over with 10 or more previous deliveries (a group of 104 women) is surprising, especially when compared with the outcome among women in the age group 35–39 years. A possible explanation might be that those women who continue to give birth after the age of 40 and reach a parity of 10 are a selection of the most fertile, most healthy and best nourished adult women.

Everett (1975) found a definite relationship in Dar es Salaam between maternal height and cephalo-pelvic disproportion. In our study caesarean sections are also clearly related to maternal height. The fact that nevertheless no increased perinatal death rate was encountered among women of short stature is a tribute to the antenatal and obstetric services. Obviously short stature is recognized as a risk and the women needing caesarean section for disproportion are selected in time and convinced of the need for hospital delivery.

Previous perinatal death is generally recognized as an indication for special care in subsequent pregnancies (Swenson, 1978; Nelson, 1975). Our impression, however, is that in the usually crowded antenatal clinics insufficient time and attention is given to taking a proper obstetric history and to explaining the implications of previous perinatal fatalities. Women who had had a previous caesarean section, however, seemed to be well aware of the need for subsequent hospital delivery.

One would like to see more attention paid at antenatal clinics to making women more self-reliant as far as their health is concerned. There is certainly no need for pregnant women to delay treatment of malaria with the consequent risk of stillbirth or premature labour when chloroquine can be bought cheaply at almost every small shop in even the most remote market centres. Similarly, a lot of time and money is spent on seeking medical help for trivial complaints, while on the other hand the symptoms of potentially dangerous diseases are often ignored for a long time or not recognized as such.

The finding that the length of the preceding birth interval does not significantly influence the outcome of subsequent deliveries does not necessarily mean that short birth intervals have no adverse effect. There may be an adverse effect on the previous child, as was suggested by Jelliffe (1955) and found by Swenson in Bangladesh (1978), or the adverse effect may only become important after infancy among 1–3-year-old children, the age group that is most vulnerable to malnutrition and infectious diseases (Morley, 1978).

A hospital stillbirth rate almost twice that for home deliveries only indicates that the hospital is at least partly fulfilling its purpose of attracting high-risk mothers. For the great majority of pregnant women it does not make much difference to the outcome whether they deliver at home or in hospital or whether they receive specialized assistance or not. Adverse conditions in hospital, like the greater danger of infections and greater anxiety for the woman in labour, are likely to be offset by adverse conditions at home, like the lack of running water and electricity and lack of knowledge and equipment to deal with complications.

Breech delivery is more than 10 times as hazardous for the baby as vertex delivery. The common habit of medical personnel of not telling a woman that a breech or transverse lie is suspected, in order not to cause undue anxiety, is a dangerous form of kindness. Too often in past years unsuspecting women have delivered a breech at home unaware of the fact that their antenatal record showed the position had been detected.

Length of gestation and birth weight are the most sensitive indices of the viability of the newborn infant (Gopalan, 1962; Susser, 1972; Omene, 1977). Cut-off points of 38 weeks and/or 2500 g as indications for extra care would be well chosen for our study population.

The great majority of causes of stillbirth, as well as of neonatal and infant death, were preventable. The same applied to three of the maternal deaths. Although the mortality rates found in this study are lower than expected there is no reason for complacency, as there is certainly scope for improvement in the medical care available to the population.

References

Butler NR and Bonham DG, Perinatal mortality, First report of the 1958 British perinatal mortality survey, Livingstone, Edinburgh, 1963.

Butler NR and Alberman ED, Perinatal problems, Second report of the 1958 British perinatal mortality survey, Livingstone, Edinburgh, 1969.

Cannon DSH, Malaria and prematurity in the Western Region of Nigeria, Brit med J, 2 (1958) 877.

Central Bureau of Statistics, Ministry of Finance and Planning, Kenya, Demographic Baseline Survey Report, 1973.

Everett VJ, The relationship between maternal height and cephalopelvic disproportion in Dar es Salaam, E Afr med J, 52 (1975) 251.

Gebre-Medhin M, Gurovski S and Bondestam L, Association of maternal age and parity with birth weight, sex ratio, stillbirths and multiple births, J Trop Pediatr, 22 (1976) 99.

Gopalan C, Effect of nutrition on pregnancy and lactation, Bull WHO, 26 (1962) 203.

Jelliffe DB, Infant nutrition in the subtropics and tropics, WHO Monograph Series No. 29, Geneva (1955).

Morley D, Paediatric priorities in the developing world, 5th Edition (1978) 303–306.

Nelson WE, Textbook of Pediatrics, 10th Edition (1975) 327.

Omene JA and Diejomaoh FME, Factors influencing perinatal mortality in a Nigerian community, E Afr med J, 54 (1977) 202.

Siongok TK Arap, Mahmoud AAF, Ouma JH et al., Morbidity in schistosomiasis mansoni in relation to intensity of infection: study of a community in Machakos, Kenya, Am J Trop Med Hyg, 35 (1976) 273.

Susser M, Marolla FA and Fleiss J, Birth weight, fetal age and perinatal mortality, Amer J Epid, 96 (1972) 197.

Swenson I, Early childhood survivorship related to the subsequent interpregnancy interval and outcome of the subsequent pregnancy, J Trop Pediatr, 24 (1978) 103.

WHO, Offset Publication, No 18 (1975), The Traditional Birth Attendant in Maternal and Child Health and Family Planning.

WHO, World Health Statistics Report, Vol 22 No 1 (1969).

WHO, World Health Statistics Report, Vol 29 No 11 (1976).

WHO, World Health Statistics Report, Vol 30 No 4 (1977).

WHO, Wld Hlth Org Techn Rep Ser no 457 (1970).

19

Use of perinatal mortality data in antenatal screening

H.J. Nordbeck
A.M. Voorhoeve
J.K. van Ginneken

Introduction

Perinatal mortality, together with maternal mortality, is the most reliable index of the quality of antenatal and obstetric care. Most deaths in the perinatal period, excluding the 4–5 per 1000 newborns that are due to congenital anomalies, are caused by complications of pregnancy and childbirth, and as such are preventable. In Europe and the USA most perinatal deaths are caused by adverse conditions in pregnancy (toxaemia, antepartum haemorrhage, placental insufficiency, unexplained prematurity). In countries less favourably situated economically, where specialized care is more difficult to obtain, asphyxia due to mechanical obstruction during labour is an important cause of perinatal mortality.

Public health programmes aimed at reducing perinatal mortality in such countries have to consider two essential questions: how can primary health care workers identify women at increased risk of experiencing a perinatal death; and how can health planners rationalize the allocation of resources such as personnel and hospital beds.

Answering these two questions involves validating a screening test to identify women who are at increased risk of delivering a child who will die in the perinatal period. The statistical validity of such a test can be defined as the extent to which it provides a true

Table 1.
Performance of a screening test.

	Outcome of pregnancy	
Screening factor(s)	*Perinatal death*	*Alive after 1 week*
Present (positive)	a	b
Absent (negative)	c	d

sensitivity: a/(a+c) predictive value: a/(a+b)
specificity: d/(b+d)

assessment of what it purports to measure (Mausner and Bahn, 1974).

A screening test has different components (Table 1): *sensitivity* (a/a+c) is defined here as the ability of the test to identify correctly those women who experience a perinatal death; *specificity* (d/b+d) refers to the test's ability to identify correctly women whose children survive; and *predictive value* (a/a+b) refers to the likelihood of a child predicted to die in fact dying in the perinatal period. An ideal screening test would, of course, be 100 percent sensitive, 100 percent specific, and have a predictive value of 100 percent.

The primary health care worker needs to detect as many true positives (cell a) as possible and thus wants maximum sensitivity; the health planner needs to limit the number of false positives (cell b) and thus needs maximum specificity; and for obvious reasons both need a test with maximum predictive value. Different screening procedures for maternal and child health that make it possible to identify women at risk of delivering infants with a higher than normal perinatal mortality have been proposed and developed (WHO, 1978).

A population-based study like the Machakos Project makes it possible to test the validity of such screening tests. The data from the project allow us also to analyse three factors: outcome of pregnancy, screening criteria and place of delivery (home or hospital). The latter needs to be taken into account as a separate variable, because it is expected to influence the relationship between the screening criteria (high-risk factors) and perinatal mortality.

The results reported in this chapter will be presented as follows. First, we shall describe generally the relationships between individual screening criteria and perinatal mortality. Secondly, we shall show how use of four sets of screening criteria makes it possible to identify high-risk mothers. Thirdly, we shall present the results of relationships between screening criteria and perinatal mortality for home and hospital deliveries separately. Finally, we shall give the results of discriminant analysis, which allow identification of the relative importance of the screening criteria or risk factors.

Materials and methods

The study included all births between 1975 and 1978 after at least 28 weeks' gestation to women who at the time of delivery belonged to the de jure population. For each woman the following information was collected:

- — age, parity, height, marital status;
- — obstetric history—previous live and stillbirths, early neonatal deaths, caesarean section, forceps or vacuum extraction, serious post-partum haemorrhage;
- — birth interval since last delivery (live or stillborn);
- — place of delivery—home or hospital;
- — mode of delivery—vertex or breech, caesarean section, forceps or vacuum extraction;
- — single or multiple birth;
- — outcome of pregnancy—stillbirth, death in the first week, survival beyond the first week.

In every case of perinatal death the mother was interviewed at home to establish the most likely cause of death.

Discriminant analysis assesses the impact of the independent variables listed above on the observed mortality pattern in discriminating between women who do and do not experience a perinatal death. This is done by constructing an equation that weighs and combines linearly the influence of the variables. It has proved its value in previous studies with mortality data (Abernathy et al., 1966; McCarthy et al., in press). The variables were scored as present or absent, in spite of the fact that the risks associated with some variables, such as maternal age and parity, are known to be U-shaped. It was realized that a logistic model would probably give slightly better results where the distribution is not normal, but it is not likely that the two methods would differ by much (Press and Wilson, 1978).

The analysis was performed in steps: first the variable that explained the greatest proportion of the variance was chosen, then the best linear combination of this with one other variable, and so on. It was decided to stop adding further variables when the next one had an F value of ≤ 3.0. The relative contribution of each variable to the equation is indicated by its standardized discrimination coefficient.

Once an equation with a set of variables allowing identification of risk has been computed, it can be used to classify mothers before they give birth into those likely to experience perinatal mortality and those not, on the basis of their scores for the discriminating variables. For each mother a score is computed that can be converted into her probability of belonging to the group with or without perinatal death, and she is then assigned to the group for which she has the higher score. As a check on the adequacy of this method, the original group of women can be scored by this method to see how many of them are classified correctly by the discriminant variables chosen. Predicted and actual categories can then be presented in 2×2 form, as in Table 1. It should be realized, however, that the results of this checking procedure tend to be too optimistic, as it is making use of the same group on which the discriminant analysis has been performed. It would have been better to split the data base into two halves and perform the analysis on one half and validate it on the other, but there were not enough perinatal deaths to allow this.

Results

There were 221 perinatal deaths in a total of 4768 births, giving a perinatal mortality of 46.4 per 1000; 141 stillbirths (29.6 per 1000 total births); and 80 deaths in the first week (16.8 per 1000 live births). Causes or circumstances associated with perinatal deaths are listed in Table 2. Thirty-eight percent of deaths were associated with complications of labour in mature infants; 25 percent with low birth weight and antepartum haemorrhage; 21 percent with unknown and accidental causes; and 8 percent and 7 percent respectively with congenital malformations and infection.

Table 2.
Causes of or circumstances associated with perinatal death.

		n	%
I	Complications of labour in mature infants	85	38
II	Low birthweight and antepartum haemorrhage	55	25
III	Infection	16	7
IV	Congenital malformations	18	8
V	Unknown and accidental	47	21
Total		221	99

Individual screening criteria

Age and parity
Age and parity of mothers are closely related and showed the well known U-shaped relationship with perinatal mortality (Fig. 1). The highest perinatal mortality rate was found in elderly primigravidae, with two perinatal deaths in 10 women aged 30 or above. Next came a group of 36 young primigravidae under age 16, with four perinatal deaths. At the other end of the reproductive period perinatal mortality increased at parities of 11 or more (a group of four women with eight perinatal deaths).

Marital status
More than half of all primigravidae in the study were unmarried. Their perinatal mortality experience was nearly twice as high as that of married primigravidae, a difference partly explicable on age. Among unmarried multigravidae perinatal mortality was somewhat lower than among the married (Table 3).

Table 3.
Marital status.

Marital status	Primigravidae N	Primigravidae n	Primigravidae per 1000 births	Multigravidae N	Multigravidae n	Multigravidae per 1000 births	Total N	Total n	Total per 1000 births
Unmarried	538	41	76	346	12	35	884	53	60
Married	452	18	40	3432	150	44	3884	168	43
Total	990	59	60	3778	162	43	4768	221	46

N = number of women n = number of perinatal deaths

Height

Height was 150 cm or less in 584 (13 percent) of 4440 women measured. The perinatal mortality in this group was 74 per 1000 as against 44 per 1000 in women over 150 cm. Perinatal mortality was particularly high (99 per 1000) among 141 primigravidae of 150 cm or less (Table 4).

Obstetric history

There were 176 perinatal deaths in the present pregnancy among 4021 women who had not previously experienced such a death, the rates being 60 per 1000 in the 990 primigravidae and 39 per 1000 in the 3031 multigravidae in the group. Perinatal mortality in 564 women who had experienced one previous perinatal death was 53

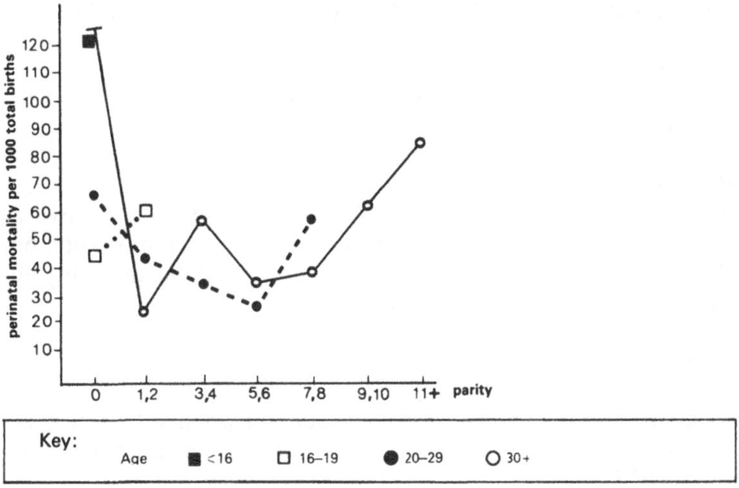

Figure 1. Perinatal mortality by age and parity.

Table 4.
Maternal height.

Height and parity	*Total births*	*Perinatal mortality* n	*per 1000*
Height >150 cm	3856	171	44
Primigravidae	720	43	60
Multigravidae	3136	128	41
Height ≤150 cm	584	43	74
Primigravidae	141	14	99
Multigravidae	443	29	65

per 1000, but this figure rose to 111 per 1000 in the group of 36 women whose only previous pregnancy had resulted in a perinatal death. In the group of 183 women who had had two or more previous perinatal deaths the rate was 82 per 100 (Table 5).

In the present pregnancy there was only one perinatal death among 71 women who had had a previous caesarean section; there were four deaths among 64 women who had had a previous forceps or vacuum extraction and nine among 182 women with a history of postpartum haemorrhage (Table 6).

Breech delivery

Thirty-three of 58 children born by the breech died perinatally (29 stillbirths and 4 first-week deaths), the rates being equally high for primigravidae (5 out of 9) and multigravidae (28 out of 49).

Twinning

There were 52 pairs of twins; 19 of these 104 children died in the perinatal period (5 stillbirths and 14 first-week deaths).

Birth interval

A short birth interval between the previous and present live or stillbirth was not associated with increased perinatal mortality, but after birth intervals of 6 years or more perinatal mortality increased steeply to 100 per 1000 (Table 7).

Combined screening criteria

From the foregoing section four groups of pregnant women at significantly higher risk of a perinatal death than normal can be identified (Table 8):

I. *Breech delivery* constituted the highest risk: two-thirds of the

Table 5.
Previous perinatal deaths.

Previous perinatal deaths	*Parity*	*Total births*	*Perinatal mortality n*	*per 1000*
0	Primigravidae	990	59	60
	Multigravidae	3031	117	39
1	Primiparae	36	4	111
	Multiparae	528	26	49
2	Two previous deliveries	5	1	200
	Three or more previous deliveries	178	14	79
Total		4768	221	46

Table 6.
Previous caesarean section, forceps or vacuum extraction and postpartum haemorrhage.

Obstetric history	*Total births*	*Perinatal mortality n*	*per 1000*
Caesarean section	71	1	14
Forceps or vacuum extraction	64	4	63
Postpartum haemorrhage	182	9	49

Table 7.
Birth interval.

Birth interval (yrs)	*Total births*	*Perinatal mortality n*	*%*
Primigravidae	990	59	60
<1 yr	60	2	33
1 yr	1174	44	37
2 yrs	1737	76	43
3 yrs	456	26	57
4 yrs	150	4	27
5 yrs	71	2	23
>6 years	80	8	100
Total	4768	221	46

Table 8.
Combined risk groups.

Riskgroup	*Total births* *n*	*%*	*Perinatal deaths* *n*	*%*
Breech (singletons)	46	1	31	14
Twins	104	2	19	9
Primigravidae at risk	160	3	16	7
Multigravidae at risk	372	8	24	11
Primigravidae not at risk	774	16	33	15
Multigravidae not at risk	3312	70	98	44
Total	4768	100	221	100

46 singleton breech births died perinatally, one percent of the women, viz. those with breech presentations, accounting for 14 percent of the perinatal deaths.

II. *Twins* formed the second highest-risk group. If women with twin pregnancy are added to group I, then 2 percent of the women account for 23 percent of the perinatal deaths.

III. *At-risk primigravidae* formed the third group. This group consisted of 160 primigravidae either aged under 16 or over 30, or less than 151 cm in height. The perinatal mortality in this group was 100 per 1000 as against 42 per 1000 among primigravidae not at risk. Adding this group to the previous two means that 5 percent of the women were associated with 30 percent of the perinatal deaths.

IV. *At-risk multigravidae* formed a group of 372 women who had experienced two or more previous perinatal deaths or one such death if this was in their only previous pregnancy, whose parity was over 10, who had a birth interval of 6 years or more, or who had previously had a caesarean section. Their perinatal mortality was 60 per 1000 as against 30 per 1000 for multigravidae not at risk. Adding these to the previous three groups makes 13 percent of the women responsible for 41 percent of perinatal deaths.

Predicted and actual perinatal deaths are presented in Table 9, in the same form as Table 1. The sensitivity of the screening test for perinatal mortality is 41 percent (perinatal deaths among women at risk divided by total perinatal deaths); its specificity is 87 percent (number of children born to women not at risk alive at one week divided by total number of children alive at one week); its predictive value is 13 percent (number of women who experience a

Table 9.
Outcome of pregnancy.

Antenatal screening	*Perinatal deaths*	*Alive at age one week*	*Total number*
Positive	90	592	682
Negative	131	3955	4086
Total	221	4547	4768

perinatal death divided by all women at risk according to the screening criteria).

Even if all perinatal deaths could be identified prospectively, not all of them could be prevented by specialized obstetric care. The deaths in group I in Table 2 could all have been prevented by timely caesarean section, and some of the deaths in groups II and III might have been prevented by better neonatal care; group IV contains only obvious congenital malformations incompatible with independent life; and it is a matter for speculation whether any of the deaths in group V were preventable. Table 10 shows the distribution of the five groups of causes and associated circumstances of perinatal death (from Table 2) over the six risk groups. Fifty of the 85 deaths in group I occurred among children of women who belonged to the 13 percent most at risk for perinatal death. These 50 deaths could have been prevented if all the women had been screened and those at risk had received good obstetric care. In that case the perinatal mortality would have been 36 instead of 46 per 1000 births.

Table 10.
Causes of perinatal death for the combined risk groups.

Risk group	*I*	*II*	*III*	*IV*	*V*	*Total*
Breech (singletons)	26	1		3	1	31
Twins	6	12		1		19
Primigravidae at risk	10	2		2	2	16
Multigravidae at risk	8	8	2		6	24
Primigravidae not at risk	16	2	4	1	10	33
Multigravidae not at risk	19	30	10	11	28	98
Total	85	55	16	18	47	221

I Complications of labour in mature infants
II Low birth weight and antepartum haemorrhage
III Infection
IV Congenial malformations
V Unknown and accidental

Table 11.
Perinatal mortality rates per 1000(numbers of deaths in parentheses) for selected screening criteria.

	Overall mortality		*Home mortality*		*Hospital mortality*		
	rate	*(n)*	*rate*	*(n)*	*rate*	*(n)*	*% hospital deliveries*
Maternal age							
≤20 yrs	47	(41)	45	(27)	52	(14)	31
21–30 yrs	44	(109)	38	(67)	58	(42)	29
31–40 yrs	49	(55)	36	(32)	97	(23)	21
≥41 yrs	55	(16)	48	(11)	82	(5)	21
Parity							
0	62	(59)	59	(36)	67	(23)	36
1–6	42	(120)	37	(80)	55	(40)	24
≥7	49	(42)	31	(21)	113	(21)	22
Marital status							
Unmarried	62	(53)	55	(34)	82	(19)	28
Married	43	(168)	36	(103)	60	(65)	27
Maternal height							
≤150 cm	70	(40)	64	(25)	84	(15)	31
>150 cm	44	(171)	35	(102)	76	(69)	25
Previous stillbirths							
None	44	(191)	37	(122)	59	(69)	27
≥1	68	(30)	48	(15)	118	(15)	30
Previous caesarean section							
No	47	(220)	—*	—	—	—	26
Yes	14	(1)	—	—	—	—	74
Previous forceps/ vacuum extraction							
No	46	(217)	—	—	—	—	26
Yes	63	(4)	—	—	—	—	53
Previous post-partum haemorrhage							
No	46	(212)	—	—	—	—	27
Yes	49	(9)	—	—	—	—	32
Birth interval							
First child	60	(59)	59	(36)	72	(23)	36
1–6 yrs	42	(154)	37	(98)	63	(56)	20
>6 yrs	100	(8)	29	(3)	143	(5)	33
Mode of delivery							
Breech	569	(33)	719	(23)	385	(10)	45
Other	40	(188)	33	(114)	59	(74)	26
Multiple birth							
Yes	183	(19)	109	(4)	241	(15)	56
No	43	(202)	38	(133)	60	(69)	27

*numbers too small

Discriminant analysis

The picture becomes more varied when the place of delivery is taken into account. Twenty-seven percent of all deliveries took place in hospital and 73 percent at home with perinatal mortality rates of 65 and 39 per 1000 respectively. We decided to do three discriminant analyses: for all deliveries combined, and for home and hospital deliveries separately. Table 11 shows total, home and hospital perinatal mortality by the previous screening criteria. Primiparity, being unmarried, height under 151 cm, previous stillbirth, birth interval over 6 years, breech delivery, multiple birth and hospital delivery all carry a significantly increased perinatal mortality and these variables were entered into the discriminant analysis. Hospital delivery per se was not hypothesized to be responsible for an increased mortality, but it was possible that controlling for this variable would change the original relationships described above. The following variables were included in the equation because they had an F value over 3.0:

Variable	*Standardized discriminant coefficient*
breech delivery	.91
multiple birth	.21
marital status	.15
maternal height	.14
place of delivery	.13
primiparity vs. multiparity	−.11

As the standardized discriminant coefficient represents the relative contribution of the relevant variable to the equation, it is clear that breech delivery is more than four times as important as multiple birth. A score that could be converted into the probability or otherwise of her child dying perinatally was computed for each woman, a cut-off point of 0.5 being chosen. Actual and predicted classifications are presented in Table 12. Only 55 of 221 perinatal deaths were predicted, giving a sensitivity of 25 percent. The specificity was 97 percent and the predictive value 28 percent.

Columns 3 and 5 of Table 11 show the mortalities corresponding to the various screening criteria separately by home and hospital delivery. The figures for previous caesarean section, forceps or vacuum extraction and post-partum haemorrhage are not subclassified because there were very few perinatal deaths in these categories. Women delivering by the breech, or with a multiple birth or a height under 151 cm appear to have significantly higher perinatal mortality rates for both home and hospital delivery. Women with a parity of seven or more, or with one or more previous stillbirths have significantly higher rates for home deliveries only.

The results of the separate discriminant analyses of home and

Table 12.
Prediction vs. outcome, all deliveries combined.

	Actual situation		
Prediction	*Dead*	*Alive*	*Total*
Dead	55	138	193
Alive	166	4409	4575
Total	221	4547	4768

hospital deliveries were to a large extent similar to those reported above and are therefore not presented in detail. Breech delivey was again by far the most important discriminating variable for both home and hospital deliveries (coefficients .98 and .69 respectively). Other variables that discriminated to some extent for home deliveries were primiparity and multiparity and maternal height. A variable—apart from breech delivery—that was of considerable importance in hospital deliveries was multiple birth; having had one or more previous stillbirths and grand multiparity were of lesser importance.

Discussion

The interpretation of the results is complicated by the delivery location factor. The higher perinatal mortality rates in hospital as opposed to home deliveries, for example, can partly be explained by the fact that many women try to deliver in hospital when they expect complications. This reduces the mortality for home deliveries but on the other hand, as some mothers reach hospital too late, it increases the hospital figures.

The absence of perinatal deaths among women who had had a previous caesar is another example. This does not mean that such woman are not at serious risk if they try to deliver at home: it means that both they and health personnel are aware of this risk and make every effort to ensure that they deliver in a well-equipped hospital.

Because of these complications none of the screening tests based on risk factors as criteria and developed on the basis of observed mortality rates was entirely satisfactory. A different approach is taken by Slooff et al. (in press), but this also involves various assumptions and it will not be further discussed here.

The researcher is left with the task of unravelling the complex interactions between the independent variables, for which two different methods have been tried and reported in this article. The

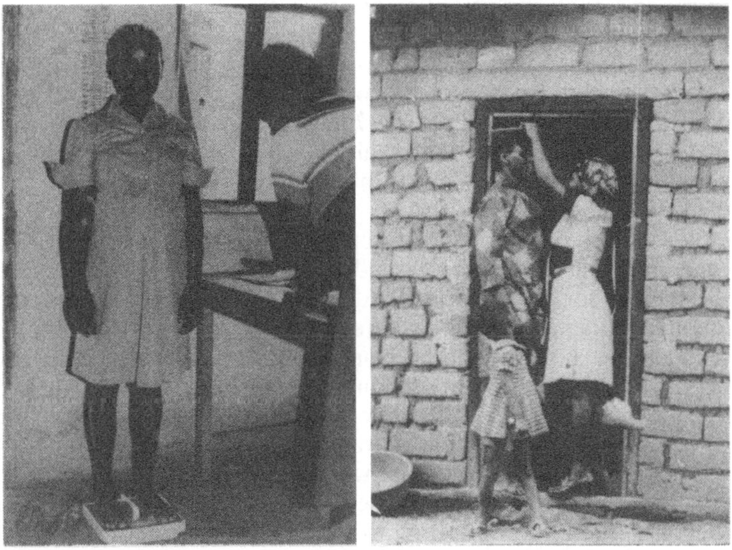

Measuring in the clinic—and at home.

following summarizes the sensitivity, specificity and predictive value of each method:

	Screening by four at-risk categories	*Screening by discriminant analysis*
Sensitivity	41%	25%
Specificity	87%	97%
Predictive value	13%	28%

The results of discriminant analysis are rather disappointing, sensitivity being particularly low. One reason for this is that the total number of perinatal deaths (221) is small for this type of analysis. Classifying a number of variables in dichotomous categories has also resulted in a loss of information, but this does correspond to a certain extent, with the actual situation, in which women are categorized as being at risk according to set cut-off points.

The results from the four-category approach are much more encouraging, although statistically less sound. It will be noted, however, that both methods largely agree on choice of variables for screening purposes.

Professor Eva Alberman (1980), in the last of a series of articles in the *Lancet* on 'Better perinatal health', said: 'In the short term the way ahead for each country might be to identify and rank causes of their own perinatal deaths in order of preventability and to set and publicize priorities of preventive action in that order.' This is what we have tried to achieve in this chapter. The data reported here should be used to design a "high risk" strategy as developed here and by means of antenatal records such as that developed by Dissevelt et al. (1976). In Kenya the situation is such that a risk strategy for maternal and child health care could be adopted without much extra input of training, manpower and medical facilities.

We would recommend concentrating initially on the risk of cephalo-pelvic disproportion and malpresentation. First because the danger for both mother and infant is high when obstructed labour occurs in a situation where obstetric care is poor or absent; secondly because the mothers and children involved are usually healthy, and timely intervention can give excellent results; and thirdly because the risk is easily understood and recognized and people without formal medical training can be taught to screen for it. It is most important for the women themselves to understand why they are selected and advised to deliver in hospital, because they are then far better motivated to accept such advice, if reasonable facilities are available.

Breech delivery is associated with a very high perinatal mortality; it is also the only factor that in practice shows a higher rate for home than hospital deliveries. Midwives at antenatal clinics are certainly capable of recognizing a breech presentation, though this needs a great awareness and careful palpation during the last month of pregnancy. In areas where traditional midwives provide obstetric care for a large proportion of mothers, this is an extremely worthwhile subject for training.

The same applies to twin pregnancies, as there is no doubt that twins' chances of survival increase considerably when their existence is known or suspected (by the mother as well as the midwife). Enquiry as to a family history of twinning should be routine at the first antenatal visit, to increase watchfulness to detect a twin pregnancy in time.

Being unmarried and primiparity were strongly interrelated: more than half the primiparae were unmarried at the time of delivery. This is also illustrated by the discriminant analysis for all deliveries combined in which, once marital status and place of delivery were controlled for, the marginal contribution of primiparity became negative. It is easier and more acceptable to screen for primiparity than for marital status.

Primigravidae aged under 16 or over 30, or less than 151 cm tall had more than double the perinatal mortality rate of taller primigravidae aged 16–29. Identifying this group of women ought to be easy as it can be done at any time during pregnancy.

Multigravidae at risk may well be the most difficult group to screen and to convince of the need for hospital delivery. Elderly women with large families in particular need special attention to ensure they can get to hospital in time (see Chapter 23).

Antenatal screening identified four groups of pregnant women (totalling 13 percent of all pregnant women) who appeared to account for 41 percent of all perinatal deaths. More than half the perinatal deaths in this group could probably have been avoided had timely measures been taken. Although the majority of all perinatal deaths in this study, and in others (WHO, 1978), occurred among women who could not really be identified antenatally as being at increased risk for perinatal death, it is difficult to envisage any other approach, within the budget available for health care in a country like Kenya, that might decrease the perinatal mortality by as much as 10 per 1000. A perinatal mortality of 46 per 1000 is only half that estimated for Kenya as a whole (CBS, 1973): one might expect that the risk strategy would be even more effective in areas where perinatal mortality is higher.

References

Abernathy JR, Greenberg BG and Donelly JF, Application of discriminant functions in perinatal deaths and survival, Am J Obstet Gynecol 95 (1966) 860–7.

Alberman E, Better perinatal health: prospects for better perinatal health, Lancet, i (1980) 189–92.

Central Bureau of Statistics, Ministry of Finance and Planning, Kenya, Demographic baseline survey report, 1973.

Dissevelt AG, Kornman JJ and Vogel LC, An antenatal record for identification of high risk cases by auxiliary mdiwives at rural health centres, Trop Geogr Med, 28 (1976) 251.

Mausner JS and Bahn AK, Epidemiology. An introductory text, Saunders, Philadelphia, 1974.

McCarthy BJ, Schultz KF and Terry JS, Identifying neonatal risk factors and predicting neonatal deaths in Georgia, Am J Obstet Gynecol, in press.

Press SJ and Wilson S, Choosing between logistic regression and discriminant analysis, J Am Stat Assoc, 73 (1978) 699–711.

Slooff R, Nordbeck HJ and Voorhoeve AM, A model for the estimation of predictability and specificity of screening criteria for hospital deliveries, in press.

WHO Offset publication No. 39, Risk approach for maternal and child health care, WHO, Geneva, 1978, pp 8–15.

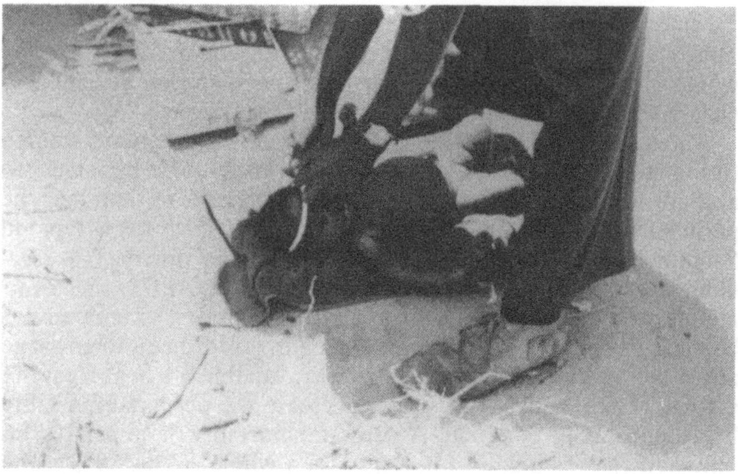

Measuring head circumference.

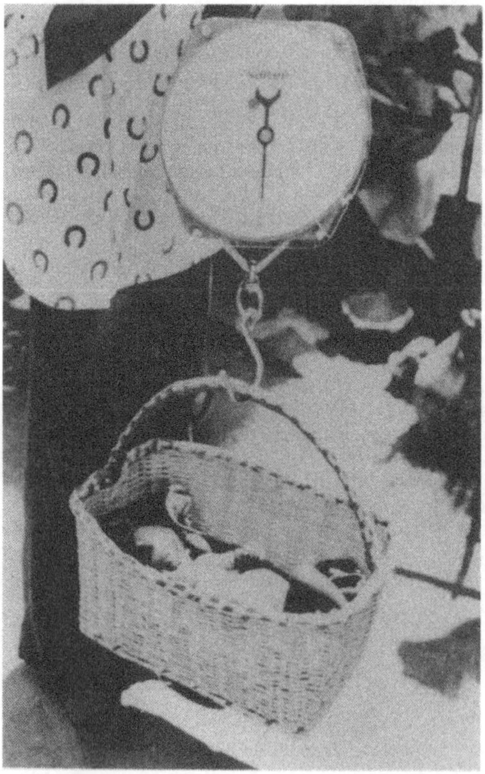

Weighing a low-birth-weight baby.

20

Factors related to infant mortality

A.M. Voorhoeve
H.J. Nordbeck
S.A. Lakhani

Introduction

Infant mortality is a sensitive indicator of the level of general health of a population and especially of the well-being of mothers and children. There is a high correlation worldwide between gross national product and infant mortality (Davis and Dobbing, 1974). In the low-income countries of Africa and Asia mortality rates 10 times those of industrialized countries in Europe and North America are found. Among low-income as among high-income countries, however, there are large differences in mortality rates. It is not so much the level of the gross national product of a country, as the distribution and the share that goes to the poorer half of the population that seems to have most effect on infant mortality (Grant, 1982). Economic development without simultaneous improvement in social organization, nutrition, hygiene, communications and literacy is likely to raise the infant death rate even more.

In the Netherlands the infant mortality decreased from 200 per 1000 a hundred years ago to 50 per 1000 fifty years ago and less than 10 per 1000 in 1980. Improved housing conditions, provision of safe drinking water and propagation of breast-feeding contributed even more to this decrease than the almost 100 percent coverage with childhood vaccinations and the developments in medical technology.

In tropical Africa infant mortality is somewhere between 100 and 200 per 1000 and the main causes of death are more or less the same in most countries: birth trauma, prematurity and neonatal tetanus in the first month; respiratory infections, diarrhoea, measles and malaria after the first month. The analysis reported on in this chapter not only seeks an answer to the question why some children in the Machakos area die, but also how it is possible for such a relatively low infant mortality to be found in such an apparently poor environment. The answer to this second question is probably more important for the implementation of health care measures than the answer to the first.

Material and methods

Data collection

This study is based on demographic data collected during fortnightly home visits by local field-workers (see Chapter 1). This framework was used to identify pregnant women and their offspring. A history of previous and present pregnancies was obtained from all women who delivered between 1975 and 1978 (see Chapter 18). The children born in that period were followed up by a contemporaneous disease surveillance programme among children under age 5 (see Chapters 6, 7, 8). During the second half of the study period an attempt was made to weigh all newborn infants shortly after birth. This weighing was done with a Salter weighing scale and locally made basket. Information relevant for this chapter collected in this study included: month and year of birth of all live-born children; maternal variables such as age and parity, sublocation, marital status, birth intervals and number of previous children who had died; sex of the child; single or multiple birth; length of gestation; birth weight and time of weighing (about 25 percent were weighed within 48 hours and another 25 percent after 48 hours but within the first month); maternal height and weight during pregnancy (approximately 30 percent); for the children who died: age at death, month of death and most likely cause of death.

Further, a cross-sectional socio-economic survey was carried out in about 80 percent of the households in 1974 and a survey on the social and hygiene living conditions of the child population covering approximately 99 percent of the households in 1975 (see Chapter 4). Variables from these surveys that are included in our analysis are shown in Table 10; these variables as well as their reliability are described elsewhere (see Kuné et al., 1979; Slooff and Schulpen, 1978).

Data analysis

The characteristics of children who were born alive during the study period but died before the age of one year were analysed in two ways:

a) at first the children who died (227) were compared with the total group of live-born children who survived beyond the age of one year (4400). The demographic, maternal and child variables previously mentioned were scrutinized and the significance of differences between both groups were calculated by means of the chi-square test;

b) next, a random sample of approximately 10 percent (411) was drawn from children who survived beyond the age of one year. The socio-economic and hygiene characteristics of this group were compared with those of children who died and the significances of differences were calculated by means of the (non-parametric) Mann-Whitney test.

Results

Longitudinal study

There were 227 infant deaths among the 4627 live births (49.1 per 1000). Of these 107 (23.1 per 1000) were neonatal deaths, 80 during the first week of life, 43 in the first 24 hours (detailed data on age at death are given in Chapter 17). After the neonatal period the numbers of children dying each month showed little variation. There were twice as many male (53) as female (27) early neonatal deaths, but after the first week the numbers of male (72) and female (75) infant deaths were about equal.

The main causes of death, as deduced from parents' histories, are also listed in Chapter 17. Complications of labour and low birth weight contributed to more than half the early neonatal deaths. After the first week infections were the most important cause of death, mainly respiratory infections, with gastro-intestinal infections becoming an important cause of death after the age of 6 months, and measles after 9 months.

Infant mortality was evenly spread throughout the year. About 9 neonatal and 10 post-neonatal deaths occurred each month for the 4 years together. Children who were born in January, however, had a strikingly higher mortality (92 per 1000) than those

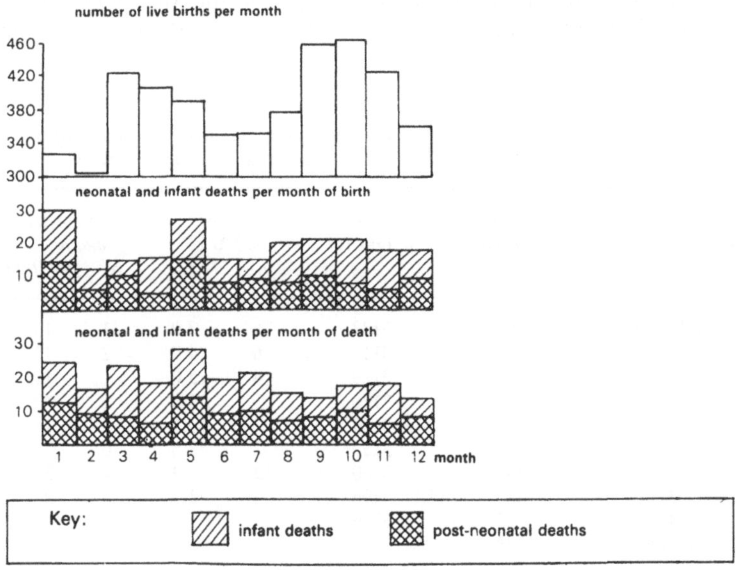

Figure 1. Number of live births, neonatal and infant deaths per month of birth and per month of death for four years together.

born during the rest of the year ($p<0.01$) (Fig. 1). No satisfactory explanation for this difference could be found.

The highest infant mortality was found in sublocations Katheka and Ulaani, the lowest in Kingoti and Katitu, with an intermediate figure in Kambusu. The difference just reached statistical significance at the 5 percent level.

Birth weight

Table 1 gives the numbers of live-born singletons weighed at different times within the first month, and their mean weights, the percentage of children below 2500 g and the percentage of children dying after the neonatal period. Although most low-birth-weight children were reported and weighed soon after birth, some only came to the field-workers' notice after several weeks. The cross-sectional increase in mean weights with time, as shown in Table 1, is what could be expected from an individual child. During the first week there is little variation. It thus seems justified to accept weights measured up to 6 days after birth as birth weights since these give similar results to those taken within 48 hours of birth.

The mean birth weight of 1091 live-born singletons, weighed within the first 48 hours, was 3133 g (standard deviation 467 g) with 7 percent below 2500 g. In Table 2 the number of children weighed within 48 hours, their mean birth weights and the percentages below 2500 g are given by sublocation. In the eastern part of the

Table 1.
Live-born singletons weighed at different times within the first four weeks of life; mean weights, percentages below 2500 g and post-neonatal mortality.

Time of weighing	*Number of children*	*Mean weight (g)*	*Below 2500 g*		*Post-neonatal deaths*	
			n	*%*	*n*	*per 1000*
First 48 hours	1091	3133	76	7.0	21	19
Day 2	150	3114	6	4.0	2	13
3	80	3129	4	5.0	1	12
4	50	3120	3	6.0	2	40
5	69	3159	7	10.1	1	14
6	52	3159	2	3.8	0	0
Week 2	360	3260	12	3.3	14	39
3	223	3496	6	2.7	5	22
4	165	3626	3	1.8	5	30
Not weighed	2288	—	—	—	64	28
Total	4528				115	25

Table 2.
Number of singletons weighed within 48 hours, mean birth weights and numbers and percentages below 2500 g, by sublocation.

Sublocation	*Singletons weighed within 48 hours*		*Mean birth weight (g)*	*Children below 2500 g*	
	n	%*		*n*	%**
Kingoti	424	28	3110	38	9.0
Katheka	66	15	2958	14	21.2
Kambusu	303	28	3134	13	4.3
Ulaani	161	20	3207	7	4.3
Katitu	137	19	3201	4	2.9
Total	1091	24	3133	76	7.0

* percentage of the total number of children per sublocation
**percentage of the number of children weighed within 48 hours

study area a lower percentage of newborns were weighed during the first 2 days of life than in the western part. This was undoubtedly due to the lower population density and more difficult communications in the eastern area. Katheka, the sublocation with the lowest percentage of children weighed within 48 hours, showed the lowest mean birth weight, the highest percentage of low-birth-weight infants and the highest neonatal and infant mortality.

Low birth weight was strongly associated with increased neonatal, and to a lesser degree post-neonatal, mortality. The neonatal mortality of children under 2500 g was 13 times, and the post-neonatal infant mortality twice, as high as that of children of 2500 g and above (Table 3).

Table 3.
Neonatal and post-neonatal mortality among infants with a birth weight below 2500 g and of 2500 g and more.

Birth weight (g)	*Number of children*	*Neonatal mortality*		*Post-neonatal mortality*	
		n	*per 1000*	*n*	*per 1000*
<2500	76	9	118	3	39
≥2500	1015	9	9	18	18
Total	1091	18	16	21	19

Length of gestation

The length of gestation was known with reasonable accuracy for 995 live-born infants. Two percent were born at less than 34 weeks; more than half of these died, all in the neonatal period. Post-mature children also had a higher neonatal mortality than children with a maturity of 38–41 weeks ($p<0.05$) (Table 4).

Table 4.
Neonatal and post-neonatal mortality in relation to gestational age.

Gestational age in weeks	*Number of children*	*Neonatal mortality*		*Post-neonatal mortality*	
		n	*per 1000*	*n*	*per 1000*
28–33	19	10	526	0	0
34–37	113	4	35	4	35
38–41	775	14	18	16	21
42+	88	8	91	0	0
Total	995	36	36	20	20

Twinning

There were 99 live-born first and second twins, of whom 14 died in the neonatal period and 5 post-neonatally (infant mortality 192 per 1000). The mean birth weight for 34 twins whose birth weights were known was 2309 g. Both neonatal and infant mortality were about twice as high for twins as for singletons of the same birth weight.

Age and parity of the mother

Only the small groups of 9 elderly and 31 very young primigravidae showed any correlation between age and infant mortality; the infant mortality in these groups was more than twice the average. The excess mortality among the children of the primigravidae under 16 years occurred only in the first week of life. In multigravidae infant mortality was not related to age or parity of the mother (Fig. 2).

Height of the mother

Both the height of the mother and the birth weight of the child (weighed within the first week of life) were known for 1186 mothers with singleton children (Table 5). The birth weights correlated with maternal height but an expected relationship with infant mortality was not found. The low infant mortality for this

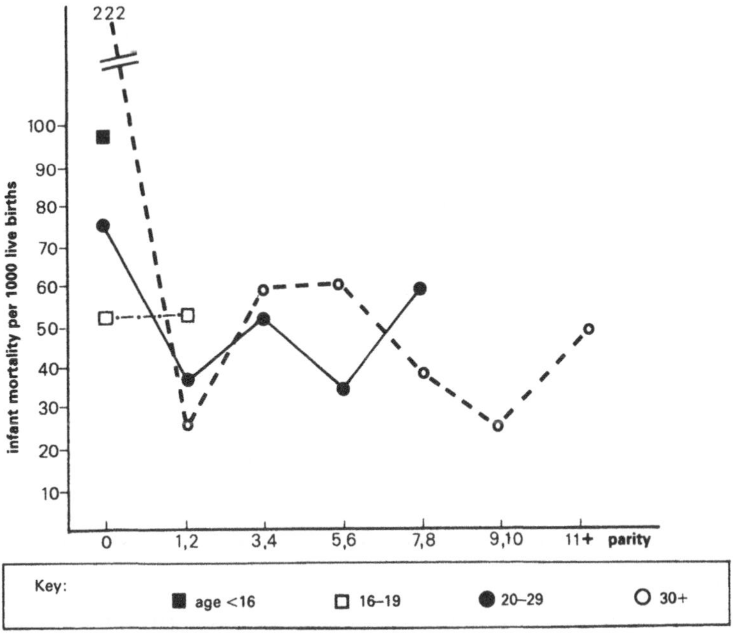

Figure 2. Infant mortality by age and parity of the mother.

whole group was due to the fact that most of the children who died in the first week of life were not weighed.

Table 5.
Birth weights and infant mortality in relation to maternal height.

Maternal height (cm)	*Number of children*	*Mean weight (g)*	*Infant mortality n*	*Infant mortality per 1000*
⩽150	138	3028	3	22
151–155	354	3069	7	20
156–160	395	3150	10	25
161–165	240	3203	11	46
⩾166	59	3239	0	0
Total	1186	3127	31	26

Weight of the mother

Weight and height were known for 1445 women. The weight was corrected for the duration of pregnancy at the time of weighing and weight for height was expressed as percentage of the standard (Jelliffe, 1966; Thomson and Billewics, 1957). Infant mortality among children of mothers whose weight for height was 80 percent or less of the standard was twice as high as among children of mothers with a weight for height over 100 percent. This difference was however not statistically significant (Table 6).

Table 6.
Infant mortality in relation to maternal weight for height.

Percentage weight for height	*Number of women*	*Infant mortality*	
		n	*per 1000*
≤80	205	13	63
81–90	553	22	40
91–100	453	19	43
101–110	156	5	31
>110	78	2	26
Total	1445	61	42

Birth intervals

Table 7 shows the relation between previous birth interval and infant mortality. Infants born after a short interval had the same mortality rate as children born after longer intervals.

Table 7.
Infant mortality in relation to previous birth interval.

Birth interval in months	*Number of live births*	*Infant mortality*	
		n	*per 1000*
Primigravidae	957	61	64
<12	59	3	51
12–23	1151	47	41
24–35	1734	78	45
36–47	437	25	57
48–59	146	7	48
60+	143	6	42
Total	4627	227	49

Previous deaths of siblings

Children one or more of whose siblings had died had a slightly higher chance of dying in infancy than children all of whose siblings were alive ($p<0.05$). Their infant mortality rate was lower than for first children, however (Table 8).

Table 8.
Infant mortality in relation to the death of siblings.

Previous death of siblings	*Number of live births*	*Infant mortality* *n*	*per 1000*
No deaths	2474	97	39
One death	779	44	56
Two or more deaths	417	25	60
First children	957	61	64
Total	4627	227	49

Marital status of the mother
Single women and women who were widowed, divorced or separated had the same infant mortality rates and there was no significant difference between primigravidae and multigravidae in this respect. The infant mortality rate among unmarried mothers, both primigravidae and multiparae, was higher than among married mothers ($p<0.01$) (Table 9).

Table 9.
Infant mortality in relation to marital status: primigravidae and multigravidae.

	Primigravidae			*Multigravidae*		
Marital status	*Number of live births*	*Infant mortality* *n*	*per 1000*	*Number of live births*	*Infant mortality* *n*	*per 1000*
Unmarried	516	44	85	331	25	76
Married	441	17	39	3339	141	42
Total	957	61	64	3670	166	45

Socio-economic and hygiene study

Table 10 lists the socio-economic and hygiene variables on which information was collected during two cross-sectional surveys (Kuné et al., 1979; Slooff and Schulpen, 1978). The longitudinal study covered the whole cohort of children born alive over a 4-year period. At the time of the cross-sectional surveys, however, some children were not yet born and others had already died; some

Table 10.
Socio-economic and hygiene variables and their relation to infant mortality.

Variable	*Mortality* T	p (2-tail)	Missing
Family structure and education:			
Presence of the father	0.56	0.57	266
Presence of a grandmother	–0.33	0.74	35
Education of head of household	0.44	0.66	35
Job level of head of household	0.37	0.71	35
Education of mother	0.11	0.92	265
Hygienic conditions:			
Drinking water	0.24	0.81	35
Place of defaecation	1.28	0.20	35
Cleanliness of the latrine	–0.70	0.48	35
Sleeping density	–0.78	0.43	266
Construction of the bedroom	0.73	0.47	266
Cooking in the bedroom	0.84	0.40	266
Animals in the bedroom	1.28	0.21	266
No. of children sleeping in one room*	2.58	0.01	266
Agricultural possessions:			
Cattle	0.62	0.54	164
Sheep and goats	0.83	0.41	164
Maize	1.52	0.13	164
Beans	0.49	0.62	164
Fruit trees*	3.64	0.00	164
Coffee	1.27	0.20	164
Household amenities:			
Quality of the house*	3.09	0.00	164
No. of sleeping rooms*	2.50	0.01	164
Possessions inside the house	1.77	0.08	164
Possessions outside the house*	2.01	0.04	164
Professional possessions*	2.43	0.01	164
Membership of a co-operative*	2.85	0.00	164
Personal observation*	2.49	0.01	164

*significant findings

households had not yet formed and others had broken up; and, moreover, the coverage of the socio-economic survey was only 80 percent. For these reasons information on a number of households was incomplete.

The variables can be considered under four headings: family structure and education, hygiene conditions, agricultural possessions and household amenities. The difference between the study group and the control group has been calculated for each variable and expressed as a T-value. T-values of more than 1.96 indicate significance at the 5 percent level ($p<0.05$).

Family structure and education

In about half of all households the father lived and worked nearby; in another quarter he worked elsewhere; in the remaining quarter there was no father or he came home less than once a month; and in approximately one in three households a grandmother lived within the household. About 60 percent of the heads of households had no job, which in most cases meant that they were self-employed small-scale farmers with not more than 3 years' formal education. Among the mothers 34 percent had no formal education and less than 5 percent had reached secondary school. None of these variables differed significantly between the study and control group.

Hygiene conditions

Two out of three households got their drinking water from a well or spring or stored rainwater; the remainder got it from a dam, river or dug hole. None of the families had tap water. About half had a latrine and used it, but a proper clean latrine was an exception. In the majority of households at least four people shared one bedroom; in approximately one house in five they shared this bedroom at night with chickens and goats. In one in three households the bedroom was also used for cooking.

A significant difference was found between the two groups in the number of children under 5 who shared one bedroom. In 20 percent of the households of the study group three or even four young children slept together: in the control group this occurred in only 7 percent of households.

Agricultural possessions

The number of cattle, sheep and goats and the amount of maize, beans and coffee harvested did not differ significantly between study and control groups, but significantly more control (55 percent) than study households (42 percent) had one or more fruit trees.

Household amenities

The houses varied from traditional circular with walls of mud or unbaked bricks, no windows and a thatched roof, to rectangular with walls of baked bricks or stone, windows, cement floor, iron sheet roof and separate sleeping rooms. 'Possessions inside the house' refers to chairs, tables, beds, cupboard, drinking glasses and pressure lamps but also to more luxurious consumer goods like sofa sets and radios. 'Possessions outside the house' mainly refers to means of transport like bicycles, motorcycles or even cars. 'Professional possessions' means items like wheelbarrows, ploughs, and ox-carts. Membership of a co-operatve society indicates that a person is engaged in growing a cash crop—usually coffee, but sometimes cotton or sunflowers; it usually means that a family lives above the economic subsistence level. Personal observation is a measure of the field-workers' impression of the economic status of the household, rated as below average, about average, or above average.

All the above variables, with the exception of the number of possessions inside the house, showed significant differences between families with and without an infant death.

Discussion

The infant mortality in the Machakos study area is only half that for Kenya as a whole (CBS, Kenya, 1975). When walking through the area, however, one does not get the impression of a particularly prosperous area: housing, sanitation, communications and basic medical provisions are poor, and a lot of badly needed money and energy is wasted by the men on alcohol. On the other hand, the qualitatively good nutrition of the people and the universal and prolonged breast-feeding of the children (see Chapters 12–14) are positive aspects, and another favourable aspect is the climate, which is, owing to the altitude, seldom really hot or oppressive although often too dry for a good harvest. Malaria is not endemic in the area.

The figures on mean and low birth weight presented in Tables 1 and 2 need to be interpreted with caution. Mean birth weight corresponds closely to the figure presented in Chapter 11, but the percentage below 2500 g may well be an underestimate in view of the finding in Table 3 that infant mortality in the sample of infants weighed within 48 hours was 36 instead of the 49 reported for all children born alive between 1975 and 1978. Likewise, it should be borne in mind that the figures in Table 2 are biased: the low birth weight percentage for Katheka may be too high and those for Ulaani and Katitu too low.

Thirty-five percent of the infant deaths occurred in the first week of life, the majority being related to obstetric problems or low birth weight (see Chapter 17) and preventable by better organization of antenatal and obstetric care (see Chapter 23). We would, however, recommend that low-birth-weight infants able to suck are kept at home; even infants with a birth weight of 1500–1600 g can be successfully breast-fed and they often fare better at home than in hospital, where infection is a great risk. Birth weights are indispensable for screening of newborns to detect those in need of some form of extra care, but it is often impractical and unnecessary to weigh them immediately after birth: a child that weighs less than 2500 g at one or more weeks is as much at risk as a child of this weight immediately after birth.

Much thought and time was put into trying to work out some form of economic or social classification of households that might be reproducible in other rural African areas, but this proved to be unexpectedly difficult, especially when trying to find some association with aspects of health. In this respect a simple classification by personal observation into below average, about average, and above average worked as well as more elaborate measures. It is not surprising that infant mortality was lower among the slightly more well-to-do families: what is surprising is that even in the poorest households most infants survived and even thrived.

Conditions in the area were fairly representative of large parts of rural Africa. The majority of the people can supply the basic needs of their family in terms of food, clothing, housing and education, but they lack reserves for times of drought and sickness. Under these circumstances it seems that parental care and foresight is more important for children's well-being than actual income or possessions. In these times of recession, scarcity and unemployment, the father who builds a decent house and the mother who plants some fruit trees around it are a sign of hope for the next generation.

References

Davis JA and Dobbing J, Eds, Scientific foundations of paediatrics, William Heinemann Medical Books Ltd, London, 1974.

Central Bureau of Statistics, Demographic baseline survey report 1973, CBS, Ministry of Finance and Planning, Kenya, 1975.

Grant JP , The State of the World's Children 1981–82, UNICEF, New York 1982..

Jelliffe DB, The assessment of nutritional status of the community, WHO Monograph Series, No 53 (1966).

Kuné JB et al., Machakos Project Studies. XV. The economic setting at the household level, Trop Geogr Med, 31 (1979) 441.

Slooff R and Schulpen TWJ, Machakos Project Studies. VI. The social and hygienic environment, Trop Geogr Med, 30 (1978) 257.

Thomson AM and Billewics WZ, Clinical significance of weight trends during pregnancy, Br Med J, 1 (1957) 243.

A water hole in Ulaani.

A tank used for the collection of rainwater.

21

Household status differentials and childhood mortality

W. Gemert
R. Slooff
J.K. van Ginneken
J. Leeuwenburg

Introduction

One of the objectives of the Machakos Project was to relate patterns of ill health to the environment of the child. This was intended to produce criteria for recognizing families with a higher than average risk of child morbidity. Such households should form the prime target for specific health promotion activities and other preventive measures (see Chapter 1).

Numerous studies undertaken in developed as well as in developing countries have produced empirical evidence indicating that environmental factors, and more particularly the socio-economic status of households, are related to mortality in under-5s. In countries in parts of Asia, Latin America and Africa certain 'favourable' environmental conditions have been shown to be associated with relatively low child mortality (Anker and Knowles, 1977; Chen, Rahman and Sarder, 1980; Meegama, 1980; Puffer and Serrano, 1973; D'Souza and Bhuiya, 1980). Analysis of data from the Machakos Project adds comparable information on a fairly typical African rural community.

The living conditions in the study area, i.e. in parts of Matungulu and Mbiuni locations in Machakos District, are characterized by a relatively high population density, marginal to medium agricultural potential and the influences of nearby Nairobi (Kolkena and Pronk, 1975 and others). Communal water supply, collective waste disposal, sewerage and electricity are not yet available. The social customs are specific for the Kamba tribe, which is the third largest tribe in the country. Ecological conditions are similar to those in other densely populated parts of East Africa. More detailed information on environmental aspects may be found in other chapters (e.g. Chapters 2 and 4).

In this chapter we shall discuss the results of an analysis of mortality in under-5s in relation to household economic, social and hygiene conditions. The existence of differentials in respect of these conditions was investigated in relation to:

— mortality due to all causes
— mortality due to specific causes
— age of the child at death

Materials and methods

Mortality levels in the study area were low. Between 1975 and 1978 the crude death rate was 7 per 1000 population, while the infant mortality rate was 49 per 1000 live births (see Chapter 5). The mortality in children 1–4 years of age was 7 to 8 per 1000 children. For reasons given in Chapter 5 we assume that these low rates are genuine and that under-reporting of infant and child deaths was insignificant. As part of a study on the outcome of pregnancy (see Chapter 14) a paediatrician obtained information on the causes of death for most of the 404 deaths occurring in under-5s between 1974 and 1978 by interviewing the mothers of the children who had died. The diagnoses thus established were classified into nine cause of death categories. Table 1 summarizes these data.

Cross-sectional data on the household environment were collected in two surveys, carried out in February–March 1974 and in May–June 1975. The first

Table 1.
Death categories and frequency distribution of child deaths, 1974–1978.

Cause of death category	*No. of child deaths*	*% of total*	*% of deaths for which component scores were available*
Respiratory infections and pertussis	92	22.8	76
Gastro-enteritis	79	19.6	77
Measles	83	20.5	81
Fever and convulsions	24	5.9	70
Malnutrition	23	5.7	83
First-week death and prematurity (excl. multiple births)	65	16.1	77
Prematurity (multiple births)	19	4.7	88
Unknown	14	3.5	70
Remaining	5	1.2	92
Total	404	100.0	77

survey was concerned with economic household characteristics. It covered 80 percent of the study population. The second survey dealt with social and hygiene aspects; its coverage was 99 percent. Out of the 35 cross-sectional variables obtained from these surveys, 21 were combined into five components, which were numbered and named as follows:

I Agricultural potential
II Wealth
III Modern orientation
IV Hygiene
V Family structure.

More information on these components may be found in Chapter 4. The status of the household of each child could be summarized by means of scores computed for each of these five components.

In order to compare the status of households in which a child death occurred a control sample was drawn. This consisted of the 619 children also studied in the context of the re-survey reported on in Chapter 4 (i.e. taken from cohort D in Figure 2 of that chapter). These were the children who had been in their second year of life in 1975 and of whom none had died by 1978. Economic data were available from the 1974 survey for 75 percent of the mortality cases. Social and hygiene data from the 1975 survey were available for 93 percent of the cases. Both percentages were significantly ($p = 0.02$) below the 80 percent and 99 percent expected respectively. This leads to the conclusion that child mortality may not have been independent of the missing household information. The right-hand column of Table 1 contains the percentages of known component scores for the various cause of death categories in the cases. For reasons inherent in the research questions discussed in Chapter 4, component scores were complete for 100 percent of the controls.

The analysis was undertaken as a case-control study with the 404 deceased children as cases and the 619 5-year-old survivors as controls. The independent variables representing hypothesized exposure to risk were formed by the five component scores. In order to facilitate the calculation of relative risks these component scores were transformed into classes. On the basis of their frequency distributions among the controls, we created four classes of almost equal size, i.e. the quartiles 'low', 'moderately low', 'moderately high' and 'high'. In the ideal situation, where each of the classes would obtain 25 percent of the controls, the ratio of the percentage of cases in any of the lower classes to the percentage of cases in the highest class would estimate the relative risk of death, standardized against mortality in the highest class. The frequency distributions for component scores among the controls were such that perfect quartiles could not be created, however, so the distribution of controls over the arbitrary component classes had to be taken into account in computing the standardized relative risk (Mantel-extension) and other parameters of risk used in the analysis. In Table 2 results for mortality due to all causes are tabulated against the four classes of component II, Wealth, to serve as an example.

In order to let one figure express the overall effect of one component we needed some form of averaging out the various risk ratios per class. For this purpose a weight was given to each component class, from which we derived a pair of *mean weight values* for every 2×4 table considered. Deducting the *mean weight value* for controls from the *mean weight value* for cases resulted in what we named a *mean shift value*. The principle of this procedure was as follows.

The choice of weights to be given to each person in a given class was based on convenience. It was considered appropriate if 'ideal' control samples, i.e. hypothetical controls arranged in perfect quartiles, would have yielded zero mean weight values. Controls in class 1 of a given component would have lower scores

Table 2.
Quartile distribution of mortality (all causes) cases and controls in respect of component II, Wealth.

Component II, Wealth, class	*No. of cases*	*No. of controls*	*Standardized risk ratio*
1 (low)	114	167	2.40
2	70	136	1.81
3	74	161	1.62
4 (high)	44	155	1.00
Total	302	619	

than approximately 75 percent of all controls. The controls in class 2 would have higher scores than approximately 25 percent and lower scores than approximately 50 percent of all controls, and so on. On this principle the values –75, –25, 25 and 75 were allocated as weights to classes 1, 2, 3 and 4 respectively. From the data in Table 2 it can be calculated that:

$$\bar{s}_m = \frac{(-75\times114)+(-25\times70)+(25\times74)+(75\times44)}{302} = -17.05$$

$$\bar{s}_c = \frac{(-75\times167)+(-25\times136)+(25\times161)+(75\times155)}{619} = -0.44$$

$$\bar{s}_m - \bar{s}_c = -16.61$$

where

$\bar{s}_m$ = mean weight value for cases

$\bar{s}_c$ = mean weight value for controls

$\bar{s}_m - \bar{s}_c$ = mean shift value.

The mean shift value is specific for a component and a cause of death. It replaces the three standardized risk ratios normally applied in this type of analysis.

The statistical significance of the mean shift value is tested as a difference between two means, under $H_0 : \bar{s}_m - \bar{s}_c = 0$, as follows:

$$T = \frac{\bar{s}_m - \bar{s}_c}{SD} \sqrt{\frac{n_m \times n_c}{n_m + n_c}} \qquad (1)$$

where

n_m = number of cases

n_c = number of controls

SD = standard deviation of the total frequency distribution.

It can be shown that in this model the normal approximation is satisfactory as long as $n_m \geq 7$.

Using the data from Table 2, the value for the SD is calculated as follows:

$$SD = \sqrt{\frac{\Sigma f_i s_i^2 - \frac{(\Sigma f_i s_i)^2}{n}}{n-1}} = 56.57 \qquad (2)$$

where

s_i =shift value per class i (i = 1,2,3,4)

f_i =frequency of shift value i

$n = n_m + n_c$.

Subsequently

$$\sqrt{\frac{n_m \times n_c}{n_m + n_c}} = 14.25$$

Therefore

$$T = \frac{-16.61}{56.57} \times 14.25 = -4.18 \ (p<0.01).$$

The mean shift value for death of all causes in respect to component II, Wealth, is thus –16.61 and this value is statistically significant at the 1 percent level.

When more than two mean weight values needed to be analysed simultaneously, the analysis of variance technique was used. In such instances the mean shift values were transformed into standardized values by means of formula (1), under the null hypothesis that the variance equals unity. As the components were treated as independent variables, all derived test values were assumed to have chi-square distributions.

A distinction between early and late deaths appeared necessary for testing whether household status components would show age differentials in terms of mortality risks. The philosophy behind this question was that the effects of household conditions on child mortality might well have been dependent on the age of the child. It was further hypothesized that if such an association with age existed it would differ among household status components and among cause of death categories. For this purpose the median age at death in each case was empirically determined for each cause of death category as well as for all causes taken together. Mean shift values were determined separately for cases who had died below this median age and cases at or above that age (relative to controls in the same ages).

The occurrence of sex differentials was tested by analysing the data for boys and girls separately. As this did not produce any significant effect, this procedure will not be discussed here any further.

The partitioning of the mortality cases into subsamples based on cause of death categories and age at death produced cells with very low numbers of individuals. In order to accommodate for the loss of power due to such small sample sizes the two-tailed probability of $0.05<p<0.10$ was considered in addition to $0.02<p<0.05$ and $p \leq 0.02$, whenever applicable.

Results

Household status and cause of death

The mean shift values for the five household status components were compiled for the nine cause of death categories and for all causes taken together, as shown in Table 3. The overall mean shift value of –12.6 is highly significant ($p<.001$). This means that for all causes of child mortality taken together household status in general was inversely related to the risk of death. Broken down by cause of death, this appeared to apply to respiratory infections and pertussis, gastroenteritis, measles, fever and convulsions, malnutrition and first-week deaths. Broken down by component, significant negative mean shift values for all causes of death together were found for components I, Agricultural potential, II, Wealth, III, Modern orientation and IV, Hygienc. The patterns of interaction between the components taken separately and child mortality due to all causes did not differ significantly in the two-way analysis of variance ($x_4^2=4.55$, $p>0.25$; bottom row). Taken as a combination of all components, household status exhibited significantly different associations with the nine cause of death categories ($x_8^2=22.11$, $p=0.005$; right-hand column). The resulting interaction between the five components and the nine cause of death categories is also significant ($x_{32}^2=51.88$, $p=0.02$; remaining cells of the table). In other words, each component was associated with different causes of death in its own peculiar way but these differences were largely cancelled out when mortality was considered as a whole. Causes of death particularly associated with low component scores for Agricultural potential were: respiratory infections and pertussis, measles and first-week death. With Wealth these associations were most significant for measles and malnutrition. Modern orientation was mostly associated with malnutrition, first-week death and the category unknown, whereas for Hygiene the associations were with respiratory infections and pertussis, fever and convulsions and malnutrition. The cause of death category most often associated with household status was malnutrition (i.e. with Wealth, Modern orientation and Hygiene).

Household status and age at death

Table 4 summarizes the mean shift values, broken down by component, cause of death categories and age of death below or above the median age for each cause of death category. Taking all causes of death together (bottom row) it appears that in most components the impact on mortality was most significant in deaths occurring

Table 3.
Mean shift values for nine cause of death categories and five household components (n values in brackets).

	Household status component					
Cause of death category	*I Agricultural potential*	*II Wealth*	*III Modern orientation*	*IV Hygiene*	*V Family structure*	*Total*
Respiratory infections and pertussis	−17 (67)**	−13 (67)†	− 9 (86)	−19 (70)**	4 (70)	−10.6 (360)**
Gastro-enteritis	−10 (59)	−14 (59)†	− 9 (72)	−14 (58)†	−15 (58)	−12.3 (306)**
Measles	−18 (64)**	−28 (64)**	3 (81)	−11 (64)	− 4 (64)	−10.8 (337)**
Fever and convulsions	− 9 (16)	11 (16)	−19 (22)	−40 (15)**	−27 (15)	−16.0 (84)**
Malnutrition	−15 (17)	−39 (17)**	−51 (22)**	−36 (20)**	6 (20)	−27.7 (96)**
First week death and prematurity (excl. multiple births)	−18 (53)*	−15 (53)†	−16 (63)*	−16 (40)†	− 4 (40)	−14.1 (249)**
Prematurity (multiple births)	1 (11)	− 6 (11)	10 (13)	1 (12)	3 (11)	2.1 (57)
Unknown	− 4 (10)	−20 (10)	−40 (13)**	8 (8)	− 5 (8)	−13.5 (49)
Remainder	39 (5)	5 (5)	−21 (5)	−24 (4)	−49 (4)*	− 7.6 (23)
All causes	−13.2 (302)**	−16.6 (302)**	−11.2 (377)**	−16.6 (290)**	− 5.0 (290)	−12.6 (1561)**

† 0.05<p<0.10
* 0.02<p<0.05
** p≤0.02

Table 4.
Mean shift values for five cause of death categories, five household components and age at death.

Cause of death category and age at death	*Household status component* I *Agricultural potential*	II *Wealth*	III *Modern orientation*	IV *Hygiene*	V *Family structure*	*Total*
Respiratory infections and pertussis						
< 6 months	– 3	–11	– 6	–24**	–17*	– 4.8
⩾ 6 months	–28**	–15	–12	–14	– 9	–15.3**
Gastro-enteritis						
< 8.5 months	–13	–20*	–12	–25**	–16†	–17.0**
⩾ 8.5 months	– 8	– 7	– 6	– 1	–14	– 7.1
Measles						
<16.5 months	– 6	–16	11	– 1	– 9	– 2.9
⩾16.5 months	–29**	–38**	– 7	–22*	2	–18.6**
Fever and convulsions						
<13.5 months	– 9	32†	– 1	6	–44*	– .7
⩾13.5 months	– 9	–12	–34*	–64**	–19	–29.0**
Malnutrition						
<24 months	–40*	–31*	–38*	–17	–36*	–32.6**
⩾24 months	6	–47**	–61**	–49**	34*	–24.0**
All causes						
< median	–10†	–13*	– 4	–15**	– 7	– 9.5**
⩾ median	–19**	–22**	–15**	–21**	– 3	–16.1**

† 0.05<p<0.10
* 0.02<p<0.05
** p⩽0.02

above the median age. This was not true for all components or for all cause of death categories. In some instances these differentials did not occur while in others they were reversed. For instance, component IV, Hygiene, had a relatively more significant impact on early deaths due to respiratory infections, pertussis and gastro-enteritis. Component V, Family structure, showed this pattern for deaths due to fever and convulsions and malnutrition. A strong differential mortality below median age would agree with hypotheses incriminating the relevant component(s) with nature rather than nurture, or vice versa.

Discussion and conclusions

This analysis has shown that household status and child mortality were in general inversely related. Although this finding is not new, it is somewhat surprising that such a relationship could be demonstrated within a rural community of such an apparent homogeneity as the Machakos study population.

The associations with causes of death differed among the various components of household status. The most significant association was with deaths due to malnutrition, followed by deaths due to fever and convulsions, first-week deaths, gastro-enteritis, measles, respiratory infections and pertussis.

Four of the five household status components showed significant associations with various cause of death categories. It was surprising that component V, Family structure, should not exhibit such an impact at any level of significance. The variables upon which the five components were based may have been less than suitable, as several variables available from the cross-sectional survey had to be dismissed on account of low reliability or low stability (refer to Chapter 4). This may have restricted the validity of certain components, in particular Family structure, which is well known to be an evasive and unstable entity.

The household variables and the components that were used were, of course, not necessarily causative or explanatory factors in themselves. The survival of a child does not depend on these factors as such but on intervening variables, in particular the nature of the disease to which the child was exposed, the knowledge and beliefs about diseases of its guardians, the motivation of the guardians, the availability of professional services and the resulting kind of care and attention it receives. We did not possess adequate information on these intervening variables and it is therefore impossible to indicate how changes in the household environment might lead to improvements of child health and a reduction in child mortality. The analysis reinforces the already existing intuition that the poorer households deserve the most attention. This conclusion should not be overrated. Our figures are based on risk ratios, which are independent of absolute mortality risks in the population at large. Even in the relatively better-off households child mortality still left ample room for improvement.

The statistics developed for this analysis differed from those normally employed for case-control studies with categorical data in multi-column tables. It is believed that this approach is more suitable than most multi-variate techniques wherever detailed breakdowns of small numbers of cases and controls lead to very small cells and much missing information. It is still possible that the missing information has produced a bias. The crude mean shift values of cases with 0, 2, 3 and 4 missing component scores were estimated to be respectively: –13 (n = 232), –19 (n = 124), –20 (n = 5) and –38 (n = 22). This means that poorer households had more missing values. Had no data been missing, the estimates of the differences between cases and controls would have been larger. In other words, due to missing information the magnitude of the household status differentials was underestimated.

Further research on the causation of child mortality should concentrate on the relationship between household status and the quality of care the child receives from its guardians. Highlighting under what circumstances the quality of care may reduce the risk of death and whether this is affected by differentials in respect of type of disease involved should also be attempted.

References

Anker R and Knowles JC, An empirical analysis of mortality differentials in Kenya at the macro and micro levels, Population and Employment Working Paper, ILO, (1977) No 60.

Chen LC, Rahman M and Sarder AM, Epidemiology and causes of death among children in a rural area of Bangladesh, Int J of Epidemiology, 9 (1980) 25–33.

D'Souza D and Bhuiya A, Mortality differentials in Bangladesh, Pop and Dev Review, 8 (1982) 753–69.

Kolkena TF and Pronk A, Report on a socio-economic survey in two rural areas of Machakos District (Kenya) 1975, Internal Report MRCN, Nairobi, (1975).

Meegama SA, Socio-economic determinants of infant and child mortality in Sri Lanka: an analysis of post-war experience, Scientific reports, World Fertility Survey, London, (March 1980) No 8.

Puffer RR and Serrano CV, Patterns of mortality in childhood, PAHO Scientific Papers, Washington, (1973) No 262.

Part VI
Modern and traditional medical care

22

The utilization of modern and traditional medical care

J.N. van Luijk

Introduction

This chapter consists of two main parts. The first presents the findings of a study on the Kamba traditional medical system and a description of the modern medical facilities available to the inhabitants of the Machakos Project study area; the second deals with the description and discussion of the findings of a survey on the utilization of modern and traditional medical care by the inhabitants of Kingoti and Kambusu sublocations in the western part of the Project area.

These studies formed part of a research project on patient satisfaction, compliance and utilization of modern and traditional medical care conducted in the northern division of Machakos District by the author from 1979 to 1982, within the framework of the Machakos Project. This research consisted of the following sub-studies:

- — a study of patient satisfaction among stratified random samples of 384 and 241 clients respectively of Kangundo subdistrict hospital and Matungulu government dispensary (1979);
- — an in-depth study of patient satisfaction, compliance and utilization of modern and traditional medical care among a group of 40 clients of the outpatient department of Kangundo subdistrict hospital, living in Kingoti and Kambusu sublocations (western part of the study area) and among a control group of 39 persons living in the same area (1980);
- — a 10-week study on the utilization of modern and traditional medical care among a stratified random sample of 110 households with 945 household members, located in Kingoti and Kambusu sublocations (1980);
- — a study among the staff of the Kangundo subdistrict hospital on their opinion

about factors related to patient satisfaction (1980);
— a survey on factors related to attitude towards and utilization of traditional medical care, involving interviews with one adult member of 108 of the 110 households included in the 1980 utilization survey (1982);
— a study of Kamba traditional medicine, especially in the western part of the Machakos Project area (1979–82).

Detailed descriptions of these studies have been or will be presented in van Luijk (1980, 1982a, 1982b, 1982c, 1983a, 1983b).

The study on the utilization of health services built on an earlier study conducted by Swinkels and Schulpen in 1976 in the area (Schulpen and Swinkels, 1980; Swinkels and Schulpen, 1980). The patient-satisfaction studies were extensions of former studies conducted in the framework of operational research studies by Vogel et al. at Machakos provincial hospital and Kiambu district hospital (Githinji, 1977; van Luijk, 1979; van Luijk and Vogel, 1979; Maneno et al., 1982).

1. The traditional and the modern systems

Kamba traditional medicine

Theoretical orientation

In his main description of traditional Kamba medicine, the author follows the ethnomedical scientific approach as described by Fabrega (1977), who stated that the ethnomedical approach tries to link ideas and principles of various sciences like biology, sociology, anthropology and history. Ethnomedical science studies the medical institutions and the way human groups handle disease and illness in the light of their cultural perspectives. One of the core concepts of this approach is the 'medical care system' as formulated by Fabrega (1977) and elaborated by Good (1980) into the 'ethnomedical care system', which can be defined as 'the whole approach of an ethnic community to disease and illness, organized spatially and changing over time'.

The study of an ethnomedical care system includes the study of a wide variety of psychological, biological, social, cultural and environmental aspects of the group and its members. The rapid and fundamental process of social and cultural change, during the colonial period amongst others, and the introduction of modern medicine and the reaction of the Kamba to this new system form part of an ethnomedical study. In the present chapter only a few aspects and facets of the Kamba traditional medical system will be presented, however. For a more detailed description the reader is referred to van Luijk (1982a).

The information on traditional Kamba medicine was collected throughout the study period by interviews and discussions with numerous key informants, traditional medical functionaries and church leaders, and the respondents in the various sub-studies, especially the in-depth study.

Kamba disease classification systems

A classification system is essentially a collection of items or concepts divided into subgroups of smaller categories by the application of certain principles. These principles are derived from the basic concepts of health and disease, of aetiology, cause, diagnosis and treatment. In the traditional disease classification system we find the way in which the Kamba themselves order or classify disease according to certain principles. It gives us also the basic explanations for Kamba behaviours in relation to health and disease.

According to the Kamba disease perceptions, there are several disease classification systems. That used in any particular setting depends on which aspect of the disease is under discussion. Only a few knowledgeable Kamba informants can describe all these systems or classify all Kamba descriptive terms for signs, symptoms and diseases. Boundaries between classes are sometimes vague or overlapping; classes within a system are not always mutually exclusive; and information is sometimes confusing and contradictory owing to informants' lack of special or esoteric knowledge, individual interpretation by informants or loss of traditional knowledge caused by the process of social and cultural change during the colonial period and after Independence in 1963.

The Kamba distinguish 10 disease classification systems, which can be subdivided into four groups:

A. 1 *System related to cause* (one system, 5 classes)
B. *Systems related to treatment* (2 types)
  1 according to persons or specialists who cure or heal the disease (6 classes)
  2 according to type of treatment (25 classes)
C. *Systems related to disease characteristics* (4 types)
  1 according to severity of diseases (3 classes)
  2 according to curability of diseases (2 classes)
  3 according to communicability of diseases (2 classes)
  4 according to hereditary characteristics of the diseases (2 classes)
D. *Systems related to characteristics of the affected person* (3 types)
  1 according to sex of the affected person (3 classes)
  2 according to age class of the affected person (8 classes)
  3 according to the part of the body affected (±19 classes)

Space does not permit us to discuss all the 10 classification systems. In this chapter we shall discuss systems A1 and B1. We have selected these systems because A1 is the system most essential to understanding the basic Kamba ideas on health and disease, as its ordering principle is related to Kamba ideas about cosmology, supernatural forces, religion and basic characteristics of human beings. System B1 is described here as it is related to the utilization survey described in the last part of this chapter. For further discussion of Kamba disease classification systems, see van Luijk (1983a and b).

Disease classification according to cause

This system consists of five classes, based on traditional Kamba beliefs and perceptions of causes of disease. These classes are:

Diseases of God
Kamba recognize *Mulungu*, the Creator and Preserver of all things. *Mulungu* is far away, beyond and above the human world; he is not involved in the 'daily life' of the Kamba. God as the Creator lives on an entirely different plane, and is not involved in the actions of human beings but, as the Creator, he has created everything, both good and bad, so ultimately he is also the Creator of disease and death. If there are no other 'nearer' or more obvious reasons for disease and death, then the cause of the disease is 'natural', indicated by the description, 'a disease caused by God himself', or in other words a disease not caused by bewitching or witchcraft. Kamba informants who spoke English almost invariably translated 'diseases of God' by the term 'natural disease', indicating the chance aspect of being struck by such a disease as, according to Kamba ideas, *Mulungu* does not punish a human being by a disease.

Herbal treatment by persons who have the knowledge is sufficient to cure the diseases of God, or natural diseases. People may pray to *Mulungu* to bless the power of herbs, but they know that ultimately, if these do not cure the patient, he may die. It is a form of *mbanga* (bad luck) to be struck by a natural disease, in the same way as it might be *mbanga* to be struck by other misfortunes, like having a bad harvest or an accident. But it can never be certain whether such a misfortune is caused by *mbanga* or by *uoi* (witchcraft).

Diseases that belong to this class include, amongst many others, measles, whooping cough, diarrhoea and teething problems of small children.

Diseases caused by the spirits of the forefathers
The *aimu* are the spirits of the forefathers. *Mulungu* is far away, not interested in the daily activities of human beings: the *aimu* are

very near, and are very much interested in the daily life of the Kamba. There are, according to Kamba concepts, two types of *aimu*. There are the spirits of people who have died recently, up to three or four generations back; these are called the 'living dead' (Mbiti, 1971). There are also the spirits of the forefathers who died many generations back. The 'living dead', especially, observe what is going on in Kamba society in the natural world. If a Kamba does not follow traditional customs, the *aimu* will punish him in various ways—he might lose his wealth, or the *aimu* might send disease and misfortune.

Traditional Kamba cosmological views are characterized by the belief that the forces in the world (both natural and supernatural) are in equilibrium within a delicately balanced system. The highest moral duty of man and the *aimu* is to maintain this balance. Infractions of moral and legal tribal rules, breaches of taboo, and malignant actions of witches and sorcerers disturb this equilibrium and compensatory actions have to be taken to restore the balance. The wrath of the *aimu* will strike a Kamba with disease in case of any breach of taboo or other form of transgression of the moral order.

The *aimu* can cause many types of disease, but they are mainly causative agents in the diseases related to *thavu*. *Thavu* is the term by which the Kamba indicate the ritual uncleanliness of a person who has transgressed certain traditional rules, mainly related to prescribed and prohibited sexual relationships. For a discussion of sexuality as a positive force according to the Kamba world view, and a description of the various types of *thavu*, see van Luijk, 1983.

When one of the parents is in a state of *thavu*, the health of a newborn child may be affected. The newborn does not grow well, becomes thin and withers away; it does not start to walk and talk like other children; and it might develop a thick belly, and ultimately die, if the *thavu* is not taken away. A child who suffers from these symptoms is called by the descriptive term, *kana ka thavu*, a child with *thavu*. When a child gets these symptoms, the parents suspect that there is *thavu* and go to a *mundu mue* (traditional medical functionary, see below), who divines the cause of the sickness. If the *aimu* tell him that it is *thavu*, he interrogates the parents until one or both of them disclose the reason for the *thavu*. If he himself does not have the gift of 'cleansing the *thavu*', then he directs his clients to a person who has this gift to conduct the cleansing ceremony.

Thavu might also be the cause of infertility or abortion. Taking into account the importance of having children, it is understandable that nowadays there are also still functionaries who carry out the cleansing of *thavu*. A famous one lives in Kingoti sublocation.

According to modern diagnostic criteria, a *kana ka thavu* would be described as a 'child failing to thrive', which could be caused by a congenital malformation such as congenital heart disease, but is most likely to be due to malnutrition.

Diseases caused by witchcraft

Witchcraft (*uoi*) is an evil power used by human beings who act as *muoi* (witches) to harm other human beings. Jealousy or pure evil are behind the use of witchcraft. A witch can cause all kinds of misfortunes and many types of diseases. Information on witchcraft is vague and contradictory. It is a secret thing and a lot of gossiping is involved. It is also an interesting topic to discuss in the evening when people sit around the fire. Many young informants stated that they did not believe in *uoi*; others, especially older informants, were convinced that witchcraft is rampant and has even increased during the colonial period and since independence in 1963 because formerly people who were suspected of witchcraft could be killed by the *kingole* (a traditional judicial council).

When a disease is caused by witchcraft, Kamba say that you are thrown together with the disease or that the disease is thrown upon you. Almost any type of disease can be caused by *uoi*, but especially when a disease does not react to normal treatment, witchcraft will be suspected as the cause. There are, however, certain types of diseases that are more suspected than others.

For any type of disease caused by witchcraft, the bewitching power has to be taken away before it can be treated by the application or use of herbal medicine. The *uoi* can be removed by the *muoi* herself or by the *mundu mue* (traditional healer).

Self-inflicted diseases

The Kamba know that certain diseases are communicable or that certain objects, animals, insects etc. may cause a disease. A person should try to protect himself against communicable diseases. If you sleep with a person who has certain types of wounds (*itau*), you know that you may also get these wounds. If you touch certain plants or insects, you know that you may get itching and certain kinds of pimples. Certain types of roots will cause diarrhoea; having sexual intercourse with a person who suffers from gonorrhoea will give you the disease; induced abortion might cause all kinds of problems; and so on. If you act or behave carelessly, the Kamba say that, 'you are in search of a disease'. Many types of disease can be caused by a person's own carelessness, especially by eating or drinking too much or not enough. If you take a risk that you should not have taken, other people will say that you yourself are the ultimate cause of the disease although the direct cause might be something else.

Diseases caused by somebody else (not including witchcraft)
This class comprises mainly injuries and other malfunctions of the brain, body or body organs caused by somebody who has attacked you physically. Many injuries and malfunctions can be caused in this way. To mention a few: when a person has been beaten on his head he might become confused or abnormal; stillbirth might be caused by harming a pregnant woman physically; vomiting blood might be due to being beaten.

It is important to note that, according to Kamba customary law, other measures besides the normal traditional diagnostic and therapeutic actions have to be undertaken to restore the disturbed equilibrium. The inflictor of the injuries has to compensate the injured person or his or her family.

From the above description we may draw the conclusion that certain diseases belong to one of the classes but that others might belong to more than one class, depending on the specific causative history. The Kamba ideas about the causes of disease are pluralistic; supernatural forces, evil human beings or carelessness might be the cause of disease. In the following description of the classification system according to persons who heal the diseases concerned we shall see that ideas about cause are related to diagnostic and therapeutic actions.

Disease classification according to functionaries

This system consists of six traditional classes. The description of these classes gives us the opportunity to describe some of the main characteristics of the traditional medical functionaries.

A selection of herbs used by traditional midwives.

Diseases healed by the traditional medico-religious specialist

At birth, certain signs indicate that an infant will become a traditional medico-religious functionary in adult life. Such a child is born with the *mbuu* (the signs) and has been given the gift of *uwe* (good or healing power) by the *aimu*. Usually after a long period of suffering from all kinds of ailments due to the calling of the *aimu*, such a person will accept the vocation. He or she might follow an informal apprenticeship with a practising *mundu mue* before starting to practise, after certain ceremonies have been conducted. Whether he will attract many clients will depend on fame and local recognition.

The *mundu mue* is a medico-religious specialist who fulfills important roles and functions in Kamba society. He is not only a person who deals with illness, but has a much wider function: he restores the balance in society when disruptive events take place, when the equilibrium has been distorted by the actions of human beings or supernatural forces. He performs prescribed actions aimed at neutralization, removal or withdrawal of the malignant forces. In case of breach of taboo or other form of transgression of the moral order, such prescribed actions are aimed at taking away the wrath of the *aimu*, so that they depart to their own spirit world at a safe distance from the human world. He keeps contact with the supernatural powers and informs the Kamba what these powers want them to do. In the field of traditional medicine, he works promotively, preventively and curatively at a personal and community level. These promotive, curative and preventive actions cannot always be clearly distinguished, as they may result from one ceremony. The cause is taken away, so the sufferer is saved from further illness and the signs and symptoms of the disease have been treated and cured. The main curative and preventive actions of the *mundu mue* are:

1. conducting of *kuausya*—divination activities to detect the ultimate cause of misfortunes and diseases;
2. officiating at rain-making ceremonies;
3. officiating at sacrifices at the *ithembo* (sacrificial grove),
4. instructing, and presenting 'the power' (*uwe*) to, apprentices;
5. administration of herbal mixtures to treat signs and symptoms of disease (in this case he acts as a herbalist);
6. removal of *nyamu* (foreign objects put there by witchcraft) from the body;
7. cleansing of a homestead when evil powers cause misfortune to happen there;
8. closing a compound to protect it from disease, misfortune and *uoi*;
9. cleansing or washing of *thavu* (see previous section);
10. officiating at the *kilumi* dance—a dance that has a certain communal preventive impact and that is conducted at night;
11. 'the escorting of the diseases'—a ceremony during which a goat (or, according to a case report, nowadays a hen) is sent away into the bush to take the disease from a certain area.

The *mundu mue* used to play an important role in traditional society. It is, however, difficult to get a clear picture of his present-day activities. Many Kamba, especially Christians, deny that they believe in the power of the *mundu mue*. Over 95 percent of the inhabitants in the Machakos study area are Christians and all church leaders interviewed declared that church members are forbidden to go to the *mundu mue*. So people will not admit that they have been to one, not only because they are Christians, but also because one does not tell other people when one goes. A large proportion of people interviewed said that Christians deny that they would go to the *mundu mue* but that they would still go secretly at night.

Concerning the types of disease for which the Kamba would still go secretly to the *mundu mue*, persons interviewed said ultimately almost all Kamba would go for any type of disease that might be caused by *thavu* or *uoi*, or that did not improve after 'normal' treatment. But this is a last resort, as the fees of the *mundu mue* are high, sometimes over 1000 Ksh.

Diseases healed by the herbalist

The Kamba herbalist is a medical practitioner who treats specific diseases with herbs or herbal mixtures. He is a distributor (seller) of these in the form of fresh or dried or ground leaves, twigs, roots etc. He might also prepare a liquid that the patient has to drink. The herbalist treats somatic diseases, because it is generally accepted that psychosomatic diseases are caused by *aimu, uoi* and *masatani* (evil spirits) and come under the *mundu mue*.

The herbalist gets his knowledge from informal apprenticeships and from experience. One should also have a certain gift, however, and this is sometimes hereditary. Many herbalists claim that they learned the job from a relative who had the same gift. Personal interest in herbs and plants and their curative qualities also plays a role.

Herbalists know the curative powers of many plants. Sometimes they also use other materials, like dirt from the side of the river, soot from the roof or extracts of certain types of meat. Charcoal from all types of wood and of different consistencies is used for many kinds of disease. Liquid medicines are sieved many times through a traditional sieve to purify them.

When a patient comes with his complaint to a professional herbalist, the latter will ask him what the signs and symptoms of the disease are; where and when he feels pain; whether he or she has observed any changes in the functions of the organs, feels hot or cold, has fever etc. If he is not yet sure of the diagnosis, he will search further by palpating any part of the body that is hot or cold or where the patient feels pain. After he has diagnosed the disease, he prepares the medicine, depending on the type of disease. The patient is given the medicine and instructed how to use it. The fee varies from a few to 40 or 50 Ksh for special cases that take a long time to cure. Sometimes a patient pays for every visit to the herbalist: sometimes he has to pay an agreed sum of money after being cured.

Most *andu awe* (plural of *mundu mue*) are also herbalists; they combine both roles. Most traditional midwives also use some herbal mixtures and some of them are fully 'qualified' herbalists.

Most Kamba informants will tell you quite openly if they have visited a herbalist; there is no secrecy about the role and function. A few said they never went to herbalists, because they did not believe in traditional herbs, but went to a modern medical facility for major complaints and bought shop medicine for minor complaints.

Diseases healed by the traditional midwife

As in most African countries, Kamba traditional midwifery still plays a very important role in the care of pregnant women and at delivery. The high birth rate in the study area (44 per 1000), and the fact that a very high proportion of pregnant women deliver at home, underline this importance. Besides assisting at delivery, the midwife also treats minor complaints and complications during pregnancy.

Taking into account that other researchers had conducted extensive research into traditional midwifery in the Project area, the author decided to restrict his research into traditional midwifery to interviewing two traditional midwives. Their information did not differ significantly from that received by the other researchers. For more information about traditional midwives, the reader is referred to Chapter 23.

Diseases healed by self-treatment

Many Kamba know some herbs or other means of treating minor symptoms. Some people know more than others because they are interested in the subject, and they will treat themselves and members of their households. Others do not know anything about it and are completely dependent upon others—relatives, neighbours or traditional medical functionaries—or upon modern medical facilities. People who know something about the use of herbal medicines will acquire some very local fame as *mukimi wa miti*; they will treat neighbours many times without charge but the latter will find an opportunity to reciprocate in some way later.

The main diseases that fall into the class of self-treatment are minor, like colds, corns, burns, dandruff, jiggers etc. Besides these, all kinds of minor pain will be self-treated by rubbing, heating or massage.

Diseases healed by themselves
The signs, symptoms and diseases that fall into this class of 'healing by themselves' are very minor conditions like a little pain, a small fever, mild diarrhoea etc. Any Kamba will say that, should such complaints become more serious, he will look for some other treatment. So, as already mentioned, the classes are fluid; signs symptoms and diseases may be classified in more than one class, depending on circumstances and severity.

Teething
Although teething (*ini*) is not really a class by itself, there is a traditional medical functionary to treat it, a specialist called the *mukii* (rubber) or *mundu ula ukiaa ini* (he or she who rubs for *ini*). The Kamba know that teething makes the baby generally uncomfortable and is sometimes accompanied by diarrhoea. It is known that these troubles can even become serious enough for the baby to die. In order to speed up the teething process, the *mukii* performs *kutita* (rubbing), formerly to the accompaniment of uttering of magical spells. The most common method of treatment by the *mukii* is to cut the gum and remove the eye-teeth, and when the blood appears, to rub the wound with *iati* (soda-ash) or another kind of herbal medicine. Many people, mainly women, know how to treat *ini*. Nowadays mothers themselves may rub the gums with some herbal medicine if they know how to prepare one, or they use soda-ash. Some informants reported that you could also apply a special kind of shop medicine. More information on treatment of teething problems is provided in Chapter 24.

Diseases healed by treatment at hospital
This is a new class, since the introduction of modern medicine. *Kisivitali* means 'from the side of the hospital', which includes all modern medical services, including those provided at health centres, dispensaries and by private practitioners. Another description for this class is, 'diseases that are healed by the treatment of these days', but this is less specific and the meaning has to be derived from the context in which it is used.

Kamba living in the Project area, nowadays, will go to the modern health services for any type of complaint or disease, however minor or serious. Whether they go depends on many factors like distance, cost, transport, satisfaction with former visits, information from neighbours and relatives and so on.

Ultimately, if traditional treatment did not cure a patient, hardly a Kamba living in the study area would hesitate to try the modern medical facilities—and vice versa.

Distribution of traditional medical functionaries

In order to assess the availability of traditional medical specialists, the respondents in the in-depth study (40) and the control study (39) were asked about traditional functionaries living nearby. The same information was collected in about 40 clusters of three to four households randomly selected in the Kingoti and Kambusu sublocations. The results are presented in Tables 1 and 2. The large number of traditional medical functionaries was surprising: 154 persons (44 males and 110 females) were reported as traditional medical functionaries, giving a ratio of 1 per 92 of the population. To assess the importance of this finding it is necessary to take into account that only 2 or 3 of the 56 midwives and 2 of the *andu awe* were more or less professionals with more than very local fame. None of the herbalists or teething specialists were professionals.

Furthermore, it is interesting to note that 55 of the 154 traditional medical functionaries combined two or three roles. All the *andu awe* combined the role of diviner with that of herbalist, and 33 of the 56 traditional midwives were reported to combine this role with other therapeutic activities, especially herbalism. The significantly higher number of female than male functionaries (110 to 44) was mainly because all 56 midwives were females. Traditionally there are also male midwives, who only assist in very special cases of difficult delivery, but there were none of these specialists living in the Project area and, as far as the author knows, there are hardly any traditional male midwives functioning in Machakos District today.

Table 1.
Traditional medical roles fulfilled by 154 functionaries living in Kingoti and Kambusu sublocations.

Type	*Total*	*Kingoti*	*Kambusu*
Herbalist	100	70	30
Midwife	56	37	19
Teething specialist	52	35	17
Mundu mue	14	12	2
Total	222	154	68

Table 2.
Combinations of traditional medical roles of the 154 functionnaries by sex.

	n
Males	
Herbalist	37
Teething specialist	2
Mundu mue + herbalist	5
Total	44
Females	
Herbalist	13
Teething specialist	24
Midwife	23
Mundu mue + herbalist	6
Herbalist + teething specialist	11
Midwife + teething specialist	5
Midwife + herbalist	15
Midwife + herbalist + teething specialist	10
Midwife + herbalist + *mundu mue*	3
Total	110

Modern medical services

The introduction of modern medical services into Kenya started in the last quarter of the 19th century. The history of the introduction has been described by Beck (1970 and 1974). General health policies in relation to national development in Kenya and the important role of church medical services, especially in rural areas, have been discussed by Hartwig (1975, 1979). Since the end of the colonial period and after Independence, the health centre has been the basis of the rural health services in Kenya (Fendall, 1963; Dissevelt, 1978). Although policy statements of the Kenya Government stress the importance of rural health, e.g. at the International World Health Organization Conference on primary health care in Alma Ata in 1978 the representative of the Kenya Ministry of Health stressed the importance of rural health care and stated the commitment of the government to the introduction of primary health care, significantly more of the health care budget is spent in urban than in rural areas. The policy of the Kenya Government on rural health is outside the scope of this chapter, however. A short listing of the modern medical facilities available for the study population should be sufficient.

At the time of the utilization survey in 1980, the following modern facilities were available for the population of Kingoti and Kambusu:

- — a 90-bed government subdistrict hospital at Kangundo, 13 km from Kinyui and 6 km from Katwanyaa;
- — a government dispensary in Kingoti sublocation near the chief of Matungulu's camp;
- — two private practitioners had clinics in Tala; two others practised in Kangundo (Tala is 8 km by road from Kinyui and 5 km from Katwanyaa);
- — the Machakos Project staff held weekly clinics for under-5s and pregnant women at Katwanyaa and Kinyui;
- — one unqualified and unlicensed private practitioner held a clinic at the back of a shop in Kinyui market, but had very few patients, according to the author's information;
- — patent medicines for fever, pain, malaria, cough, sore throat, diarrhoea and constipation could be bought at many of the shops in small local markets and in the main market-places in Tala and Kangundo;
- — up to 1979, three private clinics of qualified medical practitioners, who themselves lived outside the Project area, were managed by unqualified staff in Katwanyaa, Kinyui and Miseleni. These clinics were closed by the government before the utilization survey started in 1980;
- — a 10-bed church maternity hospital at Misyani, 4 km from Kambusu sublocation; this hospital was closed in 1980, during the survey.

Schulpen and Swinkels (1980) report that during their utilization survey in 1976, the following additional modern medical services were also available for the population living in the eastern part of the study area:

- — a government dispensary located at Mbiuni, just outside the eastern part of the study area, and three other government dispensaries situated outside the study area across the Athi River, reached by a bridge;
- — the Project staff held weekly clinics for under-5s and pregnant women at Katheka and Kathama;
- — four unqualified and unlicensed private practitioners held irregular clinics in the eastern part;
- — one church secondary school in Kabaa gave irregular services to the population living in the eastern part.

Serious patients attending government dispensaries could be referred to Kangundo hospital, from where they could be sent to the provincial hospital at Machakos town (a distance of 40 km). Patients could also directly attend the outpatients departments of these hospitals or any other private or government hospital in Nairobi or Thika (distance 30 km)on their own initiative; they could also go to one of the private practitioners in Machakos, Nairobi or Thika.

From the above description we may conclude that modern medical services for the Project area inhabitants were within relatively easy reach and of a wide variety.

2. The utilization survey

Materials and methods

Sampling and sample size

Pilot surveys and the facility-based patient-satisfaction study had shown that very few patients in the eastern part of the study area went to Kangundo hospital and Matungulu dispensary. As the utilization survey was related to the above study, it was decided to restrict it to the Kingoti and Kambusu sublocations in the western part. A 5 percent systematic random sample was selected from the households in these sublocations, the sampling areas being the villages in these sublocations. Sixty-four (5.5 percent) of the 1161 households in Kingoti and 46 (5.2 percent) of the 872 in Kambusu were selected for the study. The sampling fraction per village ranged from 4.8 to 6.3 percent. When plotted on a map, the selected households followed quite closely the geographical distribution of all households over the western part of the study area; we concluded that the average distance of selected households and of all households from 'medical service points' was the same. Nine hundred and forty-five household members of the selected 110 households were included in the study. The number of persons per household varied from one to 20.

Data collection

Three field-workers were employed and trained intensively for a period of 3 weeks with the assistance of a research assistant. A short questionnaire was constructed, translated, and tested. Registration forms were developed and assessed for field applicability. Each of the selected households was visited once a week for a period of 10 weeks to collect data on perceived morbidity and utilization of health care. All members of the 110 households were enumerated. Any available adult member of the selected households at the time of the home interview was asked to report on perceived morbidity and related health care. The data were thus mainly collected by proxy reporting.

At the beginning of the survey, profile data (age, sex, education, religion, marital status, occupation etc.) were collected for all persons included in the survey.

During each of the 10 weekly rounds, the following data were collected for each member of the selected households: absence/presence; health status (occurrence of medical complaints); type of medical complaints (a list of 210 Kamba signs, symptoms and diseases had been prepared in advance to facilitate reporting, coding and registration); duration of medical complaint (dates of onset/recovery); perception of seriousness of complaint; health actions undertaken for recovery; and perceived outcome of these actions in terms of perceived changes in health status.

Reliability of collected data

The Machakos Project population-based utilization survey of Schulpen and Swinkels (1980) used a 2-week recall period. These authors reported a high percentage of under-reporting of health actions in their survey, ranging from 25 percent under-reporting of visits to the government dispensaries to 60 percent for 'self-care actions'. To prevent such a high percentage of under-reporting, various steps were taken, such as: limiting the recall period to one week; conducting a pilot survey; careful training of field staff; close contact with field staff and regular supervision and checking of the collected data; reasonable workload for field staff; and limiting data collection to the most essential data. Owing to lack of time and resources, no further field tests (inter-observer re-interviews or re-interviewing of another proxy informant in the same household) were conducted. Excellent support and co-operation were received from the members of the selected households, mainly because the study area inhabitants were very enthusiastic about the patient-satisfaction studies, as they expected that the feedback from the outcome of the studies would lead to improvement in services at the dispensary and hospital. The author is confident that the reliability of the data of the survey is quite high, which is an important fact, considering some of the surprising results.

Results

Perceived morbidity

The survey consisted of 10 weekly rounds of 110 households with 945 members indicated as 'observed persons' (OP). The total number of household interviews was 1100. Taking into account the recorded absence of a number of OP, the total number of 'person observation weeks' was 8570 and the total number of 'person observation days' was 59 990.

The number of OP who were reported ill for at least one day varied from a maximum of 299 (34.8 percent of all OP) in the second round to a minimum of 196 (23.2 percent of all OP) in the tenth round. The total number of reported illness episodes (IE) was 792. The number of IE per OP during the 10-week survey varied from none for 441 OP (46.7 percent) to four for 12 OP (1.3 percent) (Table 3). One, two or three IE were reported for 294, 144 and 54 OP respectively. The average number of IE per OP over the complete survey period was 0.92. Extrapolating this to an annual basis, the reported number of illness episodes would be 4.8 per year for the average inhabitant of Kingoti and Kambusu sublocations.

Table 3.
Number of reported illness episodes (IE) per observed person (OP) reported during the 10-week survey.

No. of IE	*No. of OP*	%
0	441	46.7
1	294	31.1
2	144	15.2
3	54	5.7
4	12	1.3
Total	945	100.0

Table 4.
Duration of the 792 illness episodes (IE) during the 10-week survey[1].

	IE	
Duration IE	*n*	%
1– 3 days	137	17.3
4– 7 days	173	21.8
8–14 days	222	28.0
15–21 days	89	11.2
22–42 days	93	11.7
43–69 days	42	5.3
70 days	36	4.6
Total	792	100.0

[1] 132 IE (16.7 percent) started before the beginning of the survey and 36 of these (4.6 percent) lasted the whole survey period, and were still continuing at the end of the survey; 111 IE (14.0 percent) that started during the observation period were also still continuing at the end of the survey.

At the beginning of the IE (or during the first observation round for those IE that started before the survey), 464 (58.6 percent) were reported as 'serious' and 328 (41.4 percent) as 'not serious'. As to be expected, episodes varied significantly according to reported duration (Table 4). Thirty-seven (17.3 percent) were minor complaints, lasting only 1–3 days, while 36 lasted for 70 days, meaning these were true chronic complaints that started before the survey and were not reported cured by the end of it. The highest number of IE (222, 28 percent) fell into the class 8–14 days. The total number of reported 'perceived morbidity days' was 9366, 15.6 percent of the total number of 'person observation days'. The average duration of the 792 reported IE during the 10-week survey was 11.9 days. There was a significant association between respondents' perceived seriousness of an IE at the beginning of the episode and its reported duration: the longer the duration, the higher the percentage of 'serious cases'.

The reported types of signs, symptoms and diseases for the 792 IE are presented in Table 5. A total of 1159 signs and symptoms were reported for the 792 IE. A maximum of three reported signs or symptoms per IE were included in the Table, ranked according to perceived seriousness; in Table 5 these are indicated as first, second and third complaint. For example, cold/running nose was reported as the most serious complaint in 168 (21.2 percent) of the 792 IE; in 50 cases it was reported as the second most serious

Table 5.
Medical complaints of 792 illness episodes, according to ranking order of frequency of first complaint.[1]

Rank order	*Type of complaint*	*First complaint (%)*	*Second complaint*	*Third complaint*	*Total (%)*
1	Colds/running nose	168 (21.2)	50	15	233 (20.1)
2	Fever	99 (12.5)	41	14	154 (13.3)
3	Coughing	66 (8.3)	49	10	125 (10.8)
4	Stomach/abdominal trouble	54 (6.8)	17	8	79 (6.8)
5	Headache	48 (6.1)	23	7	78 (6.7)
6	Skin rashes	31 (3.9)	5	1	37 (3.2)
7	Kidney pains	25 (3.2)	1	1	27 (2.3)
8	*Kyambo*	22 (2.8)	10	3	35 (3.0)
9	Backache	19 (2.4)	3	2	24 (2.1)
10	Scabies	19 (2.4)	1	–	20 (1.7)
11	Diarrhoea	16 (2.0)	8	4	28 (2.4)
12	Ringworm	16 (2.0)	3	2	21 (1.8)
13	Eye troubles	16 (2.0)	1	3	20 (1.7)
14	Wounds/ulcers	14 (1.8)	2	1	17 (1.5)
15	Serious sore throat/ tonsillitis	12 (1.5)	7	2	21 (1.8)
16	Toothache	10 (1.3)	1	1	12 (1.0)
17	Pain in legs	8 (1.0)	2	–	10 (0.9)
18	Malaria	8 (1.0)	1	–	9 (0.8)
19	Heart beating fast	7 (0.9)	2	–	9 (0.8)
20	Boil, swelling with pus inside	7 (0.9)	2	–	9 (0.8)
21	Epigastric pain	6 (0.8)	6	2	14 (1.2)
22	Itching	6 (0.8)	1	1	8 (0.7)
23	Dislocation/sprain	6 (0.8)	–	–	6 (0.5)
24	Pain in ears	6 (0.8)	–	–	6 (0.5)
25	Vomiting	5 (0.6)	6	3	14 (1.2)
26	Pain in neck	5 (0.6)	2	–	7 (0.6)
27	Pricking pain in chest	5 (0.6)	1	1	7 (0.6)
28	Joint pains	5 (0.6)	1	–	6 (0.5)
29	Delivery	5 (0.6)	1	–	6 (0.5)
30	Worms in stool	5 (0.6)	–	–	5 (0.5)
31	Threadworms	5 (0.6)	–	–	5 (0.5)
	Other	68 (8.7)	27	12	107 (9.2)
	Total	792 (100)	274	93	1159 (100)

[1] Maximum of three complaints per illness episode.

symptom; and in 15 cases as the least serious. In the same way, fever was reported as the most serious, second most serious and least serious complaint in 99, 41 and 14 IE respectively.

The pattern of perceived morbidity in the sublocations Kingoti and Kambusu could be described from the information in Table 5. For this description the sign, symptom or disease that was reported as the most serious for that particular IE was the most important. Colds, fever, cough or stomach/abdominal complaints were reported as the most serious complaints in almost 50 percent of the reported IE; in 168 (21.2 percent), 99 (12.5 percent), 66 (8.3 percent) and 54 (6.8 percent) of the 792 IE respectively. This large number of minor complaints is not surprising, as in any well-organized study on perceived morbidity in which under-reporting is low, a high number of reported IE will consist of only minor complaints. The more serious complaints, which were less frequent, were 'hidden' in our study in the class 'other' (Table 5). This class, for instance, included: two cases of asthma, one of psychoneurosis, one of tuberculosis, one of dysmenorrhoea, one of epilepsy etc.

The information in Table 5 is not only important for the description of the pattern of morbidity in Kingoti and Kambusu, but also for further analysis of the pattern of utilization of health services. It is generally accepted that type of complaint (sign, symptom, disease) is associated with the type of 'action for health' undertaken by the sufferer. The information in Table 5 comprised the signs and symptoms as reported at the beginning of the IE. Most of these covered more than one observation round. On every round note was made whether signs and symptoms reported were the same as on the last round and whether the ranking order stayed the same. The results showed that in 652 (82.3 percent) of reported IE the signs and symptoms and their ranking order did not change throughout the complete episode; in 140 cases (17.7 percent), changes such as alteration in ranking order, cure of one or two of three reported signs, or one or two additional signs or symptoms were recorded.

Static aspects of utilization of health services

A total of 1667 'actions for health' were undertaken for the 792 IE (Table 6), and the average number of actions per IE was 2.1. Extrapolating this to an annual basis, the average inhabitant of Kingoti and Kambusu would take at least 10.1 actions for health a year. The number of actions per IE varied from none in 121 cases (15.3 percent) to 13 in 2 (0.3 percent); one, two and three actions for health were undertaken in 291 (36.7 percent), 170 (21.5 percent) and 78 (9.8 percent) of IE respectively. Further analysis showed that whether an action for health was undertaken was significantly associated with the duration of the episode.

Table 6.
Numbers and percentages of actions undertaken per illness episode in observation period of 10 weeks.

No. of actions	*0*	*1*	*2*	*3*	*4*	*5*	*6*	*7*
No. of cases	121	291	170	78	40	29	17	15
Percentage	15.3	36.7	21.5	9.8	5.1	3.7	2.2	1.9
Cumulative percentage		52.0	73.5	83.3	88.4	92.1	94.3	96.2
Total no. of actions (cumulative)		291	631	865	1025	1170	1272	1377

No. of actions	*8*	*9*	*10*	*11*	*12*	*13*	*Total*
No. of cases	11	8	6	4	—	2	792
Percentage	1.4	1.1	0.8	0.6	—	0.3	100
Cumulative percentage	97.6	98.6	99.4	100	—	100.3	100
Total no. of actions (cumulative)	1465	1537	1597	1641	—	1667	1667

The data on these actions were further analysed according to type, and the results are reported in Table 7. Several important conclusions can be drawn:
— 1528 (91.8 percent) of the actions for health came under the heading 'modern' and only 139 (8.3 percent) were in the sphere of traditional medicine;
— a high percentage (59.6 percent—994 cases) consisted of the use of shop medicines;
— 7.6 percent consisted of cases that visited the Project clinics at Katwanyaa or Kinyui, although these clinics were only open for half a day a week;
— not a single visit to the *mundu mue* was reported.
For further discussion, see below.

Dynamic aspects of utilization of health services

From the static analysis as described above, we obtained the number of actions per IE. We also knew which types were undertaken, but we did not yet know the sequence of types per IE episode, so a further longitudinal analysis was done. In order to facilitate this, the 13 different types of action from the static analysis were combined into four classes: self-modern; professional modern; self-traditional; and professional traditional. Furthermore, the author decided to analyse a maximum of nine

Table 7.
Actions undertaken for 792[1] illness episodes during observation period of 10 weeks.

Type of actions	*n*	%
Modern		
1. Bought and used shop medicine	881	52.8
2. Visit to Kangundo hospital OPD	195	11.7
3. Visit to Machakos Project clinic	125	7.6
4. Previously bought shop medicine[2]	113	6.8
5. Visit to Matungulu dispensary	76	4.6
6. Visit to private doctor in Tala/Kangundo	41	2.5
7. Visit to other big hospital	39	2.3
8. Previously obtained modern medicine[3]	16	1.0
9. Visit to private doctor elsewhere	4	0.2
10. Other modern	38	2.3
Subtotal	(1528)	(91.8)
Traditional		
11. Visit to herbalist	85	
12. Traditional home remedy	49	
13. Visit to traditional midwife	5	
Subtotal	(139)	(8.3)
Total	1667	100.0

[1] no actions were undertaken for 121 of the 792 reported illness episodes
[2] available at home from an earlier illness episode
[3] from hospital/dispensary/Machakos Project clinic for an earlier illness episode or for another patient.

actions per IE, to limit the costs of computer analysis. This did not lead to much loss of information, as actions per IE only exceeded nine in 12 cases (see Table 6).

The data from the longitudinal analysis are presented in Table 8. From this table we can, for instance, draw conclusions that:

— in 199 IE the only action undertaken was self-modern (use of shop medicine or other modern type of medicine available at home), while in 105 IE this type of medicine was used twice;

— in 5 IE the sequential use of modern medicine nine times was reported;

— in 70 IE the respondents used professional modern assistance once (health centre, dispensary, Project clinic, private doctor or Kangundo hospital); sequential use of this type of health action was reported twice for 24 IE and three times for 20 respectively;

— in 14 IE use of professional traditional help once was reported;

— 127 IE were treated by combinations of actions, which were reported less than five times; among these were all the mixed

Table 8.
Combinations of consecutive actions per illness episode, for a maximum number of nine actions per episode.[1]

No. of combinations	A_1	A_2	A_3	A_4	A_5	A_6	A_7	A_8	A_9
	Type of action per separate consecutive action								
199	1								
105	1	1							
24	1	1	1						
15	1	1	1	1					
14	1	1	1	1	1				
5	1	1	1	1	1	1	1	1	1
5	1	1	2						
19	1	2							
8	1	2	2						
70	2								
9	2	1							
24	2	2							
5	2	2	1						
20	2	2	2						
8	3								
14	4								
121	0								
127	other combinations less than 5 each.								
Total 792									

[1]—Only those combinations of actions that happened 5 or more times each are recorded.
—A maximum of nine actions per illness episode were taken into account for the dynamic analysis.
—Types of action:
0 = no action
1 = self modern　　3 = self traditional
2 = professional modern　　4 = professional traditional

combinations of modern and traditional types of treatment for the same IE.

A further step in the longitudinal analysis was to check the sequence of type of health actions for the most frequently reported diseases. For further information on this, see van Luijk (1983b).

Discussion

The data from the general utilization survey gave satisfactory information on the pattern of perceived morbidity and the associated pattern of utilization of health services. To describe the pattern of morbidity on a yearly basis, taking into account seasonal variations, the survey should be extended to cover at least 10 weeks in the rainy season and 10 weeks in the dry season. The study described in this chapter was planned to take place in the dry season but the rains started early and it was raining in the last 3 weeks of the survey.

Another problem affecting the description of the pattern of perceived morbidity could have been under-reporting owing to the social stigma of certain illnesses. Epilepsy, tuberculosis, asthma and, to a much lesser extent, venereal disease, carry such a stigma. Nevertheless, two cases of asthma, one of tuberculosis and one of epilepsy were reported. No cases of gonorrhoea were reported as such but they might have been included under the headings of 'kidney disease' or 'urinating blood'.

The author is fairly confident about the reliability of the collected data on perceived morbidity. As the data were mainly collected by proxy reporting, however, a certain number of under-reporting of minor cases had to be accepted as it could not be expected that every adult member of a household would know about every minor complaint of each of the other members of the household. To minimize under-reporting as far as possible, the interviewers had been instructed if possible to interview the head of the household or his or her partner. There was no reason to suspect any over-reporting as no medicine or any other incentives —apart from an occasional lift—were given to the respondents.

Women and children waiting at the Machakos Project clinic in Miseleni.

Real proof of the reliability of the data on perceived morbidity, however, cannot be given as, owing to lack of time and resources, no inter- and intra-observer or inter-proxy checks were carried out.

It is concluded that the data on utilization of modern medical care were reliable. No purposely under- or over-reporting was suspected. The possibility of under-reporting, of course, did exist, especially about modern self-care (shop medicine), owing to the system of proxy reporting. Nevertheless, the high frequency of reported use of shop medicine did not suggest under-reporting.

The analysis of the material from the in-depth cases studies, which is not discussed in this chapter, showed to a large extent the same pattern of use of modern medical care as the survey data, so also supporting the reliability of the survey data.

One striking outcome of the analysis was the low frequency of use of traditional medical care—with the exception of traditional midwives (see Chapter 23)—reported. Two explanations are possible: first, the author knew, when the survey was planned and carried out, that data on visits to the *mundu mue* could not be obtained in a survey. A visit to the *mundu mue* is a secret activity that hardly anyone living in Kingoti or Kambusu would openly admit or discuss. It is too secret, too private, to be reported in a survey. Christians of all denominations are forbidden by church dogma and by the church elders to go to a *mundu mue* (information received from church elders of all denominations who were interviewed). The subchiefs of Kingoti and Kambusu, who were also interviewed, told the author that the government did not forbid visits to the *mundu mue*, but both said that people would not admit going and would go secretly at night.

Of the 108 respondents in the survey on attitude towards traditional medical care, 94 (87 percent) also said that Christians were not allowed to go to the *mundu mue*, and 99 (92.5 percent) said that people would conceal such a visit for such reasons as:

— it was a sin	18 times (20.9 percent)
— to prevent loss of name	17 times (19.8 percent)
— not to alert an enemy in case of witchcraft	13 times (11.8 percent)
— people did not want to be called pagan	12 times (10.9 percent)
— Christians are not allowed to go	10 times (9.1 percent)

The author concludes, taking into account all available information, that ultimately, as a last resort in case of serious misfortune or disease, a very high percentage of the inhabitants of Kingoti and Kambusu would still go to the *mundu mue*, but as there were so many ‘thresholds’ and the price in money and social cost was so high, visits were relatively infrequent.

The use of herbalists and traditional self-care was also lower than expected. There was no reason however, to suspect any deliberate under-reporting, as there is no social stigma attached to these types of health actions. The author is sure that the low frequency of use of this type of medicine and also the relatively low frequency of visits to the *mundu mue*, as reported in the in-depth study, were the result of a very radical general process of social and cultural change that took place among the inhabitants of Kingoti and Kambusu sublocation during the colonial period and after Independence in 1963. The author is also convinced that a similar type of survey conducted among the Kamba living in other areas of Machakos District, such as Yatta, Masii and Kiteta, would give a much higher frequency of use of traditional medicine than found in Kingoti and Kambusu. The same was said in general discussions with key informants in Kambusu and Kingoti, who claimed that, especially in Kambusu, Christianity and modernization had had a radical influence on custom and behaviour, even to the extent that it was agreed that people living in the eastern part of the Project area were much more traditionally orientated.

Clear indications of such radical change were:

— only one of 108 respondents (in 108 of the 110 survey households) belonged to the traditional Kamba religion; the others belonged to Christian denominations;
— 105 of the 108 respondents were regular church-goers;
— 94 of the 108 heads of households were registered as church members, and only 2 belonged to the traditional religion;
— in 82 (72.9 percent) of the 110 households all household members were regular church-goers;
— 81 (75 percent) of heads of household could read and write;
— the degree of modernization was assessed by one interviewer living in Kingoti, and only 2 of the 108 households were assessed as being traditionally orientated;
— only 3 of the 108 respondents said they still sacrificed at the *ithembo* (sacred grove);
— all healthy children of primary school age in Kingoti and Kambusu went or would go to school around the age of 6–8;
— the almost complete absence of the traditional *kilumi* dances;
— the fact that traditional initiation rites did not take place any more; boys were still circumcised, but this was done at the dispensary in Matungulu or at Kangundo hospital. All respondents said that their boys would be circumcised at one of the modern facilities. Clitoridectomy is part of the traditional initiation rites of girls, but this does not take place any more in Kingoti and Kambusu. The author enquired very carefully about this and discussed it with informants who gave very

detailed information about witchcraft accusations, visits to the *mundu mue* and other secret and private topics; none the less, all of them insisted that they did not know of any case of clitoridectomy. They speculated that parents who really wanted to have this traditional operation done would have to go to Yatta or other area in Machakos where the people were still traditionally orientated. One informant declared that he had heard that it was possible to have girls operated on by modern medical functionaries, but that this had to be done 'through the back door'. The subchiefs of Kingoti and Kambusu both said that clitoridectomy was forbidden by law, but the author is not aware of such a regulation.

One important factor remains to be emphasized. There is a remarkable basic similarity between traditional and modern ideas about the basic cause of a high proportion of diseases. These are mainly diseases that can be treated by home treatment or by the herbalist. For the modernized Kamba, living in Kingoti and Kambusu, it is not really such a radical change to go to the dispensary or hospital or buy shop medicine, instead of using home remedies or going to a herbalist. To them the use of traditional herbal medicine against fever is in the same class as using anti-malaria medicine bought from a shop or received from the dispensary or the hospital. Taking into account the high level of expectation of the impact of modern medicine and the relative availability of modern facilities, it is not really remarkable that for a high proportion of minor and short-lived diseases and complaints, the respondents undertook 'modern actions for health'. But for chronic cases in which witchcraft was suspected, many inhabitants of Kingoti and Kambusu would ultimately go to the *mundu mue*.

The author concludes that it was the impact of the process of social and cultural change combined with relatively easy access to modern health care and the unquantifiable impact of the Machakos Project itself that was responsible for the relatively high frequency of utilization of modern services and low frequency of use of traditional services.

It is hoped that this chapter has shown that well-planned, organized and supervised utilization surveys conducted in the Machakos Project study area are important because they provide reliable data on perceived morbidity and the associated utilization of modern and traditional medical care, with the exception of the care provided by the *mundu mue*. Such data can be used by health-care planners and managers to calculate perceived morbidity rates, to define at-risk groups and to plan related health-care activities.

Finally, we would like to comment that, although this chapter has been limited to the description of the sample survey, in-depth studies are of equal importance. They provide complementary data on motivational and behavioural aspects such as reasons for satisfaction, compliance and utilization of health services. These data can be used by health-care planners and managers to decide: how to meet demands; how to improve services; how to organize promotive and preventive actions; how to introduce primary health care; and how to assess the possibility of, and eventually organize, co-operation between modern and traditional medical functionaries.

References

Beck A, A history of the British Medical Administration of East Africa, 1900–1950, Harvard University Press, Cambridge, 1970.

Beck A, History of medicine and health services in Kenya (1900–1950), In; Health and disease in Kenya, Vogel LC et al., Eds, East African Litterature Bureau, Nairobi, 1974, pp. 91–106.

Dissevelt AG, Integrated maternal and child health services. A study at a rural health centre in Kenya, MD dissertation, University of Amsterdam, Amsterdam, (1978).

Fabrega H, The scope of ethnomedical science, Cult Med Psychiatry, 1 (1977) 201–28.

Fendall NRE, Health centres: a basis for a rural health service, J Trop Med Hyg, 66 (1963) 219–32.

Githinji EM, The outpatient and the staff satisfaction with the treatment provided in a district hospital—Kiambu, MA thesis, University of Dar es Salam, Dar es Salam, (1977).

Good CM, A comparison of rural and urban ethnomedicine among the Kamba of Kenya, In; Traditional health care delivery in contemporary Africa, Ulin PR and Segall MH, Eds, African series no. 35, Syracuse University,Syracuse, (1980), pp. 13–56.

Hartwig CW, Health policies and national development in Kenya, PhD dissertation, University of Kentucky, Lexington, (1975).

Hartwig CW, Church–state relations in Kenya: health issues, Soc Sci and Med, 13C, 2 (1979) 121–7.

Maneno J, Schlüter P, Sjoerdsma AC, Vogel LC and Savage King F, Guidelines for the management of hospital outpatient services, Ministry of Health, Nairobi, 1982.

Mbiti JS, New Testament eschatology in African background, Oxford University Press, Oxford, 1971.

Schulpen TWJ and Swinkels WJAM, The utilization of health services in a rural area of Kenya, Trop Geogr Med, 32 (1980) 340–9.

Swinkels WJAM and Schulpen TWJ, A dynamic approach to the utilization of health service in a rural area of Machakos, Kenya, Trop Geogr Med, 32 (1980) 350–7.

van Luijk JN, Profile, expectations and satisfaction of the outpatients (1970–1972), Trop Geogr Med, 31, Suppl 4 (1979) S33–S60.

van Luijk JN, Patient profile and patient satisfaction. Review of outline, data analysis and first findings of a study of the clients of the OPD of Kangundo subdistrict hospital, Kenya, Royal Trop Inst, Amsterdam, mimeographed, (1980).

van Luijk JN, Traditional medicine among the Kamba of Machakos district, Kenya, Part I and Part II, Royal Trop Inst, Amsterdam, mimeographed, (1982A).

van Luijk JN, The choice of the health-care provider: preference and rejection. The utilization of different types of health care by the Akamba of Machakos district, Kenya, In; Health research in developing countries, Diesfeld HJ, Ed, Peter Lang, Frankfurt am Main, 1982B, pp. 37–77.

van Luijk JN, Utilization of modern and traditional medical care by the Kamba of Machakos, Kenya, Part I. Survey on perceived morbidity and medical care: description of the survey, Royal Trop Inst, Amsterdam, mimeographed, (1982C).

van Luijk JN, Utilization of modern and traditional medical care by the Kamba of Machakos, Kenya, Part II. Survey on perceived morbidity and medical care: static and dynamic analysis, Royal Trop Inst, Amsterdam, mimeographed, (1983A).

van Luijk JN, Health care among the Kamba, PhD dissertation, to be submitted to Leyden State University, Leyden, (1983B).

van Luijk JN and Vogel LC, Health services research: the case of the outpatient department, Trop Geogr Med, 31, Suppl 4 (1979) S61–S68.

23

Modern and traditional antenatal and delivery care

A.M. Voorhoeve
C. Kars
J.K. van Ginneken

Introduction

Every step forward raises fresh problems, and in the progress of medical science this is clearly true for obstetrics. There is little doubt that at present perinatal and maternal mortality in developing countries would be much lower if all pregnant women had the benefit of free, readily available, modern antenatal and delivery care. More and more obstetricians, however, are realizing that what may be beneficial for some pregnant women at special risk of complications is not necessarily so for the majority who are not at such risk (Kloosterman, 1978; Johnstone et al., 1978; Hellegers, 1978; O'Brien, 1978).

In technically advanced countries the decrease in maternal and perinatal mortality during the last 40 years has coincided with increase in knowledge of the causes of many serious complications of pregnancy, of improved methods of treatment and of better organization of maternity services. At the same time more deliveries have taken place in hospital, and public health and social standards have improved. Some attribute the decreased mortality rates partly to deliveries in hospital (Marsh, 1977; Hoogendoorn, 1978), but others disagree (Janssens, 1977). Recent studies in the Netherlands have shown that home deliveries generally progress more rapidly than hospital deliveries (Thomassen et al., 1979) and several authors have stressed the beneficial effect of ambulation during labour (Mendez Bauer, 1975; Flynn et al., 1978).

In the present article an attempt is made to analyse the antenatal and delivery care received by women in a rural area in Kenya.

Materials and methods

In January 1975 a survey of the outcome of pregnancy of all women included in the study population was started. When a woman was observed by a field-worker to be pregnant, a form was completed with answers to the following questions: the number of previous live and stillbirths; the number and age at death of children who had died; whether she had ever delivered in hospital and whether this had involved operation, vacuum extraction or forceps; where she intended to deliver this time and why. During the first year of the study the last question was only asked if a woman stated that she intended to deliver in hospital; later on the question was asked irrespective of intended place of delivery, as it was found equally important to know why home delivery was preferred. To avoid embarrassment for both the woman and the field-worker the questionnaire was not administered until pregnancy was obvious; once the women became familiar with the questions many volunteered the information that they were pregnant. Only a few women, mostly unmarried schoolgirls, tried to hide or deny their pregnancy.

After delivery the women were asked where they had delivered; who had assisted them; whether there had been any complications; whether they had been to an antenatal clinic; and if so their reasons for going.

The questionnaire was structured so as to classify answers on the choice of modern or traditional antenatal and delivery care into: medical reasons (current or previous illness); economic reasons (hospital too far or too expensive); sociocultural reasons (whether hospital or home delivery was considered safer or more convenient); others (custom, authority of others etc.). Information on antenatal and delivery care by traditional midwives derived from four sources:

1. one of the authors had conducted a medical-sociological investigation in 1973 on the utilization of modern and traditional forms of maternity care in two areas of Machakos district, one of which was situated within the study area of the Machakos Project (Kars, 1974);
2. while the present study was in progress a female Kenyan sociologist collected information, in the form of case studies, on ideas and practices concerning pregnancy and child-rearing from elderly members of the community (Beth Ahlberg Maina, unpublished report, Medical Research Centre, Nairobi);
3. if a perinatal death occurred at home, the first author discussed the problems that had led to the death of the child with the traditional midwife who had assisted at the delivery;
4. the first author joined some traditional midwives when they assisted at deliveries and so had an opportunity, through discussion and observation, to gain more insight into their beliefs, practices and problems; she had a particular opportunity for this during a series of training sessions for traditional midwives held in 1979.

Most women who chose modern antenatal and delivery care went to the hospital at Kangundo, a 120-bed sub-district hospital 6–26 km from the nearest and farthest parts of the study area respectively. The first author visited this hospital regularly and had discussions with the midwives and doctors working there on their views and practices concerning antenatal and delivery care.

Results

During the 4 years of the study 4716 women gave birth to 4768 children. The perinatal mortality rate was 46.4 per 1000 total deliveries; there were four maternal deaths. Twelve hundred and sixty-one women (27 percent) delivered in a hospital and 3455 (73 percent) elsewhere. The perinatal mortality rate was 65.1 per 1000 among children born in hospital and 39.4 among children born elsewhere. Details on the outcome of pregnancy are given in Chapter 18.

Modern antenatal care

Among the 4716 women in the study 3961 (84 percent) attended an antenatal clinic at least once; 613 (13 percent) never attended; and for the remaining 142 (3 percent) no information was available. The majority (82 percent) of those who had attended an antenatal clinic said that they either went for check-up or to be registered for hospital delivery; 14 percent said they had attended because of current or previous illness; the remaining 4 percent had visited the antenatal clinic because a doctor or their husband had told them to do so.

Most women went to the antenatal clinic at Kangundo Hospital. A few, mainly young women with husbands working in town, joined their husbands towards the end of their pregnancy in order to be near a hospital when labour started, and usually attended the antenatal clinic at that hospital.

Regular public transport to Kangundo was only available to people living in the western part of the study area, comprising the sublocations Kingoti and Kambusu. Women from the eastern part who wanted to go to an antenatal clinic either had to walk or to wait for a passing lorry. Table 1 gives the numbers and percentages of women who attended an antenatal clinic by sublocation and the average distance from each sublocation to Kangundo Hospital. Attendance was closely related to the distance the women had to travel ($p<0.001$).

Antenatal clinics at Kangundo Hospital were held daily from Monday to Friday. Between 400 and 500 patients were seen each week, about a quarter of these being first attenders. The staff of the antenatal clinic consisted of a registered nurse-midwife with two or three enrolled or ungraded nurses and often an enrolled public health nurse. The routine at the antenatal clinic after registration was for the women to be weighed, their blood pressure taken and the fetal position checked. At first visits a history was taken, height was measured and urine tested for sugar and albumen. Primigravidae were seen by the doctor for pelvic assessment and women with complaints were referred to the clinical officer at the general outpatient department. Tetanus toxoid was given at 24 and 36 weeks of pregnancy. Health education talks were given regularly by the public health nurse. A variety of

Table 1.
Distance from each sublocation to Kangundo hospital, antenatal clinic attendance and hospital delivery by sublocation.

Sublocation	*Average distance to Kangundo hospital*	*Number of deliveries in each sublocation*	*Antenatal clinic attendance** %	*Hospital delivery* %
Kambusu	8 km	1115	93	31
Kingoti	12 km	1603	90	34
Katheka	16 km	446	76	15
Katitu	22 km	722	78	16
Ulaani	24 km	830	69	21
Total		4716	84	27

*at least one attendance

antenatal record cards were used and for a long time the women received just a piece of paper because cards were out of stock.

Delivery intentions

Sixteen hundred and eighty-five (47 percent) of 3565 women questioned intended to deliver in hospital and 1409 (40 percent) at home; another 471 (13 percent) had not yet made up their minds when interviewed.

Table 2 shows that factors such as distance from Kangundo Hospital, previous hospital delivery and age were related to intended place of delivery: those who lived farther away were less likely to plan for hospital delivery than those who lived nearby; the majority of the women who had delivered in hospital before intended to do so again; and a greater proportion of women below than above 30 intended to deliver in hospital. Primigravidae were more and grand multiparae less inclined to plan for hospital delivery. Women who had experienced difficulties with previous deliveries, like caesarean section, forceps or vacuum extraction, post-partum haemorrhage or perinatal death, were significantly more inclined to plan for hospital delivery than those who had a history of only spontaneous births (Table 3). Women of short stature (less than 150 cm), however, were less inclined to do so. Marital status and having complaints during pregnancy were not related to the place of intended delivery.

Eighty-two percent of the women who intended to deliver in hospital gave as their reason the availability of more and better help there if something should go wrong, mentioning the presence

Table 2.
Variables that influenced intention to deliver in hospital among 3565 women questioned.

Variable	*n*	*Intending hospital delivery %*	*p*
Distance			
Kingoti, Kambusu	2068	55	<0.001
Katheka, Ulaani, Katitu	1497	36	
Age			
Under 30 years	2346	50	<0.001
30 years and over	1219	41	
Previous hospital delivery			
Yes	1281	66	
No	1639	31	<0.001
First pregnancy	645	53	
Parity			
0	645	53	<0.05
≥1	2920	46	
Grand multiparity			
≥6	891	42	<0.001
0–5	2674	49	
Marital status			
Unmarried, divorced, widowed	616	48	n.s.
Married	2949	47	
Previous caesarean section			
Yes	51	86	
No	2869	45	<0.001
First pregnancy	645	53	
Previous forceps or vacuum extraction			
Yes	52	81	
No	2868	45	<0.001
First pregnancy	645	53	
Previous postpartum haemorrhage			
Yes	152	56	
No	2768	45	<0.05
First pregnancy	645	53	
Previous perinatal deaths			
Yes	605	52	
No	2315	44	<0.001
First pregnancy	645	53	
Height			
<150 cm	269	39	
≥150 cm	3246	48	<0.01
Not measured	50	56	
Presenting complaints			
Yes	1173	48	n.s.
No	2392	47	

n.s. = not significant

Table 3.
Influence of previous caesarean section and forceps or vacuum extraction on intention to deliver in hospital among 1281 women who had previously delivered in hospital.

	n	*Intending hospital delivery* %	*p*
Previous caesarean section	51	86	
Previous forceps or vacuum extraction	52	81	<0.001
Spontaneous births only	1178	64	

of a doctor and of qualified midwives, the availability of modern medicine and the possibility of an operation. Fourteen percent of the women preferred hospital delivery because of a past or present illness. The main reasons why women intended to deliver at home were lack of transport or money and the fact that they had had no problems with previous deliveries.

Modern delivery care

Of all 4716 women 1261 (27 percent) delivered in hospital. The months with the lowest percentages of hospital deliveries were May 1975, April 1976, November 1977 and October 1978, all months with rather heavy rainfall; at other times the proportion remained fairly constant at 27 percent. Table 1 gives the percentages of women from each of the five sublocations who delivered in hospital. The difference between Kingoti and Kambusu, 8 and 12 km away from the hospital, and Katheka, Ulaani and Katitu, 16–24 km from the hospital, is highly significant ($p<0.001$).

Table 4 shows that the correlation of a number of characteristics of the women with actual place of delivery is stronger than with intended place of delivery. Almost half the women with a height below 150 cm did actually go to hospital, as did a higher proportion of primigravidae than multigravidae. Grand multiparae, who are of course usually aged 30 or more, went less frequently to hospital for delivery than younger women. Women who had never before delivered in hospital were less likely to go there for delivery than those who had; it appeared that the women tended to deliver subsequently where they delivered first, at home or in hospital. Among the women who had delivered before in hospital only those who had undergone a caesarean section went there again more often than those who had had only spontaneous births (Table 5).

Table 4.
Variables that influenced actual hospital delivery among all 4716 women.

Variable	*n*	*Hospital deliveries* %	*p*
Distance			
Kingoti, Kambusu	2718	33	<0.001
Katheka, Ulaani, Katitu	1998	18	
Age			
Under 30 years	3181	29	<0.001
30 years and over	1535	21	
Previous hospital delivery			
Yes	1689	43	
No	2044	10	<0.001
First pregnancy	983	34	
Intention			
Hospital delivery	1685	36	
Home delivery	1405	10	<0.001
Unknown	1626	31	
Parity			
0	983	34	<0.001
⩾1	3733	25	
Grand multiparity			
⩾6	1097	22	<0.001
0–5	3619	28	
Marital status			
Unmarried, divorced, widowed	1055	27	n.s.
Married	3661	27	
Previous caesarean section			
Yes	67	73	
No	3666	24	<0.001
First pregnancy	983	34	
Previous forceps or vacuum extraction			
Yes	62	53	
No	3671	24	<0.001
First pregnancy	983	34	
Previous postpartum haemorrhage			
Yes	178	32	
No	3555	24	<0.05
First pregnancy	983	34	
Previous perinatal death			
Yes	731	27	
No	3002	24	n.s.
First pregnancy	983	34	
Height			
<150 cm	316	47	
⩾150 cm	4074	23	<0.001
Not measured	326	60	
Presenting complaints			
Yes	1210	26	n.s.
No	3506	27	

n.s. = not significant

Table 5.
Influence of previous caesarean section and forceps or vacuum extraction on the place of delivery among 1689 women who had earlier delivered in hospital.

	n	*Hospital deliveries* %	*p*
Previous caesarean section	67	73	<0.001
Previous forceps or vacuum extraction	62	53	n.s.
Spontaneous births only	1560	41	

n.s. = not significant

Table 4 also summarizes to what extent the women followed their intentions. Of the 1685 women who intended to deliver in hospital only 36 percent actually did so and of the 1405 women who intended to deliver at home 10 percent changed their minds and delivered in hospital. Some of the reasons for not delivering where intended will be discussed later on.

There was nowhere near Kangundo Hospital for women to stay before delivery; the same applied, as far as we know, for other government hospitals, and women wishing to deliver in hospital had to find lodgings with friends or relatives nearby. Only the obviously ill and previous caesar cases were admitted before labour commenced. No family member or friend was allowed to stay with a woman in labour at the hospital.

Deliveries were normally conducted in the lithotomy position and an episiotomy was done as routine in all primigravidae. There was no fixed time for women to stay in hospital after delivery; once a women felt well, breast-feeding had been established and the hospital fee paid, she was allowed to leave. Breast-feeding was encouraged and women with low-birth-weight babies were kept until the child was ready for discharge, to enable them to breast-feed their babies. Major operations could not be performed at Kangundo Hospital and women who needed a caesarean section had to be transferred to the provincial hospital at Machakos, a distance of about 40 km.

Traditional antenatal care

No precise data were available on the number of women who consulted a traditional midwife during pregnancy. In a previous study it was found that, among a group of 178 women, 145 (81 percent) went for modern antenatal care only; 5 (3 percent) for

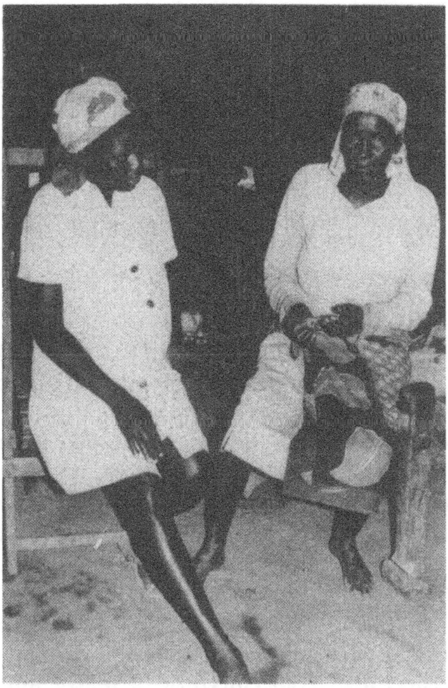

Consultation with a traditional midwife.

traditional care only; and 28 (16 percent) used both modern and traditional care (Kars, 1974).

Antenatal care was provided by traditional midwives (*mwisikya*), but in particular by traditional midwife specialists (*mwisikya mwai*). A *mwisikya* is usually an older women, past child-bearing age, who assists in the delivery at the woman's home; she does not depend on midwifery as a source of income. She gained her knowledge through experience and/or by assisting other mwisikya. A *mwisikya mwai*, on the other hand, depends entirely on midwifery as a source of income and has a special place for delivery at her home where women also come for antenatal care. Most of the traditional midwives at the time of the study were somewhere between a *mwisikya* and a *mwisikya mwai*.

Consultations with a traditional midwife took place particularly when women complained of lower abdominal pain or if they had been advised to return to the clinic to have the position of the fetus checked (Kars, 1974). The traditional midwife tended to attribute lower abdominal pain to a wrong position of either the fetus or the placenta and to treat it by massaging the woman's abdomen with warm hands smeared with butter or soap. She claimed that this turned the baby and even the placenta into the right position.

Usually this massage was done with a gentle circular movement from lower abdomen to the sides; backache was also treated with massage. For complaints like pain, weakness or swollen legs herbal medicine was often used. Most of the traditional midwives said they sent women with vaginal bleeding, painful micturition or fever to hospital. The most important aspect of traditional care is probably the comfort, reassurance and advice to a younger woman by an older one with years of experience in attending childbirths.

Traditional delivery care

Among the 3455 women who delivered at home 2122 (62 percent) were attended by a traditional midwife and 1041 (30 percent) by a friend or relative, while 292 (8 percent) gave birth alone.

Once a traditional midwife was called she usually stayed with the woman in labour until she had delivered. During the day she helped with household chores; at night she was offered a bed in the same hut or room as her patient. She spent long hours with all the women in the household talking, telling stories and praying. During the first stage of labour the mother would usually do what she liked as regards rest or activity, food or drink. There are no longer any strong food taboos for pregnant and lactating women, but most of them avoided the bulky *isyo* (mixture of maize and beans) in the last trimester of pregnancy.

When a woman felt like pushing she retired to the hut that had been prepared for the delivery. At this stage the traditional midwife often made a vaginal examination and might rupture the membranes. For this purpose some grew the fingernail on the right index finger to a length of 2 cm or more and filed it to a sharp point. During the second stage the mother would kneel on a sack with another woman supporting her shoulders and back, while the midwife sat on a low chair in front of her to receive the baby. With primigravidae, when expulsion was slow, the midwife might try to 'widen the path' by sweeping one finger around the child's head. Some claimed to perform a sort of episiotomy, probably influenced by modern hospital practice. None of the midwives ever admitted that any of their patients had had a total perineal tear. When the child was born it was wrapped in a clean piece of material and 'kept warm' on the midwife's lap. To make a baby breathe the midwife might blow on its face, sprinkle it with cold water, rub its back or slap its buttocks.

To deliver the placenta the mother's abdomen was pressed; all midwives knew that it is dangerous to pull on the cord. Some claimed to perform a manual removal in order to remove a retained placenta, but these were most likely removals of the placenta from the vagina, as none inserted her hand deeper than the wrist. The cord was cut after the placenta was born. It was tied in two places, 2–3 cm from the abdominal wall, with thread or sisal, and cut with a razor blade. The mother was then allowed to lie down, covered with a blanket and given the baby. The midwife examined the placenta and cleaned up. She did not inspect the mother's perineum but she did check for blood loss and would gently massage the uterus, tie a cloth round the woman's abdomen and give an extract of a bitter herb called *kunini* to drink if bleeding was heavy.

If all was well no special postnatal care was given. After she had rested for a while the mother would get up to wash herself and put on a clean dress. The baby was usually given some water before breast-feeding. With primiparae the midwife might remain to check and advise on breast-feeding and bathing the infant. It was not customary for her to return later.

Characteristics of women who did not deliver where intended

Table 4 shows that 64 percent of women who intended to deliver in hospital actually delivered at home. Detailed analysis indicated that in most cases this was because of inability to reach the hospital, not change of mind. Among the women with a previous caesarean section who delivered at home, three tried to go to hospital but could not get there; another who did reach the hospital only managed to do so after over 24 hours in labour. Women who had never before delivered in hospital and those who lived far away were the least likely to deliver in hospital, even if they had meant to do so.

One hundred and forty-six women who had intended to deliver at home actually delivered in hospital (Table 4). Those who had delivered in hospital before changed their minds more easily; only a few went to the hospital because of complications developing during labour.

Discussion and recommendations

The need to identify high-risk mothers and facilitate their referral to centres where they can be delivered under conditions of optimal care and safety is stressed by WHO (1977, 1978) and widely recognized in both developed (Haverkamp et al., 1976; Ferster and Jenkins, 1976; Treffers, 1978) and developing countries (Hall et al., 1976). Criteria for referral of obstetric patients have been determined and instructions sent to clinics throughout Kenya. Various excellent antenatal record cards have been designed to facilitate the selection of high-risk maternity cases at antenatal clinics (Dissevelt et al., 1976; Sims, 1978; Essex and Everett, 1977). In the present study it was found that most pregnant women attended an antenatal clinic at least once and that hospital was recognized as the safest place to deliver. Previous caesarean section and short stature are recognized as risk factors by the women themselves, their relatives and hospital personnel. So also, to a lesser degree, is primiparity. For the majority of women, however, whether or not to deliver in hospital seems to be mainly a question of opportunity.

One of the problems for nurses and midwives who want to select women at risk is that they need a yardstick to decide between high- and low-risk women. Such a yardstick could be built into a standard antenatal record card designed to differentiate between high- and low-risk cases. Our first recommendation is that such a card should be introduced on a national, or in the first instance regional, basis. An explanation of its purpose and use should be included in the training curriculum of nurses and midwives.

It is no use selecting women for hospital delivery, however, if they cannot get to hospital once labour has started. In the present study distance and public transport were obviously the most important obstacles to getting to hospital. The fact that a higher proportion of younger than older women went to hospital is probably partly due to a general modern trend towards hospital delivery. Younger women, however, have a better chance of

Far from hospital.

reaching hospital: they are usually in better health; they have fewer children to look after at home; and they have relatives not yet too old to look after the children, livestock and crops; they also have more often a husband, friends or relatives living in one of the major towns with whom they can stay towards the end of their pregnancy.

Our second recommendation is therefore that accommodation where women who are at high risk can stay until delivery should be provided near every hospital. Experience in other countries and at mission hospitals has shown that such accommodation need not be expensive: most women will feel quite happy and comfortable in the sort of house they are used to, and they can do their own cooking and cleaning and bring their own bedding if necessary. In a country like Kenya, where so much is achieved by voluntary community effort (*harambee*), such accommodation might even be built and maintained by local women's groups.

References

Dissevelt AG, Kornman JJCM and Vogel LC. An antenatal record for identification of high risk cases by auxiliary midwives at rural health centres, Trop Geogr Med, 28 (1976) 251.

Essex BJ and Everett KJ, Use of an action-orientated card for antenatal screening, Trop Doct, 7 (1977) 134.

Ferster G and Jenkins DN, Patterns of antenatal care, perinatal mortality, and birth-weight in three consultant obstetric units, Lancet, ii (1976) 727.

Flynn AM, Kelly J, Hollins G and Lynch PF, Ambulation in labour, Brit Med J, 2 (1978) 591.

Hall JStE, Lowry MF and Sparke B, A review of perinatal mortality with specific recommendations for reducing its high rate in developing countries, W Ind Med J, 25 (1976) 177.

Haverkamp AD, Thompson HE and McFee JG, Am J Obstet Gynecol, 125 (1976) 310.

Hellegers AE, Fetal monitoring and neonatal death rates, (editorial), New Engl J Med, 299 (1978) 357.

Hoogendoorn D, Ned Tijdschr Geneesk, 122 (1978) 1171.

Janssens J, Ned Tijdschr Geneesk, 121 (1977) 1241.

Johnstone FD, Campbell DM and Hughes GJ, Has continuous intrapartum monitoring made any impact on fetal outcome, Lancet, i (1978) 1298.

Kars C, The use of modern and traditional forms of maternity care among the Akamba in Kenya, Mimeographed record, University of Leyden, 1974.

Kloosterman GJ, Ned Tijdschr Geneesk, 122 (1978) 1161.

Marsh GN, Verhandlungen der Deutschen Gesellschaft für Allgemeinmedizin, May (1977) 104.

Mendez-Bauer CJ, Effects of standing position on spontaneous uterine contractility and other aspects of labour, J Perinat Med, 3 (1975) 89.

O'Brien M, Home and hospital: a comparison of the experiences of mothers having home and hospital confinements, J R Coll Gen Practit, 28 (1978) 460.

Sims P, Antenatal card for developing countries, Trop Doct, 8 (1978) 137.

Thomassen JFM, van Duyn FL and Sigling HO, Medisch Contact, 34 (1979) 1440.

Treffers PE, Ned Tijdschr Geneesk, 122 (1978) 291.

WHO Chronicle, Attempts to improve the prospects of survival of newborn infants, 31 (1977) 66.
WHO Chronicle, Something for all and more for those in greater need. A 'risk approach' for integrated maternal and child healthcare, 31 (1977) 150.
WHO Offset Publication, 39 (1978).

24

Beliefs and practices related to measles and acute diarrhoea

B. Maina-Ahlberg

Introduction

A sociological study was included in this population-based medical research project carried out in a rural area of Kenya because it was realized that social and cultural factors influence many aspects of health and disease. Such factors not only affect patterns of morbidity and mortality, but also utilization of medical care. As Suchman (1963) put it:

> 'Social factors determine the response of society and the individual to many health problems. The meaning of illness, its perception and definition, and behavioural responses to illness are basic factors influencing the reactions of the public to public health programmes.'

This implies that the existence and role of various beliefs and practices that are part of the culture of a particular population should be taken into account when designing measures and programmes aimed at improving the health situation in that population.

The present paper describes, first, part of the Kamba culture dealing with the causes, prevention and treatment of measles and acute diarrhoea. Secondly, results of a survey on patterns of utilization of modern and indigenous medical care are reported.

Materials and methods

The study was carried out in four sublocations. Two sublocations, Kambusu and Ulaani, were located in area B, where intensive research activities were carried out. The other two sublocations, Kitwii and Kivau, were in area A, a control area where the only project activity was an annual demographic survey.

In-depth information concerning matters related to measles and diarrhoea was obtained through participant observation, recording of case studies and use of key informants. The information was gathered from September 1974 to February 1976 when the author lived in the community and mastered the local language.

More data were obtained through single household visits during which mothers were questioned by means of a structured interview schedule. The bulk of the questions elicited information on what mothers think about measles and acute diarrhoea and how they behaved the last time a child suffered from these diseases. The questionnaire also asked for background information about the respondent such as age, education and composition of the household. The interviews were conducted between January and June 1975.

A systematic random sample of 304 households was drawn from the demographic surveillance system in operation in the Machakos Project. Out of the 304 mothers selected, 291 were interviewed. Twelve mothers were not interviewed because they could not be located or reached at home and there was one refusal. A total of 148 interviews took place in area B and 143 in area A. Details of the study design, sampling and data-collection procedures have been described by the author elsewhere (Maina, 1977).

Of the 291 mothers interviewed in the survey 242 (83 percent) reported that one or more of their children had had measles, a rate which corresponds with the data reported in Chapter 6. Only 121 (42 percent) reported an attack of acute diarrhoea, a lower rate than would be expected from Leeuwenburg's data in Chapter 8. This discrepancy is probably due to the fact that the questions were phrased in such a way that only serious cases of diarrhoea, e.g. those associated with rapid dehydration, were considered. A variety of symptoms were associated with diarrhoea and this may have influenced the reporting of incidence.

Medical care in this context refers to care provided by modern and indigenous medical experts as well as self-medication. The term 'modern experts' includes all modern trained health personnel, whether nurses, midwives, clinical consultants, doctors or even bogus doctors. 'Indigenous experts' in this case includes herbalists, herbalist/diviners and teething specialists. Shop medicine is referred to as modern self-medication, while preparation of herbs by mothers themselves constitutes indigenous self-medication.

Results

Beliefs and related traditional practices

Classification of diseases

The Kamba classify diseases into two major categories: 'man's diseases' and 'God's diseases'. Man's diseases are those associated with witchcraft and sorcery, commonly referred to as poisoning (*uoi*). The witchcraft and sorcery theory of disease holds that disease is put into a person by an enemy who is after his life. The enemy could be a jealous neighbour or a relative with whom the family has quarrelled.

In this community, determining sorcery as a cause of illness and identifying the sorcerer is the responsibility of a herbalist/diviner (*mundu mue*), whose supernatural connection is inherited. Usually he undergoes astounding afflictions before he becomes aware of his skills, difficulties which he freely tells to clients. Modern medicine is generally believed to be ineffective against man's diseases. Treatment involves first identifying the enemy who 'caused' the disease, then administering the cure and finally making a charm against further poisoning.

God's diseases are those whose origin may not be known, but which are believed not to result from sorcery or witchcraft. A disease that is observed to attack all children at one time or another is likely to be classified as one of God's diseases. Herbal medicine is usually administered as a cure for God's diseases. A herbalist has no supernatural powers; he learns by observing older members of his family.

Classification of a disease in this community depends largely on its perceived aetiology and on the frequency and pattern of its occurrence. (For more details on this subject see Chapter 22.) As the following sections will show, disease classification influences preventive measures practised, treatment sought and the results of treatment achieved.

Measles

This disease has been classified under God's diseases. The frequency and pattern of its occurrence may explain this classification. Because measles attacks all children, usually in epidemics, it has come to be known as a disease of wind and weather and the concept of sorcery, therefore, does not apply. The question, 'Why my child, and not my neighbour's child?' does not arise.

Measles is regarded as part of the development of a normal healthy child, so that a child who fails to contract it when young must do so later on. Measles is believed to be more dangerous to adults, mainly because their mothers can no longer control what they eat and drink. As we shall see below, it is important that certain foods and fluids should be avoided in measles.

When a mother suspects her child has measles, she does all that is considered appropriate so that the rash will erupt. The rash proves to mothers that the disease is measles and further that the disease is moving in the expected direction. To hasten the eruption of the rash, certain herbs are given to the child. Covering the child's head with a Kamba basket (*kyondo*) is also believed to hasten progress of the disease. Once the rash has erupted, it has to be cleaned. The most popular practice is to smear the child with mud prepared from an ant-hill, or with ashes from the fireplace mixed with certain herbs. The mud remains until it dries up and falls off by itself. Egg yolk is applied to eyes to prevent loss of eyesight.

Measles is believed to cause an ulcer in the stomach. It is thought that the sores which form in the mouth continue all the way to the stomach. For treatment of the stomach ulcer, indigenous herbs are prescribed.

An additional belief is that certain food and fluids like milk, fats and meat, should be withheld from the child. The stomach is believed to be the seat of the disease, and meat, which is a solid and presumably not easily digestible food, forms a covering on the stomach when eaten, thus preventing the disease from appearing on the surface. Fats and milk are believed to curdle when eaten and have the same effect. If the measles rash fails to appear on the skin, the common saying is that the disease has gone back to the abdomen, which mothers consider to be the most dangerous stage of measles. Children with measles are also not supposed to be given water. This is likely to worsen the 'cold' that often accompanies measles.

Diarrhoea

This disease, like measles, is considered to affect all children and is therefore classified as one of God's diseases. It is especially common during teething, weaning, crawling and learning to walk. Diarrhoea associated with these stages of development is commonly known as 'teething diarrhoea'.

Treatment of teething diarrhoea involves cutting the four sides of a child's gum with a sharp tool, or rubbing hard with a specialist's finger until the gum becomes sore, and then applying indigenous herbs to the cuts. The purpose of this operation is to force the teeth out more quickly, which removes the cause of teething diarrhoea. In recent times, shop medicine is replacing herbs. A manufactured medicine, highly recommended for teething, is more and more being used after the operation, instead of herbs.

It is also believed that diarrhoea burns the stomach and the intestines, causing an ulcer as in measles, for which indigenous herbs are the most effective treatment. Maize and beans should not be eaten because they are too tough for the diseased stomach to digest.

A second type of diarrhoea is identified as 'sickness diarrhoea'. A child who is not in a stage associated with teething diarrhoea is regarded as sick. For diarrhoea, and especially sickness diarrhoea, to occur, a foreign body must have entered the abdomen and disturbed the 'big worm' believed to reside there. Sickness diarrhoea is treated with herbs and prevention of this diarrhoea is not possible.

It is clear that the beliefs and related practices concerning measles and acute diarrhoea that have been described above are part of the Kamba culture. The diseases are recognized, their causes are explained, certain preventive measures are taken and appropriate remedies are prescribed. On the basis of this cultural understanding, we are in a better position to examine the actual pattern of use of modern and indigenous medical care in more detail.

Use of modern and indigenous medical care

Table 1 shows that modern medical care alone (experts and/or self-medication) was used by 50 percent of the mothers for measles and 63 percent for acute diarrhoea.

Use of indigenous forms of medical care alone (again experts and/or self-medication) was low. The Table further shows that modern and indigenous forms of medical care were frequently used together, by 48 percent of the mothers for measles and 28 percent for diarrhoea.

Table 1.
Type of medical care used by Kamba mothers.

	Measles		*Diarrhoea*	
Type	*No*	%	*No*	%
Modern care only	121	50	77	63
Indigenous care only	5	2	11	9
Modern and indigenous care	116	48	33	28
Total	242	100	121	100

Table 2 indicates that among those who used modern medical care, 94 percent consulted an expert for measles and 69 percent for acute diarrhoea. Shop medicine alone was not used for measles, but for 5 percent of mothers it was the only action taken during acute diarrhoea. Treatment by modern experts was combined with shop medicine in 6 percent of measles cases and in 26 percent of acute diarrhoea cases.

Table 3 shows that among those who used indigenous medical care, 33 percent had consulted a specialist for measles, while 66 percent had done the same for acute diarrhoea. For measles, 67 percent practised self-medication while 34 percent did so for acute diarrhoea. Only a few mothers used the services of a herbalist/diviner.

The adoption of new practices was expected to be greater among younger mothers than among older mothers, but this pattern did not appear, as can be seen in Table 4. Similarly, there

Table 2.
Modern practices followed.

Type	*Measles* *No*	*%*	*Diarrhoea* *No*	*%*
Modern expert	223	94	76	69
Shop medicine	0	0	6	5
Modern expert and shop medicine	14	6	28	26
Total	237	100	110	100

Table 3.
Indigenous practices followed.

Type	*Measles* *No*	*%*	*Diarrhoea* *No*	*%*
Self-medication	82	67	15	34
Herbalist	38	32	13	30
Herbalist/diviner	1	1	2	4
Teething expert	0	0	14	32
Total	121	100	44	100

was no relationship between age of mothers and type of medical care received for diarrhoea.

Table 5 shows that education also seemed to have little influence on the type of care preferred for measles. Mothers with at least primary education (8 years or more) used only modern care more frequently than mothers with less education, but this group of highly educated mothers was very small and there was no clear trend among the other educational groups. There was likewise no relationship between mother's education and type of medical care for diarrhoea cases.

The practice of withholding milk and water from children is related to mother's age as shown in Table 6. Except for the two youngest age groups, the percentage withholding milk or water increased with mother's age. The reason for the slightly different trend among mothers between 20 and 29 may be that they have been influenced by their mothers-in-law concerning what to do for measles. The custom is that newly married women stay with their mothers-in-law until they have been accepted by the new family.

Like age, education affects the practice of withholding fluids as

Table 4.
Type of medical care used during measles, by age of mother.

Type / *Age, y.*	*20–24* No	%	*25–29* No	%	*30–34* No	%	*35–39* No	%	*40–44* No	%	*45+* No	%
Modern care only	15	58	23	55	18	39	19	47	14	56	24	51
Indigenous care only	0	0	0	0	3	7	1	2	0	0	1	2
Modern and indigenous care	11	42	19	45	25	54	21	51	11	44	22	47
Total	26	100	42	100	46	100	41	100	25	100	47	100

Note: No information on age was available for 15 mothers.

Table 5.
Type of medical care used during measles, by years of education of mother.

Type / *Age, y.*	*Years of education* *0* No	%	*1–4* No	%	*5–7* No	%	*8+* No	%
Modern care only	53	52	30	45	33	50	5	72
Indigenous care only	3	3	2	3	0	0	0	0
Modern and indigenous care	46	45	35	52	33	50	2	28
Total	102	100	67	100	66	100	7	100

Table 6.
Banning of water or milk from children with measles, by age of mother.

Age, y.	*n*	*No. banning fluids*	%
20–24	26	16	61
25–29	42	24	57
30–34	46	25	54
35–39	41	27	66
40–44	25	17	68
45+	47	35	74
Total	227	144	64

Note: No information was available for 15 mothers.

indicated in Table 7. The percentage of mothers denying milk and water to children with measles decreased with increasing education. Table 7 also indicates that in the sample as a whole 62 percent of the mothers ban fluids. This practice was not considered as a traditional form of self-medication.

Table 7.
Banning of water or milk from children with measles, by education of mother.

Education	*n*	*No. banning fluids*	%
0	102	74	75
1–4	67	41	61
5–7	66	32	48
8+	7	2	29
Total	242	149	62

Discussion

The Kamba culture has developed a set of beliefs and practices concerning the aetiology, diagnosis and treatment of measles and diarrhoea and a number of these beliefs and practices have been described. Many of them are still common today, as indicated by the fact that, for instance, over 60 percent of mothers withheld water and milk during measles. Likewise, treatment with herbs either by herbalists or by the mothers themselves was used in nearly 50 percent of cases of measles and nearly 35 percent of cases of diarrhoea. Finally, indigenous experts such as herbalists and teething experts were consulted during a spell of acute diarrhoea in about 25 percent of the cases.

In spite of the fact that several of these practices are frequently followed during an episode of measles and diarrhoea, it is obvious that modern medical care is popular. Modern medical care provided by modern medical experts and/or shop-medicine, was used exclusively in 50 percent of the measles cases and 63 percent of the diarrhoea cases. Perhaps the most interesting finding is that modern and indigenous forms of medical care are often practised during the same illness. Mothers combined the two approaches in almost half the cases of measles and over a quarter of those of diarrhoea. Use of indigenous forms of medical care alone was rare.

One of the reasons for the popularity of modern medical care during measles and diarrhoea is that these diseases are classified as God's diseases in the Kamba culture. They occur in the form of epidemics; their pattern of outbreak is difficult to predict or to explain; and no definite remedies exist for them. This means that the Kamba culture allows for experimenting with new or alternative forms of treatment. If these work, they are easily accepted.

It might be argued that one of the reasons for the popularity of modern medicine was the presence of the medical research activities and the medical team in the study area. Detailed analysis of the data—not shown here—indicated, however, that use of modern medical care was not more frequent in area B where intensive medical research activities took place than in area A where no such activities took place (Maina, 1977).

The influence of mother's age and education was not clear. No relationship with type of medical care chosen could be demonstrated, but there was such a relationship with the withholding of water and milk from children with measles: older and less educated mothers engaged more in this traditional practice than younger and more educated mothers.

Withholding of fluids from children with measles and diarrhoea is detrimental, because it may precipitate dehydration. The same holds for the teething operation that is carried out in a number of cases during diarrhoea, because this makes it more difficult for the children to eat. It is also possible that the operation worsens existing local oral infection. Correct knowledge of the effect of certain practices on health is important and health education in the area of child health should emphasize these harmful effects. This may be more easily said than done, however, because, despite the popularity of modern medical care, certain indigenous practices are still common. This means that health education programmes should not only advocate the adoption of new practices, but should also try to find ways of minimizing the conflicts that may arise between traditional and modern practices.

References

Maina B, A socio-medical inquiry: modern and indigenous medical care utilization patterns with respect to measles and acute diarrhoea among the Akamba, MA Thesis, University of Nairobi, Kenya (1977).

Suchman E, Sociology and the field of public health, Russell Sage Foundation, New York, 1963.

Ploughing with oxen.

Planting.

Part VII
Summary and conclusions

25
Summary of findings and implications for public health

J.K. van Ginneken
P.W. Kok

This chapter summarizes the main findings of the Machakos Project and their implications for efforts to improve maternal and child health. The next and final chapter deals with a number of methodological conclusions and lessons learnt from carrying out the project.

Economic, agricultural and nutritional conditions

The economic situation in the study area is relatively favourable compared with other parts of Kenya, and with many other countries of Africa. Total household income is relatively high, being primarily derived from agricultural production, which is fairly good in the area. The altitude (1300–1700 m) and the rainfall (900–1000 mm annual average) allow two harvests of maize and beans per year, and in the western part of the area, better soil conditions than in the east make coffee-growing possible, which provides about 20 percent of total income in this part.

A second reason why household income is fairly high is that many households have external supplementary sources of income: in both western and eastern parts frequently one or more members of a family—often including the head of the household—work as migrant labourers in Nairobi or other towns. Farm income is often further supplemented in the western half by income from a second farm elsewhere bought with money from the sale of coffee.

Nutritional studies have shown that the customary diet of maize and beans supplemented by vegetables, fat and milk, is qualitatively adequate though not always sufficient in quantity. Food availability and energy intake can be precarious at times, particularly in the eastern half of the study area and in June and July, between the two harvests. Per capita food consumption is influenced by family size and is less in large than small families.

In spite of a generally favourable overall economic situation, there are still both short- and long-term problems. One of the most serious of these is the shortage of good land within the study area, a consequence of rapid population increase. The rate of natural increase, owing to high fertility and relatively low mortality, is nearly 4 percent per year. The combination of shortage of land and high population growth rate makes shortage of food an ever-present threat; this partly explains why many families have made arrangements to supplement their income. The shortage of land, coupled with limited employment opportunities within the study area itself, also explains the net out-migration from, particularly, the eastern half of the area. Temporary food shortage owing to

Fetching drinking water.

such events as a bad harvest, or shortages of fertilizer and pesticides, is always a short-term risk. A drop in the coffee price is another short-term problem causing a sudden decrease in household income.

There are a number of possible solutions for the economic, agricultural, demographic and food-supply problems, which can only be mentioned here in general terms: intensification of agricultural production within the study area; generation and maintenance of income from farming and non-farming activities outside the area; and limitation of population growth by expansion of family planning programmes.

The fairly high standard of living explains to a considerable extent the relatively high level of maternal and child health that has been described in the preceding chapters, a level attained throughout the study area in spite of a lower income level and unfavourable hygiene conditions—especially water supply, sanitation and housing—in the eastern half.

Pregnancy, delivery, lactation and the neonatal period

Nutrition during pregnancy and lactation

The energy and food intake of pregnant women was considerably lower in the third trimester than in the first and second, and energy and nutrient intakes, except for protein, thiamine and ascorbic acid, fell short of WHO/FAO recommended dietary intakes, being particularly low for calcium, retinol equivalents and riboflavine.

Weight gain during pregnancy was also low at about 4.1 kg between the third and eighth months and an estimated 5.8 kg for the whole of pregnancy. Maternal weight loss after delivery was only 300 g relative to the non-pregnant, non-lactating state. Almost all the other anthropometric measures remained the same in pregnancy. Nutritional deficiency was rarely diagnosed clinically.

In spite of their low energy and nutritional intake during pregnancy, women in the study area produced on the whole healthy babies: average birth weight was about 3100 g and the percentage of low-birth-weight (≤2500 g) babies varied between 8 and 12 percent between 1977 and 1980, averaging 10 percent. This is probably better than the average compared with the rest of Kenya. The low energy and food intake in this population is apparently still sufficient to support adequate fetal growth and to maintain maternal health, though it is not clear how such a marginal diet supports adequate fetal growth.

Food intake in the first year after birth, during lactation, was higher than in pregnancy, but energy and nutrient intakes still fell short of recommended levels. Lactating mothers of normal-birth-weight children lost on average 2.6 kg, from 54.8 kg shortly after delivery to 52.2 kg a year after delivery. The amount of breast milk produced was, however, satisfactory, and comparable with that produced by women in western countries. Again, no explanation could be given as to how successful lactation was achieved on such a marginal diet. In quality and composition, breast milk differed from western standards, however, concentrations per 100 ml milk of most nutrients (such as fat, calcium etc.) being lower. Protein, thiamine and ascorbic acid contents were similar to those in western countries.

In spite of this relatively favourable situation, there is room for improvement in the nutritional status of pregnant and lactating women. Nutrition education should emphasize a higher energy intake in lactating women through a diet of maize and beans enriched with oils or fat. Addition of green leafy vegetables is important during pregnancy and lactation and could help to increase the intake of vitamins and minerals.

Mortality levels and causes of death

The maternal death rate was 0.8 per 1000 deliveries; stillbirth and perinatal death rates were 29.6 and 46.4 per 1000 births respectively; and the neonatal death rate was 23.1 per 1000 live births per year (annual average between 1975 and 1978). No comparable figures from other parts of Kenya are available, but it is likely that these rates are lower than those in most other areas of Kenya and those in other African countries as well.

Complications of labour in mature infants were the single largest cause of perinatal mortality in mature infants (38 percent of all deaths). Many deaths in this category resulted from prolonged labour and could have been prevented by adequate use of hospital obstetric services in general and timely caesarean sections in particular. The second largest cause of mortality in the perinatal period (25 percent) consisted of sequelae of low birth weight and/or ante-partum haemorrhage. Many of these deaths could have been prevented by appropriate care antenatally, during delivery in hospital, and neonatally.

Determinants of perinatal and neonatal mortality

The following were associated with above-average perinatal mortality: breech delivery; twin delivery; maternal age >34 years;

parity 10+; primigravidity; maternal height ≤150 cm; being unmarried; and a history of a previous perinatal death.

By and large, the same characteristics were similarly associated with neonatal mortality. Low birth weight had a strong impact on neonatal mortality, which was 13 times higher in such infants than in those of normal birth weight.

Mothers and/or traditional birth attendants recognized several characteristics, e.g. very short stature (≤142 cm), a short birth interval (<18 months), complications during a previous delivery, as carrying a higher-than-average risk of perinatal or neonatal death, and they were therefore to a certain extent aware of the need to arrange for hospital delivery in such cases. They were not sufficiently aware of this need in the presence of other 'high risk' situations, such as suspicion of a breech or twins.

Antenatal screening

The information on the association between a number of maternal characteristics and perinatal mortality was used to design a high-risk strategy that identified four categories of women as being at particularly high risk of infant death during delivery or soon after birth. These four high-risk groups formed 13 percent of all pregnant women and contributed 41 percent of all perinatal deaths; it is estimated that about a quarter of all perinatal deaths could have been prevented if they had all been screened and had made use of the available antenatal and obstetric services. This would represent a reduction in the observed perinatal death rate from 46 to 36 per 1000 deliveries.

It is recommended that screening for these high-risk features be carried out partly by traditional birth attendants and community health workers and partly by nurse-midwives in antenatal clinics. Screening should preferably be carried out in the third or fourth and eighth or ninth months of pregnancy, using already developed antenatal record cards or cards specially designed for the purpose, based on the high-risk criteria referred to above.

Application of this risk strategy would give a relatively small reduction in perinatal mortality in the study area because the rate there was already low; in areas with higher perinatal mortality and more or less comparable antenatal and obstetrical facilities reductions would be likely to be greater. The screening criteria may not be universally applicable, however; elsewhere in Kenya, or in other African countries, there may be local variations both in the relative importance of the individual factors influencing perinatal mortality and in the availability of antenatal and obstetric facilities.

Low-birth-weight infants

Nutritional status in pregnancy and other maternal characteristics influenced the chances of delivering a low-birth-weight (LBW) infant. Mothers of LBW children weighed less and consumed less food in pregnancy than mothers of normal-birth-weight (NBW) children. They also scored lower on other anthropometric measures, such as height, triceps skinfold thickness and upper arm circumference.

Because of these findings it is recommended that procedures be designed to identify women at special risk of delivering LBW infants. Some of these will be for community health workers or traditional birth attendants to apply; others will be mainly suitable for staff in antenatal clinics. The importance of an adequate diet and good nutritional condition before starting another pregnancy should be emphasized, and the desirability of birth spacing should be stressed in this context.

Differences between LBW and NBW infants continued after birth. LBW children received less breast milk than NBW children and LBW children did not catch up in growth. A difference in weight between the two groups thus remained throughout the first year of life. A limitation of the type of analysis used here is that a comparison was made between surviving LBW and NBW infants. This analysis conceals the fact that the LBW infants were worse off than shown because it does not take into account that mortality for LBW children in the first year is much higher than for NBW children.

It is worth investing time, money and effort to organize appropriate neonatal and post-neonatal care for LBW infants to increase their chances of survival.

The role of traditional birth attendants

About 73 percent of mothers delivered at home and 27 percent in hospital. Stillbirth, perinatal mortality and neonatal mortality rates for deliveries at home attended by a traditional birth attendant were roughly the same as for uncomplicated births in hospital attended by trained midwives (about 23 per 1000 deliveries in both cases). Mortality rates for hospital births attended by a physician or a clinical officer were higher (44 per 1000), presumably because they were the more complicated cases.

This suggests that in this particular part of Kenya traditional birth attendants perform satisfactorily and do their work hygienically, a view borne out by the absence of neonatal tetanus. They are also apparently to a certain extent able to recognize complications needing referral to hospital.

In this area, therefore, traditional birth attendants should be respected and recognized as an essential part of the total obstetric services of the area, and local health facilities should offer them training in such tasks as, for instance, taking a relevant obstetric history and recognizing obvious maternal problems, and detection of risk factors, such as short stature and primigravidity, with a view to referring high-risk cases. Local health facilities should also organize a close liaison with the traditional birth attendants so that arrangements for them to refer cases work satisfactorily. Training of traditional birth attendant and their involvement as an integral part of the health-care system are desirable because, universal hospital delivery being unlikely to be available soon, they will continue to fulfil a role in rural areas in the foreseeable future.

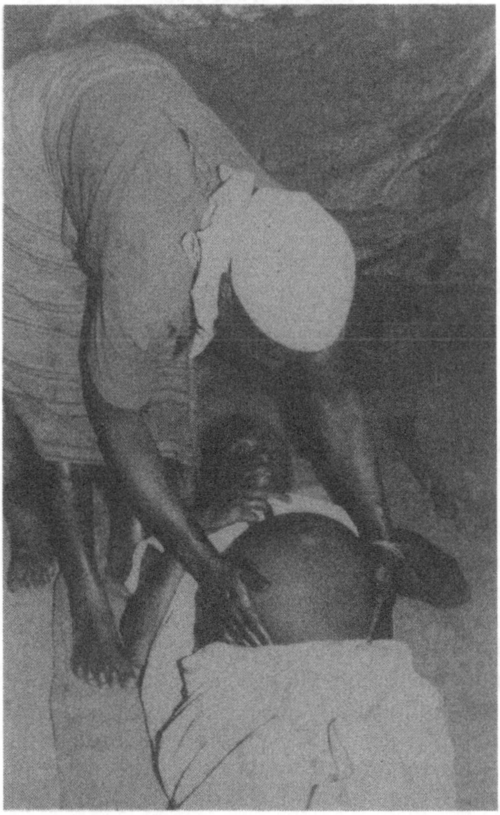

A traditional midwife at work.

Antenatal and delivery care in hospital

The large majority of women (84 percent) attended an antenatal clinic at least once during pregnancy. Screening and identification of women at special risk by use of an antenatal card should, therefore, be fairly easy to implement in this population.

Fifty-four percent of the women intended to deliver in hospital but only half of them did so. Several factors were involved: mothers who lived closer to the hospital, who were younger, nulliparous, of short stature, or who had had a previous hospital delivery, or previous delivery complications, delivered more frequently in hospital than others. This is encouraging because it shows once more that the women were to a considerable extent aware of reasons for delivering in hospital. Further improvement is definitely possible, however, because a number of women medically at high risk did not deliver in hospital. In too many cases the choice is influenced by habit and opportunity rather than by the high-risk factors. Mothers living far from hospital were not always able to reach it in time, or to travel at all. To help such cases it is recommended that accommodation be provided near the hospital where high-risk mothers, particularly, can stay, with their relatives, as their time of delivery approaches. Organization of emergency transport arrangements for women who need to reach hospital quickly if labour is prolonged would also help to decrease perinatal mortality.

Infancy and childhood

Nutrition of infants and pre-school children

Breast-feeding was nearly universal in the study area and the majority of mothers continued nursing for 18 months to 2 years. The amount of breast milk that children consumed was satisfactory, though varying with the season: it was significantly higher in the harvest than in the lean season. Supplementary feeding, with cow's milk and later thin maize-flour porridge, was started between one and four months, mostly in the third month.

Energy intake increased with age from about 530 kcal in the first 6 months to 780 kcal between 12 and 18 months. The mean energy intake between 4 and 18 months varied from 79 to 87 percent of the WHO/FAO recommended daily allowance. Intake of several nutrients, e.g. iron, calcium, riboflavine, was also below recommendations; protein intake was, however, always at or near the recommended level. After 18 months the diet and also energy intake were generally up to recommended levels and acceptable both qualitatively and quantitatively. No difference was found between the energy intakes in the two halves of the study area, probably because income from outside sources was used to compensate for inadequacies in food supply.

Severe malnutrition did occur, but much less than reported in many other African studies. Cross-sectionally, the percentage of children below 70 percent of the Harvard Standard for weight for age (W/A) in various age groups below 5 years varied from 4.9 to 6.4.

Growth during the first 6 months of life followed the Harvard Standards for weight for age (W/A) and height for age (H/A). During the second 6 months of life W/A dropped to 83 percent and H/A to 92 percent of the standards and remained there up to age 6 years. The most vulnerable age, as far as W/A and H/A were concerned, was between 7 and 12 months. Weight for height (W/H) remained close to the Harvard Standard up to age 6. Nutritional status was not constant in the years 1974–77 for which data were available, being lower in 1974, probably due to drought, than in 1975–77.

Existing breast-feeding practices are satisfactory and therefore no recommendations are called for. Pre-school children should eat more energy-rich food, in particular porridge and *ngima* (maize-flour paste) with more flour, fat and milk per unit of water than is currently used.

Mortality levels and causes of death

Post-neonatal and infant mortality averaged 26.0 and 49.1 respectively per 1000 live births between 1975 and 1978, while childhood mortality averaged 7.0 per 1000 children aged 1–4 years. Comparison of these figures with available data from the rest of Kenya shows them to be relatively low and about half what one would expect for a rural area of Kenya. A number of reasons that make these low rates plausible have already been mentioned at the beginning of this chapter. Infant mortality was somewhat higher in the eastern part of the study area, especially in Katheka, than in the western half. Childhood mortality (1–4 years) was substantially higher in 1974 (16.2 per 1000) than in later years.

The leading causes of death in infancy and childhood (excluding the neonatal period) were pneumonia (20 percent of all deaths), diarrhoea and vomiting (20 percent) and measles (15 percent). Many of these deaths could have been prevented by appropriate curative care and preventive measures, several of which, insofar as they follow from results of the Machakos Project, are mentioned below.

Determinants of infant and childhood mortality

Birth weight, twin delivery, parity (primiparity vs. multiparity), previous sibling death, and marital status all had an impact on infant mortality, though their influence on this was in general weaker than on perinatal and neonatal mortality, and some other variables that influenced these latter rates did not influence infant mortality at all.

The impact of a number of agricultural, socio-economic and hygiene variables on infant and childhood mortality was also determined. Two analyses were performed, one with respect to infant mortality alone and one with respect to infant and child mortalities combined. In the first analysis the impact of the variables was determined separately, while in the second they were grouped into several 'components'. The agricultural, socio-economic and hygiene variables were in general inversely related to infant and childhood mortality, but the relationships were not always statistically significant.

We do not see much prospect of developing a high-risk approach to identification of infants and children at increased risk of dying in infancy and childhood from these data. This is partly because of difficulties in the accurate measurement of several potentially useful screening factors and also, more importantly, because many of the variables for which reliable data are available (e.g. marital status) are not suitable as screening criteria. It is also likely that on several variables crucial to infant and childhood mortality we did not have any data at all.

Measles

The average annual incidence of measles over seven years of surveillance was 43 per 1000 children under age 5. There were more measles cases between 6 and 12 months of age than in any other age groups. Three periods of high measles incidence were observed during the surveillance period. Case fatality rates in these three epidemics were 6.2, 1.4 and 1.1 percent. The peak incidence of death was in the age group 13–18 months, while 70 percent of all deaths occurred before the second birthday. The case fatality rate of 6.2 percent during the first epidemic (between April 1974 and April 1976) means that measles was a dangerous disease at that time, especially to infants in the second year of life.

In the first and second epidemic periods (between April 1974 and April 1978) the median age of hospitalized cases was 18 months, and for all cases it was 31 months. The proportions of cases from the study area hospitalized in the first and second epidemics were 12 and 6 percent respectively, while the case fatality rate in both periods was 22 percent. During the first epidemic period nearly half the deaths occurred at home; this proportion was much smaller during the second period. These figures emphasize that hospital returns may give a very misleading idea of the impact of a disease on the population at large since they do not give a represenative picture of the morbidity and mortality occurring in the community.

Two hypotheses to explain the much higher case fatality rate in the first epidemic compared with the second and third may be mentioned. One is the poorer nutritional status in 1974 than in later years: harvests were bad in 1974 and children under 5 had a lower W/A that year than in later years. The second hypothesis is that mortality was lowered by the cumulative effect of several health interventions as part of the Machakos Project. Examples of such activities are the information on health matters provided by field-workers; early referral of sick children to clinics and hospitals; and operation of Machakos Project clinics. Many deaths from measles, particularly in the first epidemic, could have been prevented by appropriate preventive and curative care at the community level and/or in clinics and hospitals.

From the age-distribution of cases, together with already available age-specific seroconversion data, it was possible to determine accurately the optimum age for measles immunization. The recommended age is nine months. Our data show that immunization at eight months or less is not to be recommended because the number of vaccine failures to be expected is twice that at nine months, and a high vaccine failure rate jeopardizes the credibility of measles immunization programmes in the community.

Other studies concerned the most suitable route of administration. A trial comparing five routes showed that only injection by syringe and needle or by Dermojet give adequate antibody response. The other methods tried (nose drops, needle-bearing cylinder, and bifurcated needle) were not effective. The excellent results that can be achieved by multidose-vaccine administration by Dermojet are important because they mean it can be used for mass immunization campaigns. Such campaigns are particularly useful in areas that are not served by static health facilities.

The success of preventive and curative health measures against measles depends to some extent on existing beliefs held and practices carried out in a measles episode. A survey conducted among mothers who had had a child with measles between 1970 and 1975 found that 62 percent restricted water and milk. Correct knowledge of the effect of such practices on health is important and health education should explain the harmful effects of restricting fluids.

Whooping cough

The annual incidence of whooping cough was 27 per 1000 children under 5 years of age. The incidence was highest in the age group below one year but it was also high in 3- and 4-year-olds. The median age of cases was 3.5 years. In the seven years of observation two epidemic periods can be distinguished: the first from April 1974 to June 1976 and the second from June 1976 to the end of 1978. A third epidemic expected in 1979 or 1980 did not develop, probably because of an increase in herd immunity. The case fatality rate between 1974 and 1980 was 1 percent, half of the deaths occurring in the children under one year, in whom the case fatality rate was 2.6 percent.

Whooping cough was thus a widespread disease, at least between 1974 and 1978. It carries a lower mortality than measles but causes prolonged morbidity. Mortality was somewhat higher in the first than the second epidemic period, 1.3 percent vs. 0.4 percent for children under 15, and 3.6 vs. 0.9 percent in the under-ones. It is possible that the same factors as mentioned above in connection with measles were responsible.

The impact of two doses of DPT vaccine with a pertussis component of above-average potency administered six months apart was compared with three doses of DPT at three-monthly intervals, with an average follow-up of four years after the last injection. On the basis of clinical evidence it was concluded that the two-dose schedule provided the same protection as the conventional three-dose course, the (low) numbers of cases observed after each course being similar. Waning of antibody levels was more pronounced after the two-dose schedule, at several post-vaccination intervals, but this is not a reason for great concern, since children were already three to four years old at the later post-vaccination periods and mortality is very low at this age.

This trial shows that it is feasible to use a two-dose DPT schedule with a six-month interval between doses. This is important for areas not adequately covered by maternal and child health services, where immunization rounds can only be offered at six-month intervals. More research needs to be done to make full use of a two-dose schedule; in particular the effect of two doses at intervals of less than six months needs evaluation.

Diarrhoea

The two-weekly incidence of diarrhoea was 10.5 percent for under-5s, which amounts to an annual incidence of 2730 per 1000 children below 5. Two-weekly incidence was highest for children aged 6–12 months and also high in the age groups 0–5 months and 12–23 months. When the analysis was limited to episodes of diarrhoea that were considered by the mother to be an illness, the two-weekly incidence in children below 5 decreased to 2.2 percent or to 572 per 1000 children per year. Diarrhoea thus appears to be a common condition among under-5s, but mothers considered it as an illness in only about 22 percent of the cases. The above mentioned incidence figures are probably too high because two small studies carried out to validate the mothers' reports found that overreporting of diarrhoeal episodes by 15–40 percent took place.

Mortality from diarrhoea and vomiting was considerable. It accounted for 20 percent of total under-5 mortality, and the largest proportion of diarrhoea deaths (70 percent) was in children under age one. Many of these deaths could have been prevented by a well-organized community-based oral rehydration programme. Such a programme should concentrate on infants under one year, the group with the highest mortality.

A serological survey showed that all children developed antibodies against rotavirus in the first three years of life, with a peak increase in the first year. This finding suggests that rotavirus infection may be the most important contributor to the high mortality observed in the under-one age group.

Socio-cultural factors affect behaviour with respect to diarrhoea. Traditional practices that aggravate the effect of diarrhoea are the cutting of the gums and banning of food and fluids. Such practices are still in use, as witness the finding that in 1974 herbalists and teething experts were consulted in about 25 percent of episodes of diarrhoea, but there is evidence that gum-cutting and restriction of fluids have declined recently. Oral rehydration programmes should recognize the existence of such practices and explain their harmful effects.

Pneumonia

We have already mentioned that pneumonia was one of the two leading causes of death in children under five; it is highest in children aged under one year (both in the neonatal and post-neonatal periods), accounting for nearly one quarter of all deaths in that age group. Unfortunately epidemiological studies on pneumonia were not possible, and to recommend effective prevention and treatment it is necessary to have identified the bacteriological cause. Immunization against measles and whooping cough, however, should reduce the incidence of pneumonia, since this is often a complication of these two diseases.

Schistosomiasis

Schistosomiasis was another disease on which research was carried out within the framework of the Machakos Project. Epidemiological studies in one part of the western half of the study area showed 82 percent prevalence among the general population, with a peak between ages 10–19. About a third of the total population was heavily infected (≥400 eggs/g faeces), and intense infection was also commoner in the younger age groups. Clinical evidence of disease, in particular liver enlargement, was relatively rare and seen mainly in heavily infected subjects. A chemotherapy (hycanthone 1.5 mg/kg) programme, concentrating on heavily infected subjects with a mean age of 15 years, was designed. Four months after treatment, egg counts in the treatment group had decreased 97 percent (from a pre-treatment level of 1250 to 36 eggs/g), while one year later the decrease was 91 percent (115 eggs/g). The prevalence of heavy infection in the population as a whole was decreased from 33 to 8 percent by this programme.

On the basis of these results, recommendations were made for a national campaign to limit the prevalence of the disease by chemotherapy focusing on heavily infected school-age children in endemic areas. Analysis of data from follow-up two and four years after treatment, which will determine the extent of reinfection, has not yet been completed.

Modern and traditional medical care in infancy and childhood

A longitudinal survey among the general population in Kingoti and Kambusu (western part of the area) showed that about 10 'actions for health' were undertaken annually per person, for major or minor complaints or symptoms. About 60 percent of these actions consisted of taking locally purchased 'shop medicine'; 32 percent were vists to dispensaries, health centres, hospital clinics, or private physicians; and about 8 percent were 'traditional' in the sense of taking traditional home remedies, or visits to herbalists. From other sources it is known that visits to the traditional medico-religious healers did take place on a limited scale, but these were very much under-reported in the survey. A questionnaire survey is apparently not suitable for eliciting information on this topic.

These findings show that the population at large now resorts dominantly to modern medical care and it is very likely that the same applies to children under five. It is also likely that the number of health actions taken for children under five is somewhat higher than the 10 reported for the general population. (The situation is also different for maternal care during pregnancy and delivery, when traditional birth attendants play an important role.)

Traditional practices—for example the restriction of fluids in measles and diarrhoea mentioned above—are, however, still employed in infancy and childhood. The traditional functionaries consulted for infant and child ills are medico-religious healers, herbalists, and teething specialists. They are not consulted on a large scale any more but resort is made to them and to traditional customs in situations where the modern system seems not to be offering a satisfactory solution to certain health and/or social problems. The modern and traditional systems of medical care continue to exist side by side and in a number of illness episodes both systems were used.

Related studies

In the course of implementation of the Machakos Project various other studies were undertaken that are not reported here although several of them were carried out by the Medical Research Centre in Nairobi. Examples of such studies are the two- and three-dose poliomyelitis vaccination trial (Metselaar et al., 1977); a nutrition rehabilitation programme (Verkley and Jansen, 1983); a training programme for traditional birth attendants (Voorhoeve, Ndunge and Mutua, 1979); and a study of pica practices (Thiuri, 1982). On account of space limitations and other reasons these studies could not be included in this volume.

Several other studies were carried out by scientists of institutions other than the Medical Research Centre, Nairobi, who took advantage of the demographic and disease surveillance system and other facilities of the Machakos Project to conduct their studies. These included various studies on schistosomiasis; an ophthalmological survey (Sinabulya, 1976); studies on Ascaris infections (Stephenson et al., 1980; Stephenson et al., 1983); an evaluation of the traditional birth attendant training programme (Mwalali, 1982); an analysis of patterns of geographical distribution of measles (Ferguson and Leeuwenburg, 1981); application of analytical techniques to demographic data of the Machakos Project (van Vianen and van Ginneken, 1983); and studies on livestock production and in agro-forestry. Only the results of the schistosomiasis studies are included in this volume.

A number of smaller projects with research training for various scientists and students from Kenya, the Netherlands and other countries under field conditions as their main objective also took place; the results of several of these have been included in this volume. Others were, however, not included and in this group belong, for example, studies on: the reliability of recall of measles and pertussis; prevalence of poliomyelitis; prevalence of and attitudes towards epilepsy; water-contact patterns; determinants of preventive health behaviour (Mburu, 1978); the impact of urban influences on fertility; health education in schools; and attitudes towards family planning.

Several of the results presented in this volume have been used as the starting point in the design of the continuation of the Machakos Project in the form of a demonstration and research project in delivery of maternal and child health and family planning services. This project has started in the middle of 1981 with financial support from the Special Programme of Research and Research Training in Human Reproduction of the World Health Organization. It is implemented by staff members of the Department of Obstetrics and Gynaecology, Faculty of Medicine, University of Nairobi.

Conclusions

A comparison of the findings presented in the previous chapters with the five major objectives stated in Chapter 1 (objectives 1, 2, 3, 6 and 7) leads to the following conclusions.

The first objective was to obtain accurate data on morbidity and mortality from several communicable childhood diseases. The results of Chapters 6 to 9 indicate that this objective was to a large extent achieved, though owing to lack of time and manpower we were unable to carry out epidemiological studies on pneumonia and some other respiratory infections.

The second objective was to study the influence of nutritional, socio-economic and hygiene data on disease patterns. A great deal of information was collected concerning these various factors in Chapters 2–5, 10–15, and 22–24 while results on the influence of these various factors on mortality are reported in Chapters 18, 20 and 21. We were only partly successful in determining the impact of these factors; a comprehensive analysis of the whole set of data has not yet been completed.

The third objective was to obtain data on maternal and perinatal mortality in relation to antenatal and delivery care received. Chapters 17–20 indicate that this objective was achieved.

The sixth objective was to evaluate the impact of various health interventions (in particular the pertussis vaccine trial) on morbidity and mortality. Chapters 6, 7 and 9 indicate that we succeeded in determining the impact of these interventions under field conditions, while other studies dealing with other health interventions were carried out but not included here.

The seventh objective was to obtain accurate data on nutrition during pregnancy, outcome of pregnancy, lactation performance and growth of the child and to study the interrelationships among them. This objective was to a large extent achieved as shown in Chapters 10–16. The data on the impact of nutrition during pregnancy on lactation and on growth of the child have not yet been fully analysed.

Many of the results reported in this volume could only have been obtained by longitudinal or semi-longitudinal studies employing population-based data; they could not have been obtained from cross-sectional sample surveys. This and several other points made in this concluding section are further considered in the next and final chapter.

References

Ferguson AG and Leeuwenburg J, Local mobility and the spatial dynamics of measles in a rural area of Kenya, Geo Journal, 5 (1981) 315.

Mburu FM, The determinants of health services utilization in a rural community in Kenya, Soc Sci Med, 12 (1978) 211.

Metselaar D, McDonald K, Gemert W, van Rens MM and Muller AS, Poliomyelitis: epidemiology and prophylaxis 5, Bull WHO, 55(6) (1977) 755.

Mwalali PN, The effectiveness of the training of the traditional birth attendants in a rural area, Machakos, Kenya, Journal of Obst and Gyn East Centr Africa, 1 (1982) 32.

Sinabulya PM, An assessment of the extent of blindness in Machakos District, E Afr Med J, 53 (1976) 64.

Stephenson LS, Crompton DW, Latham MC, Arnold SE and Jansen AA, Evaluation of a four year project to control Ascaris infection in two Kenyan villages, J Trop Pediat, (to be published, 1983).

Stephenson LS, Crompton DW, Latham MC, Schulpen TW, Nesheim MC and Jansen AA, Relationships between Ascaris infection and growth of malnourished preschool children in Kenya, Am J Clin Nutr, 33 (1980) 1165.

Thiuri BN, Jansen AAJ and 't Mannetje, Pica practices among pregnant women in Kangundo Division Machakos District, Kenya, J Obst Gynaecol E Centr Afr, 1 (1982) 114.

van Vianen HAW and van Ginneken JK, Demographic analysis of data collected in a rural area of Kenya, Internal report, Department of Demography, State University of Groningen, Groningen, the Netherlands, (1983).

Verkley MTB and Jansen AAJ, A mixed ambulatory—home nutrition rehabilitation programme in a rural area in Kenya, E Afr Med J, 60(1) (1983) 15.

Voorhoeve AM, Ndunge BN and Mutua R, The training of traditional midwives in Matungulu and Mbiuni, Machakos, Kenya, Internal report, Medical Research Centre, (1979).

Publicizing the project.

Popularizing breast-feeding.

26

The implementation of a longitudinal, population-based study: an appraisal

A.S. Muller

General Considerations

Rationale for the study

In response to one of the first draft proposals for the Machakos Project, an interested colleague—outside the Medical Research Centre, Nairobi (MRCN)—with wide experience in community health in tropical countries asked in a letter to the author: "What is the relevance of what you propose to do in relation to the effort?"

The answer to this question is necessarily subjective but now, in 1983, 12 years after the Project's conception, an assessment of its relevance can be based on the results reported in this book and therefore be to some extent less subjective.

The major concern of the Project was to address itself to the most urgent health problems of the most vulnerable groups in developing countries: acute infectious diseases in 0–4-year-old children and the outcome of pregnancy among the population at large. These were the early days of smallpox eradication efforts and an increasing realization that control of immunizable diseases in developing countries was possible. These considerations led to the first three objectives listed in Chapter 1.

In most developing countries the impact of pregnancy and delivery, measles, whooping cough and diarrhoea on the health of mother and child is estimated from hospital statistics. Owing to the highly selected nature of cases admitted to hospital—depending not only on the severity of ill health but also on distance and means of transport to the hospital, socio-economic status and traditional beliefs—the impact can only be reliably measured in population-based studies. The effect of these selective mechanisms on hospital-based figures was clearly demonstrated by our own study in relation to median age and case fatality rate of measles patients (Chapter 6). A consequence of this approach was a need for a strong demographic component in the project, which—as is obvious from the foregoing chapters—formed its backbone.

Before embarking on the study we considered whether the objectives we had in mind could or should be met by the execution of cross-sectional surveys in a number of randomly chosen population groups in Kenya or whether a longitudinal design was required. The latter implied concentration of the limited resources of the Medical Research Centre, Nairobi, to one area.

Other longitudinal, population-based projects

Longitudinal population studies are difficult to organize and maintain; they are expensive; and the analysis of the data they produce poses particular problems. A very limited number have been conducted in developing countries. In Guatemala the research design of the INCAP (Institute of Nutrition of Central America and Panama) field study of nutrition and infection provided for comparisons between three villages with three different inputs: nutritional supplements for all children in one village; medical care and sanitation in another; while the third served as a control. Beneficial effects in terms of child mortality (but not of morbidity) were particularly apparent in the nutrition supplement village (Mata, 1978). A similar design was used in Narangwal, India, except that a fourth experimental cell was added, consisting of a group of villages where nutritional supplements *and* health care concentrating on infection control were provided. Nutrition care improved both weight and height of study children beyond 17 months of age; health care reduced the average duration of infectious disease episodes. Perinatal mortality was reduced in the nutrition-supplemented villages while health care had a beneficial effect on neonatal, post-neonatal and 1–2-year mortality; 1–2-year mortality was also reduced in the villages receiving nutritional care (Taylor et al., 1978).

In Matlab, Bangladesh, a population laboratory with a population of 260,000 (in 1974) has been maintained for nearly two decades in order to carry out a number of epidemiological studies and to test the efficacy of various health interventions (International Centre for Diarrhoeal Disease Research, Bangladesh, 1978, 1979, 1980).

The Danfa project in Ghana is one of the few major longitudinal population-based studies we know of in Africa. It was also based on a 4-cell design with various forms of family planning services as the main input. Emphasis on this design greatly diminished, however, in the course of the study; instead, efforts were more generally concentrated on the provision of integrated family planning and basic health services, epidemiological investigations and institutional development and training (Univ. of Ghana Medical School, 1979).

In spite of differences in objective and design, all four projects have the common limitation that longitudinal studies involving frequent contacts with the study population require so much manpower and money that inclusion of several representative population samples within a country cannot be considered.

From the Danfa Project it is apparent that, even when studying the whole population in one contiguous area, demographic activities may run into almost insurmountable problems in respect of both data collection and processing because of the high mobility of the people. This may be typical for tropical Africa—at any rate the Machakos Project had similar experiences. On the other hand, although these difficulties did interfere with the original study design, they did not prevent the generation of results of high public health significance that could not have been obtained without a longitudinal design.

Range of studies performed

The preceding chapters are witness to the fact that the Machakos Project produced high-quality information relevant for those concerned with health care. Examples are: age-specific incidence figures on measles on which a recommendation as to the optimal age of measles immunization was based (Chapter 6); the adequacy of two pertussis immunizations during infancy (Chapter 7); the impact of nutritional status of the pregnant woman and delivery care received on the outcome of pregnancy (Chapter 11 and 18); the relationship between intensity of schistosomiasis infection and morbidity (Chapter 9). None of these could have been established without an epidemiological and demographic surveillance system providing regular follow-up over a number of years.

Information on disease incidence and pregnancy outcome could also be collected cross-sectionally on the basis of recall by mothers but its reliability would never be known. In the case of measles—but not of pertussis—a positive or negative history can be verified by antibody tests, but serological surveys do not provide information on age-specific incidence and on mortality.

In addition, because of the Project's solid infrastructure, including complete demographic information on the total population rather than on the target groups alone, it was possible to add investigations to the programme that had not been considered at the onset of the Project but appeared useful later on and were welcomed when the opportunity arose, e.g. the measles vaccine study (Chapter 6); the agricultural study (Chapter 2); the schistosomiasis project (Chapter 9).

'External validity' of the studies

No attempts were made to make structural improvements to the health care system in the study area. Direct benefit was limited to maternal and child health (MCH) care provided by the field staff throughout the duration of the Project. As is apparent from Chapter 1, the aim was to develop methods and produce results that were of use to those involved in the delivery of health care and that could be reproduced elsewhere in developing countries. In order to be confident that results are reproducible elsewhere, they have to emanate from a population and area that are representative 'elsewhere'. In other words, one has to be certain that there is external validity. We do not know to what extent this was the case. There is no way of finding out except by doing similar studies in other parts of Kenya, tropical Africa or the tropics in general. This is obviously beyond anyone's resources.

The optimal age of measles immunization may be different somewhere else where age-specific incidence rates are different. On the other hand, it is unlikely that the pertussis and measles vaccine trials would come out very differently if done in other parts of the world. Above all, the project has developed surveillance methodologies using laymen that, adapted to local circumstances, can be used elsewhere. It has provided a valuable population laboratory through which hypotheses can be tested and the results of well-defined interventions—not necessarily purely medical—can be measured. It can continue to act as such a field instrument as long as its basic surveillance system is maintained. It has also been a training ground for multidisciplinary research bringing local and expatriate scientists from very different professional backgrounds together where the real problems are, among the people.

Accuracy and reliability

If it is accepted that a longitudinal population-based study was required to meet the objectives, the next issue is whether in fact data of maximal reliability and accuracy were required, and whether there was not too much emphasis on perfection in data collection and processing. In our view any compromise in this respect would not have been acceptable. In the field—unlike the laboratory—the investigator cannot run known controls in parallel with the actual determinations, and tests for reproducibility can only be done in a very limited way. This handicap increased the need for intensive, effective supervision in order to generate data that were as reliable and accurate as possible.

Furthermore, the Project's original fourth objective, to develop a registration and surveillance system suitable for use in the setting of a district with limited resources, could only be fulfilled if the data produced by such a simplified system could be compared with data of maximal reliability.

Reasons for not pursuing one of the objectives

To make such a comparison possible, the project design included two more or less comparable geographical areas, the study area (area B) and the control area (area A). The idea was that morbidity rates obtained with a relatively large, closely supervised field staff could be compared with rates obtained in the control area by various simplified data collection systems. Thus, the accuracy of the latter could be assessed against rates collected with maximal accuracy in the study area. The underlying assumption was that morbidity in two areas situated closely together would be of the same order of magnitude and therefore any gross disrepancies between disease rates in area B and area A would point to a failure to register an acceptable proportion of morbidity events in the latter.

If annual demographic surveys in area A picked up nearly all vital events, then any beneficial influence on death rates by the medical research team in area B would appear from lower death rates in area B.

It was recognized that this design had its inherent weaknesses: it required a degree of refinement of measurements that was difficult to accomplish, and was based on assumptions that at worst were unlikely to be correct and at best could not be verified. Mortalities in both areas for the years 1974, 1975 and 1976 when annual demographic surveys were performed in area A, were of comparable magnitude. The author feels that the presence of the research team had little, if any, influence on mortality levels in area B, although there is no conclusive evidence to support this view.

Unfortunately, the original fourth objective of testing alternative simplified disease reporting systems in the control area by comparing the information they produce with the close-surveillance data of the study area was not pursued. Only one preliminary step was made in that direction: the mothers' recall of measles among their children over the past half-year was compared with the actual recording of measles cases in the course of the disease surveillance.

Various reasons can be cited why this highly relevant issue was not addressed. The size of the task of setting up a demographic and subsequently a disease surveillance system in area B, including the required supervision of field staff, had been under-estimated when the design was drawn up. With the senior staff available it turned out to be simply impossible to divert some of their attention to a different, if nearby, area to study the same things with different methodologies. It was felt that one or two years of experience with the intensively supervised disease surveillance system in area B were needed before embarking on alternative and cheaper information systems. Meanwhile, the demographer recruited for this purpose shifted his attention to the problem of improvement of the existing civil registration system. This shift was understandable in the light of the keen interest shown by the Registrar General in the development of an improved civil registration system and the lack of interest of the Ministry of Health in simple population-based morbidity reporting systems. Unfortunately—but not entirely unexpectedly—the study to improve civil registration resulted, amongst others, in a recommendation to increase the staff of the Registrar General, a recommendation that could not be implemented due to financial constraints.

Goodwill and help were always given by the study population.

In retrospect, to pursue this issue emphasis should have been on anthropology rather than on demography. Simple health information systems will have to rely on reporting by laymen—whether modestly remunerated or not—and therefore on active, and to a large extent voluntary, participation by the community. Over the 7½ years that the project lasted, both areas A and B proved to be a fertile environment for anthropological studies that could have formed the necessary basis for voluntary lay reporting of births, deaths and diseases. The considerable amount of goodwill that we enjoyed from the population and the knowledge in respect of social structure and customs collected, almost incidentally, over the years by the research team would have provided an anthropologist with a relatively easy start. Once a feasible population-based health information system had been designed in the study area, it could have been tried out in other parts of the country as well. Doing this still remains one of the most challenging and relevant tasks to be accomplished.

Multi-disciplinary approach

The objective of studying the determinants of the observed disease pattern called for a multidisciplinary approach. In addition, it was realized at an early stage that information on health and disease (leading to better, more efficient health care) was not likely to be the only or even the most important factor leading to improvement in health status.

In this rural setting agriculture, as well as non-farm income, is obviously a major determinant of health. For this reason we encouraged investigations using the Machakos Project as an instrument to measure the impact of agricultural inputs on health and nutrition. Some results on this topic are reported in Chapter 2.

For the social scientist it was an ideal setting to study attitudes, beliefs and practices regarding western and traditional medicine (see Chapters 22–24). The sociologist-anthropologist was an indispensable member of the research team, forming the major bridge between the population and the researchers.

The project may not have been an interdisciplinary enterprise in the sense that from the beginning all participating disciplines were designed to complement each other. Rather, as an activity of a *medical* research institute, it was primarily a medical project, studying various aspects of health and disease. As a result the medical input was by far the largest. More important, however, it has been possible to create a team representing medicine, sociology and agriculture whose members were willing and able to listen to each other, to understand each other at a professional level and to share responsibility for all aspects of the project. Two essential ingredients were available: time and the right personalities.

Carrying out a sociological or agricultural survey in a medical project does not by itself signify multidisciplinary research. The project leader may be able to identify broad research areas in a discipline not his own, but the ultimate formulation of well-defined objectives and hypotheses requires intensive dialogue between the disciplines concerned. In the end, the success or failure of a multidisciplinary approach depends entirely on the way it works out among the people in the field, and much less on the way it was planned—if it was planned at all.

In summary, the project never pretended to be interdisciplinary: as a multidisciplinary undertaking it has been reasonably successful.

Aspects of field methodology

Disease surveillance

The fortnightly surveillance system constituted the basis of the project. It takes about 2 weeks for the clinical manifestations of measles to disappear completely, so an interval of 2 weeks between household visits was chosen. Our experience has confirmed that careful inspection of measles cases up to 2 weeks after the onset of the disease nearly always reveals the typical, if minimal, fine desquamation of the skin. More reliance on mothers' history of measles over the past 1–3 months would have made less frequent home visits possible but we would not have known the accuracy of the information thus obtained.

In respect of pertussis, fortnightly visits were desirable in order to increase the likelihood of isolation of *Bordetella pertussis*; the clinical manifestations of the disease usually persist for at least 6 weeks. The collection of laboratory specimens for measles and pertussis was necessary because the existence of a 'measles-like illness' in Kenya was suspected (Hayden, 1974) and in the case of pertussis the absence of physical signs on examination made it desirable to use other diagnostic methods. Besides, whooping cough has been reported sometimes to be caused by organisms other than *B. (para)pertussis*.

For both diseases, once the causative agent had been firmly established by several isolations or an antibody titre rise in paired sera, laboratory specimens were not systematically collected from all cases where the diagnosis was certain on clinical grounds

(Chapters 6 and 7). As a result it was decided to carry out surveillance monthly instead of fortnightly from September 1978. We have no evidence that an appreciable number of measles or pertussis cases were missed as a result.

Measles and whooping cough were defined according to carefully laid down diagnostic criteria that minimized inter-observer variation between the diagnosing physicians and—occasionally—the diagnosing field-worker. It was originally intended to code the presence or absence of clinical signs and to have the computer arrive at a score according to a standard programme. In practice it appeared that it would be necessary to study a large number of cases before the design of such a programme would be feasible and eventually all cases were diagnosed by one of the physicians by the agreed criteria.

As far as the surveillance of other acute respiratory infections and acute diarrhoea was concerned, 14 days between visits was an arbitrary figure; in the case of diarrhoea, the diagnosis could be based on actual observation in only a minority of cases. Limited attempts were made to relate these observations to the history as given by the mother (Chapter 8).

Although signs of respiratory tract infection were included in the disease surveillance form, their rarity made any reasonably standardized systematic study difficult and in practice only manifestations of upper respiratory tract infection (nasal discharge, cough) were considered.

Originally the screening question that determined whether specific morbidity information had to be collected by the field-worker or not, was 'Has the child been well since my last visit?' For the purpose of data processing it was easier to design the form in such a way that all questions on morbidity answered with 'No' could be ignored. As a result the screening question became: 'Has the child been *ill* since my last visit?' Although a leading question, in practice this did not draw an unjustified number of positive answers.

Population surveillance

Temporary migration in and out of the study area made the estimation of both numerators and denominators of rates difficult, while movements within the area added to these difficulties because of the inherent possibility of double registration or of omission of individual residents. Migratory movements are common among the Kamba as in many other parts of Africa.

Each study subject had a number related to the household he belonged to. Whether somebody should be considered to belong to a household was decided by the head of the household during the demographic baseline survey. This was an arbitrary decision but attempts to provide the field-workers gathering this information with guidelines as to who should or should not be considered to belong to a household, based on the length of the individual's stay with the household prior to the interview, yielded equally inconsistent results.

Problems arose in the case of internal migration when the individual was supposed to get a new number related to the household he/she had moved to. Double-counting (in the previous and in the present household) could not be entirely avoided. It also turned out that so-called 'emigrants' did in fact regularly return to the same or a different household after some months while others not marked 'emigrant' would be absent for years on end. Consequently, a somewhat different definition of emigrant was adopted at the end of 1978. Henceforth persons who had been continuously absent for more than 6 months (including the weekends) were classified as emigrants.

For epidemiological rates the de facto population did not suffice: pregnant women belonging to the study population were included even if they delivered outside the study area; a registered child returning from a temporary absence with traces of a recent measles attack was included in both numerator and denominator of the measles attack rate.

An alternative way of tracing migrant people would have been to attach a number to a subject rather than a household and use it as his/her identification number whatever his/her movements were. This might have worked for individuals moving within the study area, but would hardly have been feasible for migrants to and from elsewhere.

In order to obtain reliable information on disease outcome, patients being hospitalized needed to be traced. For this purpose all households in the study area received a numbered card to be shown to the hospital staff whenever a member of the household was admitted. The great majority of study subjects requiring hospitalization were admitted to the nearby divisional hospital in Kangundo, but the staff often did not enter the number on the hospital record because the mother failed to show the card.

Usually, however, hospitalized children could be traced by a field-worker who knew the people of the study area well and who visited the hospital wards once a week. In the case of users of outpatient services, including maternal and child health clinics, this was far less easy. Also, mothers often lost their children's vaccination cards. Reliable information in this respect simply never became available.

Data processing

Although the need for prompt data handling was repeatedly stressed from the early stages of the project onwards, the magnitude of the requirements of an ongoing, longitudinal data base was not sufficiently recognized. The technical problems of storage of such a quantity of data were much more formidable than anticipated.

Lack of feed-back of analysed data resulted at times in the collection of information that turned out to be superfluous, and in the discovery of errors at a stage when some data had already been computerized.

The lesson to be learned is that successful field pilot studies alone do not indicate that all is well. The data collected during such pilot studies should be coded, punched and stored but be retrievable until the computer produces useful tabulations with a minimal number of errors. Tabulation by hand immediately after the data have been collected in the field is useful but does not obviate the need for pilot runs of computerized data if it is known that such computerization is going to be essential in order to be able to handle a massive amount of data.

The coding system of the demographic baseline survey was very elegant and economical but ignored a number of cross-checks built into the form that could easily have been incorporated in the computer programme if a more straightforward coding of items had been adopted. The programme for updating the demographic file proved to be inadequate. This only became apparent much too late, when data collection in the field was already in full swing. Direct coding on the forms in the field was considered as a time-saving procedure but fear of an additional source of error made us decide against it. Mark-sensing was considered too vulnerable a system under the prevailing conditions.

In the final analysis of the demographic data we had, therefore, for some items to return to the raw data and to rely on tabulation by hand.

Organizational aspects

External relations

The project started in a low-key manner. As has been pointed out, it was not even clear whether its cornerstone—surveillance by school leavers—was a realistic concept. Under these circumstances it seemed unwise to surround our initial activities with too much publicity.

Among the early visitors were many competent colleagues, but most of them, however enthusiastic in the field, showed little interest after departure. Little was done to publicize the project, either in Kenya or abroad. In later years publicity came more or less spontaneously, attracting high Kenyan and Dutch officials and scientists even before the first publications had appeared.

No doubt more intensive professional contacts through site visits to other longitudinal projects in tropical Africa and through seminars and workshops at an early stage would have been of great help to the initiators of the project. By paying little attention to publicity, some valuable advice, both national and international, may have been missed at a stage that it was most needed. One favourable exception was the interest shown by investigators of the Kano Plain arbovirus study of the British Medical Research Council in Kenya: much of our demographic framework was a faithful copy of their study organization. The close co-operation between the two projects, however, came about more by accident than design.

Project organization

The Project's design and organization were built up very gradually from its original conception. It took shape as a part and not as a replacement of the existing research programme of the Medical Research Centre, Nairobi. When the decision was reached to set up a longitudinal health information system with unskilled field-workers it was not clear whether such a system could be made operational. These circumstances were not conducive to a properly integrated project organization.

The Medical Research Centre scientists had numerous other commitments and nobody was sure that the Project was going to be feasible and rewarding. It was only after some time that academic staff could be recruited specifically for the Project. The Medical Research Centre Department of Epidemiology carried the responsibility for it, whereas the Departments of Nutrition, Parasitology and Virology participated but their contribution did not become an integral part of the organization. As a result, separate nutrition field-workers were trained and supervised by the nutritionist, while a separate team for the collection of blood samples, responsible to the virologist, was formed. In retrospect, efficiency would have been increased and uncertainties occasionally leading to friction owing to differing lines of authority would have been reduced if all the above-mentioned activities had in principle been performed by one team of field-workers responsible to the academic core staff of the Project, i.e. the senior staff of the Department of Epidemiology.

The same applied to the technical department, responsible for the transport amongst other things. Its services were taken for granted but when field activities increased they were not always adequate. The technical officer handled them from his office in Nairobi where he had many other responsibilities. As a result he was insufficiently aware of the day-to-day problems arising in the field and he never felt part of the Project team. Matters improved greatly when the handling of all technical matters related to the Machakos Project was delegated to another member of his staff.

The principle of shared responsibility by academic, technical and administrative staff for all aspects of field operations should have been emphasized much more strongly than it actually was at the outset of the Project.

Academic staff

The failure to attract medically trained Kenyans has been a serious drawback. Generally they are in short supply and, if available, are not particularly interested in epidemiological field research.

The Medical Research Centre, Nairobi, an independent foreign institute until 1982, was not in a position to offer Kenyan employees any career prospects. This disadvantage was not so acute in respect of the recruitment of trainees—usually holders of a Bachelor degree—in other disciplines like biology, sociology, geography, agriculture and home economics, fields in which supply appears to exceed demand and the active interest of the various university departments has been very encouraging. The fact that only few university graduates are prepared to spend at least part of their postgraduate training period continuously in the field, however, gives cause for concern. If a relative handicap for the Project, such a tendency is disastrous for the country.

Recruitment of expatriate staff was greatly hampered by the fact that it was primarily handled by the Medical Research Centre's parent institute in the Netherlands. This resulted in a certain ambiguity in selection procedures and unnecessary delays. It was not unusual for a full year to elapse between the decision to advertise and the actual arrival of the recruited candidate.

Local field staff and field supervision

Supply greatly exceeded demand. It was therefore quite easy to be selective although it remained difficult to design adequate selection criteria.

High grades at school and number of years of schooling should not be important selection criteria. If students who have done well in their high-school exams are taken on, they soon leave because they are offered scholarships or better paid jobs in town. The quality of the performance of a field-worker depends more on his motivation than on his intelligence. If properly guided and supervised in an atmosphere of mutual trust and respect, almost any school-leaver can do well.

On-the-job training by frequent supervisory surprise visits while the field-worker is making his daily round, and weekly verbal instruction of small groups proved to be much more effective than carefully designed instruction manuals written even in simple language, as these were seldom read and understood.

Two field-workers making a home visit.

Frequent supervision of field-workers takes time and money. This was particularly so because repeated attempts failed to recruit competent local intermediate staff to whom the greater part of supervision could be delegated. Throughout 7½ years of surveillance, any relaxation of field supervision by the Nairobi-based academic staff seemed to have an immediate effect on the reliability of the data being collected. There do not seem to be any short-cuts in obtaining good field data in tropical Africa.

A similar situation has been described (Neumann et al., 1973) from the Danfa project in Ghana. As a result, supervision is expensive, in terms both of manpower and transport, but it is unwise to try to economize in this respect because it results in data of questionable accuracy. Obviously, however, as far as disease surveillance as a routine government health services activity is concerned, financial constraints will make some compromise necessary.

Efficient supervision requires accurate, detailed maps of the household clusters served by a field-worker and the availability of a daily-compiled list of households the field-worker intends to visit and in what order. This is the only way of tracing the field-worker at any time of the day. Initially maps were drawn by the field staff on the spot during the preparatory phase of the demographic survey. Later on greatly improved maps were made, based on fairly recent aerial photographs, but it continued to be difficult to have all households and their numbers marked at the right spot, especially since new houses are continually being built and old ones abandoned. It should be stressed that supervision was not aimed at scaring field-workers into a soul-destroying routine by surprise authoritarian visits and subsequent reprimands and penalties: the main objective was to make the field-worker feel that he was not being left on his own; that the physician or sociologist in Nairobi was not taking his or her work for granted; and that senior staff cared what the field-worker was doing because his work was important and an essential part of the Project. Only then can one expect the field-worker to continue to do a basically boring routine job with a certain degree of interest and motivation.

In our experience most field-workers had the capacity to perform a wide variety of tasks adequately, as long as new tasks were added gradually: these could only be properly handled when existing tasks did not create any significant problems. In general, most errors occurred through inaccurate recording of accurate observations or derived from inability of a field-worker to keep the field records of the households under his care in good order.

During the early days of the Project a number of medical

students on vacation were employed to assist in the field supervision. The results were disappointing. In respect of training and intelligence they were far superior, but in respect of maturity and motivation far inferior, to the field-workers they were supposed to supervise.

Relations with the population

For more than 8 years (including 1 year of preparations and the baseline survey) the relationship with the people and its leaders has been warm and unblemished. The response rate has been virtually 100 percent for all studies. Hospitality and co-operation were extended to field-workers, supervisors and researchers alike as a matter of course.

Throughout the duration of the Project, health care was provided to the child population through weekly clinics. Apart from the aspect of service, to which we felt the people were entitled in return for the goodwill and co-operation they accorded to the Project, these clinics offered a convenient opportunity to verify the diagnosis of cases reported for measles and whooping cough and to take diagnostic specimens. For this reason the clinics were initially conducted by one of the three project physicians. Not until 1977 was a clinical officer recruited to take over this very time-consuming activity. This could and should have been done at an earlier stage.

Conclusion

In this chapter we have attempted to make an assessment of the Machakos Project, its accomplishments, the value of the results obtained, its weaknesses and failures, its errors and its wisdom (Behar et al., 1968).

We believe that we have been able to show that this longitudinal population-based study has produced valuable information that could not have been obtained by simpler, cheaper methods, and that the results are relevant to health administrators and to the scientific community.

The Project design called for the long-term, continuous commitment of a relatively large number of scientific staff, adequate administrative and logistic support throughout and, most of all, a patient and hospitable study population. Some of these requirements can be translated into financial terms, others are a matter of motivation and mentality or purely good fortune. These requirements were met most of the time.

Field research is expensive, laborious and lacking in glamour, and does not provide the reward of immediate results, but it is essential when the health of the community rather than of the individual is our concern. In the clinical setting careful follow-up of the individual patient is the basis for good management and care. Similarly, adequate health care for the community is based on careful monitoring of its health problems. We believe that the Machakos Project has made a contribution in this respect.

References

Behar M, Scrimshaw NS, Guzman MA and Gordon JE, Nutrition and infection field study in Guatemalan villages, 1959–1964 VIII. An epidemiological appraisal of its wisdom and errors, Arch Environm Hlth, 17 (1968) 814.

Hayden RJ, Measles, In; Health and Disease in Kenya, Nairobi, Vogel et al., Eds, East African Literature Bureau, 1974, 270.

International Centre for Diarrhoeal Disease Research, Bangladesh, Annual Reports 1978, 1979, 1980, ICDDR.B, Dacca, 1978, 1979, 1980.

Mata LJ, The children of Santa Maria Cauqué: a prospective field study of health and growth, MIT Press, Cambridge, Massachusetts, 1978.

Neumann AK, Sai FT, Lourie IM and Wurapa FK, Focus: Technical Cooperation, 2 (1973) 11.

Taylor CE, Kielmann AA, Parker RL et al., Malnutrition, infection, growth and development, the Narangwal experience: final report, World Bank, Washington DC, 1978.

The University of Ghana Medical School and UCLA School of Public Health, The Danfa Comprehensive Rural Health and Family Planning Project, Ghana. Final Report, The University of Ghana Medical School, Accra, and UCLA School of Public Health, Los Angeles, 1979.

Index